FATIMA PRIEST

MW01690736

"In the Third Secret [of Fatima] it is foretold, among other things, that the great apostasy in the Church will begin at the top."

...Cardinal Mario Luigi Ciappi, 1995
Papal Theologian to Pius XII, John XXIII, Paul VI, John Paul I, John Paul II

"Suppose, dear friend, that Communism [Russia and Russia's errors, in Fatima terms] was only the most visible of the instruments of subversion to be used against the Church and the traditions of Divine Revelation ... I am worried by the Blessed Virgin's messages to Lucy of Fatima. This persistence of Mary about the dangers which menace the Church is a divine warning against the suicide of altering the Faith, in her liturgy, her theology and her soul ... A day will come when the civilized world will deny its God, when the Church will doubt as Peter doubted. She will be tempted to believe that man has become God ... In our churches, Christians will search in vain for the red lamp where God awaits them, like Mary Magdalene weeping before the empty tomb, they will ask, 'Where have they taken Him?'"

... Pope Pius XII
Quoted in the book *Pius XII Devant L'Histoire*, pp. 52-53

"Through some crack, the smoke of satan has entered into the Church of God."

... Pope Paul VI
Papal address, June 29, 1972

"We must admit realistically and with feelings of deep pain, that: Christians today, in large measure feel lost, confused, perplexed and even disappointed; ideas opposed to the truth which has been revealed and always taught are being scattered abroad in abundance; heresies, in the full and proper sense of the word, have been spread in the area of dogma and morals, creating doubts, confusions and rebellion; the liturgy has been tampered with, immersed in an intellectual and moral relativism and therefore in permissiveness; Christians are tempted by atheism, agnosticism, vaguely moral enlightenment and by a sociological Christianity devoid of defined dogmas or an objective morality."

... Pope John Paul II
L'Osservatore Romano, February 7, 1981

"Only Our Lady of the Rosary can help you."

...Our Lady of the Rosary of Fatima
July 13, 1917

FATIMA PRIEST

and

Our Lady's Message to the World

Fatima Obeyed: Promise of Peace and Prosperity

or

Fatima Ignored: Prophecy of Peril and Terror

by Francis Alban
with
Christopher A. Ferrara, Esq.

Good Counsel Publications
Pound Ridge, New York

Copyright © 1997 • 1999 • 2000 • 2013 Good Counsel Publications

All rights reserved. No part of this publication may be reproduced, stored in a retrieval system, or transmitted, in any form or by means electronic, mechanical, photocopying, recording, or otherwise, except for the inclusion of brief quotations in a review, without prior permission in writing from the publishers.

Good Counsel Publications, P.O. Box 203, Pound Ridge, New York 10576

ISBN-13: 978-0-9815357-6-0

First Edition 1997
Second Edition 1997
Third Edition 1999
Fourth Edition 2000
Fifth Edition
Volume I 2013 (revised and updated)
Volume II 2014

For extra copies of this book,
contact The Fatima Center at one of the following addresses:

In Canada:
452 Kraft Road
Fort Erie, Ontario
L2A 4M7

In USA:
17000 State Route 30
Constable, New York
12926

Printed in Canada

FATIMA PRIEST
VOLUME I
Table of Contents

BOOK I ~ The Priest and the Prophecy

Part One ~ In Person

Part Two ~ Politics vs. Prayer

Part Three ~ A Fatima Spirituality for the 21st Century

Part Four ~ A New Day for Fatima

FATIMA PRIEST – Table of Contents – VOLUME II

BOOK II ~ In His Own Words

BOOK III ~ Testimonies | Appendices

Author's Preface

A life founded upon truth is unshakeable. Only a loss of the truth can make us tremble. The Patriarchs and Prophets trembled at the thought of losing God, of not fearing Him enough, of not serving Him enough. They trembled also at seeing His truth denied. Their spiritual children, the Saints of the Church, in defense of His truth, strode singing into blood-drenched arenas, bowed gracefully to the headsman's axe, skipped up the steps to the guillotine, chanted His praises before firing squads. The catalogue of names, numbering in the thousands of thousands who willingly surrendered their life in defense of the truth is a cornerstone of our Catholic heritage. Smiling at death has been the last earthly act of many of our spiritual ancestors.

Each and every one of them, however, before they could smile at death, had an obstacle to hurdle. They had to harness the force that overcomes the mind and heart of man when truth is denied, a force human nature has in abundance, a force with which the Patriarchs and Prophets and Saints, as Sacred Scripture and Church history thoroughly testify, have been richly supplied by the Creator. They had to harness their anger.

There is great anger upon the earth today, most of it bearing the hallmark of chaos and unrelenting grief that are the gifts of Lucifer to his earthly cohorts. There is also being raised, however, a sizeable murmur, born of *holy* anger, that echoes of blood-drenched arenas, the whisper of the swinging axe, the sigh of the plummeting blade. For a lie has been told, a great lie that slanders God. A lie that cuts like a knife. It identifies the friends of God by the wounds they bear after it passes them by. The cutting edge of this fatal whisper is made of three simple words: "*Fatima is finished*".

The purpose of a lie is to hide the truth. The result of a lie is the wounding of those who are seeking the truth, the assaulting of those who are defending the truth, or the discrediting of those who are passing on the truth.

Our entire lives are built upon truths heard at our mother's knee, truths intoned gently at our bedside in childhood, truths absorbed from family tradition. Upon these foundations rest our past, our present, and our future.

There are those in the Church and State today who, for unique and specific reasons, conspire to spread the Lie by obliterating the credibility of those who defend Heaven's truth. In their wake, a plague of wounded hearts cries out to Heaven. Our Sacred heritage itself is suspect. Were we lied to at our mother's knee? At the bedside of our childhood? Is the Church not Our Mother? Did She lie to us? Most stagger under the weight of their suspicions. Some crumble. Some begin to disbelieve Heaven itself. Those who neither stumble nor fall under the blow of the Lie, but stay upright, are salting the earth anew with the secret of the Saints—the knowledge that Heaven does not lie.

When it comes to the Message of Fatima, the stakes are so high, Lucifer himself seems now to be taking a personal hand in attacking Fatima's defenders. In the forefront of the battle, constantly brandishing the banner of Fatima before the ranks of the enemies of Heaven, the International Fatima Rosary Crusade refuses to retreat, withdraw or surrender. Those who have tried to level the Apostolate in the past know that it will remain a formidable foe of the Lie for as long as Father Nicholas Gruner, its founder and director, remains its driving force. Their task then, is to obliterate Father Nicholas Gruner.

To accomplish this requires silencing a man whose insistence on the necessity of the Pope and bishops of the world to obey the requests of Our Lady of Fatima has made him, arguably, the most controversial priest in the Church today. Who is he? What is he? Why is his destruction important to the enemies of Fatima? Why are they spending so much time, money and energy to eliminate him from the scene? We must look at his personal history to discover the answer.

... Francis Alban
June 13, 1997

Foreword

by Malachi Martin

In the not too distant future, when the definitive history of the 20th Century has been written, there surely will be universal agreement that the focal point of that century's drama and the key to its meaning for the comity of nations, as well as for the salvation of mankind, was an event that took place within the first twenty years of the century, but remained largely unnoticed by the generality of men and women and willfully sidelined by many whose divine vocation it was to announce the advent of Mary's public reign in the history of nations. That keystone event was the Miracle of the Sun on October 13, 1917, at Fatima, in Portugal.

Many good and holy men and women have woven their destinies in with that Miracle at Fatima, each one contributing their share of effort to make known the glories God intends should surround the name of Mary before the eyes of mankind. We do not know any single individual who has played such a vital role as Father Nicholas Gruner in fomenting the manifest will of God for the latter days of the human race.

For in the last third of this century, there has been such a concerted effort not only to distort the meaning of that keystone event of 1917, but to nullify a divine mandate on which depend the physical safety of millions and the eternal salvation of more millions. The sole surviving person chosen by the Virgin as special witness of the MIracle and the interpretor of its meaning, Sister Lucia,* had been segregated, maligned, misquoted; she had had bogus letters forged in her name; and, we suspect, on at least one occasion, a bogus Sister Lucia had impersonated the real and living Sister Lucia.

Against all this disrespect for the Queen of Heaven and neglect of Her mandate, Father Gruner has been the foremost champion. He keeps on reminding everybody—Pope, Cardinals, bishops, priests, lay people—that the Church, in its Pope and bishops, has not obeyed the commands of Our Lady; Church authorities have not consecrated Russia to Her Immaculate Heart. Hence, the agony of the Church in the world continues. Father Gruner, the Fatima priest, will not allow any of us to forget what we neglected to do in 1960: perform the Consecration of Russia and reveal the near-future chastisements which God is about to unleash on a sinful humanity and on Christians whose faith has grown tepid.

Father Gruner has suffered ecclesiastical ostracism and persecution by calumnies and slanders, by physical bodily harm. Yet, no power on Earth has made him abandon his vocation as the premier champion of Fatima.

This book is a partial chronicle of Father Gruner`s story. It should be obligatory reading for all bishops and priests.

April 1999

---

* **Editor's Note:** Sister Lucia lived until February 13, 2005 and was almost 98 years old when she died.

Foreword to the 2013 Edition

Since this book first appeared, the landscape of the Catholic Church has undergone a dramatic transformation: Sister Lucy, the last surviving visionary of Fatima, has entered into eternity, as has Pope John Paul II. The Pope who succeeded John Paul, Benedict XVI, abdicated the papal throne in the eighth year of his pontificate, but not before making a pilgrimage to Fatima and revealing that there is far more to the Third Secret than has thus far been revealed. Succeeding Pope Benedict during one of the most turbulent epochs in the history of the Catholic Church, Pope Francis, as one of his first acts, requested that his entire pontificate be consecrated to Our Lady of Fatima.

This book was written as a testament to the heroic perseverance of a lone Catholic priest who, like Pope Francis, has dedicated himself to Her. What the priest and the Pope have in common is their recognition of the central importance of the Fatima event for the Church and the world—even now, nearly a century after the Blessed Virgin first appeared at the Cova da Iria.

Since the last edition of this work appeared twelve years ago, a series of surprising—one might say miraculous—developments has demonstrated that the drama that is Fatima has no human director, but rather is directed by One who has written the play and will infallibly ensure that the final act ends just as it was written. What has happened since 2001 now figures prominently in the unfolding of this heavenly drama, adding scenes and even entire acts that were unexpected and filled with hope.

Hence this book is, in the end, a testament to something infinitely more important than the life and work of a single priest. These pages bear witness to the ever-present action of the Lord of History in human affairs and the inevitable accomplishment of the divine plan for humanity. *The Fatima event will never be ended on human terms* but rather will reach its consummation in the one and only outcome Heaven has decreed from the beginning: "In the end My Immaculate Heart will triumph. The Holy Father will consecrate Russia to Me, which will be converted, and a period of peace will be granted to the world."

Yet the world still hangs in the balance between tragedy and triumph, for as the Virgin of Fatima warned, "various nations will be annihilated" if Russia's consecration is delayed too long. Whether the ultimate triumph of the Immaculate Heart occurs in a devastated world, or a world that is spared devastation, is the question that confronts us at this moment in history. The answer to that question lies in the hands of the Pope and the bishops who have the power to obtain what the Virgin promised, if only they will do what She requested. But, as the Message of Fatima makes clear, the answer lies in our hands as well, for the prayers and sacrifices of the simple faithful will hasten the day when the Fatima prophecy achieves its glorious fulfillment.

Christopher A. Ferrara
Richmond, Virginia
August 15, 2013
The Feast of the Assumption

This book is respectfully dedicated to

Our Lady of Fatima

and to all Cardinals, patriarchs, bishops,
priests, religious and lay persons
who have dedicated themselves
in humility and love to Her service.

BOOK I

The Priest and the Prophecy

PART ONE

In Person

Chapter 1
The Stars at Noon

In Old Montreal there is a spot beloved of all generations of Catholics in the Province of Quebec where the stars can be seen at morning and afternoon as well as at night. On the deep blue ceiling of the great church of Notre Dame, in silver and gold, handpainted stars by the thousands look down on the faithful below.

Many a child has gone home from Notre Dame with aching neck wrought from standing on kneeler and pew, turning, turning, and gazing up at that magnificent rendition of Heaven brought indoors. That the glory of the Church it represented could possibly fade in the span of a few short years would have been considered an outrageous idea in the 1940's in Quebec. The province known as the Province of St. Anne appeared as securely set in the Faith as were the stars in their blue-painted firmament.

It has been said that never in history had the Social Kingship of Christ been reflected so totally and completely on earth as it was in the kitchens of Quebec Province in the first half of the 20th Century. Here the Faith came from its supernatural height and permeated every aspect of life. To those who suggest the Church was a smothering, oppressive force in the lives of the people of Quebec it might be noted that the unique culture of the Province of St. Anne exists today precisely because of the Catholic Faith; the Church having provided the prime bulwark against assimilation by Protestant Britain.

(In fairness to Britain, however, it can also be said that the conquest of Quebec by Britain in 1759 undoubtedly saved the province from doing a brisk trade in guillotine blades when revolution turned Mother France into an abattoir a mere thirty years later.)

Whatever may be said about the history of Quebec, it is indisputable that Montreal, in 1942, was very much the center of a vibrant *La Belle Province*. To be in Montreal was to be instantly part of the most cosmopolitan city of the hemisphere outside of Rio.

The Town of Mount Royal within the greater city of Montreal was indeed an ocean removed from the sounds of the cannonade in Europe, but the soul and heart of Quebec resonated thoroughly with the dangers to France from the first moment of Hitlerian madness. The Fuehrer's broadcasts could shake radios in Northern Quebec and inner city Montreal just as readily as they did the radios of France. The fantasy of the Maginot Line came crashing to earth along the St. Lawrence as well as along the Champs Elysées. And who can doubt that the dreadful rhythm of stormtroopers marching past L'Arc de Triomphe chilled hearts in the shadow of St. Joseph's Oratory.

Even so, to be born in Montreal in the middle of the Second World War was to have one's eyes open to the most critical era of human history and yet view it from a special vantage point of security and safety. Few Canadian mothers in those dark years were unaware of their blessed distance from ringside as the curtain rose on what has appeared as Act Two of the Apocalypse.

Jessie Gruner had already borne four children to God and her husband Malcolm by May of 1942. Michael, the first, was born on the feast of St. Athanasius, that great Saint who, in defense of the Church and the Faith, justly opposed even the Pope. Peter was next, then Christopher, who was born on the eve of St. Nicholas' feast day, and then Anthony. This newest one would be called Nicholas.

Nicholas Gruner was christened in the parish of St. Malachy's, according to the tradition and law of the greatest teaching institution in the world, the two-thousand-year-old Roman Catholic Church.

He was named after St. Nicholas of Tolentino, a Catholic priest and miracle worker, on whose feast day his parents Jessie Mullally and Malcolm Gruner had married, September 10, 1930.

Is it mere coincidence that Nicholas Gruner and another Nicholas, Van der Flue, share both a name and some very similar life patterns? Nicholas Gruner, the fifth son, became a priest, as did the fifth son of St. Nicholas Van der Flue. Both, also, would oppose abuse of authority and irresponsible judgments.

In Nicholas Van der Flue's day he gave Switzerland the solution to an "unsolvable" problem. The Swiss Constitution is his masterpiece and it still stands today. Nicholas Gruner was destined to publish to the world the solution to an "unsolvable" problem, the only means of obtaining world peace.

Malcolm Gruner was one of the original five Catholic men who petitioned the Archbishop of Montreal to found the parish of the Annunciation of Our Lady where the family would live for forty years. Malcolm then served as a warden of this parish for about 30 years. Two of the children would be baptized there, three receive first Holy Communion, another three would marry there, and in time the parents would there celebrate their fiftieth wedding anniversary.[1] Malcolm was also instrumental in founding the local parish school of St. Joseph and at least four of the children went there. It had classes for both English and French Catholic school children for as long as Nicholas went to school there. More continuity. More tradition.

In 1942, Catholic continuity, tradition and law were the birthright of any future priest, all gifts he would need in abundance when, in future years, under the pressure of so-called "reformers", the Church would jettison these and other precious treasures of its sacred heritage.

Indeed, continuity and tradition marked the Gruner homefront. A statue of the Sacred Heart, displayed in the most prominent place in the house, the head of the stairs, dispensed blessings and urged caution. Year after year children navigated those stairs passing by the Sacred Heart who, as in Catholic homes everywhere, with one hand cautions don't run, and with the other says I'm here if you fall. Running on just such a staircase as this, St. Therese of Lisieux suffered the intersection of youthful emotions that would change her life forever and lead inevitably to sainthood.

In front of the image of Our Mother of Perpetual Help, in Jessie and Malcolm's bedroom, the children were taught the Memorare, that portal of rescue in times of despair.

"...never was it known that anyone who fled to Thy protection, implored Thy help or sought Thy intercession was left unaided."

Fighting the odds and testing frontiers seemed part of the family background. Grandfather Dr. Emmet J. Mullally was a prominent physician in Montreal and one of the first English-speaking commissioners on the Catholic School Board. Dr. Mullally was instrumental in founding D'Arcy McGee High, the first English-language Catholic high school in Montreal. Being an avid historian of the Irish legacy in Canada, Mullally had it named D'Arcy McGee after the dynamic Irish parliamentarian who was assassinated on Sparks Street in Ottawa in 1868. Later, a grade school in Montreal was named after Mullally himself, in acknowledgement of his contribution to education in the city.

---

1 Father Gruner, *Memories of My Mother*, "The Fatima Crusader", Issue 47, Summer 1994, p. 11.

"We had a happy, stable home," Father Nicholas Gruner remembers today, "a mother who stayed home, a father home every night and on weekends. My parents never disagreed in front of us. We took vacations as a family to Prince Edward Island and sometimes in St. Joseph de Mont Rolland, 45 miles north of Montreal, where a house was lent us." It was there Nicholas learned how to swim in a hurry shortly after a friend threw him into the water and he almost drowned.

Not a word of swearing was ever heard in the house, neither blasphemous talk nor gutter language. "The worst my father ever said was 'bloody'."

His brother Tony recalls that before Nick was born, Peter had learned some swear words when he was two, from a maid and that when he used them in front of his mother, she figured out where it came from and immediately dismissed the woman. Father relates, "My mother took her duty as a Catholic mother very seriously and saw to it that blasphemy was never even whispered in her home.

"Although we might have been considered among the upper-middle class," Father Gruner notes, "we didn't have any excess. I remember father saying if he had wealth, he would share it generously. But he was not wealthy and we knew it. We were conscious of not having excess and of working for what we had. We had to earn our own way. My sister Jenny, the youngest, recalls that when she was 10, even though our parents could have afforded to buy her a bicycle, they insisted she earn her own. When Tony accompanied my father out of town to a big construction site, he ordered only a hamburger for his meal and told my father, 'I know you don't have much money so I didn't want to be a burden.'

"We paid our own way through school, lived at home for university, but worked in the summer to pay for it.

"We were all very different, all individual, all quite aware of our independence and our own point of view." Father recounted that the person who used to babysit him was a certain Madame St. Laurent, who told him that he did not speak until he was four. But when he spoke he knew exactly what he meant. He expressed himself very explicitly and objected if he was significantly misquoted. It is characteristic of how Father Gruner speaks today.

All of the Gruner children have post-graduate degrees, except for Michael, the eldest. And, indeed, both parents put a high value on education.

Father Gruner remembers: "My father came from a long line of inventors and engineers. He had an engineering degree himself and turned down a scholarship because others more needy than himself needed it.

"His middle name and my own is Nightingale. Alice Nightingale, my father's mother, insisted that we were related to Florence Nightingale, the famous nurse.

"My mother had a great sense of justice. She was supportive if we were in the right but not if we were in the wrong. For example, despite pressure from an angry car owner, my mother would not let Tony pay for a windshield broken during a baseball game because he was not actually playing in the game but merely watching. She had been a school teacher before she married and continued to take an active role in our education. In my first year at McGill University she made me redo a paper on economic history even though I thought it was quite adequate. She said it wasn't good enough and made me work harder on it.

"Her family was well known in Montreal. Grandmother Mullally's family came to Canada in 1842, during the potato famine in Ireland, landing in Montreal.

"Grandfather Mullally could remember when Louis Riel was executed by the Government of Canada (for leading the Métis rebellion of 1885 in western Canada) and how his father explained that the hanging of Riel was bad for Canadian unity.

"Grandfather Mullally's mother knew her own mind and was very strong-willed. She was a MacDonald and despite very strong family opposition, she was the first Scot in PEI to marry an Irishman.

"Doctor Oscar Cameron Gruner, who was known to his grandchildren as 'Baba', was also a medical doctor who specialized as a pathologist and a researcher in cancer. Early in his life, his mother, Eleanor, a very strong-willed, artistic woman, determined that her son would become a famous surgeon." Her role model was that of Sir Berkeley Moynihan. Sir Berkeley was a competent surgeon to Queen Victoria. He wrote a text of surgery. In that text there was a section on the spleen, which at that time was still a considerable medical mystery. It was Oscar who wrote the chapter on the spleen though he was not given credit for it.

In 1910, Oscar, who was an assistant professor of pathology, and Alice came to Montreal with their two children, Malcolm and Douglas. He co-authored articles on pathology of various tumors with a Dr. Emmet James Mullally which were published in reputable journals such as the *American Journal of Pathology*. Mullally was a McGill graduate, and in one of the first groups of doctors to do what they now call a surgical residency. In 1913 the signs of war were obvious and Oscar felt he should be back in England. He returned and joined the British Army Medical Corps and worked as a pathologist.

Dr. Gruner pioneered a scientific test on the early detection of cancer by a simple but accurate count of white cells in the blood. He showed it to Nicholas when he was a child and taught Peter, then a teenager, how to use it. Peter is now a doctor himself.

Oscar had a very original mind in medicine and cancer research. His work in 1915 was decades ahead of his time. Indeed, it wasn't until 50 years later that the scientific community caught up with his research. They finally recognized his work and he received an award in 1965.

He, himself, opposed some of the medical establishment and was critical of contemporary theories of medicine treating the human body as if it were simply a machine. He also thought that too many medical practitioners were in the back pocket of the drug companies. He was a quiet man and would never get into a fight, but, as a researcher, held on to the truth.

In 1949, he proved that cancer can be cured. A German man called Mr. Fookes, who worked for Malcolm, had cancer and Dr. Gruner cured him with medicine discovered by another researcher in Canada.

Malcolm Gruner, born on August 22, 1905, attended Leeds Grammar School where he did quite well academically. Although encouraged by his father to study medicine, he was never really interested. Oscar was a renaissance person and intrigued by many aspects of the then new world. Malcolm was especially interested with the new finds in the various Egyptian excavations and was a well-read Egyptianology buff. One of the digs revealed the mummy of an Egyptian princess. The archaeologists sent her ringed hand to Malcolm for evaluation.

In 1926, Malcolm, a graduate engineer, emigrated to work in Montreal at Vickers. He re-introduced himself to his father's old friend and colleague, Dr. Mullally. In so doing he re-met Jessie Rosalie. Malcolm returned to England but much correspondence ensued between he and Jessie. Jessie visited England with her father and brother James in 1928. Here, Jessie and Malcolm became engaged. They would be married in Canada.

Malcolm had exhibited, early in life, a readiness not to shrink from what he perceived as a 'call'. In Rome in the 1920's, the young Malcolm, not yet Catholic, was so moved by the life of St. Cecilia, the noble Roman virgin who professed her faith courageously and gave her life for Christ, that he was converted in the very place Cecilia was martyred.[2]

His conversion is recalled by Father Gruner: "My uncle Douglas had already turned Catholic but my father was adamant in refusing to do so. Then Malcolm was invited to Rome by his parents during the Holy Year, 1925. He said he would go, not to see Christian Rome but as an avid student, interested in archaeology, to see the ruins of pagan Rome. He made his way to the Church of St. Cecilia in Trastevere because of its archaeological interest and his great love of music, St. Cecilia being the Church's patron of music. When he was in the cellar of the ruins, he heard the story of how St. Cecilia died. (She was sealed in a steam room, but she remained alive. The executioners then attempted several times to behead her but the neck wound was not immediately fatal—she lived two more days while she dictated her spiritual will, giving her house to the Roman Catholic Church so that it could be converted into a place of worship. St. Cecilia was also a great apologist for the Church.)

"When I asked my father what converted him he said he was so moved by the story of St. Cecilia, who was rich and beautiful and had everything the world could offer, but out of love for Jesus Christ gave it all up and became a virgin martyr. In 1946, true to his promise made some 21 years before, the first daughter in the Gruner family would carry her name, so that, as in all Catholic families, the spiritual legacy of the early martyrs would inspire and strengthen and direct the offspring. But whether St. Cecilia's sacrifice would actually affect Malcolm's family in future years was being determined in the late autumn of 1943 by a hand writing in a far country.

§

God must surely be the greatest storyteller of all. He certainly knows how to keep a reader's attention. No one ever put the Old Testament down out of boredom, rather it is out of the exhilaration of trying to absorb the twists and turns, plots and counterplots, throughout the whole history of God's revelation of Himself to the chosen people that causes the reader to seek rest for the eye and the soul now and then. But throughout it all He holds the reader's attention as He held the attention of the Hebrews by one perfect tactic—a promise. He promised them a Redeemer. And He held their attention for centuries until He fulfilled that promise. It was only then that the jaded, to whom He had entrusted the promise, looked the other way. And God's treasure went elsewhere.

Every teacher knows the surest way to capture a naughty child's attention is to promise something is going to happen to him soon. To the cynical, over-indulged, spoiled and arrogant people of the Twentieth Century, God presented a device that would rivet their attention year in, year out, decade after decade. He gave them a Secret. Not "to" the world at large, but "for" the Catholic faithful in the world at large. Through His Mother at Fatima, He entrusted that Secret to three illiterate peasant children: Jacinta Marto, aged seven; her brother Francisco, nine; and their cousin Lucia dos Santos, barely ten.

A vocation from God can enter the heart of a child long before adolescence. God is not restrained by lack of faith in children. He knows what their future holds. God knows

2 Father Nicholas Gruner, *A Personal Thank You From Father Gruner*, "The Fatima Crusader", Issue 30, Winter 1989, p. 1.

His own, knows that shepherds in Bethlehem would not hesitate to enter a cave, knows too that the child seers of Fatima, Jacinta and Francisco, would spend the rest of their short lives burning with love for Him. And He knows too that Lucia, the last remaining Fatima seer, would be obedient to Him and His Mother all her long life on earth.

In the spring of 1917, all of Portugal was electrified to hear that three nondescript children had apparently seen the Virgin Mary, in a pasture north of Fatima, on the 13th of May. She promised to meet them there at that spot and on the same day every month until October.[3] There would be six meetings in all. Only the three children were at the first; 70,000 men, women and youths from all walks of life and every corner of Portugal were at the last. What was played out in between was some of the richest drama in the entire 2000-year history of Catholicism.

The Blessed Virgin told the children that God was much offended by the sins of mankind and asked if they would willingly make sacrifices to console Him and for the conversion of sinners. They were promised they would go to Heaven. (Jacinta and Francisco would die within three years; Lucia, the oldest, would live for the rest of the century—in fact, until Feb. 13, 2005.) For six months the three withstood scorn, police threats, mental torture at the hands of the authorities, anger from their own families, and the suffocating adulation of enraptured spectators. Because of their faithfulness to grace, and with Our Lady's help, they survived it all. They were also helped by the two most famous ingredients of the entire phenomenon—they had been promised a great miracle in October and had been told a Secret in three parts.[4]

Over the decades, as Heaven allowed it, the first two parts of the Secret were made known by Lucia dos Santos, upon orders from her bishop, after she entered religious life.[5] The first part of the Secret contained a vision of the damned burning in Hell for all eternity, the fate awaiting many people in the world if man does not cease offending God.[6] The second part said that if mankind did not stop in its offenses against God and His law, a worse war (World War II) would break out in the reign of Pius XI and that the world would continue to be punished by means of war, hunger, persecution of the Church and persecution of the Holy Father. The Virgin stated She would return to ask for the consecration of 'Russia' to Her Immaculate Heart, by the Pope and the bishops of the Church, to prevent Russia from spreading "... her errors throughout the world".[7] The third part of the Secret, which has yet to be [fully] revealed, was written down by Sister Lucia on twenty-four lines on one sheet of paper.[8] It has been in the Pope's possession since 1957[9] and has fascinated and challenged Catholics for the balance of this century.

As for the miracle promised for October, who was going to pay any attention to a wild prediction made back in July by three peasant children? They couldn't read, couldn't write, had no social graces whatsoever and seemed downright backward when you got a good look at them.

It was too ridiculous! They even announced the day it would happen, October

3 William Thomas Walsh, *Our Lady of Fatima*, New York, The Macmilian Company, 4th printing (1947), p. 52.

4 Sister Lucia's Third Memoir, *Fatima in Lucia's Own Words*, Fatima, Postulation Centre, 1976, p. 104.

5 Ibid, p. 102.

6 Ibid, p. 104.

7 Ibid.

8 Frère Michel de la Sainte Trinité, *The Secret of Fatima... Revealed* [1985], p. 7. Even after June 26, 2000 there is still a part to be revealed. See Christopher A. Ferrara, *The Secret Still Hidden* (Pound Ridge, Good Counsel Publications, 2008) and *The Devil's Final Battle* (Terryville, The Missionary Association, 2010, Second Edition).

9 Frère Michel de la Sainte Trinité, *The Whole Truth About Fatima*, Volume III, *The Third Secret*, Buffalo, New York, Immaculate Heart Publications, 2001 edition, pp. 479-481.

13th, and the time, noon,[10] the same hour the Virgin had supposedly been appearing to them since May. Who could fall for such nonsense?

Seventy thousand people did. At noon hour, October 13, 1917, the approximate resident population of Jerusalem on the day Christ wrote with His finger in the dust, were standing ankle deep in mud, in the pasture north of Fatima, in a downpour that had lasted all night.[11]

"Look at the sun", Lucia cried at the prompting of She who had just revealed Herself to be Our Lady of the Rosary.

The rain stopped, the clouds disappeared, the sun appeared silvery, as easy to look at as the moon. It began to send out waves of color not seen since creation, to recreate the complexion of those upturned faces and of earth itself. Then to the stupefaction of the thousands transfixed below, it began to spin. Suddenly, it tore free from the heavens and threw itself earthward in a zigzagging plunge, a great ball of blazing heat, threatening to scorch the terrified spectators back into the dust from which they had come.

At the height of the terror, it stopped, just overhead, hung there for a moment, the great pendulum of time had ended its swing. Then time began again, the sun drew up, away from the thousands, and made its way back into the sky. In moments it was what it had been since it was created and once again, no one could look upon it.[12]

The seventy thousand were dry—clothes, hair, shoes, umbrellas and earth, all dry,[13] dry as the dust on the Temple floor that Christ had written in before He sent away the woman with the words, "Neither do I condemn you." Homeward bound the multitudes went that October day in 1917, hearts soaring, filled to the brim with an unparalleled reminder of God's forgiveness. Indeed, what man must do to earn that forgiveness is what Fatima is all about.

When the first two children died, the sole custodian of the Secret was Lucia dos Santos. There, within the soul of this peasant girl, the Secret has been allowed to remain out of the reach of evil men until the time was ready for it to be revealed.

By 1941, that life had already obediently shouldered the burden of her Fatima mandate for 24 years. That summer she was commanded to write what we now know as her Third Memoir.[14]

In that memoir she revealed for the first time that the Great Secret of Fatima was divided into three parts. On this occasion she also revealed the contents of the first two parts of the Secret.[15]

Lucia dos Santos, having relived the entire six months of 1917 through the writing of her Third Memoir and revealing the first two parts of the Secret by June 1943, became ill with bronchial ailments which led to a serious case of pleurisy.[16] In September, alarmed by the prospect of the seer taking the third part of the Secret back into eternity with her, her bishop, Bishop da Silva of Leiria, expressed the desire that she write it down.[17]

She explained to the bishop that on such an important matter she preferred to await a formal written order to do so.

10 William Thomas Walsh, *Our Lady of Fatima*, p. 80.

11 Ibid, p. 145.

12 Ibid, pp. 148-149.

13 Ibid, p. 149.

14 *Fatima in Lucia's Own Words*, Sr. Lucia's Third Memoir, p. 102.

15 Ibid, pp. 104-105, 107-108.

16 Frère Michel de la Sainte Trinité, Volume III, *The Third Secret*, Buffalo, New York, Immaculate Heart Publications, p. 38.

17 Ibid, p. 42.

Finally, in mid-October 1943, Bishop da Silva gave in writing to Sister Lucia the order she requested from him.[18]

Still she could not comply.

She felt for almost three months, "a mysterious and terrible agony." She related that each time she sat at her work table and took her pen in order to write down the Secret, she felt "prevented from doing so."

She wrote her director that, "Although she had tried several times, she was unable to write what had been commanded her, and that this phenomenon was not due to natural causes."[19]

1943 ended. The day after New Year's Day, 1944, Our Lady appeared to Lucia in the infirmary at Tuy. There She confirmed: "... that it was indeed the will of God and gave her the light and strength to accomplish what had been asked for."[20]

In the Chapel at Tuy, the same place where she had received on June 13, 1929 the vision of the Most Holy Trinity, Lucia wrote down the Great Secret of Fatima told to her one July day in 1917, a day when witnesses noticed the sun grow so dim that the stars could be seen at noon, a Secret so vital even the stars had come out to listen.[21]

Jacinta, Lucia, Francisco, photographed before August 13, 1917 by Father Joachim Antonio do Carmo, in the garden of the Marto family a few days before they were kidnapped and put in jail by the masonic mayor of Ourem for their crime of reporting what Our Lady of Fatima said.

An official newspaper photo of part of the 70,000 witnesses to the Miracle of the Sun on October 13, 1917.

18 Ibid, p. 44.

19 Ibid, p. 45.

20 Ibid, pp. 47, 48.

21 Ibid, p. 47.

Chapter 2

The Beauty of Thy House

Growing up in Montreal, it would be hard for a Catholic child not to be inspired by the career of Brother Andre, the humble religious who spent his life honoring St. Joseph. So many healing miracles were worked in St. Joseph's name through the prayers and hands-on administration of Brother Andre that even in his lifetime he was known as the "Wonder Worker of Montreal." Brother Andre's passion for his great patron, St. Joseph, knew no bounds. Overcoming demonic hostilities inside and outside the Church, the uneducated religious solicited the aid and financial assistance of the great and not-so-great in his grand plan. His determination and holiness caused to rise on the slopes of Mount Royal, the great edifice that would be known round the world as St. Joseph's Oratory.

Likc so many others throughout the first half of the century, Nick Gruner went to the Oratory on the slope of Mount Royal many times and prayed to the famous servant of the great Saint Joseph. Also, like so many other boys in Quebec in the first half of the century, he was a Latin Mass altar boy by the time he finished second grade.

There, amid the high drama of the Immemorial Mass, once again like many before him, he underwent a special transformation.

There was a moment, in the Mass of the Ages, when many an altar boy made the transition from being just a child listening to the "blessed mutter of the Mass," as Newman called it, as it issued from the lips of the priest, to becoming, at heart, a priest himself. The transition took place in the heart, on that landscape of innocence and trust, where, like a deer searching for a running brook, he had yearned for God, without knowing it, all his young life.

The moment was marked by the sound of running water. As he poured water over the fingers of the priest, he heard the priest whisper, '*Lavabo* ...' . At the sound of that word, decade after decade, since the Mass of the Ages was formulated, century after century, that word '*Lavabo* ... ', washed the world forever from the altar boy's heart and ushered him into the priesthood.

That moment of grace would remain a mystery all of his life, perhaps only in later adulthood could one pinpoint with accuracy the moment when the altar boy became a prisoner of Christ. Still, there must have been a moment of recognition shuddering through his soul the first time he heard the translation of the words into his own tongue:

> "I will wash my hands among the innocent;
> And will compass Thy altar, O Lord,
> That I may hear the voice of Thy praise;
> And tell of all Thy wondrous works.
> I have loved, O Lord, the beauty of Thy house;
> And the place where Thy glory dwelleth.
> Take not away my soul, O God, with the wicked:
> Nor my life with men of blood
> In whose hands there are iniquities:
> Their right hand is filled with bribes.

But as for me, I have walked in my innocence:
Redeem me, and have mercy on me.
My foot hath stood in the direct way:
In assemblies I will bless Thee, O Lord." (Ps. 25)

Of all the moments of nurturing that demonstrated the sheer genius of Holy Mother Church none surpass that moment when the Bride of Christ, so breathtaking in Her grandeur, nemesis of principalities and powers, terror of tyrants and ideologues, turns all Her attention to the littlest of Her children, the pure and trusting boy on the altar, and gives him an embrace that makes of his past, present and future, a love story unequalled in the annals of romance, the pure and utter thralldom that can exist only between a young man and God.

Powerful enough to wed time to eternity, nevertheless the love that enters a boy's heart at *'Lavabo ...'* remains within, without a pulse, until, as surely as the head is hinged to the shoulders, the boy, following an impulse he could not fathom, nor scarcely even acknowledge, leans his head back and looks up at the body of the Son of Man hanging above the tabernacle. His eye follows the line of those tortured limbs, all four of them drawing the eye toward their point of intersection, that Sacred Heart hidden within the constricted chest, and the altar boy's heart begins to throb, beating out the rhythm of the realization that floods his soul, the rhythm of the answer to the question that has haunted him since first he saw that Body on the Cross on the wall above his crib—"Why?" For a moment the boy is lost in the silence of the Cross, but then the ticking sounds are pounding, pounding, pounding within his own chest. And he knows the answer.

Somehow, he makes his way through the remainder of his duties, changes into his own clothes, rushes out into the cold winter air of morning and flies headlong homeward through the snow crying, "For me. For me. For me." And he is in love. And called to be a priest forever.

A mandate from God can come any time and when least expected. The Virgin in Nazareth was not expecting Gabriel. The shepherds in the fields of Bethlehem were not expecting a choir of angels, yet they were mandated to go seek a child wrapped in something special and laying in a manger. The shepherds on the slopes of Bethlehem, drowsy, cold, probably hungry and cranky, wanted nothing more than to doze off and be left alone. The most introspective of them might have sat gazing eastward over Jordan toward the Mount where he had been told since childhood that Moses was buried. Stories told in childhood glow with a sacred warmth that is never more welcome than in the cold heart of middle age. But, instead of being left to their rest, the shepherds were called upon to witness nothing less than the arrival of God on earth in the most unexpected of wrappings, the flesh of a baby child.

Far away from those famous shepherds in time and geography, three other shepherds—aged seven, nine and ten, had nothing more on their mind one spring day in northern Portugal, in 1917, than to rush their way through noontime prayers, when suddenly they were mandated to contemplate nothing less than the future of mankind.

So it is that greatness can enter the heart of a child and shape its future even as a boy runs home after early morning Mass, bursting to tell his mother what has just happened to him. He rushes into the kitchen, finds her at the stove, as he does every morning after Mass, but, instead of blurting out the news, he stands there speechless.

Only then does he realize the thing so recently planted in his chest is a secret, between him and God. He cannot even tell his mother. How does he know this? Well, how did the Wise Men know they could not return to Jerusalem and gossip? Heaven flooded them with the wisdom of doing otherwise.

The mother glances back from the stove to the doorway and sees the altar boy returned. Sees the snow melting from his cap onto his brow, coursing in miniature brooks down either side of the face. In a second of time so tiny only angels could measure it, she has recorded the change in him. She looks at the light in his eyes, the words shaped on his lips but arrested there by some mysterious grace with which she has always been sharing this child. "Don't drip snow on the floor," she might say. Then, perhaps, "Breakfast is on the table."

Simple banal words, spoken since time immemorial at this time of a winter morning, between mother and son. But this time by a mother to a priest.

Faith comes through the mother, said De Maistre. It always has. It always will. Who can doubt that the Three Wise Men had three wise mothers?

Padre Pio received the faith from his. Cardinal Mindszenty from his. Father Fuentes from his. They grew into three of the most persecuted priests of the Twentieth Century. One can easily suspect that it was in those silences between a mother and her son, a boy with his secret, a mother with hers, that Pio, Fuentes and Mindszenty gained the strength to stand alone against the most horrific forces this century could throw at them, and emerge with their defense of the Cross intact after years of vilification, betrayal and persecution. Is there a boy at your kitchen door? Look closely before you answer. Could he be a Fourth Wise Man, perhaps an inheritor of the mantle left on the river bank by Pio or Mindszenty? The Catholic child standing at the schoolhouse door on his first day of school in 1948 was a new creature on earth, one living under the threat of the nuclear annihilation of whole nations, unaware that his Church, too, was an endangered species.

§

A child entering grade school in Catholic Quebec went prepared with five or six years of home catechism. When Nick Gruner was five, his mother said she wanted all her children to grow up to be not just nominal Catholics, but good Catholics. She taught them about the Immaculate Conception at home, before school. It is the wise mother who reserves this precious teaching for herself in those early childhood years. The child accepts the Immaculate Conception with the greatest of ease. What, after all, to a pure child could be more natural than for God to create perfect purity to be the Mother of His Son? To learn of this treasure from a mother is to be awarded a trophy of the faith that cannot be lost to any adversary, on any battlefield.

Like Catholic children the world over, Nick learned the story of Fatima at home, long before he ever saw a school door. Just across the street from the Gruner home lived Mr. Leonard Hynes, future President of C.I.L., his wife, Jessie, and their four children, each aged within a year of four of the Gruner children, including Nick. One day, in their house, during a recitation of the Rosary, he heard them inserting at the end of each decade the prayer "O my Jesus ...", dictated to Lucia by Our Lady of Fatima. He objected to it since he hadn't heard it said before. It was then that they told him about the Message of Fatima. He took the details home and inquired about them of his mother.

It was in the 5th grade of St. Joseph's School in Montreal that the teacher told the Fatima story to the class. After hearing it, he had gone home and announced that he was pledging to say the Rosary every day for the rest of his life. He was reminded by his mother that such a pledge was a solemn promise to the Mother of God and should be entered into with great caution and even greater resolve. The presence of the Mother of God in one's life was not to be taken lightly.

Father Nicholas Gruner would later recall the legacy of Marian devotion left by his family: "On my father's side of the family, devotion to Our Lady was quite deep. My father had been an Anglican and heard the arguments against devotion to Our Lady. Still, when I was in my twenties, he defined for me his attitude towards Mary—namely, that just as a king delights in honoring his queen, Jesus, who is King, delights in honoring Our Lady, who is His Queen.

"Grandfather Mullally had founded a hospital in Montreal and named it St. Mary's, after Our Lady. He had been born in Prince Edward Island and his uncle had been a sea captain. Once, the captain had to get rid of a drunken sailor who was causing trouble. As he was about to leave the ship, the sailor cursed the captain and the crew and the ship. Afterwards, off the coast of Newfoundland, a storm destroyed the ship. Nevertheless, not one of the men were lost, for, when the ship went down, my grandfather's uncle had them all praying the Rosary.

"My grandmother, Mary Mullally, was an artist who painted pictures of Our Lady, including Our Lady of Fatima, which I now have in my house. When an art exhibit in Montreal once displayed a broken lily, symbolizing the artist's denial of the virginity of Our Lady, my grandmother severely upbraided the curator, taking him to task for including it in the display."

In the late Forties, when Nick was in early grade school, the essentials of the Fatima story and the beauty of the characters were known to nearly every Catholic. What was not known, and could not have been at that time by the father and mother catechizing their children in far away Canada, was the drama that had been still unfolding within the Church regarding both Our Lady's Message and, in particular, the Third Secret.

Pope Pius XII called himself the "Pope of Fatima". In 1950, he performed a unique and vital act of leadership. On November 1, Pius XII declared as infallible teaching of the Church that Mary had been assumed body and soul into Heaven upon Her death.[22] The Dogma of the Assumption would give a world living under the shadow of extermination a reminder that life did not end here, that no matter what evil man might bring into the world, the company of a loving God for all eternity was our true destiny.

1946 - Sister Lucia, in her Dorothean habit standing beside Bishop da Silva, where she was asked why we must wait until 1960 for the Third Secret to be revealed. She replied: "It will be clearer then."

22 Pope Pius XII, from the Apostolic Constitution, *Munificentissimus Deus*, promulgated Nov. 1, 1950; Denzinger, *The Sources of Catholic Dogma*, 2331-2333.

Chapter 3

Wound in the City

Nick Gruner was in high school from the fall of Hungary to the fall of the Church Militant. From 1955 to 1959 he attended D'Arcy McGee High School, the same school his grandfather, Dr. Mullally, had founded 25 years earlier.

Few young men of that era could savor such continuity in family tradition. For Nicholas Gruner it would last a lifetime. Indeed it would have to, for tradition as it was known by home, school and family, was about to be swept away by a wind created outside of nature.

Nick had always been considered serious in nature even as a teenager. Not that he was totally immune to stimuli, but fads never seemed to touch him. Rock and roll, for instance, was popular, but it seldom consumed his interest. Fonder of Chopin and other classical favorites that Malcolm Gruner played at home in the evening, he became even more appreciative as he grew older.

"He was a bit of an entrepreneur in school," his brother Tony recalls, "organizing ski trips, selling magazine subscriptions to raise money for school projects. He wasn't into a lot of sports but he did play hockey in the Parish hockey league after he left high school." He had two sisters younger than himself. The last and seventh born, nine years Nick's junior, was named Jennifer. A classic moment of sibling co-existence is contained in her childhood memory of him.

"He was very good to me. He even taught me to ride a bike. I used to make him sandwiches, three cheese sandwiches every day. He'd pay me 10 cents. It was my first job. He was my first employer. But he'd complain to classmates when he got tired of them. By the time my older sister joined him in school she was jokingly blamed for making the sandwiches."

As a family, they followed the practice of visiting seven churches in one day the week before Easter on Passion Sunday. It was one of the first great Catholic family traditions swept away by the changing times.

At university, Nick was voted in as president of the Newman Club, winning by one vote. He put a lot of effort into it, showing his characteristic willingness to lead the way even when unpopular, against opposition.

Though there was little time for it in his always busy schedule, he enjoyed playing hockey and football.

Always, he exhibited a lifelong character trait.

"He had a strong sense of right and wrong," Jennifer recalled. "When Jehovah's Witnesses came to the door there was a strong family tradition of talking to them, not just for courtesy sake, but at length, to teach them. He seriously defended their attacks against Our Lady's virginity to which they were unable to argue. He would talk to them and they would go home to check out what he said, hopefully to think things through. But he did not talk about the religious life in the sense of his being interested in it."

Looking back and reflecting on those early days forty years later, Father Gruner explains some of this secondary family and school formation: "I learned to 'make it on my own' very early on." As the fifth child and the fifth son, he was in the middle of the family. "Of course, my sister's friends were not my friends. My older brother Tony was, and still is, a charming man. He made friends easily and was invited everywhere but, as older brothers are wont to express, he did not want his younger brother tagging along. Plus, we had different characters. As a result, I made my own way.

"That continued after leaving grade school. All my companions went to Loyola, which was run by the Jesuits. But my father insisted that, unlike my older brothers, I would not be taught by the Jesuits. Reputedly, they did not excel at teaching math and, as there was a possibility that I might go on to engineering as he had, he felt I would fare better at D'Arcy McGee, the school my grandfather Mullally had founded. It was then run by the Christian Brothers.

"D'Arcy McGee was in the heart of downtown Montreal, quite a different setting from where we lived. We weren't a rich family but we lived in what might be called a good neighborhood in what had originally been my grandfather's home. Though we wanted for nothing, and the house was well kept, we still did not have the extras that the neighbors had. Going to school in downtown Montreal at the age of 13, having no friends there, forced me to adapt to people of different cultures and diverse backgrounds."

It might be said that like many who are considered more mature than their years, there were certain stages of growing up he never went through. The trajectory of his future career had already begun, one that would constantly pit him against superior numbers.

He came by that dynamic honestly, as Tony Gruner relates—his parents tended to be politically Conservative in a province that was, at that time, historically Liberal, the Gruners taking advantage of the option of voting against the party in power. Even as he entered school, he was developing a resistance to being outnumbered, no doubt in part a result of being raised in a non-French family surrounded by the French-speaking population of Montreal.

§

Montreal itself had been founded by a special act of providence, although most Montrealers would not know that today. It began as a missionary outpost, the result of a dream interpreted as coming from God, the seeds of Montreal being sown by a small population of French pioneers who accurately believed their endeavors, sacrifices and sufferings were in the service of the Gospel and the Catholic Church.

As a Montrealer, it was not lost on Nicholas Gruner that his native city could have had a very different history had Louis XIV consecrated France to the Sacred Heart in 1689, as requested by Our Lord to St. Margaret Mary Alacoque.[23] If the powerful Sun King had obeyed, Protestant Europe might have been converted back to the Catholic Faith through France, and French North America might never have fallen to the English. As Nick Gruner learned later, these possibilities would dramatically parallel those promised by Our Lady of Fatima in return for the consecration of Russia. In retrospect, the parallels were even more poignant to him, when recalled, that his student days were lived during the collapse of the Church in Quebec. Would it have happened anyway? Would the Church in his native Quebec have withstood its almost total disappearance, along with the old Quebec, under longtime Premier Maurice Duplessis?

For all his faults, Duplessis understood the importance of keeping the province Catholic. He had even passed a law which kept the Jehovah's Witnesses out of Quebec. And, indeed, less savory aspects of Duplessis' reign made a profound impression on

---

[23] *The Life of Saint Margaret Mary Alacoque*, Bishop Emile Bougaud, pp. 263-273, Tan Books and Publishers, Rockford, Illinois.

the young Nick Gruner.

A saintly Archbishop, the Most Rev. Joseph Charboneau, had confirmed him, the same bishop who soon got into trouble with the Vatican because he crossed a line drawn in the sand by Premier Duplessis. The famous strike of Quebec's asbestos workers struck the province like a cataclysm. It devastated incomes, starved families.

"Bishop Charboneau took the side of the union workers," Father Gruner today recalls. "I remember him as a man of great courage and moral fortitude."

Experiencing a unique brand of hellfire, Charboneau raised money to feed the starving workers.

"He saved lives," Father Gruner points out. "Literally, Charboneau was a pastor feeding his sheep. Whether the strike was right or wrong did not matter, he would not see families destroyed by hunger."

Duplessis was outraged that a mere Archbishop should be siding with the union workers against the government. He apparently enlisted the aid of some well-placed Vatican bureaucrats.

Charboneau was removed, sent packing, a broken man, to Victoria, as a confessor of nuns. He was the Archbishop of Montreal yet he was summarily dismissed and replaced. His departure left wounds in the city for a long time.

Charboneau's feeding of the poor was his downfall. There can be little doubt that the incident still reminds one to be cautious regarding careerist Vatican bureaucrats. The reality at the bottom of the crisis should never be forgotten.

Charboneau's replacement was Paul Emile Leger, later to be made Cardinal. Leger's transformation throughout his career mirrors with sad irony the disintegration of the Church in Quebec. In the beginning, Leger's presence and determination were edifying. In the early Fifties he had caused a sensation at 10 o'clock one night by approaching a roadside pornography stand downtown, taking magazines off the racks and throwing them into a bonfire.

By the time he died, thirty-some years later, women in long priestess gowns stood along the steps of Notre Dame Cathedral holding aloft coffers of burning incense in their hands as his coffin was carried down the steps, at the avant-garde Offertory, with baskets of bread on their head, all images of the post-conciliar Church Leger personally shaped in Quebec.

There were, admittedly, abuses of power executed by various Churchmen in Quebec over the centuries but overall this unique bastion of the faith in North America had been preserved. Then on October 8, 1958, Pius XII died. Pius had predicted Communism would strangle the Americas 'at the neck'. The noose was tightening before Pius was laid to rest. Few had seen it coiling into place. The election of John XXIII was felt in every city, hamlet and classroom in the world. Then came 1960. In Quebec, Duplessis and his two political successors died in the same year. It set the province spinning. On February 8, 1960, the curtain rose on the most catastrophic decade in the history of the Church. That day, the Vatican anonymously announced that the Third Secret of Fatima, the details of which Catholics worldwide had eagerly awaited, would not be publicly revealed that year.[24] The Sixties had started with a lie. Nick Gruner was still studying at McGill University in the critical year, 1963, when Pope John XXIII died, John Kennedy was assassinated, and Pope Paul VI reconvened the Second Session of the Vatican Council. Life seemed more serious suddenly.

24 Frère Michel de la Sainte Trinité, Vol. III, *The Third Secret*, Buffalo, New York, Immaculate Heart Publications, pp. 578-579.

Nick Gruner considered himself blessed to have gotten through the Catholic school system in Quebec before governmental attacks on education changed it forever. Ten years later, he would teach within that system, see how schools had been reorganized into large impersonal classes, both unwieldy and unwholesome. The public education system was not organized any better, and worse, it wasn't Catholic. By 1970 both systems would be destroyed, with few remnants of Catholicism surviving.

The priesthood had always been there. But even at 21, on retreat in Montreal, he had been cautioned, 'Finish your degree first and then consider the priesthood'. He was then two or three years into his degree, with no thought of abandoning his studies. Basic to his plans was to enter the seminary with a degree in business. He earned his Bachelor of Commerce Degree at McGill University in Montreal, finishing in 1964. Then it was time off to see a bit of the world.

1964 - Nicholas Gruner graduating from McGill University in Montreal, Quebec with a Bachelor of Commerce Degree.

1971 - Nicholas Gruner as a seminarian, in conversation with Pope Paul VI.

1972 - Seminarian days at San Vittorino. Left to right: Andrew Winchek, Brother Gino, stigmatist (with the wounds of Christ), Ron Tangen and Nicholas as he completed his final year of his Bachelor Degree in Theology. Brother Gino dubbed him "Doctor".

Chapter 4

Gethsemane

After graduating from McGill, Nicholas Gruner decided to head to Europe and visit places of importance to his father's English roots.

These were personal pilgrim years for Nicholas Gruner, filled with travels in honor of Mary's Motherhood of Men. He began his journey as a deck hand on a freighter to Europe, in 1964, cleaning and painting, until the officers' cook got sick and he took over the job.

Because Baba had a great devotion to Our Lady, he wanted his grandson to visit Aylesford, Kent, in England. Nicholas recalls why Oscar Cameron Gruner had such great devotion to Our Lady. "My uncle Douglas died in Australia when he was only 18 years old, trying to stop a team of horses that were running wild through the town. Douglas took after them on his motorcycle and the horses trampled him to death in January 1926."

Many times it has occurred to Father Gruner that his father's sudden conversion was not only due to St. Cecilia, but also to Douglas, his brother, whom he believed offered his life to God to obtain this grace for Malcolm.

"This spirit of self-sacrifice is also reflected in my father who, after his conversion, made the heroic offering of allowing God to take all the merits and prayers for his soul in Purgatory to be offered to other souls before him.

"Shortly after Douglas' violent death, my grandfather Gruner had a dream about Douglas, who was the younger of his two sons. He described how, in his dream, he saw the way saints greet the newest one among them. First, the saints receive him, then afterward, Our Lady welcomes him to their number. He recognized Our Lady in his dream because She resembled the image of Our Lady as She is depicted in the chapel of Hartley, a small chapel in Kent, England. My grandfather described his special dream as follows:

> "The picture began by the appearance of a small glow of light... and the picture was of the altar rail and the altar of the Oratory here at Hartley... Very rapidly it became evident that there was a solitary young figure kneeling in the middle of the rail. It was Douglas. His head was bowed low over the rail...
>
> "...The form of Our Lord became evident; robed in brilliant golden light; the raiment and He were one... the upper part of our boy's body being quite lost to view in the blinding light of Our Lord's presence.
>
> "Then I perceived His Face, sharply visible in semi-profile, among the brightness which extended beyond and all round, almost like thick rays; and as He stooped over the boy, and seemed to embrace him, his shoulders, He seemed to be soothing him and comforting him, and embracing him, as a father might...
>
> "...One felt absolutely secure; it was not an atmosphere; it was peace itself; it was living peace...
>
> "...That odor of Peace was all between the place I saw, and right across the gulf down to me, and I was filled with it during the whole time His Form was visible...
>
> "...Suddenly, at his left side, appeared the form of a most beautiful Lady; Her face was in semi-profile; there was a wonderful expression on it; infinite

motherhood; the face was not young; the light She gave round Her was extremely intense, much more than that of the angels; and yet it was less intense than that of Our Lord, different really, it was not that peculiar sense of Almighty—security.

"She stooped down to our boy and seemed gently to lift him up, his head lying in Her left elbow; I could not see his features; he was like a babe; and yet I was sure it was still he—still Douglas; he seemed to be sleeping, and yet aware of being in Her arms. His form was indistinct. As She held him thus, the circle of angelic forms rose a little with Her, and there seemed a movement of them all—away from the rail, and towards the Gospel side of the altar, and it was as when a person is carried from among a crowd and the crowd slowly makes as if to follow. At the same time She stood erect, nearly; and was in full profile; and for a moment I saw that Her profile was now exactly the profile of Our Lady of Hartley; but it was not a fancy; She was living; one could tell it was not a statue. The light of the whole scene centered in Her as She moved from the altar rail.

"The details became indistinct for a short time now; but when it was all clear again, I saw that Our Lady had handed the soul of our boy into the care of a great multitude—a very great multitude of bright forms, forms like the angelic ones at the altar, but paler; where their features were visible, one could see they seemed sad—but a happy sadness.

"They seemed to move greatly as She came; they moved eagerly forward to their new companion; it was a very active movement; and yet they did not seem to move away from their place. It was the movement of a sudden intense interest and eagerness to minister to the newcomer. But when the newcomer was among them he became like unto them; not like a baby—form; and he was quite lost to view to me; so dense was the crowd of beings who came round him..."

Father Gruner remembers: "When Baba heard of my trip to England, he insisted I go to Aylesford, which is also in Kent, where Our Lady of Mount Carmel appeared to St. Simon Stock and presented him with the Brown Scapular in 1251.[25]

"Saint Simon Stock's cell was flooded with light when Our Lady appeared to him. She held the Scapular in Her hand, even as She wore it full size on Herself, and She made this, the Scapular, a sign of Her special love and protection for them.

"She said to Saint Simon, 'This shall be to thee and to all Carmelites a privilege that whosoever dies clothed in this (Scapular) shall not suffer eternal fire. It shall be a sign of salvation, a protection in danger and a pledge of peace.'

"My grandfather had always been gentle with me but was unusually adamant in insisting I go to Aylesford. So I went there, staying from December 1964 to March 1965. I was enrolled in the Scapular during that time and have not taken it off since. That was the beginning of my pilgrimage to Marian shrines." And since putting on the Scapular, Nicholas almost immediately started to pray the Rosary daily. He has only missed a few days over the last forty-five years.

He lived as a volunteer at the shrine for three months, until March 1965. From there he crossed over to France, heading for Rue du Bac, Lourdes and also to Garabandal.

[25] This shrine is unique among all Our Lady's shrines. The Carmelites prayed to Our Lady, their perfect example, for guidance, and She led them to Aylesford, England, in 1241, with the help of Saint Simon Stock. One day, July 16, 1251, Simon Stock went to his cell there in Aylesford and prayed with all his heart for Our Dear Mother's intercession. Saint Simon Stock's cell was flooded with light when Our Lady appeared to him. She held the Scapular in Her hand, even as She wore it full size on Herself, and She made this, the Scapular, a sign of Her special love and protection for them. She said to Saint Simon: "This shall be to thee and to all Carmelites a privilege that whosoever dies clothed in this (Scapular) shall not suffer eternal fire. It shall be a sign of salvation, a protection in danger and a pledge of peace."

§

Can any priest look back over his shoulder at the grace that has shaped his life and pinpoint with exact precision the moment he first recognized the call to the priesthood? What is the call? What exactly is it calling the young man toward?

A priest is set aside from other mankind by one single fact, he is born with a vacant chamber in his heart that he can fill only after giving it a name.

Breathes there a man who claimeth not
One lonely spot
His own Gethsemane,
Whither with his inmost pain
He fain
Would weary plod,
Find the surcease that is known
In wind a-moan
And sobbing sea,
Cry his sorrow hid of men,
And then —
Touch hands with God.

(*Gethsemane* by Edmund Leamy)

The young man who touches hands with God never forgets the touch, and spends the entire treasure of his life trying to earn that touch again.

Once, in Paris, shortly after visiting the shrine of the Miraculous Medal on Rue du Bac, praying before the incorrupt remains of the silent Saint, Catherine Labouré, and contemplating the famous chair in which Our Lady sat and held Catherine's head in Her lap, Nick Gruner made his confession to a French priest, not in the chapel itself, but in a makeshift confessional corner.

The priest asked about his vocation and explained, "When God created each individual human being, He, at the same time, gave that soul a vocation. Now if we are faithful to God's call, we will, in fact, be much more happy in this life because we shall fulfill in our lives what God intended us to be." The priest emphasized, "God created us in a way in which we will be more fulfilled, more ourselves, if we accept the call from God. It is a great obligation, a high vocation, but there is sacrifice."

The priest put a uniquely French perspective on it, 'la gloire'—sacrifice. Added to it was the promise that if one does what God wants, one will become more of what God wants one to be, and ultimately more happy.

Father Gruner would remember this promise throughout his life. By 1965, he was in Portugal, where he tried to hitchhike to Fatima but was unable to catch a ride. Eventually, he made his way north to Pontevedra and Tuy, from there to Santiago. He went to Garabandal in March, where he stayed for several days. He came back to Garabandal on June 18, 1965, when St. Michael reportedly gave the last message which told us to have greater charity and more love for the Most Blessed Sacrament and which also warned that many Cardinals, bishops and priests were on the way to hell and dragging many more souls with them.

His journey there really began to take more definitive shape in July, upon returning to Aylesford for Cardinal Carmel Heenan's official re-opening of the Shrine which had been lost to the Church since 1549 under the Protestant revolt in England. While walking behind a young pilgrim couple, he overheard the woman say to her husband, "I'm not sure about this Garabandal business. Is it really Our Lady appearing here? The miracle hasn't happened yet." Nick introduced himself and said: "You don't have those problems with Fatima. Fatima is approved. The miracle has taken place. The popes have approved it. Fatima is valid, Fatima is good." Nick also said: "If we listen to Fatima then we need to pray the Rosary, wear the Scapular, these are the message of Fatima. So at least you can resolve to obey Our Lady of Fatima. If you do all She said at Fatima, you need not worry about any, as yet, unapproved apparitions."

Yet even as he said those words, he was conscious of the difference between Garabandal and Fatima. Fatima was so uncomplicated because it was approved by the Church and thus so easy to promote.

At Garabandal, a pilgrim put into his hand a booklet on the Rosary by an American. It contained the statement of Our Lady regarding Russia: "If My requests are not granted Russia will spread her errors throughout the world raising up wars and persecutions against the Church. The good will be martyred, the Holy Father will have much to suffer, various nations will be annihilated."[26]

Interestingly, it was the only thing about Fatima in the booklet, amid meditations on the mysteries of the Rosary. He became preoccupied with what Our Lady's Fatima requests actually contained.

He finally returned to Montreal in August of 1965. His brother Tony notes that although even in high school Nick was similar in nature to what he is now, serious, with his humorous moments, after he came home from Europe there was a difference in him.

"In Europe," said Tony, "he had made the decision to become a priest."

He entered the seminary that September and was sent by the diocese of Montreal to Resurrection College in Kitchener to do his year in philosophy. He took as many courses as time would allow, passing them all with flying colors. In September 1966, he went to the Grand Seminaire, the major seminary in Montreal, for his first year in theology. Most of the classes there were conducted in French. While there, he expressed himself emphatically about the outright atheism on the campus at the University of Montreal, to which the "Grand" was affiliated, and argued forcefully against a group of students, with modernist leanings, who were promoting the idea that Catholic divorce would be permitted in the future.

They claimed that Cardinal Garrone, the new Prefect in the Vatican in charge of all Catholic seminaries, was on their side. Undaunted by prestigious names, Nick Gruner said: "I don't care if 10 Cardinals hold that position, it is still heresy. Divorce for Catholics can never be approved by the Church." The rector, in May 1967, told Nicholas he did not agree with his intellectual position though he acknowledged they were argued intelligently and forcefully, but were not shared by him, and told him to try his vocation elsewhere.

By 1968 he was once more in Italy. He was, in fact, riding a train to San Giovanni Rotondo when he first heard of *Humanae Vitae*. He vigorously defended it against the naysayers. It was probably the first papal encyclical since the *Syllabus of Errors* that raised tempers in trains, buses and coffee shops worldwide.

He was to live in San Giovanni during the last six months of Padre Pio's life and was

26 Frère François de Marie des Anges, Book One, *Fatima: The Astonishing Truth*, Immaculate Heart Publications, Buffalo, New York, p. 104; also, *Fatima in Lucia's Own Words*, Sister Lucia's Fourth Memoir, p. 162.

present for the funeral of the man called 'a living crucifix' who had suffered so cruelly from the ill will of Vatican bureaucrats, the indifference of Pope John XXIII and the financial exploiters of his name. Few men in this century suffered more for the love of his priesthood, few men were subjected to more suspicion and vilification, than the pious Franciscan of San Giovanni Rotondo.

His lesson to all seminarians might well be that any priest contemplating a new apostolate receives no peace on this earth. Vilification, libel and slander will rain down upon him with relentless force. Only knowing that Christ suffered worse slander allows men like Padre Pio to find strength to continue.

The list of priests, some of whom would later be canonized, who have so suffered is endless. St. John Vianney, St. Louis de Montfort, St. John Bosco, Damien the Leper. Is there a good priest alive today who has not been subjected to the malice of the relentlessly pious of today's Church and most especially from that ingredient of Church life few priests escape—the Catholic matron who considers all she needs to be canonized in her own lifetime is the friendship of a unique man of God, preferably one much in demand and the center of world attention?

Padre Pio showed all too clearly what fate lies in store for the priest who becomes a lightning rod for pious assassins ever active on the phone lines of the current day Church. Nick Gruner lived in San Giovanni from April to September 1968, when Padre Pio died.

On October 13, 1968, he saw Fatima for the first time. The most startling characteristic of the shrine in the Cova da Iria is its masculinity. This is no mere gathering place for sentimental housewives. Here, uniformed Portuguese soldiers, having returned home from the horrors of war in Angola, did the army crawl on their stomachs from the edge of the esplanade to the azinhiera tree to thank the Madonna for bringing them home safely. Here young men walk along the highway in packs with all the panache and swagger of gangs in any big city in the world, but here they carry Rosaries. Here men, young and old, join the women petitioners for the long sojourn on their knees, along the Penitential Way, from the edge of the Cova to the capelinha. Men walking the street with a Rosary in hand is as common as men fingering worry beads in Greece and the Middle East. Men come here to lay down their lives for God. Some never leave, content to pass the remainder of their days, living saintly hidden lives, serving the Virgin in the shadowed laneways spreading out from the shrine. Nicholas Gruner would come back many times. But for now there were more pilgrimages, to Lourdes, to La Salette, and finally to the Holy House of Loreto, in Italy.

§

During the years when Vatican II had been in session, Nick, like most of the world, did not follow it daily. He was aware of it, but was preoccupied with his seminary studies at that time. Indeed the sacrifice spoken of by the priest confessor at the Rue du Bac had not been long in coming, for by the Sixties the attack on the seminaries was already in full swing. The domino effect, the Council inadvertently set in motion for Catholic education and theology itself, was already threatening to unbalance the spiritual and intellectual foundations of the priesthood. It was during these years that the ideologies that had haunted the Church since Pius IX ceased being mere specters and seized control of seminaries, colleges, high schools, and even began to filter down to the Catholic grade school level. Americanism, Leo XIII had labelled it. Modernism, Pius X had called it. Democratic socialism and secular humanism were its classroom euphemisms.

In the resulting confusion spreading everywhere in the dogmatic, hierarchial, sacramental Church, a seminarian had little but his own spiritual instinct (*sensus fidelium*) to help him discern what was true from what was not. Our Lady had promised those who prayed the Rosary daily, would not fall into heresy. Father Gruner reflected in later years, "How fortunate I had rediscovered the Rosary as an adult, before entering into the seminaries in those days of confusion."

For him the determination to always fight for what was true had been founded long ago. His entire educational trajectory reveals an independent mind prepared to stand alone regardless of the cost.

Political and organizational abilities which would be so crucial to his own future apostolate had been already in evidence as early as 1956.

Throughout those years, his sister Jennifer recalled, Nick remained thoroughly involved in the normal activities of day to day life. In 1956, he became president of Annunciation Teenagers Club (A.T.C.). The older teens were letting it close down but Nick took it over and made it flourish for many more years, despite jeering opposition from the older teenagers.

> "The older teens basically despised the efforts of the founder, a Mr. Coleman, a Vice-President of Kraft Food in Montreal, and talked about closing the club down. I wrote that we would like to keep it open. As a result of that letter, I was elected president and we were allowed to try one more time. In spite of the jeers of the older teens, we were able to revive the club, making it active within the parish once more." This initiative of his also helped others, he recalls, "I recruited Eric McLean, who was one year lower in school, to work on our executive committee. He became the next president of ATC and later went on to join the Jesuits. Today [1998] he is the Provincial for the English-speaking Jesuits in Canada."

At McGill University, he became president of the Newman Club, winning the election by one vote—that of the returning officer, who had the deciding vote since the vote had been tied. He found himself in a leadership role responsible to and for people who had, to some extent, opposed him. The experience foreshadowed future battles.

In October 1970, he was offered a position with a small Mexican religious community housed in Rome. He took them up on the offer, staying a year. While there, he completed his second year of theology, taking his courses at the Pontifical University of St. Thomas Aquinas.

That brief stay with the Mexican Community would ultimately involve Nick in the drama of initiating a new and unique seminary. At the Mexican Community, the founder, Father Morelos, urged the novices to work on Sunday in the orchards. Gruner chose not to engage in physical labor on Sundays and so, after exams, in June, he departed, at the insistence of Father Morelos. Thereafter he was left to find his own way, relying on some money he still had left in his bank account from teaching.

As Father Gruner recalls:

> "In the summer of 1971, I used to go to Mass near St. Paul's Outside the Walls, and pray there every day with some Franciscan friars who were just beginning to form their own community. I had just left St. Paul's Basilica to go back to my room when I noticed the car from the Mexican community that I had left one month before.
>
> "I met a Father Carlos and two other visitors to Father Morelos' community, Ron

Tangen and Les Stelter, who had come looking for me at my previous address, having been directed to me by a friend in London, England. They were looking for a seminary.

"I told them about Brother Gino, a religious well known in Rome as a stigmatist and miracle worker and, as many said, the successor to Padre Pio. Some days later they came by and wanted me to take them to Brother Gino, which I did. I translated for them and told Brother Gino they were looking for a seminary, and Brother Gino suggested that all three of us join his Order, the Oblates of the Blessed Virgin Mary (O.M.V.), and study there, at San Vittorino, where Brother Gino lived. Ron was overjoyed with the suggestion. Brother Gino told me to be their 'guardian angel'. I refused to translate this at first, since it wasn't addressed to them, but at the guys' insistence I finally translated what Brother Gino had said. Brother Gino told us there was going to be a general chapter of the order in mid-August and to not apply now, but come back after the general chapter had been held.

"Brother Gino had the gift of foretelling the future sometimes and was a prudent counsellor. They took his advice. As Brother Gino appointed me to be their guardian angel, they invited me to go with them to Garabandal, Fatima and Lourdes. They had a third companion, Mike Larshack. They were all over six feet tall and somehow all fit into a Fiat Seicento, much smaller than a Volkswagen. I took the fourth seat.

"On the pilgrimage trip that followed, we travelled over 1,000 miles and we stopped at a number of places including San Damiano, where it was reported Our Lady was appearing. There we met Andy Winchek (who later became a priest) and picked him up to bring him to Rome. In Garabandal we met Jim Shelton from Ohio (who was ordained a priest in 2002), who was 39, 10 years older than I and we brought him back to Rome as well. In Rome, we met a third American, Jim McArdell, from New Jersey. They all agreed to join the Oblates.

"Although Brother Gino suggested we stay at San Vittorino, and we were welcomed when we went there every so often, we continued to be stationed in Rome at the OMV parish of St. Helen's.

"Shortly after joining the Oblates, five of us English-speaking seminarians went on another trip to Eastern Europe with Father Michael, the priest in charge of the seminarians, along with three other Italian-speaking seminarians. We visited the OMV house in the same city where the Council of Trent was held. We also visited Austria where the Oblates had a parish and a house in Vienna. From Austria we went to Hungary."

It was during their stay in Hungary that Father Gruner gained a first-hand view of what Communism was really like.

"Early in September 1971, eight of us seminarians and a priest drove to Hungary. Visas to enter the country were only issued for 36 hours and the fee was the largest I had ever seen for such a brief visa. As we approached the Austrian-Hungarian border, I took a closer look at the landscape. In both directions the fields were ploughed up and mined and steel watchtowers were planted every half mile or so. The whole country was like a giant prison camp with miles of barbed wire fencing. The sentinel scrutiny towers seemed high enough to watch for anyone trying to make a run across the minefields, making escape virtually impossible.

"There was a heavy steel barrier at the Hungarian border that you would not dare to try to run through with your vehicle. As if that wasn't bad enough, once inside that barrier you found you were trapped between that and yet a second steel barrier. We noticed something very unusual when the immigration compound was changing guard. There were not just two military border patrol men being replaced by two others. There were three guards, all with machine guns drawn, replaced by three other men, also with guns drawn. The third, Father Michael told us, was to shoot the first two guards if they should ever try to escape. Was he serious? I don't know. But none of us were about to start testing them.

"After some time, we were finally released and allowed into the country. We had 36 hours to drive to Budapest, look around and get out before we were officially breaking the law and liable to some fine or imprisonment. We drove to the capital and noted how empty the streets were, hardly any cars. But there were long lines of people at the grocery stores waiting their turn to buy bread.

"That evening, around 9:00 p.m. we went to a restaurant. Again, hardly anyone was there except for an older woman who started to speak to us. She raised her voice and spoke excitedly in Hungarian for a minute or so. Quickly she was surrounded by two or three men in trench coats and without ceremony hurried out of the restaurant. No one moved or did anything—and, we did not see her again. We decided, then and there, not to experiment in free speech in a public place.

"The following morning five of us went to the American Embassy to see if we could visit Cardinal Mindszenty. It was watched by two Hungarian plainclothes police who paced in front of the embassy all the time. I had never had any trouble entering an American Embassy anywhere else around the world, but here I was not allowed in as I was not an American citizen. I was told it was because of the ever watchful Communist police who were looking for some pretext to accuse the Americans because of the high profile exile, Cardinal Mindszenty, who had been living inside the embassy for the last 15 years.

"The Hungarian Communist police outside were there as spies to ensure that Cardinal Mindszenty did not escape and to see who was going in to visit him. He represented a real and continuous threat to the morally bankrupt regime that had imposed itself on the Hungarian people for the past 25 years.

"That one man represented such a threat shows what moral authority the Church had and would have if it would follow the courageous example of that great witness to the Catholic Faith.

"I learned afterwards that not even the four American seminarians who were let inside the Embassy were able to meet Cardinal Mindszenty. Obviously, access to him was near impossible. Cardinal Mindszenty had come freely to the Embassy in 1956 when he was released from the clutches of his Communist torturers and prison guards during the brief Hungarian uprising. He stayed there as a symbol of resistance, resistance against the religious and civil oppression his countrymen had been and still were undergoing.

"The Cardinal was, no doubt, treated humanely inside the Embassy, but it was clearly a crucifixion for him. May he pray for us today, now that he is in Heaven. I believe his case will be introduced shortly for sainthood. We need many more Catholics of all levels from laypeople to Cardinals like him.

"One of the Americans with us spoke German, which is the international language of Eastern Europe and thus we were able to communicate and find the address of an old acquaintance of his living in Budapest. The man and his wife had not dared to have their children baptized because they would have lost their good-paying jobs. They both were like middle managers in a State-run concern, part of a small fortunate group who would own their own home after paying the mortgage on it over 35 years.

"This home was a very small apartment on the 8th floor of a very large and run down apartment complex. The toilet top was made of wood with tin to prevent the water from leaking out of it. The concrete beams and columns in the stairwells were crumbling to dust. We estimated the building would not be standing in 35 years, but this was the 'workers paradise'.

"Obviously they were getting neither the kingdom of God nor much else on earth. It is indeed sad that people do not realize how true Our Lord's statement is: 'Seek first the kingdom of God and all things will be added unto you'. One could say, by way of implication, 'Seek first the paradise of man on earth and you will get hell here and hereafter'. To us this point was clearly made in Hungary.

"On Saturday morning after we went to the U.S. Embassy we looked at more of the sites in the city. The historic Church of St. Stephen had been turned into a museum by the Communists. We saw it for the historical record of what it had been in the past and also to see what Communism did to famous churches. Creeping secularism in the West also has the effect of turning our famous cathedrals into mere tourist traps and quasi-museums, but in Hungary the effect was achieved by a deliberate state policy.

"Saturday afternoon, our Hungarian host took us to the monument built in honor of the Russian soldiers who 'liberated' the city. It is a massive monument placed in the prime location of Budapest overlooking the Danube River which runs through the city. It is an historic spot, not just because of the 'liberation' monument, but because it is symbolic of the glorious days of Hungarian history before Marx, Lenin and Stalin were even heard of. Here at this monument stand not only several giant statues of Russian soldiers laboring to take over Budapest, but also several live flesh and blood Russians with real guns standing guard.

"Les Stelter decided to have his picture taken in front of the Russian monument. There he stood, 6'2" with his arms upraised holding in his hands a giant sized wooden rosary for all to see. Several pictures were taken when our Hungarian host called me over to him and quietly but firmly said: 'Tell your friend to take down his rosary. You see that Russian soldier over there?' 'Yes' I said. 'Well he might think your friend is mocking the Russians and he will have me imprisoned.' Les took his rosary down in this city supposedly 'freed' by the Russians, yet not free enough to display a rosary in public.

"We left that afternoon in a hurry because our 36-hour visa was running out. Thanks to our two guides, we had seen more than most in that short period of time. We made it back to the border with only half an hour to spare. After our luggage was thoroughly inspected and rummaged through, we were allowed to leave."

When they returned they saw first-hand that the writing was on the wall for conservative and orthodox seminarians. Father continues:

"We went to St. Helen's parish where Father Michael was in charge of seminarians in Rome, 25 km from San Vittorino, in the Casalina district of Rome, close to the heart of the city. They were renovating the seminarians' chapel. The altar was not going to be left against the wall but put in the center. Father Ron, who had spent four years looking for a good seminary and had been invited by Brother Gino himself to join the Oblates, was not about to take this chapel renovation lying down. He objected quite strenuously and went to Brother Gino and told him his objections. Brother Gino told us to ask to be transferred out to San Vittorino and take seminary training there and take a car in, every day, to the Angelicum.

"The Superior General, Father Ottello Ponzanelli, who was about to leave for a three-month tour of the Oblate houses in South America, said he did not want the seminarians to go to San Vittorino. He left the decision to us English-speaking seminarians but strongly counselled against it. I said I would stay with the majority, since I was the translator.

"Then Ron and Les and a third seminarian decided to go to San Vittorino, I then said I would go as translator. The other two Americans also then agreed to go. This was the beginning of a seminary that would rock the Vatican.

"By September 1972 we had 50 new seminarians and would have had 100 had the Oblate middle-managers allowed us to accept the Nigerian applicants. I was authorized by the Superior General to speak on behalf of the Oblates, in the summer of 1972, on vocation-gathering trips in the U.S. and Canada. I acted as the official translator and travel companion of Father Capello. He was opposed to what we stood for, was very 'modern' but I suppose that was the Superior General's way of maintaining control and placating the strong opposition he was getting from some of the 'modern' Oblates.

"My role in the founding was getting professors who were orthodox and conservative, the distinction between conservatism and traditionalism hadn't been made yet. We found Father Buckley, Father de Voss and Father Vansteenkiste to teach philosophy.

"Basil, Ron and I drew up and printed a brochure about the seminary, with the Superior General's approval. Ron wrote a letter explaining his experiences. He started as follows, 'I am writing before the Blessed Sacrament exposed' and went on to describe his experience looking for a seminary for four years, and how they were all bad ones, and how his dream was fulfilled by going to San Vittorino. Over several months, it got published in eleven small journals. We circulated our brochure, especially in Ron Tangen's mailings, to prospective seminarians who had written him as a result of his letter being published. The brochure explained that the seminary was based on the rule of the saintly Father Lanteri, a humble Italian priest from the Piedmont district of Northern Italy, who lived through the troubled period during and after the French Revolution, and died in 1830.

"One of the purposes of Father Lanteri's congregation was to fight current errors. Alas, the modern Oblates' attitude was, 'We don't fight current errors anymore.' Father Lanteri spoke of St. Thomas as the first choice as teacher of dogmatic theology and St. Alphonsus as first choice as teacher of moral theology, both being Doctors of the Church.

"During the fall of 1971, while living at San Vittorino, I heard from my friend, Nimal Mendez, about his brother Basil's plight. Basil had been a professor of philosophy in Ceylon, who decided to become a priest, and entered a diocesan seminary in Ceylon.

"Basil's agony was not unlike my own persecutions at the hands of seminary administrators. I told Brother Gino about Basil, and in keeping with Father Lanteri's spirit, Brother Gino agreed for us to pay for Father Basil's plane ticket to bring him over. Father Basil had fought against heresy in the Ceylon seminary and told the Cardinal there, quoting St. John Eudes: 'When heresy is taught in the seminary, there will be blood flowing in the streets.' And indeed, sad to say, there has been blood flowing in Ceylon almost ever since Father Basil left the country. In fact, recently, they had a strike in nearby Madras, India, in sympathy for the ongoing bloodshed continuing in Ceylon."

In their brochure, the young seminarians promised a rich prayer life to others interested in the priesthood: 15 decades of the Rosary every day, and one hour before the Blessed Sacrament, Mass and Communion; and a spiritual apostolate afterwards, giving the sacraments, preaching the gospel, saving souls, as well as being taught St. Alphonsus and St. Thomas.

"The brochure struck a nerve." Father Gruner recalls, "We got hundreds of letters. The seminary was written up around the world, thanks to the prayers and sacrifices of Brother Gino and, of course, the fact that we were offering a genuine Catholic training to serious young men who knew that finding a true Catholic seminary was becoming very difficult.

"We operated our outreach on a shoestring with only a few dollars donated here and there which, after six months, started to be more sizeable. By October 1972, one year after we had started to recruit seminarians, we had collected and spent $25,000 to promote Oblate vocations. This was only one quarter of what the Archdiocese of New York had, just for their vocation outreach."

Nick, Ron and Brother Gino had demonstrated by October 1972 that there was no lack of vocations in North America.

At the same time, in 1972, the North American College in Rome, sponsored by the National Bishops Conference of the USA, was openly talking about closing down because they couldn't get enough seminarians to fill it. The whole hierarchy of the USA couldn't find enough seminarians to keep the North American College going, even though at the College each seminarian had a private room, bathroom and office, which by any seminarian's standards are palatial. The Archdiocese of New York alone had a $100,000 budget per year to find seminarians but was not successful in finding many, if any, while that year with only $25,000 the apostolic zeal of these Oblates brought in fifty new seminarians.

Then the fight began. As has happened so very often in this century, a success story attracting the attention of the Vatican upper echelon spelled trouble. Specifically, it brought into the picture Cardinal Garrone, at that time the head of the Congregation for Education. Father Gruner continues the story:

"When I returned to San Vittorino on the feast of St. Francis, September 17, Vini Young, a personable young seminarian, said how relieved he was that I was back. Four seminarians suspected of being Communists, and who were not part of the movement we had generated, had turned the Superior against the vast majority of seminarians. They insisted we remove all outward signs of piety, such as medals worn on the outside, crosses on our briefcases, and what have you.

"Our Lady helped us in this crisis through Brother Gino. God gave Brother Gino a vision of the Communist seminarians phoning a Communist priest in the Vatican at 2:00 a.m. Brother Gino went downstairs and surprised these Communist infiltrators as they were on the phone in the kitchen where they thought no one would find them at that late hour.

"After this, Brother Gino took me aside and said, 'If you don't stand up to them now, you will lose the seminary you want to form. Stand united'. That's how Communists work, a small number can overwhelm a larger number too intimidated to stand up to them.

"I explained his words to the others and we did stand united. The four Communist seminarians saw the ranks closing in on them, saw that they could not carry the day in modernizing the seminary and finally gave up. They were ultimately shown the door."

Brother Gino said later, "Because of the presence of one person (Gruner) and the absence of another (who had supported the four), we were able to get rid of four Communist seminarians."

Brother Gino was asked by the seminarians, after the Communists left, why this was allowed to happen. He replied that it was because God wanted them to be trained and aware that these things were going on. "The training was not lost on us and not lost on me today."

The lesson was: be too successful and they'll try to shut you down. Either by infiltrating your operation or...

"We wanted to have philosophy as well as theology at the seminary taught by orthodox professors. Not all professors at the Angelicum were orthodox. There were among them professors who promoted heresy, even though the Angelicum was reportedly 'the best' of all the Roman theological universities. Our aim was to get a degree from the Angelicum with our own professors. The Dean of Philosophy agreed to it, as did the Dean of Theology, the Rector of the university, and the Superior General of the Oblates. A confirming vote by the Senate of the Angelicum was merely a formality in such a situation.

"Thus in the spring of 1972, we took their word for it and did what they told me. Then a few days later, the closed door meeting of the Senate was held and shot down our proposal. I had not been invited to be present. The Dean of Philosophy apparently stood up and said the Congregation for Education under Cardinal Garrone would not accept it. With that remark from the Dean of Philosophy, no one else said or did anything in our favor and then the Senate voted us down.

"When I found out the next day, I asked the Dean of Theology, Father Salguero, what happened. I reminded him that he personally had told me not to worry about our proposal for Angelicum professors teaching at our seminary and that he had reassured me that the Senate, the supreme governing body of the Angelicum, would easily accept our proposal.

"I believe it was Father Salguero who then told me that it was the Dean of Philosophy who had intervened, as I described above, to shoot it down.

"I then went to the Rector Magnificus, Father Gieraths, and I asked him why I had not been told of the problem before the meeting. Perhaps I could have done something to prevent the negative vote.

"Father Gieraths told me I should have talked to the student president beforehand, who could have represented our proposal, had he wanted to. No one ever told me that before our proposal was torpedoed, and I did not even think the student president had much to say in anything, up to that time. Well, I decided the Rector cannot have it both ways, when it came to the election of the student president a few years later.

"The upshot was we could not give degrees for those studying theology in the internal school. They had to go to the Angelicum and be exposed to heretical and less-than-orthodox teaching but we kept our hopes that in September we could have an internal school for theology and philosophy.

"We knew from the Legion of Christ that their Superior General had gone into the Dean of Philosophy's office one day and said, 'Get rid of that professor or I will take my students out tomorrow.' Only then did the dean get rid of him. This proved we knew what we were talking about in choosing our own professors.

"We didn't need their degree to be ordained. The Oblates had the right to train their own and they didn't have to graduate with university degrees to be ordained. But come September, we ended up studying theology at the Angelicum but managed to save our philosophy school by having philosophy under Father Buckley and Father de Voss, but even that wasn't acceptable to the powers that be. Over the next three months they managed to have Father Buckley removed and then over the next few months succeeded in totally closing down what remained of our internal philosophy school. But they did not rely only upon internal agents in the seminary to close it down, the Vatican's Cardinal Garrone got involved.

"Cardinal Garrone was reliably reported, at a meeting in the Vatican, to have become angry upon hearing in early fall 1972, that there were 50 seminarians at the school, and of all the things we were trying to do. 'That place must be closed' he said, pounding the table with his fist. At first, the young seminarians could hardly believe this report, but in time it was proven to be true.

"Before 1972 was over, the Superior General of the order came to visit me in the Novitiate near Turin, after his visit to South America." Father Gruner recalled, "I was in far Northern Italy because by October, I was identified as the leader in getting the seminary started and holding it together, plus, I did have a track record for getting rid of the four bad seminarians that Father Capello had sided with. Thus the local Superior insisted I do my Novitiate up north.

"I did not know much of the details of what was going on in San Vittorino after I started my Novitiate on November 21, 1972. I got my largest dose of news in December from the Superior General, Father Ponzanelli.

"The Superior General said the pressure on him was tremendous. Even though he was somewhat modernist, he was sympathetic to getting vocations. Father Buckley was bounced. An investigating team from the Vatican came to look at what was going on in the seminary. There was nothing to investigate. (The investigation was merely window dressing for what they intended to do.)

"By the spring of 1973, our internal school was closed. All the seminarians had to go to the Angelicum, with good and bad professors.

"In September 1973, I was still in the novitiate of the Oblates of the Blessed Virgin Mary. The Superior General had just come back from some lecture where a professor denied that Christ rose physically from the dead. He agreed with this heretical teaching and repeated it to me and as well to all the Fathers and

> novices, including Basil. I simply said, 'That is heresy.' The Superior General repeated his point and I repeated 'Heresy'. He still kept it up and after the third time I remained silent as this was not a child's game. A few months later, I was out on my ear, a conclusion that is not surprising. In reference to my saying it is heresy, their reasoning was 'Since you have no confidence in your superiors, it is not reasonable you stay with us in this order'.
>
> "In the mid 1980's, Father Basil, now editor of *Christ To The World*, a small journal sent to 1500 people, published an article by an English priest demonstrating that Garrone's tenure in charge of Catholic education around the world was a disaster. Garrone was furious and expressed his fury in a letter to Father Basil. Shortly after, Garrone was replaced."

Long-time friend Jean Fioretti of New York recalls meeting Gruner in those early days when he was not yet 'Father', merely 'Nick'.

> "My husband Bob and I knew another seminarian who was studying at the Oblate seminary in San Vittorino who invited us out for a visit. That was in November of 1972. There was a gathering at which Brother Gino received people from many different countries. Nick, as it turns out, was Brother Gino's interpreter and right hand. We became friends and remained in touch with him throughout his studies and his ordination.
>
> "It's a custom in Italy for seminarians to go home for the summer and so, sometimes, he visited with our family here in New York. Many of the young men stayed at our home in the summer. The other seminarians all used to say Nick was too rigid. But nobody could argue with him and prove him wrong. They had all gone into the seminary with a very strong faith. But it was the Seventies. Things were changing."

§

By 1975 Nick was in St. Thomas Aquinas University in Rome, where once again he found himself in the role of challenging election irregularities—a candidate with the lesser count of votes had been declared the winner. The vote was 66 to 63 on the first two ballots with only two candidates running. Still the Dean and Rector called for a third ballot.

> "It meant challenging the Dean of Canon Law and the Rector, Father Gieraths; addressing the 'fixing' of an election; studying the existing constitution and discovering the law was on our side; petitioning against the validity of the election, then, appealing over the heads of the Dean and Rector to the Master General of the Dominicans who still upheld the Rector."

Undaunted, that encounter saw Nicholas Gruner taking the kind of direct and positive action that has long since become his trademark.

> "We sent the documentation to *Si Si No No* when Father Putti was still editor and publisher there. Whether or not this had anything to do with the future of the Angelicum, the fact is the Rector, Father Gieraths, was never re-appointed."

Gruner received his Bachelor's Degree in Sacred Theology and the Licentiate Degree in Sacred Theology from the Pontifical University of St. Thomas Aquinas, in Rome. Achieving ten out of ten on all courses and papers save one, where he obtained a nine out of ten, he successfully completed all required courses for his doctorate in Sacred Theology. His doctoral thesis alone remained.

The subject of his Licentiate thesis was Mary's Motherhood of Men in the Supernatural Order of Sanctifying Grace. A good part of the thesis dwelt on this teaching of the Church prior to and during Vatican II and the post-conciliar teachings of Pope Paul VI. In part it read:

"'For the glory of God' and at 'the most solemn and most opportune moment', Pope Paul VI proclaimed Mary Most Holy to be 'Mother of the Church'. The Holy Father did this to satisfy his own desire, and the requests of many Council Fathers, to make an explicit declaration of the maternal function which the Blessed Virgin Mary exercises towards the Christian people.

"Paul VI gives the dogmatic foundations of this title: 1) It is a title widely used by the faithful and the Church; 2) Her Spiritual Maternity is based on Mary's Divine Maternity. Because She is the Mother of Christ, She is also the Mother of the Mystical Body of Christ.

"It seems to me", Nick Gruner wrote, "that this affirmation by Pope Paul VI that Mary's Divine Maternity is the foundation of Mary's Spiritual Maternity should stop all further discussion which tries to say that Mary is only the most excellent member of the Church and no more, since only She is the Mother of the Whole Christ."

As an elected student representative at St. Thomas Aquinas for the doctorate year in Theology, this meant being invited to faculty meetings and he found himself with a vote in the election of the dean.

> "When the current dean, Father Salguero, stated with, shall we say, 'official humility', that he should not run again, I took him at face value and began to seek other members of the faculty's help in getting a better dean. Even so, I was soon prompted to bear in mind that they still had some say in whether I graduated or not.
>
> "In faculty meetings, we student representatives had not only a consultative but a decisive vote. In other words, our vote would count toward whether or not a decision would be made. Father Salguero, Dean of Theology, wanted to appoint Father Barnabus O'Hearn, C.P., as a visiting Professor of Scripture, in the Angelicum. I inquired around about him and was given an article by a priest, a recent Doctoral graduate, which was published in the *Wanderer*, against O'Hearn, by Msgr. Bandas, who had impeccable theological credentials. His degrees included a degree higher than Doctor of Theology. He pointed out that O'Hearn was suspect of heretical writing. When the item came up on the agenda at the next meeting, the Dean of Theology asked if there were any objections to appointing Father O'Hearn. I then proceeded to distribute copies of the article. After reading his copy, Salguero became very angry and yelling at me, said, 'Gruner, don't ever bring anything like that in here again.' I was centered out and felt like crawling under a table. The dean regained his composure and insisted on a secret ballot. When the vote box had only been three-quarters circulated, some of the voters opened the ballot box and saw the votes up to that point, thus making the vote invalid. The dean however declared it valid and that the vote went against us. We lost the battle but we won the war because O'Hearn, some weeks later, claimed health problems and did not come."

A former dean of the faculty, Father Lemeer, who had participated in the meeting, told Gruner afterward that he agreed with him that the article he had circulated was fair comment and his circulation of it did not deserve the criticism it got. Nicholas Gruner reflected on that: "I wondered to myself why, then, did he not stand up at the meeting in defense of the article and my position?"

The reality is—the way business is conducted at faculty meetings demonstrates clearly why professors who are orthodox, and know better, do not stand up when they should. They are simply afraid that they themselves will be thrown out, as was Father Giuliani, an orthodox professor of Christology, who was dismissed by the modernists who were in control.

Personalities on staff at the Angelicum merely confirmed the unhealthy dynamics at work in Catholic education in that era: "A visiting Spanish Professor of Theology went out of his way every class to take many shots at St. Paul, saying St. Paul discriminated against women, basing it on his admonition that women should obey their husbands." After hearing this many times, Nicholas Gruner felt it his duty to speak out, even though he was endangering himself. He countered with, "Do you have to obey your superior? Do I have to obey a legitimate order from a bishop? Is that discrimination against us?" The debate, conducted in Italian, in class, ended after 20 minutes, with the Professor left with nothing to say. Except for one or two passing remarks, he never spoke about it again in Nicholas Gruner's hearing. Neither did he return the following year.

Father Gruner reflecting on this incident, says: "The victory was all Our Lady's—I was so mad at his scandalous comments that I prayed one Hail Mary after another—asking for the right words, and they came to me even as I was speaking, just an instant before I needed them."

In mid-1975 his spiritual director was the famous Father Gabriel, a Servite Father who had a following of thousands of faithful in Rome. He advised Nicholas not to join any religious order unless they obtained his ordination first. When the Conventual Franciscans of Frigento offered to take him in, he told them the conditions laid down by Father Gabriel. Gabriel had the reputation of being a holy, gifted man, so they conformed to his advice and found a bishop for him on November 21, 1975, the Feast of Our Lady's Presentation in the Temple, in the diocese of Avellino. In the same manner, they had already ordained one Father Paolo, a seminarian from Padua, whom Gruner had met on pilgrimages around Rome.

The Bishop of Avellino, Pasquale Venezia, a short man, five-foot-five, had a heart attack shortly before Nick Gruner arrived for his incardination. The whole diocese had turned out en masse to pray for his recovery. When the young seminarian was incardinated into the diocese on April 15, Holy Thursday, 1976,[27] the bishop jokingly said: "I blame all the priests. It's your fault. If you've got me for longer now, it's your fault because you prayed for me."

On the Feast of Our Lady's Queenship, on the Octave of the Assumption, August 22, 1976, his father's birthday, and also the day designated by Pius XII in 1946 as the Feast of the Immaculate Heart, at the Sanctuary of Our Lady of Good Counsel in Frigento, Italy, Nicholas Gruner received Holy Orders, conferred upon him by Bishop Pasquale Venezia.[28] Among those present at the ceremony were Malcolm and Jessie Gruner, as well as Fathers Manelli, Pelletiere and Sutton.

§

Immediately after, Malcolm Gruner, whose early years in Italy, and his conversion at the tomb of St. Cecilia, had forever linked his family to that country, celebrated his

27 Copy of document maintained in the diocese of Avellino.

28 *Congratulations, Father Nicholas Gruner*, "The Fatima Crusader", Issue 53, Summer 1996, pp. 1-2; also, *Picture of Father Gruner's Ordination*, "The Fatima Crusader", Issue 18, Oct.-Dec. 1985, p. 13.

71st birthday by receiving Communion from his own son's hand at his first Mass. It is the moment the parents of a priest await for their entire life. Much of the salting of the ensuing apostolate had already been determined by the people and the events of that day. When Malcolm had converted, under the influence of St. Cecilia, the faith came to him with its abundance of treasures in a sudden flash of knowing, so that soon after, he was able to say to those who charged that devotion to Mary competed with devotion to Jesus, that it was Jesus Himself who delighted in honoring His Mother.

As it so often does with a new priest and his parents after ordination, the ensuing months were devoted to family. All priests know that time will never come again. In this case, they went on pilgrimage to the shrines of St. Anthony of Padua, St. Francis of Assisi, St. Michael of Mount Gargano, St. Leopold in Padua, St. Gemma Galgani's burial place, St. Peter's in Rome and St. Nicholas of Tolentino, to commemorate the Saint on whose feast day, September 10, in 1930, his parents had married and in whose name he had been christened.

After ordination to the priesthood, but before entering the Novitiate, Father Gruner lived and worked in the house of Our Lady of Good Counsel, Casa Mariana, the Marian House of the Franciscan Friars, under the direction of the local superior, Father Stefano Manelli.

The work included some travel, with permission from the bishop. He entered the Novitiate on October 4, 1976, and received his name, Father Nicholas Maria. He remained at the Novitiate of the Franciscan Friars until February 1977. At that time, he began inquiries, with the permission of the provincial, to see if he could continue his Novitiate in North America, in one of the provinces of the Conventual Franciscans.

With permission of his superiors, he travelled to the USA and Canada.

By May, after talking to and visiting with provincials of two of the four Franciscan provinces, he was directed to Marytown in Kenosha, Wisconsin. The provincial there could not promise that he would incardinate him. He would only consider it after he completed his Novitiate in Italy. But there were language difficulties, for, in Avellino, the bishop would not let him preach unless he had written out everything. And to hear confessions in Italy, the bishop wanted him to first learn the difficult local dialect. That would have taken years.

§

The possibility of forming an English house in Italy, at that time, seemed pretty well hopeless. There was nothing left for Father Gruner to do but write to the Bishop in Avellino, asking permission to seek a bishop in North America.

He travelled across North America introducing himself and seeking incardination, seeking a bishop who did not order his priests to give Communion in the hand: Washington, D.C., New Mexico, Texas, Florida, North Carolina, New York, Kentucky, Wisconsin, all to no avail. Then in August of 1977, acquaintances in Ottawa asked him to come help save a Fatima Apostolate centered in that city. He arrived on the Feast of Saint Clare, August 12, 1977.

By 1977, little remained of the pontificate of Paul VI. In the sixteen years since John XXIII's 'inspiration' the Church had become barely recognizable. Virtually nothing remained of the moral authority it had wielded in the past. A sneering triumphalism was assumed by the enemies of the Bride of Christ. Any attention paid to spokesmen for Roman Catholicism by the Left Wing establishment of the Ecumenical Church was an exercise in sheer condescension.

In the waning months of Paul VI's life, traumatized Catholics hoped and prayed for a successor who would strengthen the primacy of the Chair of Peter and promote the rights of Christ over those He redeemed with His Blood on Calvary. The knowledge that Paul VI was nearing the end spurred many who had suffered myriad varieties of martyrdom in defense of the faith during his pontificate. Restoration movements sprang up around the world. In anticipation of the inevitable conclave, grief-stricken Catholics began offering nothing less than the balance of their entire lives for the salvation of their sacred heritage.

On June 5, 1978, Bishop Pasquale Venezia officially granted Father Gruner written permission to live and work outside the diocese of Avellino.[29] With that blessing, Father began his full time commitment to Our Lady of Fatima's Apostolate.

On August 6, 1978, Paul VI died. Grief was the legacy left the Church. Grief for the passing of treasured aspects of the faith that were consigned to oblivion. Grief that the truths of the faith had been lost by poorly educated clergy in theology chairs.

Those fatal years coincided with the most dangerous time in history for the unborn children of the planet. A New World Order was on the horizon. Population controls were on the agenda of world health organizations. The new missionary to the Third World was the contraceptive salesman. A slaughter of the innocents of the world was about to be launched supposedly to harness mankind's growth down to a manageable number. In the Western hemisphere, mass infanticide would be launched in the most unlikely country on earth.

August 22, 1976 - Ordination of Father Nicholas Gruner by Bishop Pasquale Venezia, Bishop of Avellino, at Frigento, Italy in the Diocese of Avellino, in the Conventual Franciscan Sanctuary of Our Lady of Good Counsel. Father Gruner, center, kneeling. Left to right: Vicar General of the Diocese, a newly ordained young priest, Father Stefano Manelli, Bishop Venezia, the Pastor of Frigento, Father Gabrielle Pelletier and Father Alphonsus (William) Sutton.

29 Father Nicholas Gruner, *A Canonical Recourse to the Sacred Congregation for the Clergy*, "The Fatima Crusader", Issue 53, Summer 1996, pp. 19-20; also Father Nicholas Gruner, *Father Gruner's Letter to Cardinal Innocenti*, "The Fatima Crusader", Issue 29, Sept.-Nov. 1989, p. 34.

Chapter 5

Whose Hands are Full of Bribes

The results of a mid-1960's survey run by the *New York Times* claimed that the three most boring words in the English language were 'weather, budget and Canada', but not necessarily in that order.

Even the people of Canada were amused, demonstrating that at least the non-violent, non-revolutionary, non-strife ridden country north of the 49th parallel still had a sense of humor.

By 1968, Canada would have another distinction. It would be the first country in North America to legitimize the murder of children in their mother's womb. A high price to pay to be interesting.

If ever a country needed a soul-stirring, it was in those years leading up to the fatal act of entrenching judicial slaughter of innocent babies in the Canadian Constitution.

In June 1978, Father Gruner became the Vice-President and Executive Director of the National Committee for the National Pilgrim Virgin of Canada[30] and shortly thereafter published the first issue of *The Fatima Crusader*. Immediately after, in this position, he launched the first of his nation-wide Rosary tours.

During those early pilgrimage days of 1978, crisscrossing Canada with the statue of the Pilgrim Virgin, the true heart and soul of Marian devotion revealed itself to be very much alive in Canada. In the warm reception afforded the statue of Our Lady of Fatima, it was clear that the romance of Catholicism still remained in peoples' hearts, that same yearning that once prompted artisans to raise the great stones of Chartres above the plains of France.

Those escorting the Pilgrim Virgin on the mid-Canada portion of the tour must surely have thought, from the evidence, that it was not too late for the world to return to God. There was the procession through the streets of half-English, half-French Hawkesbury, on the Quebec-Ontario border, recalling to mind the great Corpus Christi and Christ the King processions of now distant memory. Then, in Ottawa, a triduum at St. Mary's, with Father Whelan, the all-night First Friday, First Saturday vigil at St. Martin de Porres, with Father Heffernen.[31] At St. James Church, in Oakville, Father Lima's parishioners lined up for one and a half hours to venerate the statue. At Cobourg, the parishioners asked to accompany the statue's travels, in their own vehicles, to the next town of Port Hope.[32]

The recollection of the Pilgrim Statue visit to the parish of St. Stephen the Martyr, in Dowling, Ontario, by the pastor, Father Marcel Nault, provides a close-up of Father Gruner's early priesthood days.[33]

Father Nault recalled: "It was 1979. Father Gruner called me and said: 'My name is Father Gruner and I have with me the Pilgrim Statue of Our Lady of Fatima. I go from church to church wherever I am travelling. Would you like me to come to your church?'

"I asked why he wanted to. He answered, 'Because people know you as a Marian priest'.

"I could not help but smile when I saw him getting out of his van wearing a black

30 *Introducing the new Executive Director*, "The Fatima Crusader", Issue 1, Summer 1978, p. 1.

31 *Recent Events*, "The Fatima Crusader", Issue 3, Summer 1979, p. 3.

32 *News of the Apostolate*,"The Fatima Crusader", Issue 5, Spring/Summer 1980, p. 3.

33 *Recent Events*, "The Fatima Crusader", Issue 3, Summer 1979, p. 3.

cassock. I was not in the habit of seeing a priest in a cassock.

"I helped him bring the statue of Our Lady inside, all his scapulars, everything. He had not yet celebrated his daily Mass and asked permission to say it there.

"I invited him to say either the Mass on Saturday night or Sunday morning for the Parish. He said, 'If you don't mind I prefer to say it by myself.'

"I then said, 'If you're not saying Mass, will you help me distribute Holy Communion?' He said, 'I'd rather not, if you don't mind.' You see, he would not give Communion in the hand.

"I thought, what kind of a priest is this? I found out the answer as I watched him say the Tridentine Mass, with his own chalice and his own traditional vestments, listening to him when he was praying the Rosary on his knees, teaching the message of Fatima, giving out the Brown Scapular to my parishioners, praying with his hands extended over the head of those being invested in it. All his prayers were in Latin.

"I took note that he was very serious about everything he was doing, especially in teaching the message of Our Lady. He was outside of the new way of saying Mass. I was inspired not to condemn him because of that.

"He asked permission to visit the two schools in the parish, one French and one English, to distribute hundreds of Brown Scapulars.

"A year later, in 1980, he asked again to come back to my parish. This time, after his visit was finished, I shook hands with him and said, 'Father Gruner, I have the feeling Our Lady of Fatima wants me to work for Her.'

"Later, he invited me to preach in Montreal at a conference at the Sheraton Hotel. I talked on the Catholic dogma of hell and he printed it in his *Fatima Crusader* magazine.

"When he asked, 'Why don't you come and work with me?' I decided to wait for a sign from the Lord. Then he invited me to go to Fatima and there I had the privilege of addressing Cardinals and bishops on the dogma of hell. I decided to work with him."

Father Nault was instrumental in establishing one of the most noticeable characteristics of Father Gruner's appearance. As Father Gruner recalls: "Father Nault assigned me the penance of wearing the miraculous medal outside of my cassock. I still wear the one he gave me to this day. Our Lady promised that those who wear the medal would get great graces. I began wearing the medal around the time I started to write on the issue of the Consecration of Russia. Is it because of these special graces, for wearing the miraculous medal publicly around my neck, that I have been able to concentrate on the consecration? Is that why I was selected to do this job? If so, I wish more priests would wear it, then more work on the consecration would get done."

On the tour of Western Canada, the statue arrived in the diocese of Mackenzie-Fort Smith in the Northwest Territories, geographically the largest diocese in Canada, by way of a special courtesy, free air passage given on all jet flights for Our Lady's travels in the north.

At Black Lake, people flew in from over 1000 miles away. Hundreds received the Sacraments during the visit. The parish priest, Father Mowka, O.M.I., kept saying it was like Christmas or Easter. Father Mowka heard confessions all day for three days. "I only saw him briefly during meals. He was always hearing confessions. I could not help because I didn't speak the Indian languages. When it came time for us to fly out to our next scheduled visit, the entire town came to see the seaplane off and to wave a final farewell." [34]

At Fort Norman, they gathered at the landing strip to greet its arrival, then walked

34 *Recent Events*, "The Fatima Crusader", Issue 2, Spring 1979, p. 4.

back to the church in procession. Once inside, they individually chose to approach the Pilgrim Virgin statue on their knees, to pay homage and petition for favors. Official government meetings scheduled for the district had to be cancelled because of the great numbers who chose instead to go to the church to see the statue.[35]

In Prince Albert, at the Cathedral, Bishop Morin crowned the Pilgrim Virgin and formally consecrated his Diocese to the Immaculate Heart. Forty parishes were visited by the Pilgrim Virgin when Edmonton hosted the tour in November.[36]

She travelled 20,000 miles, as 38,000 Scapulars were given away, 22,000 Rosaries, 170,000 leaflets, 40,000 pamphlets, 10,000 *Fatima Crusaders*, and thousands of Peace Plan booklets.[37]

During stop-overs of the Pilgrim Virgin, the Blessed Sacrament would be exposed all day to the accompaniment of those ingredients of Catholic life that are, alas, now but a thing of memory—school processions, five-hour vigils, all-night vigils. At Holy Trinity, in Vancouver, the Stations of the Cross were said at 2:30 a.m. These are the things by which Catholic culture was once nourished.

With such style were the signs of a vibrant traditional Catholicism made evident that in 1978, Bishop Remi De Roo of Victoria would give his "...wholehearted support for the further promulgation of the devotion to Our Lady through the practice of the Fatima Rosary." [38] My, how times would change! In a mere ten years, a marathon 'people's synod', lasting just slightly shorter than the Jurassic Period, would conclude that Remi De Roo and his Diocese of Victoria were on the cutting edge of a New Church, that Thing set up to replace the Church of Rome.

"I am not a lackey for the Pope," De Roo would repeatedly claim while blithely and heretically announcing that, "Transubstantiation was a thing of the past." His diocese, the synod said, would no longer be needing input from Rome. Would no longer, in fact, have any need of the Pope. But that was still one Pope away.

The Pilgrim Statue was in downtown Vancouver when news flashed around the world that the newly-elected Pope, John Paul I, after reigning only thirty-three days, was dead.

§

Meanwhile, back in Ottawa, the Trudeau government, who in legalizing homosexuality had declared that, 'the government had no place in the bedrooms of the nation,' had proposed omitting a clause in the long-awaited new Canadian Constitution. That omission in effect said not only did the government have a place in the wombs of the nation, but that once it got there, it could do whatever it darn well pleased to the unborn voter slumbering peacefully under her mother's heart.

His 1968 Omnibus Bill had, as far as Trudeau was concerned, justified abortion. Before 1968 it had been recognized in law for the crime that it was in fact. Trudeau decriminalized it and by 1981 was attempting to enshrine the murder of unborn babies in the Canadian Constitution by leaving out the necessary clause protecting the unborn.

Canadians who recognized the omission for what it truly meant were traumatized and propelled into action. One of the most daring and, it turned out, most troublesome of all the obstacles thrown in the path of the government brought attention to Father

35 Ibid.

36 Ibid, p. 5.

37 "The Fatima Crusader", Issue 6, Christmas 1980, p. 15; reprinted from *The Catholic Register*, an article written by Stan Koma.

38 *Recent Events*, "The Fatima Crusader", Issue 2, Spring 1979, p. 4.

Nicholas Gruner from people in rather high places.

1981. Parliament was preparing to vote on the Constitution. With little time and a meager few hands to help, Father Gruner set about to make the Catholic Members of Parliament an offer they would not soon forget. In a twenty-five page letter informing Catholic Members of Parliament of the real meaning behind the constitutional terms, Father Gruner quoted Pius XI's *Casti Connubii* condemnation of abortion and made the point that it was a parliamentarian's moral obligation to defend the unborn. Failure to do so would make them guilty of the abortion death of Canadian babies through the sin of omission. With the help of an unnamed Member of Parliament, Father Gruner managed to place on the desk of every Catholic MP the reminder that if they voted for the proposed constitution, that was without protection for the unborn, they were going to be guilty of mortal sin and would end up in Hell, eventually, unless they truly repented.

To succeed in positioning an outside paper on the desk of each MP was almost unheard of and the reaction from the Speaker of the House was swift. In his bruised and battered mini-office in downtown Ottawa, Father Gruner received a phone call from no less a personage than Jean Sauve, then Madame Speaker of the House, who demanded to know how he gained access.

Jean Sauve was Catholic. Prime Minister Pierre Trudeau was Catholic. Cabinet Minister John Turner, later to be Prime Minister, was Catholic. Jean Chretien, another future Prime Minister, was also Catholic. All of them, together, were about to carve in stone a constitution that did not protect the unborn, in direct opposition to the requirements of their Faith. All of them proceeded to make it *de facto* legal to suffocate, burn and scissor a baby in half inside its mother's womb. The image of a cassock-wearing priest gaining access to the inner sanctum of Parliament to challenge the consciences of Catholic MPs was intolerable to them.

After all, had not Archbishop Emmett Carter of Toronto, a spokesman for the Canadian Conference of Catholic Bishops, himself pulled back from challenging them by telling his brother bishops in Canada that they had no business interfering with government? Yet Father Nicholas Gruner had published, to the embarrassment of His Eminence, the fact that twenty-four Western bishops had condemned the lack of protection for the unborn.

It is now part of Canadian history that Cardinal Carter, shortly after, was granted the highest honor in the land, the Order of Canada, by Trudeau, Sauve, Turner, Chretien et al. It can be truly said that the government of Canada never forgets a favor. Nor, for that matter, would they ever forget the cassock-wearing troublemaker who had almost upstaged them in their triumphant moment, and to whom possibly might go the blame for causing their critical vote to be delayed a few hours. Not to worry, it was passed into law anyway. And Canada was, at last, interesting.

The errors of Russia, where legalized abortion had been enshrined for six decades, had seduced the quietest, most peaceful country on earth and lulled it into becoming the blood-spattered midwife of a soon-to-be eugenics industry. Hitler would have blushed.

What the Parliamentarians of Ottawa had encountered in that month so crucial to the abortion holocaust in the West was the new reality of the Catholic Church. The defense of Roman Catholicism was now up to the man in the street, and to the priest with a sense of purpose.

Chapter 6

Power Play of a Locket Cult

Perhaps the years of touring had been too successful, had drawn too much attention, not from, say, a hostile media, but rather from hostiles within the Church, specifically, in Ottawa, where the Trudeau, Sauve, Turner, Chretien abortion endgame was in play. The high altitude from which the first invectives were launched at Father Gruner conjures up images of hotlines and unlisted numbers and secretaries dialing.

The first attack had actually come in October of 1978, when Father Gruner was on the road with the Pilgrim Virgin. In Edmonton he received a letter from Archbishop Angelo Palmas, the Papal Pro-Nuncio in Ottawa. The letter was in French, even though Msgr. Palmas knew Father Nicholas Gruner spoke English as his first language. In it, Msgr. Palmas accused him of being a 'vagus', that is, a priest who is not incardinated anywhere.[39]

In fact, Msgr. Palmas didn't address him as Father Nicholas Gruner in the letter at all, but as Father 'Colas' Gruner. Father Gruner phoned Ottawa, objecting strenuously to the accusation, telling Msgr. Palmas he was most definitely in possession of permission from his bishop, Pasquale Venezia, in writing. He asked if Msgr. Palmas wanted him to come back to Ottawa immediately, to set the record straight.

Msgr. Palmas told him: "No, no Father, stay where you are. As soon as you complete your statue visits we'll talk about it."

Meanwhile, Father Gruner sent Msgr. Palmas a copy of the letter from Bishop Venezia which granted him official permission to be away from the diocese of Avellino. The document was a mere five months old, still perfectly valid, and eliminated *any* possibility that he was a 'vagus'.

The trail of this first notable complaint lodged against Father Gruner by the Pro-Nuncio, led, incredibly, to a strange fringe group claiming allegiance to the anti-Pope, Clemente Dominguez Gomez, a Spanish so-called 'seer' living near Seville.

Of all the factions, movements, groups, that had come into existence to fill the void in Church leadership, few were more bizarre than this Spanish cult that had founded a foothold in Ottawa in the 1970's. Its symbol was a locket worn around the neck. A very special locket.

Clemente supposedly had a vision of the Blessed Virgin, soon after which he enthroned himself as 'Pope' Gregory XVII. And so was added to the arsenal of the anti-Catholic press yet one more bizarro who discredited yet anew any authentic mystic soul. This same group was dabbling in what Father Gruner perceived as satanic sacrilege against the Holy Eucharist. But who were these people?

Among other titles, they called themselves the Brothers of Saint Joseph, and also the White Army. The 'Army' was founded by one Maria Concepcion, whom the Portuguese bishops once charged with sacrileges against the Blessed Sacrament. There was also a Madame Bouff, who based herself in Marseilles, and who would go to visit Maria Concepcion every so often in Portugal. At the center of their cult were supposedly consecrated hosts which Maria Concepcion said she got from the Archangel

39 Correspondence between Father Gruner and Archbishop Palmas.

Michael, who, during an apparition, was supposed to have dropped them on the ground. Concepcion picked them up, so the story goes, and in time began sharing them with Madame Bouff from Marseilles.

Madame Bouff visited Canada in 1975 and again in 1976, recruiting people into the White Army. The "Army" had a hierarchy, a commander general for Canada, who was higher than the rest of the Canadian members, the next rank underneath were the 'apostles'. The 'apostle' was to wear a locket which could be bought in any ten cent store. Madame Bouff bestowed upon each 'apostle' a host, allegedly consecrated. Inside the locket she would affix the host with glue and, once bestowed, the Body and Blood of Christ was, supposedly, thereby transmitted through the daily workaday world. The "soldiers", the next lower rank, were to gather around an "apostle" and to adore the contents of the locket.

Father Gruner's first-hand knowledge of the cult came about when one of the 'apostles', reasonably enough suspecting there was something not quite proper about the required item of apparel, asked Father Gruner if he would relieve him of his locket. He did so, opening it up himself. Inside was a piece of host about thumbnail size.

Father Gruner recalls vividly that, during his possession of the locket, he sensed pains in his chest that he had not experienced before or since. He considered the locket to be 'of the devil'. Besides the pains Father Gruner experienced, he had already come to this conclusion for 9 different theological reasons only after reflecting on the locket story and Maria Concepcion's tale. He told two other priests, each of whom had more than 30 years' experience, of his findings and they concurred that the locket was diabolical. One of the most compelling reasons that told him the locket was of the devil was the fact that the White Army types order their followers to never tell any priest outside the White Army about the lockets. St. Ignatius says such a command of secrecy about the spiritual life is one of the strong signs that a mystical experience is of the devil.

"Just as the Church has sacramentals," Father Gruner comments, "the devil too has his 'sacramentals'. The locket clearly represented a sacrilege against the Blessed Sacrament."

The locket, Father Gruner perceived, was literally a devilish sacramental. Was it a consecrated Host that had been desecrated? He could not be sure. Was it something that gave the devil power over the people? Most definitely yes.

An unsettling string of horrific physical accidents befell locket wearers. Marriages were rent asunder. Families broke apart, polarized into hate camps, children were lost, seemingly forever, to their parents.

Father Gruner's first precaution was to bury the locket in salt that had been blessed with the blessing in the Roman Ritual which is used particularly to control the power of the devil. Then he asked another priest to relieve him of it and dispose of it according to the rites required by the Church in cases such as this. The priest who received it from him was so afraid of the evil aspect of the locket he drove the forty miles back to his home on a four-lane highway at twenty miles an hour. Once home, he took the host out of the locket and put it in a jar of water to let it dissolve. There was no way of ascertaining that the host had, in fact, been consecrated. The safest thing to do was to assume that it had been and treat it as such. As well, the priest in question put a second host, unconsecrated, of comparable size, in a second glass of water. After five days, the second one was dissolved. The first one lasted another 15 days.

When Father Gruner denounced the locket cult publicly, in Catholic papers in the U.S. and Canada, he instantly became the cult's number one enemy. He was soon vindicated when the cult was publicly denounced by Archbishop Plourde of Ottawa in the front pages of the *Ottawa Citizen*. The *Montreal Gazette* followed up with a lengthy series of articles about this bizarre aberration.

One of the locket wearers declared her intention of destroying Father Nicholas Gruner, boasted, in fact, that she would have him run out of the country and immediately proceeded to shop for a journalist who would print her personal rendition of Father Gruner's concocted failings. Nothing suited her purpose more than to have at her disposal the ultimate tool for discrediting Father Gruner at every turn, the vague and scary-sounding term 'vagus'.

§

The tour of Western Canada had drawn considerable attention to the young priest. The actions of his enemies would ensure that everything he would do in the future would attract even more attention. Ironically he was generating a public profile that belied the personal conditions under which he labored. A uniquely qualified witness to the spiritual climate of Ottawa in those days, Father Victor Soroka, rector of the Basilian Seminary in the late 1970's, recalls the conditions under which Gruner toiled.

"He worked in one room rented from an elderly lady. In the front section of the room he slept on a bed without springs. There were hardly any facilities. He had to ask neighboring pastors for a place to say his Mass. At that time he was publishing *The Fatima Crusader* with the help of one pious lady by the name of Debbie. But when it came to sending out the issues, he rented a hall basement and asked for volunteers to help with the envelopes.

"He was our guest quite often at the seminary. It was not possible for him to stay there as we had twenty-six seminarians then and all the rooms were occupied, except when we had a vacancy. (The seminary has since been destroyed by fire.)

"His finances were so slow in coming he could never pay in full for one edition, he was always running behind, and had a lot of trouble with the post office. They didn't want to give him the right rate, said he wasn't entitled, which wasn't true.

"Father Gruner went to different bishops but he didn't find any co-operation. Why? Because of jealousy. You see, he hardly had enough for food and yet he was promoting Our Lady through *The Fatima Crusader* and the Pilgrim Virgin Statue. He was willing to live in a rectory and help out but no one would have him. Why? Because they didn't want to acknowledge Marian devotions or have the Rosary in public. Churches neglected the Stations of the Cross and they were all giving Communion in the hand. Father Gruner's biggest crime was saying the old Mass. He was probably the only priest in Ottawa who did so at the time.

"He never made a cent, and he drove one of the poorest cars on the road. Everybody said, 'let's let him have it.' And they let him have it. But he won after all these years. Just look at what he's accomplished in contrast to them."

For those who wanted to destroy him, Father Gruner himself had provided the necessary ammunition. The focus of his apostolate was Mary. The agenda of his apostolate was simple and direct—take Mary's message straight to the people. After 18 years of the smoke and mirrors of some modernist bureaucrats who were smothering the Church, Rosaries and Scapulars were practically revolutionary. The response of the people to the Western Canada tour suggested that such a 'revolution' was, though unwelcome by the powers-that-be, apparently not unthinkable. The thing to do then was to stop it.

Why? Because of Mary, that's why. There was no place for Mary in the plans of those who were deforming the Church to fulfill their own agendas. Mary had to go. To understand clearly why Mary had to go, one has only to turn to one of the most fascinating Scotsmen of the 20th Century, Hamish Fraser.

Hamish had been a devout Communist until 1947, responsible for the work of the party in the west of Scotland, especially responsible for seeing to it that the soul and heart of the labor movement remained forever opposed to the government of the day and the Church of all time. In 1943 his conversion began.

By 1947 he was a Roman Catholic. By 1950 he was attending Fatima Conferences.

In the January 25, 1953 issue of *L'Homme Nouveau*, Abbé Richard, later to become President of the Blue Army in France, recounts a moving incident in which hereafter Hamish would be dubbed "The Dove Man".

> "Is it impossible that the cosmic rays of charity should bring about the resurgence of authentic humanity in a world made monstrous by brutality and hate? On the contrary, such a rebirth may be confidently counted on as the result of prayer, penance, holiness, and the consecration of ourselves to God through Our Lady. For these things are real, and, in consequence, have the power to set in motion, with a new vigor and a new orientation, all the potentialities of modern man.
>
> "That is the lesson taught us once more at the Parc des Expositions by our friend Hamish Fraser, the Man of the Dove. ... A friend of ours, a priest of the diocese of Cherbourg, had in his possession two doves, the offspring of the doves which in such an extraordinary fashion accompanied the statue of Our Lady of Fatima during its progress in Portugal and Spain. This priest unleashed the couple, which had never known freedom, into the Great Hall of the Parc des Expositions at the very moment when, to the music of hymns, Our Lady's statue made its entrance. The doves, frightened out of their wits, flew two or three times about the hall, and then hid in the rafters.
>
> "But one of them circled around as if looking for someone, and, out of the thousands of people who filled the hall, selected Hamish Fraser and calmly perched on his head [see photo on page 59], in the midst of his bushy hair, and there it remained, apparently quite undismayed by the flashes made by the photographers who were vying with each other in their efforts to get a shot of the scene. Then, after about three minutes, it went along to rejoin its companion.
>
> "Some moments later, Hamish Fraser was beginning his speech and declaring: 'I do not say that I believe that prayer can convert Communists; *I know* that prayer can convert Communists.' The dove seemed to have vouched for the declaration of this man in advance. A miracle? Not, certainly, a miracle for unbelievers. But, to adopt an expression of St. Paul, it may well be a sign for the faithful: *in signum fidelibus*."

Hamish watched the hijacking of the Church take place at the Second Vatican Council, saw the confusion being sown by confused theologians, witnessed the humanists outwit the bishops, observed the misguided modernists planning their strategy. Saw it all. He wondered why others could not recognize what was occurring. The tactics of confusion and well-planned 'spontaneity', the endless appeals to the dignity of man, for compassion, for liberty, equality, the endless insertion of brotherhood slogans into speeches, the relentless demands for more involvement of the people—all this was a strategy he knew and recognized. It had been his job to make this very strategy work within the labor movement in Scotland.

At the bottom line of all the changes these strategies wrought in the Church, he pointed out, there was one single prime directive, the necessary effort required to move Mary out the Church door, for according to the Communists, if Mary goes, the Catholic Church, sooner or later, will go.

Why did Mary have to go? Hamish explains:

> "It was necessary to assault the Mother of God for the simple reason that there was no other way possible whereby the Son could be effectively exiled from Society and Man. Get rid of Mary and you would have dismantled forever any notion of institutionalizing within the Church the Social Kingship of Christ." Which would mean annihilation of Communism.
>
> "Mary had to go because there was no other way of uprooting the Incarnate God from the consciousness of the people.
>
> "Mary had to go because it was in Her womb that God had become flesh and blood.
>
> "Mary had to go in order that God could be transformed into a meaningless abstraction. An impersonal being remote and entirely divorced from the affairs of the work-a-day-world.
>
> "Mary had to go because it was from Her womb that God issued forth into human society.
>
> "Mary had to go because She had mothered and suckled the author of the old moral order of society, which the revolutionaries were seeking to destroy.
>
> "Mary had to go because She was the mother of Christendom, the mother of unity of Christians.
>
> "Mary had to go because no less than the Mass itself, Her Immaculate Conception was literally an insuperable barrier to the rise of the lay state.
>
> "Mary had to go because Her blessed name was the last remaining obstacle to the development of that 'laissez faire' society wherein relations between man and man were no longer based on brotherhood but on the cold and utterly forbidding cash nexus.
>
> "Mary had to go because the reformers recognized Her for what She was and is," what the popes have always called, "... the Mediatrix between God and human society".[40]

And once She was gone, anyone who dared try to bring Her back would have to be annihilated, i.e. Father Gruner and The National Pilgrim Virgin Apostolate. The last thing the new Church needed was another Blue Army.

§

For decades, the original Blue Army, the militant-sounding association of Catholics devoted to Fatima, had been impressing upon popes and princes the worldwide interest of Catholics in the cause of Our Lady of Fatima. Its organization was firmly entrenched in Fatima with an impressive onion-domed headquarters just east of the edge of the Cova da Iria. It was situated in that direction from the azinhiera tree where the light first flashed in the sky to announce the impending arrival of the heavenly Visitor to the Cova. It had been difficult enough for the enemies of Mary to infiltrate the Blue Army.

40 Hamish Fraser, *Fatal Star*, Long Prairie, Neuman Press, 1986, p. 159.

They didn't want another Fatima Apostolate and feared Father Gruner might prove to be just that.

They were wrong to expect him to form another Blue Army. In the beginning, however, relations with that historical organization had begun cordially enough, and with the best of intentions. However, the movement begun by Father Nicholas Gruner would ultimately neither represent, operate the same, nor imitate the Blue Army. In time, his own Apostolate would come to oppose the Blue Army's U.S. leadership's disinformation about the request of Our Lady.

With time, the Blue Army and *Soul* magazine, its official publication, had lost its edge, its leadership had aged, mellowed, and seemed to lose its independence from the *Ostpolitik* (the political overture to the East) of the Vatican. They became willing participants in a nearsighted vision of the future:

A few months before the Second Vatican Council began, Vatican diplomats negotiated an unprecedented restriction on its deliberations: Metropolitan Nikodim of the Orthodox Church, a puppet of Moscow, would accept the Vatican's invitation to send Orthodox observers to the Council, if the Council would promise to refrain from any condemnation of Communism. A written agreement to this effect was signed between Nikodim and the Vatican's representative, Cardinal Tisserant. The Orthodox observers, KGB operatives in the garb of priests, waited in Moscow for Pope John's opening speech, which promised a new era of "dialogue" with the world and an end to condemnations. The next day the observers arrived at the Council.

The "Vatican-Moscow Agreement" established *Ostpolitik*, "East politic", as the touchstone of Vatican diplomacy, influencing the Holy See's relations with the entire world. In exchange for silence in the face of evil, the Council would be favored with the presence of KGB operatives representing a puppet church controlled by the Kremlin. Where once there had been steadfast papal condemnation of Communism, there would now be dialogue and negotiation with the forces of world atheism.

The properly filed written canonical request of over 450 Council Fathers that Communism be placed on the agenda of the Council was somehow "lost" in the conciliar bureaucratic apparatus. During the Council, Cardinal Tisserant would rise to silence any discussion of Communism by a Council Father, saying that it was forbidden. A human plan of diplomacy had collided with the divine imperatives of Fatima. Some 16 years later Father Nicholas Gruner and the Apostolate would enter the zone of collision. Not so the Blue Army.

In matters of the Vatican-Moscow Agreement, the Blue Army seemed to be almost too agreeable, too eager to toe the party line. Its new sense of compromise, its currying of favor with the Secretariat of State earned it the epithet—The "Bl'Army", and the chunk of the Berlin wall enshrined in glass on the edge of the Fatima shrine's esplanade—the "Bl'Army Stone".

Father Gruner and *Soul* and the leadership of the Blue Army had gotten along very well in the beginning. An occasion for collaboration in the early 1980s demonstrates the case clearly: For years the International Council of the Blue Army had observed the fragmentation of its leadership in several countries, Canada among them. John Haffert, in *Soul* magazine, wrote: "At first we attributed Canadian fragmentation to French-English differences. But as we look back over thirty years of experience, many other factors emerge ..."

In January 1980, Mr. Setz-Degan, the International Secretary, invited Father

Gruner to the Blue Army meeting in Rome to help the International Council resolve problems in Canada. Father Leoni, chairman of the Blue Army in Montreal, was not able to be there, but Father Nick Gruner was. Asked his opinion of Father Leoni, by the vice president of the Blue Army, Monsignor Galamba, Father Gruner remembers answering, "He's a nice guy."

In retrospect, it now seems what really lay behind the effort to unify the various Blue Army groups in Canada was the desire to bring *every* Fatima apostolate under the influence, if not control, of the Blue Army, which in turn would be controlled from the top through the Vatican's Secretary of State.

Father Gruner's instinct was to aid in the effort to create a unified Fatima Apostolate in Canada. As was reported by John Haffert in *Soul* magazine, "Father Gruner ... gave an overall report of his meeting with various Canadian leaders." (Gleaned from his touring the Pilgrim Virgin across Canada.)[41]

The Council officers decided that Father Peter Leoni, President of the French Section in Montreal, "... be given full authority to bring the various factions in Canada together and to prepare a single National Executive Committee ..." with the help of Father Gruner, "whose proven devotion, availability for the work full time, and his ability to speak English, French and Italian made him the ideal choice."

The Canadian leaders from Montreal, Toronto and Ottawa agreed to meet on January 17, 1981 at St. Mary's Cathedral rectory, Kingston, midpoint between the cities under the chairmanship of Father Leoni. One of the Canadian leaders, Mr. Wally Stafford, refused to go, holding to the position that he was already the Blue Army president of Canada.

A National Executive of the Blue Army in Canada was formed with full power to form a national center, to publish its own magazine, to call for recognition from all Blue Army Centres in English-speaking Canada and to establish Toronto as the National Blue Army Centre in Canada for the time being, with Father Nicholas Gruner being chosen President of the National Executive Committee in English-speaking Canada.

In July of 1981, the Blue Army met in its Fatima headquarters for the election of officers for its international organization. Although the meeting had been planned for some time, it was conducted in the traumatic climate immediately following the attempted murder of the pope.

At the time, Father Gruner, with one secretary, was occupied full time with the Apostolate, working out of a small, cramped office in the ground floor of a monastery in Ottawa. In advance of this gathering, Father Leoni (President of the Blue Army in Montreal), after a visit to the Pro-Nuncio, Msgr. Palmas, in Ottawa, paid a call on Father Gruner and insisted in a friendly manner that he accompany Leoni to Fatima, offering him one of the two votes allotted to Canadian delegates that year.

Father Gruner was unprepared for a trip to Fatima at that exact moment, to the point of not even having a current passport. Leoni, however, insisted, offering to pay Gruner's way, including the hotel expenses. Father Gruner did not at first see the importance of it but a priest friend, Father Victor Soroka, advised him to go.

Neither of them could possibly have dreamed that the long arm of the locket cult was already stretching ahead of them, all the way to Fatima. Unknown to Father Gruner, Father Leoni was carrying a letter in his pocket indirectly connected through its writers to the locket cult, a poison pen manifesto of former disgruntled volunteers.

It would be a summer of confusion and crisis. It seemed that the progress Father

41 *New Hope for the Fatima Apostolate in Canada*, "The Fatima Crusader", Issue 6, Christmas 1980, pp. 13-15.

Gruner was making in serving the cause of Fatima was eliciting nameless and faceless opposition. Just before leaving for the Fatima meeting, he was informed by a priest serving in the diocese of Avellino, where he himself was incardinated, that word was out that he, Father Gruner, was about to be suspended.

Once again, as seemed to be becoming habitual, the enemies of Fatima were guaranteeing that his attention would be divided at crucial moments in the history of the Apostolate.

Father Leoni and Father Gruner flew together from Montreal, landing first in the Azores, then proceeding on to the mainland and to Fatima. Seated together, they talked for about ten hours throughout the trip. What was not spoken about, however, was that a meeting had recently been conducted from which Father Gruner had been excluded, at the insistence of John Haffert, and decisions made in the Kingston, January meeting had been overturned.

Monday, in Fatima, Father Leoni rose to announce not only in his own name, but also in the name of Father Gruner, certain supposed changes from the January meeting in Kingston. Listening to Father Leoni, Father Gruner now realized that the trip to Fatima was intended to get him to acquiesce to these unauthorized changes.

Father Leoni also had another card to play. In the event that Father Nicholas Gruner should be nominated as a candidate for any position during the elections, Father Leoni had come prepared. The *coup-de-grace* to any such plans was in his pocket. Taking Father Gruner aside at one juncture, Father Leoni informed him that he was carrying a letter, received in Canada, that contained accusations by some disgruntled persons in Ottawa. Father Gruner and Father Soroka had already replied in person to these libels sent to Father Leoni several months earlier. Father Leoni had indicated his satisfaction then but now he was going to use this letter as a concocted blackmail weapon to make Father Gruner conform to Father Leoni's orders. A rear-guard action, and relentless phone calls to the Pro-Nuncio by Father Gruner's White Army opponents in Ottawa, had brought the ugliness of Ottawa politics to Fatima. 'The Letter', Leoni stated, 'would be revealed if necessary.' Later on the letter writers were to become plaintiffs against Father Gruner but all three of them dropped their claims.

'The letter' ploy is one well known to anyone who has tried to establish an apostolate in the service of the Church. Pious opportunists, poison pen letters, the telephone, are the nemesis of many a volunteer organization. This 'letter' had been circulated with the thoroughness at which poison pen letter writers are wont to excel, one copy of it having gone to the Nuncio in Ottawa.

Father Gruner was compelled to resume a familiar role, that of measuring and weighing the procedures of the elections as in the seminary days in Rome several years earlier. In attendance were some illustrious veterans of the Cold War. One of the more notable, Bishop Constantine Luna, had been a prisoner of the Red Chinese in 1951. Father Peter Leoni himself had been in a Communist prison in Russia in 1955. Yet, in spite of their histories both were, from their vantage points within the Blue Army, supporting the Vatican-Moscow Agreement forged from the 1962 meeting of Nikodim and Tisserant.

When it came to the issue of elections, three names were nominated for the post of president—Luigi Scalafora, (the future president of the Republic of Italy), Father John Power, from Ireland, and Bishop Luna. In what seemed a clearly overt attempt to control and direct the voting, some twenty plus delegates who had been guaranteed a vote were disenfranchised when Mr. Setz-Degan and John Haffert announced the vote would be limited to one vote per country instead of the two. Setz-Degan, as international secretary, had formally promised, in writing, there would be two votes per country, in the official notice of the meeting, dated January 1981, six months prior to the meeting.[42]

To this obvious infraction Father Gruner voiced a legal objection on constitutional grounds, speaking in English, French and Italian.

> "The unilateral decision to disenfranchise half the delegates was totally illegal, even if it was backed by the majority of those who kept their votes. I would not have wasted my time, had I known that Haffert and his cronies would change the rules of procedure and of elections as it suited them and without any regard to law, justice or charity.
>
> "One delegate from Brazil, who was a lawyer, talking to those beside him said plainly, 'This is a circus'. I urged him to speak up to all the delegates but he refused. He later on was elected as one of the members of the international board of directors.
>
> "During this manipulation of the Blue Army and its highest governing body, which claimed itself as the Vatican-approved Fatima apostolate, the fact emerged that despite its founding in 1947, it did not by 1981 have a constitution that had been ratified by the Vatican.
>
> "So not feeling bound by its own rules and with no one overseeing its proceedings, it continued to change the rules as it suited the insiders, who were clearly afraid of the democratic rule which they so proudly proclaimed.
>
> "The election of officers and directors came. Instead of having one vote all at once, each office was nominated and voted on one at a time. It was not long before a new fraud was attempted by Setz-Degan.
>
> "The constitution absolutely called for a clear majority of votes in the first ballot. With the 50 originally promised votes, the majority would have been 26. Even with Setz-Degan's elimination of half the votes down to 25, a majority would have been 13. With all this maneuvering, Bishop Luna still only got 12 votes, Father John Power of Ireland and Mr. Luigi Scalafora between them got 13 votes. Yet in total disregard for their own constitution, Setz-Degan tried to claim that Bishop Luna had thereby been elected."

It was at this juncture Father Gruner felt bound to speak once more. This time he did not expect them to understand or follow fundamental rules of procedure or laws since they had shown dismal lack of understanding and respect for it in his first intervention.

> He said again in English, French and Italian, "I don't care what you do, but in case you are interested, you are breaking your own rules that you claim you are guided by, your own constitution calls for an absolute majority in the first ballot."
>
> "Then, Setz-Degan said, 'We are all friends here, let's not go through another ballot, let's not bother with formalities. Let's just declare Bishop Luna as elected.'
>
> "Obviously Setz-Degan and his close personal friend, John Haffert, wanted Luna to be the new international president.
>
> "This was even more obvious because they had insisted on nominating him despite the fact that it was publicly announced that Cardinal Rossi, the Cardinal in the Vatican in charge of the Council on the Laity, had formally told the Blue

42 Letter of invitation to delegates with original signature officially signed by Albert Setz-Degan, International Secretary of the Blue Army, dated Jan. 31, 1981, sent from Basel, Switzerland.

Army leaders, 'We do not want any bishop to become International President.' They formally went against this order while they claimed to be so obedient to the Holy See. They further acknowledged this Congregation as having jurisdiction over them since they, as a body, were seeking a special recognition which they had not, as yet, received.

"Despite all this, they went ahead and nominated Bishop Luna. John Haffert, in public, said in French several days later to the Bishop of Fatima that there were no other qualified candidates. This was clearly not true since Luigi Scalafora, then a member of Parliament in Italy, and who later became the President of Italy, had allowed his name to stand for nomination."

In response to Setz-Degan's appeal to break the rules again, the famous Spanish priest and Fatima archivist, Father Alonso, rose and spoke out plainly and with controlled but obvious anger. He told all present they could not change the rules in mid stream. After Father Alonso spoke, they held a second ballot and gave 15 votes to Bishop Luna.

Later, Father Gruner, himself, was nominated for one of the next ranking positions. It was then that Father Leoni pulled out the letter in question and told him that, if he ran, he, Father Leoni, would make public 'the false letter' causing sufficient confusion to lose the vote.

So Bishop Luna was finally elected with a majority after several ballots. That he would toe the party line, play down the worldwide petition campaigns to the Pope for the consecration of Russia, do nothing to upset the directives coming from the Secretary of State, was proven later in an all-day meeting between Father Gruner and John Haffert in the spring of 1985. Haffert was an open admirer of Cardinal Tisserant, prime architect of the Vatican-Moscow Agreement. Father Gruner offered to publish a positive news story on Cardinal Tisserant in *The Fatima Crusader* magazine in exchange for Haffert restoring in *Soul* magazine, the campaign of petitions for the Consecration of Russia. Haffert replied, "I can't. Luna won't let me."

Had the Blue Army by that time been subverted by the Secretariat of State to the point where it had lost its independence? There was no way to prove it. Father Gruner, however, resigned in protest from the organization.

In 1986, the President of the Cleveland, Ohio division of the Blue Army also resigned over the illegal maneuvers used to keep the National Council of the Blue Army from discussing and resolving to promote the Consecration of Russia. He said "It is quite apparent that the Blue Army is controlled by a few entrenched people and is not governed according to its constitution." The facts surrounding this continued to raise suspicions in this regard.

The attempt to silence Father Gruner with the letter-in-the-pocket trick, no doubt, at other times in Church history, had sent other priests running for cover, never to be heard from again. The attempt was a study in the arrogance of old power, power corrupted from being too long in office, revealed in the tired tactics of men who were unaccustomed to being challenged. They presumed one opponent of the Vatican-Moscow Agreement had thus been dispensed with. They presumed too much.

§

Rome, August 1981. Within days of the Blue Army meeting Father Gruner was in the Eternal City, following up a letter of appeal sent through Father John Magee, at that time personal private secretary to the Pope. It was intended for John Paul II. It was read to him in the hospital in early summer 1981.

Before Father Gruner's letter reached the Pope, His Holiness was already learning more about Fatima. Pope John Paul II had sent for and read the Secret of Fatima immediately after an assassin's shot rang out in the Piazza of St. Peter's on May 13, 1981.[43] The exacting requirements of the terms of the Consecration of Russia that would, apparently, ward off the consequences of the Third Secret were also detailed to him at that time.[44]

As Abbé Caillon, head of the Blue Army in France, explains: "The question of the consecration of Russia to be made by the Pope in union with the bishops is governed by two texts written by Lucia a long time ago. The first important text: 'The Good God promises to make an end of the persecution in Russia if the Holy Father deigns to make, and orders to be made, by all the bishops of the Catholic world, a solemn and public act of reparation and consecration of Russia to the Most Sacred Hearts of Jesus and Mary and if, in return for the end of this persecution, His Holiness promises to approve and to recommend the practice of reparatory devotion (the Five First Saturdays).'

"Lucia gave this text to her confessor, the Portuguese Jesuit Father Gonçalves, on May 29, 1930. As Father Gonçalves posed still further questions, Lucia gave him another text a fortnight later, on June 12, 1930, along exactly the same lines. As for the Bishop of Leiria, Msgr. da Silva, he decided to write to Pius XI in March 1937 reproducing exactly what she had said. This text is therefore beyond all doubt." Father Caillon continues:

"Let us recall that between 1929 and 1939, Stalin was at the apogee of his cruelty. All the Russians whom one met in Paris or elsewhere, at that time, spoke with one and the same voice, in effect saying: 'Lenin was responsible for 20 million corpses in seven years; Stalin has been responsible for 46 million in 29 years; i.e. a total of 66 million corpses. Lenin is therefore worse than Stalin.'

"Pius XI was therefore informed in 1937 of the duty of effecting the collegial Consecration of Russia. He did not do so. And we have had corpses in tens of millions.

"In May 1936, in the course of an intimate communication, Lucia asked Our Lord why He would not convert Russia without these two so difficult conditions: that Russia should be the sole object of the consecration; and that this consecration should be made by all the bishops of the world, on the same day, each bishop doing so in his own cathedral in a solemn public ceremony.

"Our Savior replied: 'Because I wish all of My Church to recognize this consecration as a triumph of the Immaculate Heart of Mary, in order, thereafter, to extend and place alongside devotion to My Divine Heart, devotion to this Immaculate Heart.'

"Lucia replied: 'But, my God, the Holy Father will not believe me if You do not move him by special inspiration.'

"Christ replied: 'The Holy Father! Pray much for the Holy Father. He will do it, but it will be late! However, the Immaculate Heart of Mary will save Russia. It has been entrusted to Her'."[45]

It has been broadly reported that Pope John Paul II wept when he read these lines shortly after the attempt on his life.

The Pope, at the time Father Gruner presented the letter to Msgr. Magee, had returned to the Gemelli hospital for further rest after initially being discharged. As Msgr. Magee

---

43 Frère François de Marie des Anges, *Fatima: Tragedy and Triumph*, first edition, p. 153.

44 Ibid.

45 Frère François de Marie des Anges, *Fatima: The Only Way to World Peace*, p. 91.

testified later, he read the contents of Father Gruner's 15-page letter to the Pope. The letter outlined the threat of "suspension" that Father Gruner had been subjected to, and the fact that there was no crime committed and only anonymous accusers. The pressure was being applied against him by nameless bishops of various ranks who were against Our Lady of Fatima. Father Gruner's letter had concluded with a promise to correct any errors if there were any with a reminder that he could not stop spreading the truth just because he was subjected to political pressure.[46] The letter was sent by the Pope to the Secretary of State who sent it to the Congregation for the Clergy.

Father Gruner then proceeded to the Congregation to find out, in person, why he was being harassed. At that time, Msgr. Usai was the official in charge of the file. He told Father Gruner that it was not the Congregation that wanted to intervene, that, in fact, the Congregation was really not interested in the matter, but that the Pro-Nuncio to Canada had spoken face-to-face with its head, Cardinal Oddi, about him. Msgr. Palmas apparently had told Cardinal Oddi that no Canadian bishop would have Father Gruner. (Prior and subsequent facts demonstrated that Msgr. Palmas' claim was false.) Msgr. Palmas had strongly urged therefore that Father Gruner should be made to return to Italy.[47]

Father Gruner immediately sought out his bishop, Pasquale Venezia, who had incardinated him in Avellino. Bishop Venezia also made clear that it was the Pro-Nuncio, Msgr. Palmas (and by extension the Secretary of State), who was interfering with his efforts to find a benevolent bishop.[48]

When Bishop Venezia was asked by Father Gruner to make a contract between Father Gruner, Bishop Venezia and a benevolent bishop, for a period of five years, Bishop Venezia said he could not do that. "The Nuncio," (meaning Msgr. Palmas) "will not let me do that."

Father Gruner returned to Rome to speak to the third in command at the Congregation for the Clergy, Under-Secretary Msgr. Guglielmo Zannoni. Msgr. Zannoni told him, "The Pro-Nuncio cannot forbid your bishop from making a contract with you and another bishop—it is none of his business. It is strictly a matter for you and the two bishops concerned."[49]

Nevertheless, the pressure brought by Msgr. Palmas on Bishop Pasquale Venezia held. It would result, from 1981 to 1989, in Father Gruner not being allowed to find, without hindrance, a benevolent bishop to incardinate him.[50] Still, during most of this time, he obtained faculties from local bishops to preach and hear confessions.[51]

46 Letter of Father Gruner to Pope John Paul II, June 1981, on file with Father Gruner's personal records.

47 Father Nicholas Gruner, *Father Gruner's Letter to Cardinal Innocenti*, "The Fatima Crusader", Issue 29, Sept.-Nov. 1989, p. 35.

48 Father Nicholas Gruner, *Canonical Recourse to The Sacred Congregation for the Clergy*, "The Fatima Crusader", Issue 53, Summer 1996, p. 23.

49 *Fr. Gruner's Letter to Cardinal Innocenti*, The Fatima Crusader, Issue 29, Sept.-Nov. 1989, p. 35.

50 Ibid.

51 Written faculties from Archdiocese of Ottawa, of St. Catharines, and others for various times in the 1970's and 1980's are still on file with Father Gruner's personal records. Also present on file are faculties given in the 1990's.

Chapter 7

Before Communism Changed Its Name

To Father Nicholas Gruner, the moral authority of the Catholic Church worldwide was tragically neutralized through the disastrous Vatican-Moscow Agreement of 1962. The Agreement—arrived at in Metz in 1962 between Cardinal Eugene Tisserant, representing the Vatican at the explicit direction of Pope John XXIII, and Metropolitan Nikodim of the Russian Orthodox Church—paved the way for Russian Orthodox representatives to sit as observers at the Second Vatican Council on the condition demanded by the Russian Orthodox, that no condemnation of Communism would take place at the Council,[52] such a condemnation being equated by the KGB puppet Nikodim as a condemnation of the Russian people themselves.

Father Gruner elaborates on the dismal failure of this Agreement to protect the Church in the East, or around the world, wherever Communism held power: "No part of the Catholic Church existing in the territory of Communist control exists in freedom at all comparable to anywhere in the West. Persecution has not disappeared. Catholic priests are forcibly detained by Communist agents on a regular basis simply because they are Catholic priests; loyal Catholic lay people because they practice their Catholic faith are discriminated against, unable to work at the jobs and at the pay that they are due; the Church has little freedom in appointing bishops. All this in those countries which have negotiated with the Vatican.

"Communists in these countries have temporarily lessened some of their fury against the Church which they displayed at the time of Stalin. This apparent lessening of persecution in some countries had been granted in return for some extremely significant concessions given by the Vatican.

"But in those Communist-dominated countries which have not been willing to negotiate with the Vatican, the persecution of Catholics continues as ruthless and relentless as anything that existed under Stalin. In Albania, China, North Korea and Vietnam the Catholic Church suffers open, bold and vicious persecution."

To this Father Gruner applied one specific indisputable explanation: the Consecration of Russia still remained undone.

In recent years, so much has been said about the 'Consecration' of Russia, from so many points of view, so often, with such passion and with such futility, people scarcely listen when it is mentioned. The controversy over its form and substance had divided the Church and ignited internecine warfare. The degree of boredom now exhibited whenever it is mentioned represents a major triumph for the anti-consecration forces. But, in fact, in the early 1980's many people had never heard of the consecration. It was in great part through Father Gruner's efforts that it was brought to the world's attention.[53]

In spite of the familiarity of its terminology, the copious rhetoric for and against, it is necessary to include the details of the consecration 'requirements' here and now. The need to do so highlights a much-overlooked fact in the career of Father Gruner, namely, that his enemies like to paint the picture that he is isolated, alone in his opinions, and therefore to be ignored. But Father Gruner is anything but alone. His beliefs regarding

52 Jean Madiran, *The Vatican- Moscow Agreement*, "The Fatima Crusader", Issue 16, Sept.-Oct. 1984, p. 5; originally published in *Itineraires*, Feb. 1984, Paris, France.

53 Frère François de Marie des Anges, *Fatima: Tragedy and Triumph*, p. 183.

the Fatima Message and the consecration are thoroughly confirmed and strengthened by the most respected and familiar names in the entire Fatima arena. For example, to secure the exactitude Our Lady deserves, one need only turn to the testimony, insight and research of two of Her greatly respected servants, Abbé Caillon of the Blue Army in France and Father Joaquin Maria Alonso, for many years the official Fatima archivist.

One year to the day after the attempt on his life, His Holiness Pope John Paul II, at the shrine in Fatima, consecrated the world to the Immaculate Heart of Mary. Sister Lucia herself was there to witness it. *Soul* magazine, the Blue Army of USA's official journal, reported that at last the consecration of Russia was completed according to the requirements. Surely the Pope wouldn't come to Fatima and not follow the criteria set down by the Virgin. But Abbé Caillon shows why the act of May 13, 1982 did not, in fact, meet the demands of Heaven.

He begins by recalling the events leading up to the Pope's shrine visit May 13, 1982.

"In March 1982, Pope John Paul II wanted to know precisely what he should do on the occasion of his pilgrimage to Fatima."[54]

And so a special envoy for the Pope, the Lisbon Nuncio, Archbishop Sante Portalupi, was sent to Coimbra.

"This historic interview which took place during the afternoon of Sunday, March 21, 1982 lasted for two hours. On the one side of the grille there was Lucia; on the other side there was the Lisbon Nuncio, the Bishop of Leiria, Cosme do Amaral and Dr. Francis Lacerda."[55] When it was proposed by Bishop Amaral that the consecration the Pope had already done was indeed what Our Lady had asked for, Sister Lucia, while not saying a word, did wave her finger back and forth, making it very clear that no, it had not been done properly.

Sister Lucia then made crystal clear what was required: to the question what exactly should the Pope do, Lucia explained that "the Pope must select a date on which to order the bishops of the whole world to arrange for a public solemn Act of Reparation and of consecration of Russia to the Most Sacred Hearts of Jesus and Mary, each in his own cathedral and at the same time as the act of consecration effected by the Pope."[56]

In spite of the high-level involvement of men hand-picked by the Pope to hear these words from the seer, "... in the text which was sent to the Holy Father by diplomatic bag, it was not spelled out that each bishop must, each in his own cathedral, and on the same day as the Pope, arrange for a solemn public ceremony of the consecration of Russia."[57]

Why was the exact message not passed on to the Holy Father? On March 21st of 1982, when the Pope's envoy, Archbishop Sante Portalupi, went with Bishop Amaral and Dr. Francis Lacerda to see Sister Lucia, John Paul II knew that Our Lady of Fatima had saved his life. He was asking through Portalupi, 'What does Our Lady want of me?'

Father Gruner, in reporting the causes of the misinformation, said: "After the visit, Archbishop Sante Portalupi sent his message back to the Vatican. However, Bishop Amaral intervened to see to it that the full message was not sent in the papal diplomatic bag, and that the requirement ordering the bishops to join him was not included." In

54 Abbé Pierre Caillon, *Regarding the Consecration of Russia, Sister Lucia's Recent Authorized Statements*, "The Fatima Crusader", Issue 13-14, Oct.-Dec. 1983, p. 3; also, Abbé Pierre Caillon, *Fatima May 13, 1982 What Actually Happened? Was Russia Consecrated to the Immaculate Heart of Mary?* "The Fatima Crusader", Issue 16 Sept.-Oct. 1984, p. 22; also, published in *Fidelite Catholique*, April 1983, BP 217 - 56402 Auray Cedex, France; also, *Stella Maris*, No. 170, June 1983; also, *Ephemerides Mariologiae*, 1983, pp. 461-462.

55 Ibid.

56 Ibid.

57 Ibid.

fact, Abbé Caillon, in November 1985, in Rome, told Father Gruner point blank that Bishop Amaral had told Portalupi not to put into the message to the Pope any mention of the bishops joining the Pope in his act of consecration.

"This same kind of interference in 1952 caused Pope Pius XII to be badly informed. In 1952, Pope Pius mentioned Russia specifically, the only time that a pope has ever done so.

"What he lacked was the bishops. In 1982, Sister Lucia specified there must be the bishops, it must be the same day, the same hour, either all in Rome or Tuy or anywhere else they want, one location all together or they can be in their own dioceses, in their own cathedrals, and do it at the same hour of the day."

Abbé Caillon takes up the story again following the May 13 consecration by John Paul II at the Fatima shrine: "In the days after May 13, 1982, a Brazilian advocate, the Blue Army Representative for Brazil, presented himself at noon one day at the Carmel at Fatima (where the 75-year-old Lucia who had travelled there for the papal event still rested, before returning to the Carmel at Coimbra) seeking to be received by Lucia in order that they might know precisely what to make of the act of consecration ... effected on that day.

"Poor Lucia, having no authorization to speak concerning the essentials of the matter, could do no more than make some trite observations that would sound encouraging, appeasing and hopeful. But the Brazilian advocate believed that from these observations it was possible for him to infer that a statement based on what she said could be broadcast worldwide. In effect, his text was reproduced almost everywhere, misleading opinion everywhere."[58]

As a result, diverse sources began to report that the May 13, 1982, consecration fulfilled Our Lady's request for the Collegial Consecration of Russia to Her Immaculate Heart, this, in spite of the fact that the Pope himself was saying otherwise: In the Bull of January 6, 1983, announcing the Holy Year, the Pope seemed to be taking his cue from what Lucia said to the Lisbon Nuncio on Sunday, March 21, 1982. Clearly the Pope was planning for the future:

"A special ceremony of prayer and penitence could be celebrated by the bishops of the entire world in their respective cathedrals on the same day, or on a date which would follow immediately, in order that after the solemn inauguration of the Jubilee, the entire episcopate of the five continents with the clergy and the faithful could manifest their spiritual union with the successor of Peter."[59]

But he still made no move to order the bishops to do it. The Holy Father only said 'could be'.

Father Gruner recalls that year, 1982, as the one in which the consecration emerged in its full importance to him: "When I heard for the first time in 1980, in Toronto, that the consecration of Russia would bring peace to the world, I thought, that's too simple. It doesn't fit. What about all these other works that need doing. So I more or less dismissed it."

In the summer of 1982, John Haffert in the Blue Army *Soul* magazine added immeasurably to the confusion of the general public by publishing a supposed interview with Sister Lucia by an 'unidentified' anonymous interviewer saying that the consecration was done.

58 Ibid; also, see the important footnote on this matter, Frère François de Marie des Anges, *Tragedy and Triumph*, Chapter 4, footnote 125, p. 226.

59 Abbé Pierre Caillon, op. cit.; also see the Papal Bull announcing the Holy Year, promulgated January 6, 1983.

"About a month later I read Hamish Fraser's comments on the *Soul* magazine statement saying that John Haffert had done great work in promoting Our Lady of Fatima up until then but all the good Haffert had done previously was outweighed by the evil of publishing as true this false statement. Hamish stated Haffert had it all wrong. But how could he get it all wrong?"

Father Gruner had known Hamish since 1969 and John Haffert since meeting him in Rome in 1971-72. He published both their stories in the same issue of *The Fatima Crusader*.[60] The John Haffert piece was the only time the *Crusader* ever carried an article declaring the Consecration was done. From that point on, the issue of the Consecration would remain center stage of Father Gruner's apostolate.

From a much respected voice in Rome came a complete refutation of the Blue Army's claims. Father Joseph de Sainte-Marie was a Professor of Sacred Theology at the Teresianum. It was he who had drafted the speech delivered by John Paul II at Fatima during his 1982 visit. Father Sainte-Marie addressed the misleading statements in a letter to Hamish Fraser on January 16, 1983.

"I profoundly deplore all these more or less authorized declarations made in the wake of the Pope's visit to Fatima on May 13 last. Until now, they have given rise only to confusion of minds, a division of hearts and the dissipation of forces ...

"It is therefore necessary to confine oneself exclusively to statements by the Blessed Virgin ... They are known, and concerning what we are at present discussing, the consecration of Russia to Her Immaculate Heart, the two principal ones are the following:

July 13, 1917: 'To prevent it (war, hunger, persecution of the Church and persecution of the Holy Father), I shall come to ask for the consecration of Russia to My Immaculate Heart, and the Communion of Reparation on the First Saturdays ... In the end, My Immaculate Heart will triumph. The Holy Father will consecrate Russia to Me; it will be converted and a certain period of peace will be granted to the world.'

June 13, 1929: 'The moment has come for God to ask the Holy Father to make, in union with all the bishops of the world, the consecration of Russia to My Immaculate Heart, promising to save it by this means'.

"On May 19, 1982, on his return from Fatima, in the course of a general audience, the Pope declared: 'I tried to do everything possible in the concrete circumstances to emphasize the collegial unity of the Bishop of Rome with all his brothers in episcopal ministry and service in the world.'[61]

"Reading this," Father Caillon continues, "we observed that, curiously, the Pope had made no allusion to the necessity of proceeding to the consecration of Russia according to what had been prescribed by the Blessed Virgin Mary, both in 1917 and 1929, and transmitted by Lucia. But we could not imagine that on May 13, 1982 the Pope did not already know what we ourselves know clearly and what is also known by millions of rank-and-file Catholics who are somewhat familiar with the history of Fatima. We can still less imagine that, after having made investigations, the Pope was as badly informed as all that ... We know, moreover, that the Pope was to meet Lucia on May 12. He was prevented from doing so by a delay in the implementation of his program. Lucia could speak to the Pope only just before the ceremony of May 13. The interview lasted 30 minutes. No one knows what was said, but by then the Pope's talks had already been

60 John Haffert, *A Reported Interview with Sister Lucia*; also Hamish Fraser, *Last Minute News Flash*, "The Fatima Crusader", Issue 9-10, Oct.-Dec. 1982, pp. 4, 5, 31.

61 Father Joseph de Sainte-Marie's January 16, 1983 *Letter to Hamish Fraser*; published in "The Fatima Crusader", Issue 13-14, Oct.-Dec. 1983, pp. 10-13.

printed. It would have been difficult to change anything."

Abbé Caillon takes up the story again in the spring of the following year.

"A second historic interview also took place. Sister Lucia was sought out by Archbishop Portalupi again. (This time Bishop Amaral was excluded, very likely, because he had caused the 1982 message to be incomplete in its version sent to the Pope. He was replaced by a priest instead, Father Messias Coelho.)

"The Lisbon Nuncio, accompanied by two Portuguese experts, returned to see Lucia the afternoon of Saturday, March 19, 1983. This interview at which Lucia, the Nuncio, Dr. Lacerda and Father Messias Coelho were present lasted for two and a half hours, from 4 p.m. until 6:30 p.m.

"Lucia had prepared a text which was read officially and on which she commented. The Consecration of Russia (it made clear) had not been effected because Russia was not clearly the object of the consecration and because each bishop had not arranged a public, solemn ceremony of Russia's consecration in his own cathedral.

"The text prepared by Lucia concluded with these words: 'The consecration of Russia has not been made as Our Lady has demanded. I could not say so because I did not have the permission of the Holy See'."[62]

Father Gruner points out that much of this confusion continues to exist today because Sister Lucia is not allowed to speak in public. "When allowed to speak, she has consistently said the same thing—in 1929, 1931, 1935, 1940, 1943, 1946, 1952 and again in 1983—*always* the same thing. The message is very clear, very specific."

Father Alonso completes the picture, demonstrating again that the conditions for the consecration are exact and well known. Father Alonso presented the following texts which are certainly composed by Sister Lucia herself, at different dates:

June 13, 1929 - "The moment has come in which God asks that the Holy Father make the consecration of Russia, in union with all the bishops of the world."

May 29, 1930 - "If the Holy Father deigns to make and command that the bishops of the Catholic world do it likewise..."

April 1937 - "... if Your Holiness deigns to make and commands that all the bishops of the Catholic world do it likewise ..."[63]

§

There it is. No one can doubt or deny the conditions. Even the reader with the most rudimentary knowledge of Fatima can judge for himself whether the consecrations that took place in 1982 and 1984 meet all of these requirements.

"Make it known to My Ministers," Our Lord said to Lucia, "given they follow the example of the King of France in delaying the execution of My command, like him, they will follow him into misfortune. It is never too late to have recourse to Jesus and Mary".[64]

In spite of all the specifics available, all the confirmations required, and the living eyewitness testimony of Lucia herself, whom Heaven had seen fit to leave on this earth for the purpose of contradicting error and thwarting interference, the bishops of the world have not met Heaven's demands.

Again and again, Father Gruner has published and broadcast on radio and TV the warning to the 'ministers' of the Church that the scaffold of the King of France looms

62 Father Pierre Caillon, *Sister Lucia's Recent Authorized Statements*, "The Fatima Crusader", Issue 13-14, Oct.-Dec. 1983, p. 3.

63 Father Joaquin Maria Alonso S.T.D., Ph.D., Official Archivist of Fatima, *Meaning of the Consecration of Russia*, "The Fatima Crusader", Issue 50, Autumn 1995, p. 13. Previously published in Madrid, Spain in 1979.

64 Frère François de Marie des Anges, *Fatima: The Only Way to World Peace*, p. 78.

on the horizon unless they fulfill the demands of Heaven.

"The word 'bishop' is Greek for watchman," Father Gruner reminds us. "The prophet Ezechiel, in the Old Testament, was told of the duties of the watchman. God said to Ezechiel: I've appointed you watchman. Now, if I put you as watchman on the watchtower and you see the enemy coming and you do not sound the alarm, you do not warn your fellow citizens that they are in danger, then I will hold you, watchman, personally responsible for the deaths of any one of your fellow citizens.[65]

"What's that got to do with the Vatican-Moscow Agreement? It has everything to do with it. Each and every bishop has a duty to cry out when he sees the enemy attacking the city of God, the Church of God. He is in a watchtower. He can see them coming and if he doesn't warn his fellow citizens, then the deaths—spiritual or even physical—of his fellow citizens are held to his account.

"What our watchmen did in 1962 was make a compact, an agreement, to not cry out when they see the enemy coming. Communism is an intrinsic evil. That is a definition of Pius XI speaking as a representative of Christ. 'He who hears you, hears Me',[66] Christ said. "Communism is intrinsically evil and no one who would save Christian civilization can co-operate with it in any way whatsoever."[67] So spoke Pius XI.

"He also said at the same time, 'During Our Pontificate We too have frequently and with urgent insistence denounced the current trend to atheism which is alarmingly on the increase. In 1924 when Our relief-mission returned from the Soviet Union We condemned communism in a special Allocution which We addressed to the whole world ... to this hour the Papacy has continued faithfully to protect the sanctuary of the Christian religion, and that it has called public attention to the perils of communism more frequently and more effectively than any other public authority on earth.'[68]

"In 1937, he said it was his duty to raise the cry again. If it was the duty of Pius XI to raise the cry again, how can we countenance an agreement from 1962 to 1998 in which Communism has not been denounced?"

During the Second Vatican Council, 450 bishops went through the legal procedures to put the topic of Communism on the Council agenda;[69] yet, the petition was illegally sabotaged so that it would not be brought to the floor.[70]

From the very beginning, in 1962, it was understood by the parties to the agreement that for the agreement to have its effect, it could not be revealed nor could any denouncement be tolerated from any corner of the Church, particularly from bishops, but also from priests.

There, in the simplest terms, is the reason behind the targeting of Father Gruner from the highest levels of the Vatican bureaucracy. Even in the early days of his apostolate for Fatima, unbeknownst to himself, he was breaking the Vatican-Moscow Agreement by denouncing Communism. Couple that with the fact that Father Gruner has focused on delivering this message repeatedly to the bishops and the pot begins to boil over.

Father Gruner has written to the bishops of the world thirty-five times and, out of all that correspondence, less than twenty-five bishops have actually said they disagreed with him about joining the Pope in consecrating Russia. This is less than one percent of

65 Ezekiel 33:1-7.

66 Luke 10:16.

67 Pope Pius XI, Encyclical Letter, *Divini Redemptoris*, paragraph 58.

68 Ibid, paragraph 5.

69 Ralph M. Wiltgen S.V.D., *The Rhine Flows Into the Tiber*, p. 274.

70 Ibid, pp. 274-275.

the world's bishops. For all intents and purposes, aside from these few negative replies, there appears to be no opposition outside the Vatican.

Does this mean they would join in the consecration if the Pope demanded it? Father Gruner believes they would. The vast majority who respond are positive. Of the 1700 bishops who have written to Father Gruner, 1500 positively support, in general, the Fatima initiative of Father Gruner. It seems whatever opposition exists, is found within the Vatican bureaucracy itself. The obvious preoccupation of a small group of bureaucrats with Father Gruner's apostolate suggests that he must be making some serious headway in gathering support for the true consecration. To effect the Consecration of Russia as it was requested clearly requires the dismantling of the Vatican-Moscow Agreement of 1962. A deliberate breaking of it.

How could John Paul II do this when in 1981, being pressured by Cardinal Casaroli, he accepted and renewed the Vatican-Moscow Agreement?[71]

"We can't make a promise to do evil," Father Gruner points out. "Such a promise, vow, or oath is not binding. I can't take a vow to disobey God's law, to not denounce evil. It is my sworn duty. By becoming bishop, by becoming pope, one has taken on the job of watchman.

"Why pay the man in the watchtower who won't sound the alarm? It would be a betrayal of the sacred office of the papacy, of the sacred office of the bishop, to engage in or agree to or to carry out the terms of the Vatican-Moscow Agreement. There is no moral obligation to live by it. In fact, there's a moral obligation to break it. Every Catholic priest should denounce it publicly, not just by saying how terrible it is, but by pointing out that Communism, as evil, is still here. We can't take a vow to do nothing in the face of evil."

On Friday, June 4, 1948, Hamish Fraser went to Confession and was accepted into the Catholic Church. He had been a secret agent for the Communist Party and as such fought against the Catholic Church for many years. On Dec. 8, 1952, Hamish spoke at the Fatima Rally in Paris, France, at the Paris Parc des Expositions, before the famous Pilgrim Virgin Statue.

Hamish was heard by the immense crowd present that day to declare: "I do not **believe** that prayer can convert Communists; I **know** that prayer can convert Communists." It was before that same crowd of many thousands which saw this Fatima dove land on Hamish's head and remain there for some time. In the view of some witnesses, it was a sign to the faithful to pay attention to Hamish's speech.

71 Malachi Martin, *The Jesuits*, pp. 85-88.

Chapter 8

The Scaffold Rises

It is an oft-repeated fact of history that one single individual working out of one single room can change the course of history. St. Philip Neri, St. Therese of Lisieux, Marie Curie, Louis Pasteur, Alexander Graham Bell, Edison, Marx, Lenin.

Father Gruner had made his entrance onto the international stage and the Message of Fatima was being spread around the globe as a result. The conditions under which all this was being generated deserve special note.

From the very beginning, volunteers invited to undertake key roles were overwhelmed by the Apostolate's need for the basic necessities. This was not merely an operation with its ribs showing, this was one of bare bones for everyone.

Jane McAuley, who met Father Gruner on his tour with the Pilgrim Statue in Niagara Falls in May of 1983, answered his call for help and soon found herself arriving at the Ottawa bus terminal later that year, at 5:30 on a July morning, with nothing but his phone number on a scrap of paper to indicate what the future might hold.

He was living and working out of four small rooms on Rochester Street, two up, two down. She remembers the windows were covered with a faded purple material someone had given him.

"I'm not in Purgatory yet," was her first remark.

Working conditions seemed to contradict her words. He had a small workroom for himself with a desk or two, the kitchen housed three filing cabinets, a refrigerator, teacher's table, an oil stove and sink with a chipped mirror cabinet. Her new boss ate one meal a day.

"Got any rules?" she asked, to which he replied, "Three Rosaries a day and daily Mass."

Forces natural and supernatural gnawed at the nerves of the workers on a daily, hourly basis. The Old Boy with the red tail was always on the hunt to get the volunteers in-fighting, fill the rooms with tension, jettison patience, crave escape from co-workers. And the devil was not above staging a little high drama.

> "After doing a mailing one day, Pearl Garneau, her daughter Cathy Sene, and I went out for food," Jane relates. "I was driving, missed my turn, and took another. Suddenly there was a person in the middle of the road ahead of me. They yelled, 'Stop, you're going to hit him!' But I knew I wasn't to stop. I said, 'No, I'm not. I'm going to go right through him'."

And so she did, but not before glimpsing an image that has stayed with her to this day.

> "A ball of fire came out of the mouth of this man and straight at the van, then he was gone. Just like that. I drove through where he had been standing, without even slowing down. In the morning the windshield wipers were twisted."

Down and dirty melodrama, however, didn't need the devil as executive producer. It came quite readily from one of those piety-dripping antagonists who lurk on the fringe of new Apostolates, bent on destroying them if the game is not played their way. This particular individual, infamous for shredding the reputation of priests who failed to recognize that person's habitually self-confessed sanctity, adopted the strategy of following Jane around town.

"Trying to psyche me out," Jane recalls, "when we went, for example, to the post office. They would sit in the parking lot watching our every move."

The tactic is a familiar one, a staple maneuver of the pious assassin who feels compelled to let people know they are being watched and considered 'suspect' in an attempt to unnerve them. But it didn't work.

As Jane said: "We learned how to outwait that person and it finally stopped."

By mid-1984, though no one knew it at the time, the later relocation of the Apostolate from Ottawa to Fort Erie, Ontario (across the Niagara River from Buffalo, New York), was being initiated by people and circumstances in small, seemingly insignificant ways.

Coralie Graham, editor of *The Fatima Crusader*, describes the preliminaries leading up to the move.

> "Our little group (in Fort Erie) worked at bringing the Rosary and devotion to Our Lady back to our church and privately prayed for a Tridentine Mass. We organized a Wednesday night novena to Our Mother of Perpetual Help at St. Michael's Church, along with Father Patrick Norton. We were not the most welcome addition to the church schedule and had to carry the five-foot statues of St. Joseph and Mary back and forth from home every week. We wanted some traditional material for the people attending. Through St. Michael's Cathedral in Toronto we encountered Father Gruner's booklet called *Our Lady's Urgent Appeal*. The phone number listed on it was Shirley and Don Pennel's, who told us about Father Gruner and gave us his number in Ottawa.
>
> "After phoning him we received *The Fatima Crusader* and booklets we ordered to give out along with cartons of books on St. Alphonsus. Father could never resist the opportunity to promote St. Alphonsus' holy work. That was the beginning of the book service in Fort Erie.
>
> "I was attending daily Mass at the Redemptoristine Convent on the Niagara Parkway every morning, by special permission of the bishop, before going to work. Father Norton, who was chaplain and was preparing to go to Ireland for a trip, announced one morning that a visiting priest would be bringing a statue of Our Lady of Fatima to the convent and would be saying Mass in his absence.
>
> "The visiting priest was Father Gruner. My first introduction to Father Gruner was a Godsend as he proceeded to offer the Tridentine Mass. I was giving my thanksgiving before Communion, for this wondrous answer to my prayers, when I felt a tremendous enveloping warmth filled with peace and glowing happiness. It literally permeated the room. It was so intense, I looked up from my prayers as if I were expecting to see what I so intensely felt. But I could not determine the cause. Minutes later, as I fell in behind the Communion line, it hit me like a thunderbolt. All except one or two of the Contemplative nuns that normally received Communion in the hand, standing, were kneeling and receiving the Host on their tongue. It is as crystal clear in my mind today as it was at that moment that Our Lord gave a sign of how pleased He was at this appropriate act of adoration and respect. The statue of Our Lady of Fatima, as always with Father Gruner, was prominently placed at the foot of the cross on the altar and Her sweet smile seemed to also radiate with warmth and pleasure at this small act of adoration.
>
> "With such an introduction to Father Gruner, my future working for Fatima, it seems, had already been decided.

"Father Gruner continued his pilgrimage through the Niagara Region to the various churches and our little Rosary Group attended the first one. Then the second, then the third, until we were attending all of them. The combination of Father Gruner's Mass and the appeal of the Pilgrim Virgin Statue was a magnet drawing us in spite of times when we had not planned to go at all, for God had answered our prayers, we had Mary back and the Tridentine Mass.

"In May of 1984, he took me up on my offer to do volunteer work for the Apostolate and called from Ottawa to ask if I would handle Canadian book orders. I converted my spare bedroom into an office. Two others, Bernie Dumelie and Frank Timms offered to list orders on their computer. By autumn we had a smooth enough volunteer operation going to prompt Father Gruner to consider establishing the Apostolate in Fort Erie."

They went to Ottawa to see what his set-up there was like. It was as Jane McAuley had described it—bleak.

"In one small apartment he had a card table, metal shelving along the wall piled with paperwork, and a door off its hinges, propped up on cartons of *The Fatima Crusader*, as his desk. In his fridge was a bowl of rice and a can of tuna which he did not hesitate to offer to share with us."

Father Gruner went through a period of doubt about moving to Fort Erie and for a time considered crossing into the States to work out of Constable, New York instead. Jane McAuley encouraged him to choose Fort Erie, adding that her relatives there also would act as volunteers.

In March of 1985, they moved the office to Fort Erie and Father Gruner followed a month later.

"I moved to Fort Erie with the bishop's own personal permission," Father Gruner explains. "He knew I was coming not just for a visit, but to buy property for the Apostolate. Before coming to the St. Catharines Diocese, I wrote the Bishop of St. Catharines, Bishop Thomas Fulton. I said I was thinking of moving the office down here and did he have any problem with that? Basically, he wrote back asking who wanted us. I replied in person by going to visit him in the Chancery office. I was relieved to find out when I met him, near Christmas 1984, his reply to my proposed moving of my office. 'It's a free country', he said clearly, indicating he had no objection to my proposed move. In fact, he then lamented I had not moved earlier so that he could have sold me some property the diocese had just disposed of. Later, he recalled to me his freely given permission when I went to visit him at his Chancery office in August of 1988.

"Coralie Graham, representing her Rosary group, also contacted Bishop Fulton and offered to furnish him with ample signatures of petition to allow the Apostolate and Father Gruner to settle here, to which His Excellency replied, 'That would not be necessary'.

"Regarding the permission, in August of 1988, Mary Sedore, a staff worker since 1986 and a personal friend of Bishop Fulton, together with Coralie Graham and myself, visited the Bishop of St. Catharines to discuss matters of mutual concern. During this discussion the bishop's permission of 1985 came up and Bishop Fulton, after reflecting on it a bit, did recall giving his permission to us to move the Fatima Apostolate to Fort Erie, within his diocese.

"After June of '85, as I was living down in Fort Erie by that time, the faculties in Ottawa expired. Bishop Fulton extended them to me, by phone, every month thereafter until November 1987. I finally got them in writing in November of '87, but only for six months, till June of '88. In January 1988, he then wrote me a second letter saying that there was a typing mistake by the secretary ... so he extended them to only three months and then he extended them again. In effect they went to June 1, 1988."

Coralie Graham recalls the early days after the move:

"A month after Father moved to Fort Erie I was volunteering evenings and weekends to ship books and do office work. Ultimately, I quit my job to work full time for the Apostolate. I have never regretted it nor even once looked back. Actually, I learned very fast that when you work for Our Lady your life becomes an express train."

There were major disappointments along the way. The Apostolate wanted to put in an offer to buy an abandoned school in Crystal Beach, not far from Fort Erie. At first they were stopped by the town which was about to claim special privileges and purchase it for themselves so they could give it to a group in Fort Erie. Their plan was contested as contrary to law and abuse of municipal privileges. The town then withdrew.

The Apostolate was told the suggested price for the school but a private consultant counselled to bid higher as the building and property were worth much more. The counsel was followed and a bid was made for several thousand dollars higher than the suggested figure.

The next day, the Apostolate found that the purchase was awarded to another group who bid a mere forty-five dollars more than the Apostolate despite the thousands of dollars difference between their bid and the suggested price. This was suspicious, particularly as the Apostolate was denied the right to be present for the opening of the bids.

Father and the staff learned to measure how effective an issue of *The Fatima Crusader* was going to be by the amount of trouble encountered getting it out. Every *Crusader* worked on was beset by crises. They felt very close to the Curé of Ars. The very day they would decide to start on a *Crusader* pandemonium would ensue—staff off sick, water pipes burst, furnace breaking down, vehicles breaking down, the entire ceiling leaking from a torrential rainfall—once it was so bad they hired two students to empty trash cans full of water throughout the night. The electricity has been outed by storms—Father Gruner has worked on the *Crusader* by the light of vigil candles propped up on soft drink cans. When machines wouldn't work, the staff would tape a Miraculous Medal or St. Benedict Medal to them, have Father bless them, and they would start up again.

The editor of the *Crusader* recounts:

"When Father was around, the devil worked overtime harassing him. When he was away on business, the devil switched his focus to those left behind.

"Before we grew to our present size, sometimes I worked until 2, 3, 4 in the morning, alone in the building. At times, others have worked with me but they went away saying, 'I don't know how you can work at night.' They kept hearing footsteps on the roof.

"When Father is away and phones to ask, 'How are things going?', I learned that as soon as I said, 'Fine,' pandemonium would break loose again. If he called one hour after departing, it would start then. If he didn't call for three weeks after leaving, it wouldn't start until then. I began not answering, 'Fine,' to the question. But just recently, I slipped, said, 'Fine,' and 60 seconds later there was a line-up outside my office of people with grave problems to overcome.

"Yet, it seems that Heaven always helps the Apostolate survive the gravest crisis, so long as we persevere and never give up. Our faith did not let us down. When we owed $750,000 and had not a cent to pay for services or make a mailout, St. Joseph brought in the funds to bail us out."

A Director of the Apostolate tells us of a side of Father Gruner often not seen except by those working closely with him.

"Father takes very seriously his position as 'steward' of the donations that come in. Though he does not have a spare minute to answer everyone's personal concerns, for years he helped open the mail himself. He would be quite overwhelmed at the hardships and sacrifices of our people and would be fierce at not allowing any volunteers or staff to squander a penny.

"Father practiced what he preached. Since I met him, and 13 years later, to this day, Father has only drawn a paltry sum of $500 a month to live on, and this for laboring 18-hour days, hardly ever taking any leisure time off for himself. It has become a common practice for our *Crusader* staff, including Father, to work two days and nights straight through with no sleep to make our deadline. On at least one occasion we even persevered to the third straight day. That was the time Denise, our Production Manager, was so tired that when she stopped at a stop sign on the way home, she forgot where she was.

"No task was too menial for Father. He always joined the staff to lick stamps, stuff envelopes, drive trucks, whatever it took, to get the job done—to get another step closer to the goal of consecrating Russia.

"In the first year in Fort Erie, we rented an old factory that had been abandoned for ten years. The roof had leaked and on the floor were huge puddles of water. We moved in and Bernie and Frank, always there with their sleeves rolled up, did a tremendous cleaning job to make it as fit as possible. And Bernie's sister, Virginia Halbach, and 'mother', Martha Halbach, were our prayer powerhouse, offering Rosary after Rosary to pray us through our trials.

"Money was scarce and Father would not spend a dime more than necessary, so he made a room for himself in the warehouse. His first year there, he had no bathtub, no hot water, no furnace, no kitchen stove or sink. We put a small electric heater in his room. He had only the staff washroom to bathe in. His stove was an old oil heater in the office. His table was an old bed board propped up on cartons of *Crusaders*.

"Never did he complain. We all worried, but he just kept shuffling on, like St. Louis de Montfort.

"Now and again those who act like a pack of wild dogs tearing and pulling at a morsel of food would publish remarks, 'What does Father Gruner do with that money?' and I'd smile, thinking if they only came and saw. The donations Father Gruner receives go to promoting the full Fatima Message. Anyone who comes to visit sees it does not go to luxuries.

"When Rome bureaucrats tried to get Father Gruner out of the Apostolate and prevent him from preaching on Fatima by threats, innuendoes, and branding him a 'vagus', we became an endangered species. But we are still here."

§

It is also a fact of history that the intensity of opposition directed at people who work for Our Lady is in direct proportion to the effectiveness of their efforts. The efforts to confuse and control Father Gruner's Apostolate were a mirror image of the confusion that was attempting to distort Our Lady's Message worldwide.

The Blue Army has long held an emotional hammerlock on the hearts of believing Catholics who remember when it started in 1947 and was the only voice promoting the Message. It still remains a formidable foe of the critics because of the historical sentiment that it earned from supporters over the decades.

In the early 1980s, however, it appeared the Blue Army was losing its characteristic independence and fortitude. Most evident in their change of attitude was the manner in which, to the exacting demands of Heaven for the consecration, they suddenly applied a sort of political relativism.

In extracts from an interview with Sister Lucia, published September 1985 in *Sol de Fatima* (the magazine of the Spanish section of the Blue Army) the Fatima Secret was considered in the light of events unfolding within the Church in 1985. The article was a vital one. The bogus interview of Sister Lucia in the 1982 *Soul* magazine[72] had already been exposed and ridiculed by Abbé Caillon and Father Paul Leonard,[73] among others.[74]

Extract From The Interview:

Published September 1985 in *Sol de Fatima*, Spain.

Question: At what moment of the Fatima mystery do we find ourselves?

Sister Lucia: I think we are living in the time when Russia is spreading its errors.

Question: By that, are we to understand that Russia will take possession of the whole world?

Sister Lucia: Yes.

Question: John Paul II had invited all the bishops to join in the consecration of Russia, which he was going to make at Fatima on 13 May 1982 and which he was to renew at the end of the Holy Year in Rome on 25 March 1984, before the original statue of Our Lady of Fatima. Has he not therefore done what was requested at Tuy?

Sister Lucia: There was no participation of all the bishops, and there was no mention of Russia.

Question: So the consecration was not done as requested by Our Lady?

Sister Lucia: No. Many bishops attached no importance to this act.

So stood Fortress Blue Army before it underwent some fundamental changes in direction in 1985-86. The changes took place against the backdrop of very definite and very specific concerns of the Holy Father. Hamish Fraser explained:

> "Concerning one thing at least there is no possible room for doubt—the Holy Father's awareness of the need for the Collegial Consecration of Russia ... For already within two years he has three times consecrated the world ... and on the third occasion (March 25, 1984) he invited the bishops to join with him ...

---

72 Father Pierre Caillon, op. cit., pp. 22-23.

73 Father Paul Leonard, *The Plot To Silence Our Lady*, "The Fatima Crusader", Issue 20, June-July 1986, pp. 9-13; also Father Paul Leonard, *The Vatican-Moscow Agreement Has Silenced Our Lady*, "The Fatima Crusader", Issue 22, April-May 1987, pp. 12-15; also Father Paul Leonard, *The Blue Army Leadership Has Followed a Deliberate Policy of Falsifying the Fatima Message*, "The Fatima Crusader", Issue 22, April-May 1987, pp. 26-28.

74 Father Joseph de Sainte-Marie's January 16, 1983 *Letter to Hamish Fraser*; published in "The Fatima Crusader", Issue 13-14, Oct.-Dec. 1983, pp. 10-13.

in making the Act of Consecration.

"Moreover, on each occasion he indicated that he realized ... the consecration demanded by Our Lady had yet to be made.

"Let no one therefore pretend that the Collegial Consecration of Russia ... is not very much on the mind of the Holy Father."[75]

Why then has it not been properly done?

"Given on the one hand the Holy Father's anxiety concerning the ... consecration ... and on the other hand the scandalous hostility elicited by the (his) request for episcopal participation in the consecration of ... March 25, 1984, it can be inferred, with moral certainty, that one thing in particular has so far prevented the Holy Father from ordering the bishops of the Universal Church to join with him in ... consecrating Russia; *his fear that to do so might well provoke formal schism*." (italics added)

Why are the bishops resisting Our Lady of Fatima? Once again Hamish Fraser provides a stunning explanation.

"There are several reasons why so many bishops quite literally see red whenever the Message of Fatima is mentioned:

"1) Fatima condemns the new catechetics! In many episcopally approved catechetical texts, Hell is scarcely even mentioned, and certainly not as something to be taken very seriously, in spite of the fact that the Virgin in the Cova ... felt it necessary to give the three young seers a terrifying vision of Hell:

"2) Fatima Condemns Sex Education! Ignoring both *Humanae Vitae* and *Familiaris Consortio* which stress the necessity for modesty and chastity as well as the grave sinfulness of contraception, many bishops have imposed most questionable forms of 'Sex Education', some of which border on pornography, on the Catholic schools for which they are responsible. Our Lady ... went out of Her way to emphasize the need for strict fidelity to the Church's moral teaching, and in particular the need for both modesty and chastity, telling Jacinta, youngest of the three seers: 'The sins which lead most souls to Hell are sins of the flesh'."[76]

As Jacinta herself subsequently reported: "The Mother of God wants more virgin souls bound by the vow of chastity. Woe to women wanting in modesty."[77]

Hamish continues: "The Pope's fear is grounded in his realization that material episcopal schism is already widespread in various parts of the world ... at a time when great numbers of the bishops are obsessed with the notion of collegiality, nothing rouses many of them to greater fury than to be reminded that the Queen of Heaven has demanded that, together with the Holy Father, they collegially consecrate Russia to Her Immaculate Heart.

"In other words, the first and foremost reason why Fatima is intolerable to so many bishops, and why they also intensely resent papal authority, is that whereas prior to Vatican II the Popes had consistently condemned Communism as 'intrinsically evil', since Vatican II most episcopal conferences now appear to act on the assumption that it is not Communism but anti-Communism in any shape or form that is 'intrinsically evil'.

"Why has this change of episcopal attitude dated from Vatican II? It is primarily

75 Hamish Fraser, *Address to International Fatima Rosary Crusade Symposium*, Vatican City, Nov. 24, 1985, published in "The Fatima Crusader", Issue 19, Feb.-April 1986, p. 7.

76 Ibid, p. 13.

77 Ibid, p. 13.

because of the Vatican-Moscow Agreement which assured the Kremlin that if Russian Orthodox observers were sent to Vatican II, Communism would not be discussed at the Council. Nor was it. It is because of this criminal omission that after the Council, it became possible to pretend that Communism had become licit and to do so in the name of the Council. This criminal omission is why it became possible to advocate an alliance of Catholics and Communists and even to espouse a 'Theology of Liberation' that is simply revolutionary Marxism in a 'Christian' disguise.

"In short," says Hamish, "if so many bishops detest the Message of Our Lady of Fatima it is because its reference to Russia's errors condemns the policies of virtually all episcopally approved 'Justice and Peace Commissions' and also of Catholic 'Development Agencies' such as CAFOD (England), SCIAF (Scotland), Trocaire (Ireland) and CCFD (France). For these organizations today provide 'the revolution' with a basis for the kind of 'popular front' which it was at such pains to engender against the determined opposition of the pre-conciliar Church; a 'Popular Front' which everywhere promotes subversion by mobilizing Christians, particularly Catholics, in support of the Revolutionary Cause, but particularly in such areas as the Philippines, South Africa and Central America which Moscow is determined to destabilize in order to foster its imperialist ambition.

"To be perfectly blunt, if so far the Holy Father has not found it possible to fulfill the demands of the Queen of Heaven, it is because he realizes that, as a consequence of policies pursued by post-conciliar Nuncios and Apostolic Delegates, he has now to contend with a host of modernist bishops who are Catholic in name only.

"For that reason there is only one means whereby the Holy Father could now fulfill the demand of Our Lady of Fatima. He would be required to order all bishops to join him in collegially consecrating Russia to Mary's Immaculate Heart on pain of demitting office forthwith, in the event of their refusing to do so ...

"Indeed, it is doubtful if any Pope in history has ever been confronted with circumstances so prejudicial to the exercise of papal authority as now exists in the wake of Vatican II. Certainly, no one who fully understands the present situation would be so foolish as to upbraid, or in any way belittle, the Holy Father, because so far he has not found it possible to do what is manifestly necessary in order to restore Catholic order.

"And this despite the fact that such action is manifestly necessary. It is imperative, because the longer material schism is tolerated, the more intractable will the bishops become, for each day they are becoming ever more greedily accustomed to having their cake and eating it; that is to having all the advantages of material schism with none of the disadvantages of formal schism.

"Moreover, the longer material schism persists, the greater the likelihood of those bishops being able to take their flocks with them in the event of formal schism."[78]

Hamish stated this in November 1985 at the first Fatima conference sponsored by Father Gruner held in Vatican City. Much has happened in the Church and the world in the past twenty-eight years to change the bishops' attitude toward the Consecration of Russia. Not the least of which is the ongoing campaign by Father Gruner and his associates to inform the bishops about Our Lady of Fatima's command to them to

78 Ibid, pp. 13-14.

consecrate Russia.

Hamish died in October 1986. No doubt today some bishops are still influenced against the Consecration for the motives Hamish outlines above. Nevertheless, had he still been alive today, he might be inclined to conclude, as Father Gruner has from his extensive correspondence and personal visits with bishops, together with their participation in the Bishops' Conferences, that once properly informed about Fatima, most of the bishops would, in fact, join the Holy Father in consecrating Russia, if asked by him to do so. This point of view was publicly upheld by Archbishop Milingo in his talk at the Fatima Peace Conference for Bishops held in Mexico in November 1994.

In 1985-1986, in spite of all the evidence to the contrary, "semi-official" sources and the Blue Army began to publish and insist that the consecration had at last been completed as of March 25, 1984, in Rome.

Why then, with all the evidence available, does the Blue Army continue to spread confusion? It would seem that the Blue Army had been infiltrated and compromised. According to Father Paul L. Kramer, "The leadership of the World Apostolate of Fatima (alias Blue Army) has stubbornly and impenitently falsified Our Lady's message, in their unholy campaign to bring the Fatima message in line with the Vatican-Moscow Agreement."[79]

The March/April 1986 Issue of *Soul* magazine, on page 22, states: "The Collegial Consecration (was) ... made with the bishops of the world by Pope John Paul II in St. Peter's Square on March 25, 1984 ... There the Pope in union with all the bishops of the world made the consecration to Mary's Immaculate Heart. *As requested in the apparition of June 13, 1929.*

Then, on page 9 of the same issue *Soul* magazine states: "The Holy Father proceeded to consecrate the world to the Immaculate Heart of Mary ... in compliance with the request of Our Lady when She said 'I will ask for the consecration of the *world* to My Immaculate Heart ...'"[80]

In view of the publication of such an obvious misrepresentation of the known facts, Father Paul Leonard Kramer, encouraged by Father Gruner, hastened to the defense of Our Lady, stating dramatically and emphatically that Our Lady never asked for the consecration of the *world* but clearly specified Russia. Father Paul Leonard saw the reasoning behind the misrepresentation in stark terms:

"Our Lady's real Fatima Message has been suppressed because it is at variance with Cardinal Casaroli's ... pro-Communist Vatican-Moscow *Ostpolitik*."[81]

The point that Father Paul Leonard Kramer makes also is that this misinformation is deliberate so as to inject enough confusion into the consecration issue[82] as to dissipate the laity, so that there be no groundswell of support for the Pope. In accord with Father Kramer is Father Joseph de Sainte-Marie, who said about the consecration confusion caused by the Blue Army and *Soul* magazine in 1982/83: *"Until now, they have given rise to confusion of mind, division of hearts and the dissipation of forces."*[83]

Their sowing of confusion, said Father Paul Leonard Kramer, of the Blue Army leadership, is "cunningly conceived to achieve a hidden but nevertheless very definite

79 Father Paul Leonard Kramer, *The Vatican-Moscow Agreement Has Silenced Our Lady*, "The Fatima Crusader", Issue 22, April-May 1987, p. 12.

80 *Soul* magazine, March-April 1986, p. 9; cited in "The Fatima Crusader", Issue 22, April-May 1987, p. 12.

81 Father Paul Leonard, *The Vatican-Moscow Agreement Has Silenced Our Lady*, "The Fatima Crusader", Issue 22, April-May 1987, p. 13.

82 Ibid, pp. 12-15; also, Father Paul Leonard, *The Blue Army Leadership has Followed a Deliberate Policy of Falsifying the Fatima Message*, "The Fatima Crusader", Issue 22, April-May 1987, pp. 12-15, 26-28.

83 Père Joseph de Sainte-Marie, *Letter to Hamish Fraser*, "The Fatima Crusader", Issue 13-14, Oct.-Dec. 1983, p. 10.

purpose to put an end to the public campaign for the Collegial Consecration of Russia to the Immaculate Heart of Mary."[84]

It seemed even the most highly respected of American bishops, when under the Blue Army mantle, felt obliged to direct the faithful away from Our Lady's dramatic demand to the hierarchy for the consecration and to instead place the onus on the faithful who are already obeying Our Lady. U.S. Blue Army President, Bishop Jerome J. Hastrich, in *Soul* magazine March/April, 1984, page 5 stated: "... We might pray explicitly for Russia if we wish to do so, *but in our public message* ... avoid upsetting the delicate balance of international affairs which the Holy See is trying so hard to control and direct." So there we have it. According to Bishop Hastrich, it seems we must desist from working for the fulfillment of Our Lady's request so as not to offend the Communists, or even Russians who are not Christians, who would resent the notion that they are in need of conversion.

In a statement that would make them few friends in the Vatican, Fathers Gruner and Paul Leonard responded with the following summary, "The Blue Army has been turned into an instrument of Cardinal Casaroli's Vatican-Moscow *Ostpolitik* which would prohibit the Pope and bishops from fulfilling Our Lady of Fatima's request for the sake of the shortsighted politics of appeasement, compromise and surrender to Communism."

Father Gruner continued to press home his main point throughout: God demands the solemn public act of Consecration of Russia by the Pope and all the bishops of the world. God insists upon this solemn act in our time.[85]

The Vatican-Moscow Agreement in fact had raised a drawbridge between the Blue Army and Father Gruner's Apostolate.

"We cannot agree with Mr. John Haffert that the Vatican has outsmarted Moscow in this agreement and that, because of this agreement, the Church is better off," said Father Gruner.[86]

"Communism is conducting more than just a war of ideas. It is a total war on all fronts against God ...[87]

"The fight by the militant atheists of the East and West converges upon the Catholic Church. Both concentrate their efforts towards drawing the faithful away from the practice of their faith, away from the Word of God, from prayer and the Sacraments, the means of Grace necessary to save our souls."[88]

Father Paul Leonard Kramer added: "Cardinal Casaroli, who as Secretary of State is at the head of the entire Vatican diplomatic corps, still adheres to the Vatican-Moscow Agreement. He recently demonstrated this when he made it clear that he had no responsibility for the anti-Communist content of the Instruction on Liberation Theology issued on September 3, 1984, by Cardinal Ratzinger and he denied that he was even consulted about the Instruction."[89]

Blue Army President for the U.S., Bishop Hastrich, stated in that March/April, 1984 Issue of *Soul* magazine (which came out before the 1984 consecration) that instead of praying for the conversion of Russia, "... We are rather to pray that members of the Blue

84 Father Paul Leonard, *The Vatican-Moscow Agreement Has Silenced Our Lady*, "The Fatima Crusader", Issue 22, April-May 1987, p. 12.

85 Father Nicholas Gruner, *World Enslavement or Peace ... It's Up to the Pope*, Fort Erie, Canada, Fatima Crusader Publications, 1988. This book is a well-documented source of information to gain an indepth understanding of this vital point.

86 *The Catholic Church Betrayed*, "The Fatima Crusader", Issue 17, Feb.-April 1985, p. 7.

87 Ibid, p. 9.

88 Ibid, p. 10.

89 Father Paul Leonard, *The Blue Army Leadership has Followed a Deliberate Policy of Falsifying the Fatima Message*, "The Fatima Crusader", Issue 22, April-May 1987, p. 27.

Army would so pray and fast that they themselves might be thoroughly converted ... to pray for the 'conversion' of Russia may seem like waving a red flag in front of a bull ... and so it might be more prudent to pray for peace in the world."

So intense was the craving to have the campaign for the Consecration over and done with, the wishful thinkers were willing to overlook anything the Soviets did. Or said. In late November 1986 Soviet leader Mikhail Gorbachev, in a speech in Tashkent, called for a 'firm and uncompromising struggle against religious phenomena'. So much for change in the Soviet Union. So much for the conversion of Russia. So much for the 1984 consecration.

Gorbachev declared, "We must be strict above all with Communists and senior officials, particularly those who say they defend our morality and ideals but in fact help promote backward views and themselves take part in religious ceremonies."[90]

The timing of the speech and the location reflected Moscow's concern for the Islamic fundamentalist revival, Tashkent being the center of a predominantly Islamic population. Knowing the media's fondness for Gorbachev, it was no surprise that they failed to publicize this gaffe in the General Secretary's otherwise smooth public utterances. Yet imagine the headlines if he had made his pronouncement in, say, Rome itself.

There can be little doubt that even those bishops still entranced by the disorientations resulting from the Vatican-Moscow Agreement would have found reasons to applaud Gorbachev's speech.

In response, Father Gruner's message has, in recent years, become increasingly more pointed. He says: "*ONLY* Our Lady can help us as She, Herself clearly emphasized at Fatima. Only when the Pope and the bishops obey the request given at Fatima by consecrating Russia to the Immaculate Heart of Mary at the same time in a solemn and public manner, can there be peace. There surely is no other solution whatsoever."

By the mid-1980's, then, Father Gruner had fixed a course for himself and the Apostolate which would bring them within the ambit of the Vatican bureaucracy's radar. In fact, the surveillance had already begun.

Father Gruner has personally delivered to the Vatican, tens of thousands of petitions asking the Holy Father for the Consecration of Russia.

90 Mikhail Gorbachev, *Speech in Tashkent*, Richard N. Ostling, *Time* magazine, Jan. 12, 1987; also published in the Uzbek daily *Pravda Vostoka*, and the report was cited in the Keston College News Service of December 11, 1986.

PART TWO
Politics vs. Prayer

Chapter 9

The Network

In late July of 1989 Father Gruner received a most unusual letter from Antonio Cardinal Innocenti, Prefect of the Congregation for the Clergy. It was the ecclesiastical equivalent of a letter-bomb:

"This Congregation has been following for a long time your case which arouses serious preoccupation on the part of the Holy See..."

Case? *What* case? And why was the "Holy See"—that is, certain elements of the Vatican bureaucracy—"seriously preoccupied" with him? As Father Gruner read the rest of the "Innocenti intervention" he saw a pattern which would repeat itself over and over again in the years to come.

The letter did not bother to answer the questions it raised; it did not define its own terms. There was no explanation of what the "case" of Father Gruner consisted of, nor any reason given for the "serious preoccupation on the part of the Holy See." Instead, Cardinal Innocenti simply declared the result he desired, and Father Gruner was evidently expected to comply without benefit of due process of Canon Law: Father Gruner was to find another bishop by September 30 or else return to Avellino. Naturally, this would mean the end of the Apostolate.

A basic point of Canon Law occurred to Father Gruner as he read the "Innocenti intervention". The Bishop of Avellino had given no such order himself, and Cardinal Innocenti had no right to issue it in the bishop's stead. A bishop is the ruler of his own diocese, answerable only to the Pope, not to the Congregation for the Clergy. The intervention was, quite simply, void.

Father Gruner replied to the intervention in a letter which pointed out, among other things, that a Cardinal sitting in the office of a Vatican Congregation had no right to run the Diocese of Avellino. For good measure, Father Gruner placed a copy of a formal appeal against Cardinal Innocenti into the hands of the Pope himself at a general audience in January of the following year. Thereafter the "Innocenti intervention" vaporized. Cardinal Innocenti was never heard from again in the "case" of Father Gruner. It was later reported to Father Gruner by a friendly Vatican insider that Cardinal Innocenti had stated that the name of Father Nicholas Gruner was never to be mentioned again in his presence.

Although the "Innocenti intervention" went nowhere, it prefigured later developments in the "case" of Father Gruner. Many of those developments would be unprecedented in the annals of Canon Law, but they would not be without parallels in the prior abuse of priests and prelates who had posed an impediment to the executors of *Ostpolitik*.

To comprehend the suffering many priests endure today at the hands of the bureaucracy of the Church they have vowed to serve until death, we need look no further than Father Augustine Fuentes and Cardinal Mindszenty. Their history is useful to discuss here in an effort to appreciate the startling parallels with Father Gruner's case.

On December 26, 1957, Father Augustine Fuentes conducted a famous interview with Sister Lucia which was published in July 1958 with explicit written ecclesiastical permission and reprinted thereafter by various magazines around the world.[91] A full

---

91 For text of this interview of Sister Lucia with Father Fuentes see *La Verdad Sobre el Secreto de Fàtima*, page 107. Most Reverend Sanchez, Archbishop of Veracruz, gave the imprimatur; Dec. 26, 1957 interview with Sister Lucia by Father Fuentes—her last official statements allowed to be made public, Coimbra, Portugal; also, Frère François de Marie des Anges,

year passed before anyone in "authority" suggested it was not authentic. On July 2, 1959, nine months after the death of Pope Pius XII, an anonymous chancery official (who has not been identified to this day) suddenly published in the Diocesan bulletin of Coimbra that Father Fuentes had lied and had made up the interview out of thin air.[92] In response, Father Fuentes' own Archbishop of Veracruz, and the Cardinal Primate of Mexico, publicly stated that Father Fuentes was an honest, good priest who did not merit the charges being leveled against him by the anonymous "news" bulletin.[93] Nevertheless, the anonymous bulletin of the Curia of Coimbra was successful in suppressing Sister Lucia's statements and having Father Fuentes removed as vice-postulator for the cause of beatification and canonization of Jacinta and Francisco.[94] Oddly enough, he was replaced by the very person Frère François now accuses of being behind the bogus letters of Sister Lucia in 1989, Father Luis Kondor.[95]

As Father Paul Leonard points out: "Of course, it is manifestly dishonest and unjust what was done to Father Fuentes. Obviously if that Curia official of Coimbra or anyone else is not willing to stand behind his words, if he won't even take responsibility for his own 'official' acts, then clearly no one else should take his anonymous words and acts seriously either. This is clearly a case of some powerful figure who does not want anyone to question, rebuke, examine or subject his actions to judicial review but who wants to impose his opinion, judgment and decision. In other words, it is the action of a man who recognizes no authority over himself but who forces his will on others when he has no real authority to do so. All authority by men over other men comes from God, but God gives no one, not the President, not the Prime Minister, not the Pope nor the Supreme Court Judge any authority to command or judge unless the person in authority takes personal (and therefore not be anonymous) responsibility for his authoritative, official acts."

As Father Gruner notes: "The whole nature of law, which must be observed if a society is not going to be subverted by a secret society, is that those in authority must take *personal and public responsibility* for their official acts. This posture is a fundamental requirement of the natural law."[96]

Incredibly, a similar attempt was made on no less a personage than a Cardinal of the Roman Catholic Church. In 1975, a statement was published declaring that Cardinal Mindszenty had resigned from being Archbishop of Esztergom, Primate of Hungary. The Cardinal issued an immediate rebuttal stating, "I have not resigned and I presently cannot resign because of all the things going on in Hungary today which endangers souls."[97] Here was a Cardinal, one of the electors of the Pope, a prince of the Church, but even this did not deter certain Vatican bureaucrats from removing him from office and, at the same time, giving the public the impression that he had left his post willingly.

Due to Cardinal Mindszenty's courageous stand, the truth won. He wrote:

Fatima: Tragedy and Triumph, pp. 26-32; also, Frère Michel de la Sainte Trinité, Vol. III, *The Third Secret*, pp. 503-509.

92 Frère François de Marie des Anges, *Fatima: Tragedy and Triumph*, p. 31.

93 Frère Michel de la Sainte Trinité, Vol. III, *The Third Secret*, p. 551.

94 Frère François de Marie des Anges, *Fatima: Tragedy and Triumph*, p. 31; Frère Michel de la Sainte Trinité, Vol. III, *The Third Secret*, p. 551.

95 *The Catholic Counter-Reformation in The XXth Century*, Issue 251, Oct. 1992, p. 4; Frère François de Marie des Anges, *Fatima: Tragedy and Triumph*, p. 30; Frère Michel de la Sainte Trinité, Vol. III, *The Third Secret*, p. 551. For more information regarding the accusation against Father Kondor, see *Following Our Lady's Path to Her Triumph*, "The Fatima Crusader", Issue 100, Autumn 2011, pp. 51-53 (on the web at http://www.fatimacrusader.com/cr100/cr100pg3.pdf). See also photo and caption on page 197 of this book.

96 See Father Gruner's article, *Schism and the Common Good*, "The Fatima Crusader", Issue 57, p. 24.

97 Cardinal Mindszenty, *Memoirs*, pp. 412-413.

"On February 5, 1975, the announcement of my removal from the See of Esztergom was published. Next day, to my profound sorrow, I found myself forced to issue a correction through my office:

"A number of news agencies have transmitted the Vatican decision in such a way as to imply that Jozsef Cardinal Mindszenty has voluntarily retired. The news agencies furthermore stressed that before the papal decision there was an intense exchange of letters between the Vatican and the Cardinal-Archbishop, who is living in Vienna. Some persons have therefore drawn the conclusion that an agreement concerning this decision had been reached between the Vatican and the Hungarian primate. In the interests of truth, Cardinal Mindszenty has authorized his office to issue the following statement:

Cardinal Mindszenty has not abdicated his office as Archbishop nor the dignity as Primate of Hungary. The decision was taken by the Holy See alone.

After long and conscientious consideration the Cardinal justified his attitude on this question as follows:

1. Hungary and the Catholic Church of Hungary are not free.

2. The leadership of the Hungarian dioceses is in the hands of a church administration built and controlled by the communist regime.

3. Not a single archbishop or apostolic administrator is in a position to alter the composition or the functioning of the above-mentioned church administration.

4. The regime decides who is to occupy ecclesiastical positions and for how long. Furthermore, the regime also decides what persons the bishops will be allowed to consecrate as priests.

5. The freedom of conscience and religion guaranteed by the Constitution is in practice, suppressed. "Optional" religious instruction has been banned from the schools in the cities and the larger towns. At present, the struggle for optional religious instruction in the schools is continuing in the smaller communities. Young people, contrary to the will of their parents, are being educated exclusively in an atheistic spirit. Believers are discriminated against in many areas of daily life. Religious teachers have only recently been confronted with the alternative of choosing between their professions and their religion.

6. The appointment of bishops or apostolic administrators without the elimination of the above-mentioned abuses does not solve the problems of the Hungarian Church. The installation of 'peace priests' in important ecclesiastical posts has shaken the confidence of loyal priests and lay Catholics in the highest administration of the Church. In these grave circumstances, Cardinal Mindszenty cannot abdicate.

This is the path I have traveled to the end, and this is how I arrived at complete and total exile."[98]

Father Marcel Nault,* reflecting on the above experiences of Father Fuentes and Cardinal Mindszenty, said:

"In Acts of the Apostles, Chapter 20 (verses 28-31), St. Paul warns the bishops that, from among their own number, perverse men will arise to draw the faithful after them. And urges them to watch therefore and not be taken in. St. Jude, in verse 4 of his Epistle, says that infiltrators will enter the Church. In the Apocalypse

98 Ibid.

* **Editor's Note:** Father Nault worked for Father Gruner from 1992 to 1997, when he died.

we can read about the false lamb with two horns. This false lamb represents bad bishops. The two horns symbolize the two points on the miters of bishops who, while giving the appearance of a lamb, are actually false.[99] In fact, as we have learned from Frère Michel's painstaking research, the Third Secret clearly refers to the responsibility of a number of members of the hierarchy for the present state of apostasy within the Catholic Church today.[100] And as we have seen, this infiltration of the hierarchy has been predicted in Sacred Scripture.

"Thus, it seems we have here the terrible 'burden' of the Third Secret, namely, the infiltration of the upper hierarchy and their complicity in the apostasy sweeping across all Christendom. That would explain why a few members of the upper hierarchy seem to work so hard to discredit priests like Father Gruner. Simply stated, if Father Gruner succeeds in bringing to the attention of the Catholic faithful the existence of these false lambs and their plans, so that the faithful are able to protect themselves from these false prophets, and if he were to succeed in getting the Third Secret revealed, then, of course, their game would be up and Catholics everywhere would rise up to defend themselves against these interlopers.

"These same false shepherds are certainly going to do whatever they can to protect themselves from the exposure that revealing the Third Secret would bring."

Sister Lucia herself had been silenced since 1960. Would they attempt to silence Father Gruner? They certainly knew that he was not bound by obedience to remain silent about the Vatican-Moscow Agreement. The pretense that "Father Gruner must obey our commands" had not worked in the Innocenti intervention. But there were other ways of getting rid of an inconvenient cleric. The cases of Father Fuentes and Cardinal Mindszenty made that clear.

Father Gruner and Cardinal Mindszenty's cases would prove to be strikingly similar, although Father Gruner would shrink from any comparison with the great prelate. By the manner of the trap set for them, by the type of isolation they suffer and by the intensity of their resistance to it, these two cases would illustrate what Father Paul Leonard calls "the decay of the moral leadership in the bureaucracy of the Catholic Church in this century."

The great St. Athanasius was exiled from his diocese by the Conference of Bishops of Egypt five separate times. He spent at least 17 years in exile. He was even "excommunicated" by Pope Liberius, who ended up being the first Pope in the early Church not to be canonized. Athanasius continued to preach and ordain priests despite the "excommunication".

Another Saint, St. John Gualberto, went to the bureaucrats in Rome and complained to them regarding the Archbishop of Florence, who had actually bribed certain bureaucrats to get himself appointed bishop. To this Saint the Vatican bureaucrats would not listen. So he took his case directly to the people, and God worked a public miracle, at St. John Gualberto's request, to prove that what he was saying was true. The people drove the corrupt bishop out of town. From such lessons of Catholic history we learn that God expects clerics to go to the people to protect the Church when Vatican officials will not pay attention. It now appeared that "front line" clerics would have to rally the Catholic faithful in the current confusion and deception. They must go to the people so the people

99 Acts 20:28-31.

100 Frère Michel de la Sainte Trinité, Vol III, *The Third Secret*, pp. 701-702.

can wake up to what they can do to resist and overcome the crisis.

(There is also, of course, the example in Sacred Scripture of St. Peter being rebuked by St. Paul to protect the Faith and the Church. Saints and Doctors of the Church all concur that St. Paul was absolutely right.)

What secret strengths sustain a priest when the bureaucracy of the Church for which he has laid down his life seeks to erase the good he has done, prevent the good his memory might yet do, and eradicate from the record any reference to the bureaucracy's part in the deed? Heaven alone knows.

It is a sad and oft-overlooked fact of Conciliar Church history that the two bishops "excommunicated" over their defense of the Mass of the Ages, Archbishop Lefebvre and Bishop de Castro Mayer, were also the two loudest voices among the International Group of Bishops raised in opposition to Vatican II's hush-hush policy on Communism.[101] It cannot be mere coincidence.

The showdown between Father Gruner and the bureaucrats was inevitable. In view of the confusion deliberately generated by the anti-Fatima forces regarding the consecration, Father Gruner had gone directly to the world episcopacy in issue after issue of *The Fatima Crusader* during the late 80's and early 90's. The printed headlines sent again and again around the world had a much more lasting effect than a television broadcast or radio could possibly have had. Statistics prove that the printed word receives eight times as many repeated viewings as any other form of media expression. *The Fatima Crusader* headlines continued to repeat the danger: "Lucia Silenced", "He (the Pope) Will Do It But It Will Be Late" "Make It Known to My Ministers" "They Will Follow Him (the King of France) Into Misfortune".

Many had predicted that Vatican bureaucrats would step up the attack and take direct action to silence Father Gruner, to mute his insistence that the Consecration must be done, to prevent the public airing of his well founded perception of who was directly responsible for it not being done and, especially, to permanently prevent him, or anyone else, from effectively obeying the command of Jesus to "Make It Known to My Ministers".

To those who might suggest that it was presumptuous of Father Gruner to undertake to obey the command "Make it Known to My Ministers", the reply ought to have been self-evident:

First of all, the command of Our Lord to Sister Lucia extended to all the ministers of the Church, including Father Gruner. What would be the point of making the message known to all the sacred ministers of the Church, if they were not to preach it?

Secondly, how could the message be preached effectively without including the bishops, whose pressing duties as heads of their dioceses might preclude a study of the message in all its implications?

Third, how could any of the sacred ministers remain silent in the face of Our Lord's command, merely because a few Vatican bureaucrats had deemed it inexpedient to speak any longer of the conversion of Russia as the only means to avoid annihilation of nations?

What is more, if certain Vatican bureaucrats had undertaken a global campaign to bury the Message of Fatima, did not the sacred ministers who had been ordered by Our Lord to preach it, have a sacred duty to mount an opposing campaign to keep the message alive?

---

101 Dr. David Allen White, *The Mouth of the Lion*, p. 79.

The anti-Fatima forces in the Vatican had their work cut out for them. To destroy Father Gruner's Fatima Apostolate would be the objective. But that would mean silencing his continent-wide weekly television show, his daily radio broadcasts, and *The Fatima Crusader* magazine, of which he was the publisher. To eliminate all of them would be a formidable task. A much easier solution to the "Gruner problem" would be to take the outspoken priest out of contention with one simple masterstroke. The tactic chosen in the summer of 1989 would anticipate a more elaborate effort later on: The bureaucrats would make Father an offer he couldn't refuse. A new bishop in Canada would be offered on the condition of silence!

This ploy would involve the Secretary of State, Cardinal Casaroli; the active participation of the Nuncio to Canada, Archbishop Palmas; Cardinal Innocenti from the Congregation for the Clergy and the current Bishop of Avellino, whose predecessor had ordained Father Gruner and given him written permission to reside outside the diocese of Avellino. Also drawn into the campaign was Bishop Fulton of St. Catharines, Ontario, Canada, in whose diocese the Pilgrim Virgin Apostolate was housed. For some years, Bishop Fulton had accommodated the Apostolate, at first by granting his permission to move the head office into his diocese, and then by simply leaving it alone. Now, Bishop Fulton was to become a pawn in a game he did not initiate.

On August 9, 1989, a letter from Bishop Fulton arrived at the Fort Erie Fatima Center address.

"I have just received documentation from the present Bishop of Avellino, His Excellency Gerrardo Pierro," the letter read, " in which he raises the question of your possible incardination in the diocese of St. Catharines ...

"As far as incardination is concerned, I would require ... that you would promise total obedience to me as bishop and that you would accept an appointment at my bidding, which would require you to abandon the present apostolate which you have chosen for yourself."[102]

Pope John Paul II said: "The Fatima Message is more relevant and urgent than ever. It is addressed to every human being ... The Message of Fatima imposes an obligation on the Church".[103] Obviously, it is not optional nor can priests take a vow of silence about it. It appeared that just as the Vatican-Moscow Agreement immorally and illegally but *de facto* imposes silence on priests, bishops and Cardinals, they would now pressure Father Gruner to make his own personal pact of silence regarding the full Fatima Message. The offer of incardination came with a string attached: "promise to keep silence about Fatima and all it implies."

It was clear as lightning in a Canadian sunset—we'll put up if you shut up! But such an agreement would be immoral. How could any priest in good conscience agree to be silent about a public revelation which the last five Popes have publicly promoted? How could any priest simply ignore the command of Our Lord Himself: "*Make it known* to My ministers"? And why was this pact of silence not being demanded of Father Fox? It seems that the Fatima Message propagated by Father Fox had been "dumbed down".

The response to the offer was taken up, on Father Gruner's behalf, by one of the finest honed, and best aimed pens in the Catholic world, Father Paul Leonard.

"It would be the easiest thing in the world for Father Gruner to succumb to the

102 Bishop Fulton, *Letter to Father Gruner*, dated August 9, 1989, published in "The Fatima Crusader", Issue 29, Sept.-Nov. 1989, p. 40.

103 *L'Osservatore Romano*, May 17, 1982, English Edition; also published in "The Fatima Crusader", Issue 9-10, Oct.-Dec. 1982, pp. 5-8.

machinations of Vatican bureaucrats and abandon the apostolate he has carried out for more than ten years. [Now in 2013, over 35 years.]

"How easy it would be to abandon Fatima to assume the much easier life of a small town curate, earning more pay for less work."[104]

"However, it is canonically illegal for Church authorities to attempt in this manner to silence a priest from carrying out his priestly task of preaching the truth. In Sacred Scripture, St. Paul tells the bishop, St. Timothy, to impose silence on false shepherds who depart from the teaching of the Church and thereby dissipate the Faith. (1 Tim. 1:3-7) It is high time that those clergy and laity who are faithful to the Magisterium of the Church resist the abuse of authority whereby the holders of ecclesiastical office tolerate and permit the Faith to be dissipated, destroyed and expunged from the hearts of men by modernist priests, while they unlawfully attempt to impose silence on those who remain in steadfast conformity to the Gospel of Christ, the Magisterium of the Church, and the pontifically approved message of Our Lady of Fatima.

"The pressure applied by Cardinal Innocenti (the July 1989 intervention) is not merely against Father Gruner as a single individual, but is really against the Apostolate of *The Fatima Crusader*, *Heaven's Peace Plan* radio program and the TV program, *Fatima: "The Moment Has Come"*. All stressing the need for the Consecration."[105]

As Father Gruner had pointed out in his reply to the void intervention of Cardinal Innocenti, there was no need for him to obtain a new ordinary in Canada:

"There are many priests working in Canada who are not incardinated here, yet that does not appear to arouse any 'serious preoccupation on the part of the Holy See'. Canon Law does not *require* that all priests be incardinated in the diocese where they reside, and therefore, I would like to know what is the reason for this extra-legal requirement ...[106]

"If the Secretary of State and some bishops are displeased with my activity in promoting the Message of Our Lady of Fatima, then the burden of proof is on them to prove any wrongdoing on my part. I have sent my magazine to every bishop in the world for years. I have sent my book *World Enslavement or Peace ... It's Up to the Pope* to all the bishops of the world. No bishop, Cardinal, or any official of the Holy See has even suggested there is anything doctrinally wrong in anything that I have ever published.

"It is to silence us from denouncing the Vatican-Moscow Agreement that you unlawfully inflict this injustice."[107] Cardinal Innocenti never replied to these arguments. They were, in fact, unanswerable.

Sister Lucia herself gives us the key to understanding the persecutions of faithful priests while modernist wolves in shepherds' clothing roam at will: "The devil is in the mood for engaging in a decisive battle against the Blessed Virgin. And the devil knows what it is that most offends God and which in a short space of time will gain for him the greatest number of souls. Thus the devil does everything to overcome souls consecrated to God because, in this way, the devil will succeed in leaving the souls of the faithful abandoned by their leaders, thereby the more easily will he seize them."

To those who suggest that the faithful should simply wait for the "competent authorities" to address the crisis, Sister Lucia had a pointed reply: "We should not wait for an appeal to the world to come from Rome on the part of the Holy Father to do

104 Father Paul Leonard, *Incardination Offered on Condition of Silence*, "The Fatima Crusader", Issue 29, Sept.-Nov. 1989, p. 39.

105 Father Paul Leonard, *Some Vatican Officials Attempt to Silence and Suppress Our Lady of Fatima and Father Gruner*, "The Fatima Crusader" Issue 29, Sept.-Nov. 1989, p. 4.

106 Father Nicholas Gruner, *Letter to Cardinal Innocenti*, "The Fatima Crusader", Issue 29, Sept.-Nov. 1989, pp. 37-38.

107 See Sister Lucia interview with Father Fuentes – see Chapter 9, footnote 1 above.

penance. Nor should we wait for the call to penance to come from our bishops in our diocese, nor from the religious congregations. No! Our Lord has already very often used these means and the world has not paid attention. That is why, now, it is necessary for each one of us to begin to reform himself spiritually. Each person must not only save his own soul but also all the souls that God has placed on our path."[108]

§

The Innocenti intervention and the "strings-attached" offer of a bishop for silence were the opening moves in a bureaucratic chess game which began after eleven years of dramatic growth for the Apostolate from 1978, when Father Gruner became its vice president, to 1989, when the opening moves of the chess game were made in Rome.

Understanding the importance of the Fatima Message, despite all the controversy, Father Gruner's Apostolate had neither changed direction nor slowed down during that period. In 1985, Father Gruner had begun restoring a fast-disappearing aspect of Catholic culture, a mission to India, with the Pilgrim Virgin Statue of Our Lady of Fatima. To the average Catholic, India represents a subcontinent of non-Christians, prone to hostile expressions regarding any missionary invasion ever since the time of St. Thomas the Apostle. In fact, the fervor for Catholicism sown by the Apostle was at a fever pitch in the mid-80's, far surpassing even the devotion expressed in the Western Canada tours of the late Seventies.

On May 13, 1985, having installed the Pilgrim Virgin Statue at the high altar built over the tomb of St. Thomas the Apostle, in the Cathedral of Madras [now Chennai], India, Father Gruner joined the Archbishop of Madras, His Grace Archbishop Rayappa Arulappa, to preach to the multitudes drawn by Her presence.[109]

The faith in Mary is still strong, beautiful and simple in India. Following this pilgrimage, Father Gruner supplied the newly opened Fatima Rosary Crusade mission office in Madras with hundreds of thousands of scapulars, rosaries and holy cards.

By November 1985, he was in Rome to chair the first Symposium at the Vatican specifically on the Message of Fatima: "Is the 1985 Extraordinary Synod the Last Opportunity for World Peace?". This important meeting coincided with the opening of the Extraordinary Synod called by the Holy Father. The Apostolate hosted influential members of the clergy as well as such Fatima scholars as Frère Michel de la Sainte Trinité (France); Hamish Fraser (Scotland); Abbé Pierre Caillon (France); Professor Emilio Cristani (Italy).

There were also various bishops in attendance. Especially notable was the following: the Latin Patriarch of Jerusalem, His Beatitude Giacomo Beltriti, who was quite familiar with the consecration of Russia request and who acknowledged it had not been done properly by the time of the November 24, 1985 symposium. His Beatitude had publicly, at the Roman Synod of Bishops in October 1983, from the Synod floor asked the Pope and the bishops to consecrate Russia as Our Lady of Fatima requested. He agreed to be an honorary chairman of the Symposium. He told Father Gruner he would continue to work towards the consecration of Russia through diplomatic channels within the Church and he encouraged Father Gruner to continue to openly publicize the need for the consecration of Russia as Father Gruner had been doing for several years.

The other notable bishop present was Bishop Gabriel Ganaka, President of the

108 *Father Gruner in India*, "The Fatima Crusader", Issue 18, Oct.-Dec. 1985, p. 13, caption.

109 "The Fatima Crusader", Issue 39, Winter 1992, p. 20, caption.

Bishops' Conference of Nigeria. Bishop Ganaka was deeply impressed with the meeting and told Father Gruner that as a result of the presentation, he would talk to the Holy Father about the request for the consecration of Russia. A few days later, Bishop Ganaka arrived in the papal apartments for his appointed lunch with the Holy Father and a number of other bishops. He got there a few minutes early and in the sitting room on the coffee table was a magazine that headlined, "the consecration of Russia is already done." This confused the bishop who did not have enough background on the Fatima Message, and consequently felt it "prudent" not to bring it up with the Pope.

It became increasingly clear to Father Gruner, after Bishop Ganaka reported this experience to him, that a deliberate campaign of disinformation was preventing the consecration of Russia from being done. The Pope simply did not know just how many bishops would be loyal and obey him if he requested it.

In advance of a new pilgrimage to India, Issue 19 of *The Fatima Crusader* had drawn a letter of encouragement, support and prayers from Mother Teresa of Calcutta, April 7, 1986: "May Our Lord continue to bless your dedicated efforts to spread devotion to the Immaculate Heart of Mary." Her handwritten postscript, the cornerstone of her own apostolate, went straight to the heart of the India Pilgrimage, "Keep the joy of loving Jesus through Mary and share this joy with all you meet".

By May 1988, the International Fatima Rosary Crusade had expanded Father Gruner's radio program, begun in 1987, which was already reaching a potential 200 million people through 43 radio stations in the U.S. and Canada, via regular short-wave radio broadcasts to more than 40 nations overseas.[110]

By August of 1988, Father Gruner's book *World Enslavement or Peace ... It's Up to the Pope*, a comprehensive analysis of the Fatima Message, had been published. It became a staple for Fatimologists, paving the way for the English translation of the three volumes of *The Whole Truth About Fatima*, the definitive examination of Fatima by Frère Michel de la Sainte Trinité which Father Gruner's own publishing house printed in the late 1980's and early 90's.

The explosive growth of the Apostolate from 1978 to 1989 had greatly alarmed the anti-Fatima establishment. Here was a genuine movement to keep alive a message most unpalatable for the executors of the new order—a message that Russia must be converted, and that locked in what had become known as the Third Secret were answers to the crisis which had spread throughout the Church since Vatican II. Clearly, something had to be done about the man leading the movement.

§

The pressure from various opponents of Father Gruner started to take on a frantic Keystone Cops pace. In *Soul* magazine, the voice of the Blue Army, Bishop Luna declared that "The Holy Father is disturbed by the many letters being written demanding a consecration of Russia. The work in *The Fatima Crusader* by Fr. Nicholas Gruner is creating worldwide confusion. Pope Pius XII made a consecration of Russia; Pope Paul VI repeated the consecration when he went to Fatima in 1967 for the fiftieth anniversary. Pope John Paul II repeated the consecration in 1982 during his visit to Fatima and again when Our Lady's statue was brought from Fatima to St. Peter's Square in Rome in 1984."[111]

Then began the harassment that would continue for years. Bishop Luna wrote a

110 *Father Gruner Speaks World-Wide on the Only Daily Radio Program Dedicated to Our Lady's Fatima Message*, "The Fatima Crusader", Issue 30, Winter 1989, p. 34.

111 *Soul* magazine, Jan.-Feb. 1990, p. 29.

letter to Bishop Legaspi, President of the Philippine Bishops' Conference, to which Father Gruner's Pilgrim Virgin tour was headed. In it, Bishop Luna lamented the fact that so many Blue Army members received *The Fatima Crusader*, because, he said, "its philosophy promotes ideas against the Holy Father and against the Holy See."[112]

Never has this claim of Bishop Luna been substantiated, nor could it be, as there is absolutely no evidence of any disloyalty or disrespect towards the Pope in any of the Apostolate's activities or publications. Nevertheless, this letter was put to a very specific use in the city of Ilo Ilo in the Philippines. Father Gruner had been invited to bring the Pilgrim Virgin into the Cathedral of Ilo Ilo. Archbishop Piamonte, based on the Bishop Luna letter, informed the faithful of his diocese that Father Gruner had canceled the visit and would not be arriving there with the statue.[113]

When the tour actually arrived at the Cathedral with the statue, the doors were closed. No official was on hand to welcome the Pilgrim Virgin as there had been at eight other cathedrals in the Philippines. Nevertheless, they entered the Cathedral and brought the statue into the nave. While the Cathedral was packed for Mass, the Archbishop and the vicar were out of town, and the two young priests left in charge did not bother to even acknowledge Our Lady's presence in their midst. The Vicar General refused to speak with the tour organizers.[114] At the end of Mass, their enthusiasm and devotion was not lost. The people crowded around Our Lady, paying homage to Her and enthusiastically demonstrating their appreciation at having Her in their midst.

The islands of the Philippines are half way around the world from that little island of knowledge and inspiration wherein is deposited the key to the secrets of Fatima, one Carmelite nun in a convent in Coimbra. Yet it was in the Philippines that the long anticipated guerrilla-style harassment of Father Gruner's Fatima Apostolate first showed its face. The setting itself could only prompt one to wonder how much simpler life for the Church would be if only the Holy See's order of silence was lifted and the world could hear the truth from the voice of that one specially chosen woman a half a world away.

Meanwhile, the Apostolate continued its initiative in India. In October 1991, Father Gruner had received a pressing letter from Victor Kulanday of the All India Laity Congress urging him to return to the subcontinent to meet with bishops and Catholic lay leaders to explain the urgent need to consecrate Russia in the manner Our Lady specified. Many of the 140 Indian bishops had already indicated their willingness to consecrate Russia as Our Lady asked.

Included in the pilgrimage were plans to meet with two Cardinals, two Archbishops, and the hope to meet again with Mother Teresa and that other legend of the Church in our time who had spent more than 60 years among the poor of Bombay, Father Maschio.[115]

According to Bishop Amalnather, 200,000 people welcomed the Pilgrim Virgin statue at Sacred Heart Cathedral in Tuticorin in mid-November.[116] The November 24, 1991 edition of *Mid Day* also reported that more than 200,000 pilgrims welcomed the Pilgrim Virgin statue in Bombay, some several thousand miles away.

The fervor for, love of and devotion to the Mother of God evident in grassroots Catholic movements in India was of the type not seen in decades in North America or

112 Father Paul Leonard, *The Plot To Silence Our Lady Thickens*, "The Fatima Crusader", Issue 31-32, March-May 1990, p. 5.

113 Ibid, pp. 5-6.

114 Ibid, p. 6.

115 "The Fatima Crusader", Issue 39, Winter 1992, p. 13, caption.

116 Ibid, p. 28, caption.

Europe. In city after city, tens of thousands came out bearing flowers and gifts for the Pilgrim Virgin, leaving forever impressed upon the mind's eye hundreds of thousands of outstretched hands reaching for scapulars and rosaries.

How much effect would this 'Garment of Grace' have on the Catholic culture of India? Bishops walked with thousands of their flock in procession to honor the Pilgrim Virgin. On at least one occasion, a bishop, after hearing Father Gruner's sermon on the message of Our Lady of Fatima, consecrated his diocese to the Immaculate Heart of Mary.[117] One priest commented after Father Gruner had spoken to a rally of 60,000 people that the visit of the Pilgrim Virgin had revived the faith of hundreds of thousands.

Father Marcel Nault, who had hosted the Pilgrim Virgin Statue at his parish of St. Stephen the Martyr in Dowling, Ontario, and who would later join forces with Father Gruner, accompanied him on that pilgrimage to India.

"In 1991," he said, "I went with him to India. I have never seen such poverty and yet so much modesty among the people. The Indian people are very pious, religious, peaceful, and dress with great decency.

"I was very much impressed by Father Gruner's extraordinary ability to preach for hours on the message of Fatima to millions. His is a marvelous holy work. He is a true crusader for Our Lady of Fatima.

"I stood alongside him for hours giving out Brown Scapulars."

The pilgrimage returned to Canada with the goal of providing in the first months of the following year one million Scapulars and scapular booklets to India's 25 million Catholics, with a special emphasis on Catholic school children.

At the end of 1991, the movement started by the Apostolate showed no signs of distress, and its leader had so far fended off the first few thrusts of the bureaucratic forces which had yet to implement their definitive strategy.

In Portugal, in 1992, however, the effort to derail the Apostolate and discredit Father Gruner would descend to the theater of the absurd.

Bishop Paul Vasylyk, Ukrainian bishop imprisoned by the Communists several times for defending the Catholic Faith, and Josyp Terelya, a prisoner of conscience for 23 years, pictured here on the TV set of FATIMA: "The Moment Has Come." It was Josyp who had an appointment for Father Gruner and himself, in January 1990, to meet the Pope. After paying the expenses to get both of them there, the meeting was cancelled mysteriously, after they arrived in Rome, by someone the day before the meeting.

117 Ibid, p. 10, caption.

Chapter 10

To Make the Guitars Laugh

Coimbra appears as if out of nowhere at a surprise turn in the road and the imagination instantly catapults back to the age of martyrs and saints. The incorrupt remains of St. Elizabeth of Portugal are preserved in the Basilica there on the hillside. Atop the hill, where the renowned fado festivals occur each spring, the University of Coimbra resonates like an exquisitely crafted guitar to the murmur of the heart of Portugal. Coimbra is proud. With good reason. Here in this fabled city rising upon the banks of the Mondego River is housed the Secret. The sole surviving seer from the Cova da Iria did live here behind very high walls until her death on February 13, 2005.

The Carmel of Coimbra rests on the side of the hill, a massive white enclave with emerald green doors, a bejewelled rock on one finger of this historic mountain. Here where Rua Santa Teresa intersects with Avenida Dias da Silva, Lucia dos Santos had withstood the curiosity of the world through the second half of the most rapidly changing century in history.

Born seven months before Pius X published his condemnation of modernism, she had seen seven other popes take the Chair of Peter. Indeed, she had met several of them in person. Arriving here at this cloister shortly after the end of the Second World War, she had followed the Korean War, Vietnam, and the Persian Gulf conflict. She had watched Communism devour much of the world. She even later observed its supposed and much publicized 'collapse.'

Born before the birth of radio, she had lived to see pictures radioed back from Pluto. She had survived the countless tyrants, dictators and madmen who have promised the world thousand-year reichs, the burial of capitalism and the extermination of the Church. Of her life lived in private, away from the prying eyes of media entrepreneurs and religious fanatics, we know next to nothing. Time may bring us precise details of her hidden life in written accounts but of her actual life we can be sure of only one thing—she prayed her Rosary each day.

Photographs of this unique Carmelite taken in adult life reveal a dramatic face exuding confidence in the presence of popes and pilgrims—on occasion she had returned to the great monumental shrine now surrounding the azinhiera tree. There was in her face an obvious joy, the source of which must surely have reached all the way back to that day in October 1917, very near the Feast of Tabernacles that Jesus so loved, when the sun left its tent in the sky and educated the souls and hearts of 70,000 people in that famous Cova in Portugal.

There was in her countenance ample evidence of a lifetime of conscientious responsibility. But one special ingredient outshined all others. In her eyes there was freedom. Freedom born of the miniature winds that move the trees on the hills of Aljustrel, cool the rocks of the Cabeço, bend the flowers in the Cova da Iria. Freedom like the crafted winds spun by the flashing fingers of the fado players. Freedom from this world. It is the secret of the saints. It is this that makes the guitars laugh.

Upon beholding the Carmel of Coimbra one is reminded that God is the greatest of all storytellers. Behind these towering walls of Carmel, He put this specially chosen woman. And there He kept her very well. Like a princess in a castle keep, she gripped our imagination, held us in wonder, lest the rest of the story He is telling be tugged from our minds.

Many have tried to scale the heights of the Great Secret. None can prove they have succeeded. Many have tried to lure the keeper of the Secret into the light of day to unfurl those '24 lines on one lined sheet of paper' which contain the Secret. All have failed.

For 65 years, since departing her previous convent in Tuy to arrive here, she had been the focus of relentless scrutiny, outrageous speculation, misplaced devotion, political and ecclesiastical pressure. But at no time was her resolve more challenged, her personality more taxed, her very integrity more threatened, than in the year 1992, when it seemed all the world wanted to breach the white walls of this Carmel.

The concentration of pressure resulted from one reality—the fact that Sister Lucia had been silenced since 1960. Yet those who refused to acknowledge that John Paul II had clearly and publicly said that the Consecration of Russia as requested by Our Lady of Fatima is not done, continued to try to bolster their position by fraudulently claiming that Sister Lucia agreed with them. They were only able to do this because she could not respond and defend herself publicly without the permission of then-Cardinal Ratzinger himself.

As J. Kaess explains, "The Fatima establishment keeps insisting" that the consecration has been done. But "they cannot produce a single shred of evidence." First, "Russia was not mentioned in the (1984) ceremony and they can't prove that any more than a few hundred bishops were involved." Second, "the 1984 Consecration was not a public act. Even though there was a public ceremony, not a single person in the world knew anything about it having anything to do with the Collegial Consecration until five years later when the 'writing was on the wall' in the Soviet Union."[118]

Alas for the establishment, the Catholic world has a longer memory than the establishment banked on. After waiting 40 years for the Consecration of Russia, Catholics were suddenly being told in the late 80's, "Oh, by the way, that was done back in '84." But, of course, the whole world knows that it was not done in '84. The most devout, attentive, loyal supporters of the Pope had not heard a thing about it. Suddenly, in 1989, pictures and articles appeared in publications far and wide showing the consecration by John Paul II that took place in St. Peter's Square, March 25, 1984.

It was as if the FBI issued a news release in 1989 saying, "Oh, by the way, Walt Disney killed Kennedy. We proved it back in '84."

Cardinals, bishops and priests, and the faithful knew full well it had not been done. And as Father Gruner keeps saying, "... time is running out".

Whoever the individual was behind that very transparent maneuver, he is a man never to be envied. In the circles where hoodwinking is a fine art, the supposed consecration whitewash was worse than a hoax, it was a *faux-pas*, a terrible mistake. By 1992, the establishment was dangling naked at the end of its tether. People wanted an explanation. The ruse of '89, designed to convince the faithful that the consecration was done, had exposed the Big Lie at home. By November of that year, the "Fatima Establishment" had been proclaiming that, in five letters supposedly written by Sister Lucia, the last living Fatima seer was confirming the Consecration of Russia had been done. The establishment now found that it had to scurry to provide more specific proofs that Fatima is finished.

March 21, 1992, the first incident. The chain of events this day triggered would turn 1992 into a rollercoaster ride for the establishment. That it was the direct result

---

118 J. Kaess, *Strange Goings on in Fatima*, "The Fatima Crusader", issue 44, Spring 1993, p. 35.

of the pressure applied relentlessly by Father Nicholas Gruner and his Apostolate was clearly confirmed from the onset by one of the most credible voices of the entire Fatima phenomenon.

Abbé Caillon writes, "The event was triggered off by a certain Father Gruner who *'runs a review on Fatima'* (author's emphasis) *in North America and who maintains that the consecration of Russia has not been made*."[119]

Father Messias Coelho explained (to Abbé Caillon), "This interview took place on the initiative of Doctor Lacerda, who was irritated with Father Gruner's campaigns."[120] In a letter dated December 20, 1991, addressed to Father Gruner's representative, Doctor Lacerda stated: "Pope John Paul II effected this consecration on March 25, 1984. And what Gorbachev has done since 1985 can only be explained by this consecration".[121]

"It was necessary, therefore," says Abbé Caillon, "to go to the source."

On Saturday, March 21, 1992, a delegation of four people went to the Carmel of Coimbra to consult with the seer. It was the Feast of St. Benedict, no longer much celebrated or even noted in the new liturgical calendar. But there was irony in the date. The obliteration of Monte Casino in World War II was nothing compared to what this meeting would do to the credibility of Fortress Lucia.

The group was comprised of the Apostolic Delegate to Portugal, Monsignor Luciano Angeloni; his secretary, Doctor Francis de Lacerda; and Father Messias Coelho, a longstanding Portuguese Fatimist who had, up until 1988, steadfastly maintained, along with Father Gruner and so many others, that the act of consecration of the world made on March 25, 1984, had not met the requirements given by Our Lady of Fatima.

Abbé Caillon reports: "The interview lasted one and a half hours. Sister Lucia declared that the consecration of Russia has been made."[122]

What? Sister Lucia says the consecration has been made? Even the most bold of the anti-Fatima forces hesitated crowing the news to the world at large. One would expect such world-shaking words to be immediately blasted from the housetops *ad mare usque ad mare*. They were not. Instead, a peculiar calm followed what should have been a grand victory for the anti-Fatima establishment. But an event was fast approaching that would provide a stage for the announcement.

Between May 8-12, 1992, an international congress on 'Fatima and Peace' took place in the Paul VI Center in Fatima as a build-up to the 75th anniversary of the first apparition in the Cova. About five hundred persons attended. It was the ideal setting for the great announcement.

Among those attending was Father Gruner, who was invited to endure hearing his entire life's work being dismissed by one particular speaker. Bishop Jose da Cruz Policarpo characterized those who still work for the consecration of Russia (such as Father Gruner, although his name was not mentioned) as "... inclined to a simplistic reading of history and with a taste for myth and the pseudo-eschatological ..." who accuse "... the popes and bishops of being responsible for the world's calamities through failing to accomplish the request of Our Lady of Fatima." (Bishop da Cruz Policarpo, formerly Auxiliary Bishop of Lisbon and now rector of the Portuguese Catholic University, has

119 *The Catholic Counter-Reformation in the XXth Century*, Aug.-Sept. 1992, p. 4.

120 Ibid.

121 Doctor Lacerda, Letter to Father Gruner, dated Dec. 20, 1991, published in *The Catholic Counter-Reformation in the XXth Century*, Aug.-Sept. 1992 issue, p. 5.

122 *The Catholic Counter-Reformation in the XXth Century*, Aug.-Sept. 1992, p. 4.

been characterized as a '... man of the Left, known for his progressive positions ...')[123]

But no great announcement of the supposed words of Sister Lucia of March 21 was made from the podium.

In an address on May 13, Cardinal Sodano, the newly-appointed Secretary of State, mentioned the past consecration attempts of the Popes but did not mention that the only Pope to formulate an explicit (albeit incomplete) consecration of Russia was Pope Pius XII in 1952.

No great announcement of the words of March 21 followed this address either.

In a private conversation with Abbé Caillon, Father Messias Coelho reported part of the contents of the March 21 meeting: "Lucia said that the consecration had been made, that she has always said so, that she had never asked anything concerning Russia, but only concerning the union of the bishops. And since this union was imperfect, the fruits will not be as good as might have been imagined."[124]

Father Coelho added, "That there were things that Lucia said which he could not report because *the Nuncio had forbidden him*."[125] So now there was a *fourth* secret of Fatima. No matter how strenuously the anti-Fatima forces tried to bend Sister Lucia to the shape demanded by their program, she would always say something which had to be hidden from the faithful. This would suggest, later on, that perhaps what was needed was a Sister Lucia whose words would be *entirely* theirs.

Entering into this debate was a brilliant young religious from France whose dramatic analysis of the people and events of the Fatima story reveals a talent that is part John le Carre and part G.K. Chesterton—Brother François de Marie des Anges of the Catholic Counter Reformation.

Brother François dissected Father Coelho's report with razor sharp precision.

"It is in fact unlikely that Sister Lucia declared on March 21, 1992 that she had always said that the consecration of Russia had been made when a series of concordant testimonies going back to 1984, 1986, 1987 and 1989—a good number of them collected by Abbé Caillon himself—shows that during those years she often stated that the consecration of Russia still had not been done as willed by Our Lady. Besides, how is it possible to believe Sister Lucia confided that she had never said anything about Russia? There we have travestied both the request made at Tuy and Our Lady's promise!

"We know, in fact, that on several occasions during the last decade she explained why the acts of offering of May 13, 1982 and of March 25, 1984, which were practically identical, do not correspond with Our Lady's request, at the same time affirming that 'God wants Russia to appear as the sole object of the consecration'. For the Divine plan to be fulfilled, the consecration of Russia alone is in fact necessary 'because Russia is an immense, well defined territory, and her conversion will be seen and will thus be proof of what can be obtained through consecration to the Immaculate Heart of Mary.'"[126]

Then Brother François added his most convincing argument.

"Furthermore," he said, "if Sister Lucia had really said on March 21, 1992 that the consecration of Russia had been done, her declaration would not have remained secret, or 'hidden' to repeat the word used by Abbé Caillon. Firstly, the Apostolic Nuncio, Monsignor Luciano Angeloni, would have made it known on emerging from this parlor.

123 Ibid.

124 Ibid.

125 Ibid, p. 5.

126 Ibid.

Secondly, Father Messias Coelho would have published it in his review *Mensagem de Fatima*, and to be precise in his issue which appeared a few weeks later for May (No. 189). Then Father Fox would not have failed to mention it in the July issue of his quarterly periodical, *Fatima Family Messenger*. Thirdly, Doctor Lacerda would have used this declaration of Lucia's as an unanswerable argument in his controversy with Father Gruner's representative at Fatima. Fourthly, the Rector of the Fatima Sanctuary (Monsignor Guerra) would have referred to it when questioned by Abbé Laurentin.

"Fifthly, Abbé Caillon would have learned this news, not in the corridors of this Congress, but from the mouth of Monsignor Policarpo when he delivered his communication 'Fatima, Peace and Russia' mentioned previously."[127]

The accusation demanded a response. One came.

Monsignor Luciano Angeloni's letter to Brother François of August 4, 1992 seems to let the steam out of the kettle: "On my last visit of this March 21st, I was accompanied by two specialists in Fatima affairs, who had asked me to provide them with the opportunity of returning to see Sister Lucia (whom they had not met since 1983). Without it being necessary to make known the news in question, I can tell you that there was no conversation. There were no special declarations. It was simply a visit on my part, during which those who had asked to accompany me wished to see Sister Lucia again. They spoke with her about various current matters—matters, for example, which have been published in her *Memoirs*."[128]

In other words, not the kind of exchange that would spawn a grand announcement at the Congress. In fact, nothing worth even a whisper. So—someone lied.

Ironically, at the same congress, Cardinal Casaroli admitted to the result of his 30 years of *Ostpolitik*. "The Church, who seemed to pay so much attention to the great questions of disarmament and tensions between the two blocs, now seems powerless before the mosaic of conflicts breaking out in the world. The fact that the highest international authorities prove to be equally powerless affords us no consolation."[129]

Brother François notes, regarding Cardinal Casaroli, that we have total collapse! but the former Secretary of State is not going to abjure his faith in Masonic humanism for all that.[130] Nor, we might add, his decades of faithful service to the Vatican-Moscow Agreement.

Who could have guessed that all that had transpired so far in this busiest of years was merely a prelude to the drama to unfold on the 75th anniversary of the Miracle of the Sun?

---

127 Ibid, p. 5.

128 Ibid, p. 5, footnote 2.

129 Ibid, p. 4.

130 Ibid.

Chapter 11

Ambush in Fatima, October 1992

The invitation to attend was simply worded: "The Fatima Crusader Magazine respectfully requests the honor of Your Excellency's attendance at an International Conference to publicly discuss the Collegial Consecration of Russia as requested by Our Lady of Fatima as a condition of World Peace."[131]

The note added, "As funds allow, accommodation and airfare will be provided through the generosity of thousands of supporters of Our Lady's Fatima Apostolate who have sacrificed for this intention, for those bishops from poorer dioceses who otherwise could not attend."

To bishops of the poorer nations who received this invitation in June of 1992, it was a generous offer. To those better off, who might be able to afford their own trip, it was a chance to mingle with brother bishops in the Cova da Iria on the 75th anniversary of the Miracle of the Sun. One hundred and ten bishops accepted the invitation.

Those returning to Fatima might well have anticipated the hospitality they would receive. Those coming for the first time must ready themselves for a warm surprise. The courtesy of the Portuguese people, specifically in the northern half of the country, may be one of the great mysteries of this century. How they have kept their sense of humor, their gentility, their irrepressible dignity in the wake of endless waves of humanity descending on the terrain of Our Lady is a question that was partially answered by Senor Vincente of the Virgin Maria Hotel where many of the bishops were billeted. When asked for the recipe to the justifiably famous soup he served to start each day's dinner Senor Vincente shook his head, admonishing the inquirer with a wagging finger.

"No, no, no," he warned. "That is the Fourth Secret of Fatima." Unwittingly, the genial proprietor had revealed the core of the Portuguese character in the north—a reserve, prudence, confidence, pride, and humor that comes from living in a world completely mantled by the things of Heaven.

What occurred, then, upon the arrival in Fatima of the one hundred plus bishops from 23 countries heading for the International Bishops Peace Conference, would shine a very stark light, indeed, on the Shrine management and on its rector, Msgr. Luciano Guerra himself. Shrine officials should have known better. But who, after all, had ever financed the gathering in Fatima of over one hundred bishops?

Bishop Alberto Cosme do Amaral of Leiria was hosting his own Pastoral Conference in the Paul VI Center for the laity, to which only a selected handful of bishops had been invited. The Fatima Peace Conference, to which all the bishops of the world were invited, in no way conflicted with Bishop Amaral's gathering. At most 50 bishops were in attendance at the Paul VI Center, most of which were drawn from those who had accepted the invitation of Father Gruner and whose passage to Fatima was paid for by *The Fatima Crusader*. More than one hundred bishops had come to meet at the Floresta Hotel which comprised the largest private gathering of bishops in the century. It was a veritable motherlode of Church Fathers that could hardly be ignored.

To assemble such a body of bishops had never been done before by any single organization. Its purpose was clear to all. The very words of the invitation contain the

131 *Invitation to International Peace Conference*, photographically reproduced in "The Fatima Crusader", Issue 43, Winter 1993, p. 16.

entire raison d'être of Father Gruner, 'Consecration...Russia...World Peace,' and his movement by now is one of the largest lay apostolates in the Church.

No one could claim ignorance of the motives for the gathering. It was, rather, because someone in a high place understood the purpose of it all too well that the opposition released its deadly whisper the moment the first plane touched down.

Efforts to discredit the entire Conference included one of those bureaucratic gestures that reek of overconfidence and arrogance. Wednesday, October 7, Cardinal José Sanchez, prefect of the Sacred Congregation for the Clergy, signed a declaration specifying that Father Gruner, "... does not have faculties from the Diocese of Leiria-Fatima to perform his ministerial acts ..." and "... his Congress has not been approved by competent ecclesiastical authorities."[132]

Yes, and so what? No "permission" or "faculties" were required under Canon Law, but the Cardinal neglected to mention this. The declaration was nothing but an imperious act of sabotage.

The sabotage continued at the airport. As the bishops arrived, they were intercepted by Shrine representatives attempting to hijack them to Bishop Alberto Cosme do Amaral's conference at the Paul VI Center and telling them that Father Gruner's conference at the Floresta Hotel was "cancelled" and "not authorized". Indeed, Shrine representatives were so brazen that they did this before the very eyes of the official welcoming party of *The Fatima Crusader* who were on hand to greet the bishops and transport them to Fatima.

The whisperers, however, did not include in their diversionary tactics the offer of accommodation and meals, for which Bishop Amaral had no intention of providing. Only when it came time to provide for the bishops they had diverted, did they send them back penniless, as bishops "without funds" were useless to them! A miscalculation that exposed the shrine officials for the cold and cunning pharisees they are. The assault on the dignity of these bishops, the majority of them from impoverished countries, was not considered, apparently, by the Shrine detractors. They had only one thing in mind, ambush the Reverend Father Nicholas Gruner.

The confusion generated in the local dailies and the publications of the international press by the movers and shakers of the Sanctuary had its effect. On Wednesday, October 7, the day before the Conference opened, 25 of the bishops met with Father Gruner to have their questions and concerns answered. Having received frank replies, they then decided to send representatives to seek an audience with Bishop Amaral to, in effect, state their intention to proceed according to their original agendas.

That evening Archbishops Limon of the Philippines, Toppo of India and Cardoso Sobrinho of Recife, Brazil drove the 18 kilometers to meet with Bishop Amaral.[133]

The road to Leiria stretched out over the northern plain of Portugal beneath an autumn sun reddening the sky and turning the mind of October pilgrims back in time to the Miracle of the Sun 75 years earlier. Archbishops Limon, Toppo and Sobrinho were at that moment navigating their way through the thorn-ridden thicket of conflicting agendas that had separated the world famous apostolate of the Blue Army and *The Fatima Crusader* for over a decade, hurrying headlong toward that very seat of authority where the Great Secret had remained hidden from 1944 to 1957. In the beginning, the office was held by the friend of the seer of Coimbra, Bishop da Silva, ruling the diocese of Fatima from Leiria. Now it was Bishop Alberto Cosme do Amaral.

---

132 *L'Osservatore Romano*, Oct. 7, 1992, Italian Edition; also *L'Osservatore Romano*, Oct. 14, 1992, last page, English Edition.

133 "The Fatima Crusader", Issue 43, Winter 1994, p. 13, caption.

Shortly before 9:00 p.m., the three travellers were ushered into the bishop's chamber. Also attending with Bishop Amaral was Coadjutor Bishop Serafim who would soon replace Bishop Amaral as bishop. After the usual flurry of 'Brother Bishop' exchanges, the small assemblage got to the issue that had brought them to Leiria. The air needed to be cleared if only for the sake of the brother bishops. The actual facts facing Bishop Amaral were crystal clear. One hundred bishops whom he had not personally invited were, nevertheless, on his threshold. Among them were many with Canon Law expertise. The most knowledgeable among them had made it perfectly clear that, according to Canon Law, they had no need of official recognition from Bishop Amaral or the Vatican to gather in private and confer, as they were doing. What could he do to them after all? Especially on the 75th Anniversary of the Miracle of the Sun? The events unfolding in Fatima would, for better or worse, become part of Church history before the sun set on October. Not surprisingly, Bishop Amaral agreed to make the Peace Conference an official part of his own Pastoral Conference on the provision that Father Gruner's Conference attend plenary sessions of Bishop Amaral's conference and the concelebrated Masses. It is important to note here that, obviously, Father Gruner was also invited to attend.

The return to Fatima along those 18 night-blackened kilometers provided an opportunity for the Archbishops to weigh the elements of the equation. They had come to Portugal with the best of intentions, to honor the Mother of God on this most meaningful of all anniversaries. They had been caught up in the vortex of lies and more lies that had long been multiplying over the crucial issue of the Consecration of Russia. They now found themselves on the soft shoulders of that very roadbed long ago sketched out by the designers of the Vatican-Moscow Agreement.

They arrived at midnight to announce an 'accord'. Come morning, Thursday, October 8, Archbishop Cardoso Sobrinho took to the podium and announced the meeting of the previous night, extending Bishop Amaral's welcome to all present, inviting everyone in the conference room at the Floresta to join in the Eucharistic celebrations of the next three days with the 50 bishops at Bishop Amaral's Pastoral Conference and to attend, as a sign of unity, the primary sessions of the Pastoral Conference. With those provisos in place, the Peace Conference in the Floresta could proceed with Bishop Amaral's blessing. In short, they were to consider themselves Bishop Amaral's guests as well.

Father Gruner and the Apostolate immediately agreed to this proposal but not without grave inconvenience and upset to the schedules of speakers and events that had been months in preparation. Nevertheless, the Apostolate immediately proceeded to change the entire schedule of the conference (sometimes twice daily!) in order to work in Bishop Amaral's agenda.

Not too surprising, however, this gracious attempt by the Apostolate was not reciprocated. The Apostolate had honored every one of the requests and more. In return, every promise made to the Apostolate was broken. Amaral changed schedules at the last minute and created havoc for the Peace Conference. Deirdre Manifold, who came all the way from Ireland to speak, was on the podium only five minutes when a spokesman bishop from Bishop Amaral's court got up and announced that they had to all leave now for another "appointment" with Bishop Amaral, and this after they had returned one and a half hours late that very morning from another "unscheduled Bishop Amaral appointment".

Father Gruner's group did not give up. They responded graciously and went without sleep most nights to replan amidst the havoc caused by Shrine officials (in charge of

Bishop Amaral's conference) to ensure the bishops' comfort and reasonable scheduling for the following day.

But the maneuvers of the Shrine official had their effect. By the time the first session opened, the number of bishops present was down to sixty. It would eventually dip to forty-five.[134]

Oh, unity, the things bishops do in thy name! Indeed, Father Gruner might well note, "Unity without truth is merely a compromise with sin."

Saturday, October 10, 1992

The esplanade of the Fatima Shrine is one of the great gathering places in the world. With as much love and care as the faithful could provide, the Cova da Iria has been paved over to provide for the millions who pray here in a gathering area four times the size of the Piazza of St. Peter's in Rome. Crowning the east end of the esplanade, with open arm colonnades extended to embrace the upper slope of the Cova, is the basilica containing the two precious jewels of Fatima, the bodies of Jacinta and Francisco. There, too, Lucia does rest since February 2006, one year after she died on February 13, 2005.

To the west of the esplanade, reached by an underpass from the shrine enclosure, is the Paul VI Center. Architecturally, it is yet one more exercise in the dreariness the self-proclaimed new "experts" have imposed on the Catholic world for fifty years. The quest for excellence in architecture had ever been a hallmark of the Roman Catholic Church until the "architects" of Vatican II unleashed on the Church a seemingly relentless pursuit of the mediocre.

No one looking at this bleak structure could possibly suspect that throughout history the Church has been the foremost patron of artists, architects and poets. It is a concrete container for bureaucrats. Nothing more. An edifice designed by accountants. Something every bureaucrat in the Church today would be comfortable entering, for there is absolutely nothing Catholic about its exterior.

To reach it from the esplanade, one must first pass by a mammoth statue of Paul VI, kneeling, hands posed in prayer, dwarfing much better and more artistic representations of Pius XII and Bishop da Silva of Leiria, he to whom was confided in writing, the Third Secret.

To the north of the esplanade stands the tree under which the children stood in 1917 to await the warning flash in the heavens announcing the impending arrival of the Mother of God. Almost within the shadow of the tree is the miniature chapel, the Capelinha, so tiny, one is tempted to tuck it inside the heart and make off with it. It marks the spot where the azinhiera stood. On its very leaves She to whom the Incarnation was made known by the Message of an Angel rested six times between May and October, 1917. She who received the Three Wise Kings, received here three peasant children. She Who said at Cana, "Do whatever He tells you,"[135] spoke equally specific words here. She Who stood 'by the Cross Her station keeping', here wept for all mankind. She Who at the age of 49, at the foot of the blood-drenched Cross, received into Her arms the lifeless Body of the Son of God, came here for the sake of His Mystical Body, now afflicted with the neck-stiffening heresies of Modernism, and delivered the antidote for theological rigor mortis, a recipe for healing, namely the formula for an act of total unconditional faith in Her role as Mediatrix of All Graces.

Here, on the exact circle of earth on which the shadow of the azinhiera was drawn by

134 Ibid.

135 John 2:5.

the movement of the Fatima sun, a marble enclosure surrounds a table. On it the liturgy is said continually throughout each and every day. Marble benches allow concelebrants to sit in a circle around it, almost always dressed in white. Ironically, their circle sits atop the very circumference of earth that opened to reveal to the three children the vision of Hell that would haunt the Church for the rest of this century.

The Indians of New Mexico had a name for that opening into the earth through which evil spirits are supposed to enter the world. They called it Sipapu. On October 10, 1992, a Sipapu opened in front of the Capelinha.

On that day, and the previous one, the Conference had adjourned so the bishops could partake of the major public ceremonies preparing for the main anniversary celebrations of the 13th. On both days, the bishops vested for Mass in the vestry of the north colonnade. On both days, Father Gruner assisted the elderly Anthony Cardinal Padiyara of Ernakulam, India, and several other bishops in getting vested, and accompanied him from the main altar, at times holding the Cardinal's arm to assist him as he walked.

On October 10, after Mass ended at the Capelinha, Father Gruner walked alongside Cardinal Padiyara and was about to enter the sacristy when a layman, with no arm band or any other insignia of authority, blocked his way. In spite of him, Father Gruner managed to enter the sacristy, moving quickly indoors. There he was slowed by a gathering of bishops awaiting their turn to ascend the few stairs and narrow passageway into the larger room inside. In the meantime, the unidentified man, speaking Portuguese, ran in and blocked the stairway on the left side, in the process also momentarily obstructing the way of several bishops, among them, Maronite Archbishop Chucrallah Harb of Jounieh, Lebanon.[136]

Father Gruner, having dropped his sandals in the confusion, stepped up onto a chair. From there he spotted Bishop Amaral seven feet away. What happened next was one of those frequent, seemingly comic, moments in the career of Father Nicholas Gruner that are, in fact, all too often a prelude to something decidedly sobering. Here he was, a priest in the very prime of his Apostolate, standing in socks on a chair in Fatima, appealing for Christian charity from the Bishop of Leiria. He called out to Bishop Amaral, asking if this was how he treated his 'guests'.[137]

Bishop Amaral, who can speak English, did not respond, though he clearly saw and heard the priest on the chair. Turning his back, he hurried up the steps with the other bishops. The room emptied. When the stairs were clear of all bishops save one, Father Gruner, once more in his sandals, proceeded up the steps on the right side. The mysterious layman, who was talking to Archbishop Chucrallah Harb, left the Archbishop abruptly and flew after Father Gruner. Father Gruner had reached the first step when he was seized by his pursuer and thrown against the wall, the shocking sound of a ripping priestly cassock marking the moment. Then, a second assailant grabbed him, spun him around, and threw him against the wall again.[138] Witnesses recall that the second assailant disappeared almost as fast as he had appeared.

From behind, arriving at the top of the stairs, was Archbishop Cardoso Sobrinho and Father Francesco Pacheco, also from Brazil. They confronted the first attacker, in Portuguese. Later, Father Pacheco related that, incredibly, the attacker had openly

136 *Police Report*, "The Fatima Crusader", Issue 43, Winter 1993, p. 9.

137 Ibid, p. 9.

138 Ibid, p. 9.

admitted he was acting on *explicit directions from Msgr. Luciano Guerra*, who had ordered him to prevent Father Gruner from entering the sacristy.

Father Pacheco had demanded, "Why are you doing this? You know you cannot do this ... *this man is a priest!* Who told you to do this? Did the Rector tell you to do this?" To this the assailant nodded 'Yes'. It would emerge later that the attacker had been present at Bishop Amaral's residence in Leiria the night Archbishops Limon, Toppo and Cardoso Sobrinho met with Amaral.[139]

The bruises and abrasions resulting from the assault on Father Gruner were documented by Doctor Olinda Moura Almeida in the hospital at Ourem. Meanwhile, spin doctors at the sanctuary offices were fast denying that the assault had ever taken place. Once again, the Fatima faithful were subjected to the embarrassing display of power-proud Shrine bureaucrats surrendering to self-grown fantasies of their own importance. When they heard the attack had been witnessed and part of it video-taped, the shrine officials just as quickly dropped their denial. Their sad performance was not over, however. They limply claimed Father Gruner had staged it himself, "for publicity". No one wondered why when, within a year and a half of the supposedly choreographed spectacle, the new Bishop of Leiria-Fatima, Bishop Serafim de Sousa, replaced Bishop Cosme do Amaral. Perhaps it was the fulfillment of several Archbishops' promise, after the assault on Father Gruner, that they would sign and circulate a petition to the Pope for do Amaral's retirement because he appeared to have lost control of the diocese.

Faithful priests, like Father Gruner, have been victimized over the centuries by appalling rumors planted and spread by bureaucrats jealous of the victim's following, support and personal appeal: Padre Pio, Father Gino, St. Maximilian Kolbe, St. Louis de Montfort, the list goes on and on.

In Fatima and Portugal, the scuffle drew the attention of the faithful and the bishops mainly because of its profoundly sacrilegious nature. A priest had been manhandled on orders of a representative of honor of the Holy Father within a stone's throw of the very spot the Virgin had sanctified by Her presence. Shortly after the beating of Father Gruner, Cardinal Padiyara sent for him urgently, and when Father Gruner came, the Cardinal took him aside and warned him that his life was in danger as long as he was in Fatima. Father Gruner had not returned until May 11, 2000 for the occasion of John Paul II's third visit to Fatima and his beatification of Francisco and Jacinta.

The conflict between Father Gruner and the authorities of the Shrine had entered a new phase. What would happen next would challenge the imagination of even the most daring of fiction writers.

An "Oscar" Winning Performance

The unthinkable began to take shape Saturday, October 10. Why not ask Sister Lucia herself, it was suggested, whether the consecration of Russia had been done according to the requests of Heaven. At first glance, it appeared that the bishops who had congregated in Fatima might actually produce something of value by this request. It was agreed that a delegation would be sent to Coimbra—Cardinal Padiyara, Bishop Michaelappa, and to ensure proper understanding, the Portuguese-speaking priest, Father Pacheco from Brazil.[140]

As a Cardinal, Padiyara needed no permission from either then-Cardinal Ratzinger, or from the Bishop of Fatima, Cosme do Amaral, to request a meeting with the seer. It

139 Ibid, pp. 9, 28; also J. Kaess, *Strange Goings on in Fatima*, "The Fatima Crusader", Issue 44, Spring 1993, p. 34.

140 "The Fatima Crusader", Issue 46, Winter 1994, p. 15.

was agreed they would travel to Coimbra in the morning. Meanwhile, in advance of their visit, Father Kondor was presenting the Lusa news agency with a communiqué announcing that Sister Lucia had declared the Consecration of Russia had been done.

While the communiqué was being published by the Portuguese dailies, Cardinal Padiyara, Archbishop Michaelappa and Father Pacheco were on their way to the Carmel of Coimbra, chauffeured there by a Carlos Evaristo.[141] Evaristo did some logistical work for the Apostolate in its Fatima office. He would prove to be an embarrassment of mammoth proportions.

Travelling the sloping streets of Coimbra to the Carmel that contains the most famous religious of the Twentieth Century must surely have a profound effect on Cardinals and bishops as well as priests. This is no mere convent. This gleaming white building with emerald doors has the hand of the Mother of God holding fast its doors and its secrets.

Just before noon the high green portals of the Carmel of Coimbra opened to admit the travellers. They entered a stark, high-ceilinged foyer, plain and unadorned, befitting Carmel. The doors to the cloister stand directly ahead. Immediately to the left, off the foyer, is the convent chapel.

The initial gloom of the chapel interior is soon pierced by threads of light where the chocolate brown interior is highlighted with gold trim. The high altar rising above the communion rail supports one of those stairways to Heaven so common to the altars of Portugal on the top of which the ostensorium holds the Blessed Sacrament for adoration. Kneeling at the rail, one can look up, to the left, and see the second floor grille through which the Carmelites observe the Mass. Below and to the right of the grille is the breathtaking statue of the Immaculate Heart, specifically sculpted for this chapel. Facing it across the chapel is the equally awe-inspiring statue of the Sacred Heart as He appeared to Sister Lucia at Rianjo.

The certainty remains, that here, within these high walls, the voice of the Virgin remains inviolate in the memory of the last seer from the Cova. Here, at least, truth is protected, defended, and honored.

The Players:

Enter the "Oscar" nominee performers: Mother Superior and Carlos Evaristo. Enter a woman in a Carmelite habit who had the appearance of being Sister Lucia. Enter supreme guests of the command performance: Cardinal Padiyara, Bishop Michaelappa and Father Pacheco, allowed "on set".

The Play Begins:

"Sister Lucia will receive you," says an extern sister, returning from making the arrangements.

The doors open to the audience room. Two Carmelites are waiting just inside. On the left stands Mother Prioress. The nun on the right was presented as Lucia dos Santos, the most famous nun of the Twentieth Century. She turned ten years old seven months before the 1917 November Revolution in Russia. A tiny peasant child from Aljustrel. Now she is eighty-five. 'Much shorter' than was expected, Evaristo reported. She wears the habit of the Carmelites which, amazingly, does not properly fit her.

After initial introductions, the "players" move to an adjacent room where they sit down facing each other with no grille between them, totally contrary to the customary rule adhered to for the past 400 years both here and at all Discalced Carmelite Convents since their founding by St. Theresa in the 1560's.

---

141 Ibid.

Mother Prioress, according to her script, would begin, "Sister Lucia would you like me to leave you alone with the guests?" and on this cue, Sister Lucia would reply, "No, no, Mother, please stay here." And like any suspense novel cleverly planned to confuse the reader, the naive would be led to believe, why my goodness, this must mean Sister Lucia is not silenced! Mother Prioress, during the rest of the visit, would come and go throughout the interview that was to follow, although Sister Lucia had said she would like her to stay.

The Cardinal and the bishop were 'very nervous' according to Evaristo.[142] And well they should have been. Unable to speak Portuguese, they were unknowingly about to participate in a great work of fiction, the likes of which had never been heard in the whole history of Fatima. It would be entitled *Two Hours With Sister Lucia*, the pamphlet Evaristo would fabricate claiming to be based on the "interview" with Sister Lucia. The answers to their questions, as reported by Evaristo, would go to the very roots of the azinhiera tree and tear them free of the millions of hearts from which they had drawn nourishment since first the Virgin stood upon it. The performance that would follow, the words about to be spoken, would starkly and cruelly suggest that Catholics who grew up believing in Fatima had been lied to at their mother's knee and been the victims of disinformation for 75 years.

But before we actually hear the words, the manner in which they were delivered must be addressed. By that is meant that the question of familiarity with this most unique and protected woman must be considered. For seven and a half decades this dear nun has been sheltered, shielded, protected by the Church. The labyrinth of authorities one must traverse to get permission to see her have not surrendered to any coherent mapping, but rather have become increasingly complex. Thus anyone inquiring about seeing her is told first, "Oh, that is impossible." Then follows the long list of addresses and bishops and Cardinals all standing in line to say 'No' to you, all, apparently on behalf of the man truly in charge of access to her, then-Cardinal Ratzinger. And, in spite of all that, the two-hour interview about to take place occurs while this secluded nun, cloistered for all of her adult life, sits facing and holding hands with a man she has never laid eyes on before, who is neither Cardinal nor bishop, but rather one Evaristo, a minor employee of Father Gruner's Apostolate, who has chauffeured the dignitaries to Coimbra.

From the moment the group entered the audience chamber, the function of Evaristo as interpreter (he does speak Portuguese) and what we might, perhaps, call 'stage manager' of the event, emerged.

Arguing that it was indeed Sister Lucia they saw, Evaristo said to Brother François de Marie des Anges, "It was her. There is no doubt about it. I touched her face. I embraced her."[143] Touched her face? Embraced her? A Carmelite whom mere bishops and Archbishops cannot approach without Vatican approval? A nun who was not able to see her own blood-sister Caroline for over forty years except through the grille and then only when surrounded by half the community. Embraced by a stranger?

Regarding Cardinal Padiyara, Evaristo reported to Brother François, "The Cardinal asked your questions (Brother François, upon being told of the impending visit, had sent two questions to be answered) and then seemed to be almost asleep."[144]

When Brother François challenged him, "You have no decisive proof that you were

142 *The Catholic Counter-Reformation in the XXth Century*, Oct. 1992, p. 1.

143 Ibid, p. 2.

144 Ibid, p. 2; also, "The Fatima Crusader", Issue 44, Spring 1993, p. 36.

in the presence of Sister Lucia," Evaristo made the astounding reply: "She was sitting in front of me. She held my hand like this for two hours."[145]

For any cloistered nun to hold hands with a stranger for two hours is a curious business. For this particular cloistered nun it is unimaginable.

The Evaristo pamphlet presents a new Sister Lucia who serves as the pathetic ventriloquist's dummy of the anti-Fatima forces, obediently repudiating everything Sister Lucia of Fatima had said before. The pamphlet is a veritable cavalcade of capitulation in which the new Sister Lucia finds a way to consign to oblivion what the old Sister Lucia had told the entire world.

The old Sister Lucia had mentioned that Our Lady many times told her about the conversion of Russia as a nation and the old Sister Lucia had repeated this Divine requirement orally and in print over and over again to priests, historians, correspondents, and on the pages of *L'Osservatore Romano* during the previous 60 years and more. Ah! But this was all a terrible misunderstanding, explained the new Sister Lucia! She had not been speaking of the nation of Russia at all!

Evaristo: "But didn't Our Lady want Russia to be specifically mentioned?"

New Sister Lucia: "Our Lady never requested that Russia be specifically mentioned by name. At the time I didn't even know what Russia was. We thought she was a very wicked woman."

So, there we have it: the three Fatima seers believed that Our Lady appeared at Fatima and God performed the Miracle of the Sun before 70,000 people simply in order to bring about the conversion of a very wicked woman who happened to be named "Russia". It was all a case of mistaken identity. Our Lady had neglected to inform them that Russia is a nation, not a lady by the same name!

The old Sister Lucia had told the world that Russia must convert according to the Virgin. Naturally, the world took conversion to mean the embrace of the Catholic faith. Not quite, says the new Sister Lucia.

Evaristo: "But is the conversion of Russia not interpreted as the conversion of the Russian people to Catholicism?"

New Sister Lucia: "Our Lady never said that. There are many misinterpretations around. The fact is that in Russia, the Communist, atheist power prevented the people from carrying out their faith. People now have an individual choice to remain as they are or to convert. This they are now free to do."

You see, Russia had already converted without becoming Catholic!

"Converted" really means that Russia is now free to choose the Catholic faith, therefore, Russia has "converted".

But one might consider that the Americans are free to choose the Catholic faith, yet no one had ever suggested that the word "converted" applies to America, the land of "Roe vs. Wade", abortion on demand, and partial birth infanticide.

Such considerations do not trouble the new Sister Lucia: her lower jaw moves up and down on its metal hinge as the ventriloquist throws his voice into the dummy, making it utter things unheard of in the history of Fatima, or indeed, the history of the Church.

A conversion without a conversion. Imagine that! All we needed was democracy, not a change of heart.

The old Sister Lucia had told the world again and again,—in letters, interviews

---

145 *The Catholic Counter-Reformation in the XXth Century*, Oct. 1992, p. 2.

and other statements, that *Russia* had not been consecrated in the manner prescribed by Our Lady and as a consequence, had not converted. But the new Sister Lucia has a surprise announcement:

Evaristo: "Has the conversion of Russia then taken place?"

New Sister Lucia: "Yes, news speaks for themselves."

So, the cloistered seer of Fatima reads the news! One could envision a surreal spectacle: the new Sister Lucia sipping her morning coffee and reading the headlines in *Diario de Coimbra*, which, of course, is delivered to her daily so that this consecrated soul, locked away from the world under a vow of enclosure, could keep abreast of current events! Or was this perhaps the case of a ventriloquist projecting his reading habits as well as his voice, into the dummy?

New Sister Lucia: "That man in Russia, unknowingly, was an instrument of God in the conversion ..."

Evaristo: "What man? Gorbachev?"

New Sister Lucia: "Yes, when he visited the Holy Father in Rome, he knelt at his feet and asked pardon for all the crimes he had committed in his life."

The old Sister Lucia had spoken of the triumph of the Immaculate Heart of Mary bringing about the conversion of Russia and peace to mankind. But the new Sister Lucia has found a new instrument for the accomplishment of this miracle—Mikhail Gorbachev!!

But was not the new Sister Lucia aware that after Mikhail Gorbachev had knelt before the Pope in the Vatican, he returned to his chairmanship of the Gorbachev Foundation which promotes a New World Order of zero population growth and a New World Religion whose sacraments are contraception and abortion? To be fair to the new Sister Lucia, she could not possibly have been aware of the evil undertakings of "that man in Russia" because the new Sister Lucia is made of wood and has no brain, but only a jaw which mouths the words projected into her by others. That is, the new Sister Lucia is not Sister Lucia at all, but a new product to go along with "Fatima Lite": "Lucia Lite".

The other three witnesses to this "interview" of the new Sister Lucia knew a travesty when they saw one. Father Pacheco, the only Portuguese-speaking witness besides Evaristo, fired off letters to Evaristo and to all concerned parties denouncing the pamphlet as "notorious", full of "gross lies" and "inventions".

Cardinal Padiyara made it clear that he could attest only to having been present during the "interview" but could not authenticate anything "Sister Lucia" had said since he did not speak Portuguese. Bishop Michaelappa went further: he ordered Evaristo not to publish the pamphlet. The fraud was summed up by Father Pacheco: "I categorically do affirm that the booklet, *Two Hours with Sister Lucia* published by Carlos Evaristo contains lies and half-truths and is not to be believed."

Brother François, unquestionably the most exacting investigator at work on the Fatima story today, summarizes the appalling possibility behind the catastrophic interview.

"In order to discredit the work of Father Gruner and to stop Pope John Paul being *'importuned'* with the request for the Consecration of Russia, did the authorities at Fatima, after circulating the apocryphal letters from Lucia, organize a parlor with a 'false Lucia' at the Coimbra Carmel on this 11th October 1992? Until proof to the contrary, we are not rejecting such an hypothesis. For on this there is no possible doubt: if Cardinal Padiyara and his three companions actually met a person in the Carmel who spoke the words they have reported, then the person was not the seer of Fatima, Sister Maria-Lucia of the Immaculate Heart."[146]

So what did happen in the Carmel of Coimbra on the nearest Sunday to the 75th anniversary of the Miracle of the Sun? Did Sister Lucia make statements that completely and blatantly contradicted 75 years of previous statements? It is not merely a matter of Sister Lucia being out-of-character that day. To Lucia dos Santos was made the promise on June 13, 1917, by the Mother of God Herself, that the Immaculate Heart would never abandon her. The reportage as it stands is simply not believable. And the only other Portuguese-speaking witness present at the interview, Father Pacheco, has repudiated Evaristo's account.

Are there alternatives to the mendacity of Evaristo? Was there a deliberate mistranslation of her responses? Was Sister Lucia under duress to confirm the consecration? Surely, after a lifetime of fidelity to the Immaculate Heart, Sister Lucia would not suddenly resort to lying to cover up the failings of Vatican bureaucrats. The term 'mellowed' was used at the Fatima shrine these days to explain why Sister Lucia, in her ninth decade of life, was not pushing harder to make the truth known. Did Heaven leave the last Fatima seer alive all of this century so that she could 'mellow' picturesquely on the hillside of Coimbra? Perhaps many of these riddles could be put to rest if it was clearly understood how and why Carlos Evaristo managed to publish and distribute his booklets without any bureaucrat at the Shrine, or the Vatican, or any member of the Carmelites of Coimbra raising as much as a whisper of complaint or caution. Some light did filter onto the mystery when Evaristo, acting with more casual familiarity than members of her own blood family are allowed to, publicly interrupted Sister Lucia as she walked from the Carmel to cast her vote in the Portuguese elections, to introduce his wife and child and relatives. He claims also that he had returned to the Carmel to *interview her again*, without the benefit of a Cardinal on hand or the permission of the Holy Office. Someone, somewhere, has seen to it that this individual was allowed liberties. Why? Clearly the misinformation poured onto the unsuspecting faithful through this manipulated interview is satisfying someone's agenda.

Before the infamous October interview ended, nearing two o'clock in the afternoon, it was suggested that Father Gruner should come with Cardinal Padiyara, the next day, to hear these words for himself. Sister Lucia agreed. As did Mother Prioress.

The interview concluded. Cardinal Padiyara, Bishop Michaelappa, and Father Pacheco left the Carmel for the return drive to Fatima. After the meeting, as it is recorded in the *Diario de Coimbra*, the regional newspaper for Coimbra, Mother Prioress telephoned to Fatima for instructions.

Meanwhile, the Pastoral Conference at the Paul VI Center continued throughout the long afternoon of Sunday, October 11.

Brother François de Marie des Anges was present at this session. He brought into the midst of this high establishment occasion the accusation made in his book, *FATIMA Joie Intime Événement Mondial*, regarding the earlier "letters" of Sister Lucia. The accusation reads: "Under the authority of Bishop do Amaral, three ecclesiastics, residing in Portugal, were directly implicated in the fabrication and spreading of these artificial letters—Father Luis Kondor, Father Messias Coelho and Monsignor Luciano Guerra. We think that Monsignor Guerra personally wrote several of these letters, including

146 Ibid, p. 5.

one dated November 21, 1989."[147]

At 5:30 p.m. Brother François, from the stage, addressed the head table at which sat Father Fox and Father Kondor. He denounced the five bogus letters supposedly written by Sister Lucia, the message of which Father Fox and the Blue Army had been propagating since the Fall of 1989, letters claiming the consecration of Russia had been done by Pope John Paul II on March 25, 1984.

"These letters are fake," said Brother François. "I have already published the demonstration of it and my demonstration has not been refuted. I am ready to justify my actions and if necessary to retract them if my criticisms are refuted in a decisive manner."[148]

Neither Father Fox nor Father Kondor gave a reply. Instead, the session was swiftly closed. The following day, Abbé Laurentin expressed surprise when he learned that both Father Fox and Father Kondor failed to give any response to these serious allegations against them.

§

Evening. One of those blissful October Sundays when it seems the whole world is either gathered in or headed to the esplanade to have one last look at the Capelinha before sundown. Cardinal Padiyara must have wondered how he came to play the role thrust upon him that day. He expected no such chore when he boarded the plane for Portugal a few short days before. Now he was preparing to announce tomorrow to the gathered bishops what he had been led to believe had transpired in the Portuguese language during the interview—namely, that Sister Lucia had apparently confirmed that the consecration of Russia was done, that the Third Secret was intended exclusively for the Pope.* The announcement would, without doubt, add yet another layer of confusion to those already accumulated throughout the 1980's regarding the Fatima Message. Clearly, he could be relieved of the onerous task once Father Gruner met with Sister Lucia in person the following day. That would provide a solution.

Alas, Cardinal Padiyara would be granted no such reprieve.

Early Monday morning, October 12, 1992.

Seventy-five years ago this morning, all over Portugal, people were rising and gathering belongings for the trip to a shepherd's field near Aljustrel, where the Voice of the Virgin, repeated by three peasant children, promised a great miracle. It was one of the truly great spontaneous movements of a people in all of recorded history. Seventy thousand people on the move.

That morning, 75 years ago, Portugal was on the alert. To those who fear God, there was no doubt He was going to do something never before done in all of salvation history. To the godless, there was no doubt the Church was about to try to manipulate away from the Masonically-controlled state the uneducated masses of people.

It was the fear of God in those 70,000 that drew down from Heaven the unparalleled blessing of the Miracle of the Sun. To the innocent hearts of Portugal, God showed a sign which He had refused to the haughty Pharisees. To the latter, none but the sign of Jonah. Truly, the very willingness of the Son of God to die at the hands of men was sign enough of what was in His Heart. Raising Himself from beyond death to, among

147 *The Catholic Counter-Reformation in the XXth Century*, Aug.-Sept. 1992, p. 3, footnote 4.

148 *The Catholic Counter-Reformation in the XXth Century*, Nov. 1992, p. 9.

* **Editor's Note:** The Third Secret is not meant exclusively for the Pope. This is proven in *The Secret Still Hidden* and *The Devil's Final Battle* (2nd edition).

other things, confirm the forgiveness He offered them from His Cross, was more than the human mind could script. Certainly a dance of the sun was more than man's imagination could entertain.

Seven and a half decades later the day began, as it does in most hotels and hostels of Fatima, with early risers, almost always American, looking for a waitress, a coffee pot and an ashtray for that all important first cigarette. For the hour preceding the customary 7:30 breakfast serving, line-ups form in lobbies and hallways throughout this one-of-a-kind hamlet. Non-muttering line-ups. Not even hungry tourists would dare to complain in Fatima.

In the rooms above the foyer of the Virgin Maria Hotel, bishops prepare for the descent to breakfast. Is it true, they wonder, are they all being encouraged to travel to Coimbra for a visit en masse with Lucia? They will find out more at breakfast.

Breakfast ends. Time speeds past. Watches are wound furtively. 'Is the appointment not for 10 o'clock? When do we leave?'

Corazon Aquino is in Fatima. The former president of the Philippines is going to Coimbra. Her appointment is for 11 o'clock. Two of the most remarkable women of the century will be meeting immediately after Sister Lucia grants her audience to Father Gruner. The solution to the mysteries that have spurred on *The Fatima Crusader* Apostolate for fifteen years are to be sandwiched into what communication can be exchanged within one short hour.

Aquino is on everyone's tongue. Few women in the 20th Century can command such heartfelt approval. It is akin to heresy to detract in any way from the legend she has become in the few short years since her husband was shot to death on the tarmac of a Philippines airport.

On any other occasion, her presence in Portugal would bring the press to a standstill. But this is the 75th anniversary of the Miracle of the Sun. Fatima is crowded with legends and legendaries.

10:05 a.m. Outside the entrance to the Carmel of Coimbra, journalists and photographers await the arrival of Corazon Aquino.

10:10 a.m. A bus holding fifty bishops from the International Peace Conference makes its way down the slope of Coimbra toward the Carmel.

10:25 a.m. Twenty-five minutes of the precious time allotted to meet with Sister Lucia have ticked by before a taxi carrying Father Gruner, Father Paul Leonard Kramer, Archbishop Michaelappa and Cardinal Padiyara pulls to a stop below the high doors of Carmel.

10:28 a.m. The car driven by Evaristo veers into a parking space in front of the Carmel. He had been an hour and a half late arriving to pick up his intended passengers. What happens next makes nonsense of the centuries of protocol and security for which the very word 'Carmel' is justifiably famous. Kings, Emperors, Popes have had their footsteps chosen for them by the precise and well thought-out design of Carmel entrances. In this case, the large square foyer previously described as having three doors, determines what anyone entering must do. The high green entrance door admits the visitor. The door to the left looks in at the chapel. The door to the wall immediately ahead leads to the enclave. History itself takes off its hat in this precious space. It is impossible to stand in such an intersection of pathways and not be moved to silence by thoughts of the countless gifted women who have chosen to live out their lives completely shielded from outside interference by the very specific blueprint of their convent fortress.

Nevertheless, Evaristo, having rushed past the delegation, strides across the foyer, past the chapel entrance to his left, and, unbelievably, swings open the door to the enclave. Totally unchallenged, he proceeds to the door in the far wall of the next room. He is now directly adjacent to the parlor in which the most protected woman of the 20th Century has met with a thoroughly screened select few over the decades. Not until he is about to throw open the door in front of him does a voice call out to stop him. Two men dressed in lay clothes have appeared. One refers to himself as the chaplain of the Carmel, even though he wears a shirt and tie. The other layman is a doctor. Words are exchanged. Evaristo returns and immediately begins to usher from the foyer back into the street those who had followed in his wake. The meeting, he announces, has been cancelled.

During these bewildering moments, Father Paul Kramer had been assisting Cardinal Padiyara through the doorway. Suddenly, a layman grabbed the Cardinal's arm in what was perceived by onlookers as a threatening gesture intended to prevent him from entering. The only words to accompany this manhandling of a prince of the Church were that, 'Sister Lucia was not feeling well', and is unable to receive visitors.

The acts of Evaristo secure him a unique place in Church history. For the greater part of this century the words, actions and security of Sister Lucia have been treasured by Catholics. This gifted woman, grown from an illiterate peasant child into the most sought after woman religious in the Church, is practically a member of each and every Catholic family. She had been with us for so long, her life recognized as so humble and admirable, that she was, to Catholics the world over, simply 'Lucia'.

She is one of the most precious ingredients of the Catholic legacy the next [21st] century will inherit. To understand the real import of what was permitted to happen that morning in Coimbra, one must contemplate a tragic fact—namely, that not even the Immemorial Mass, the Mass of the Ages, the Gregorian Carlovingian Mass was spared in the attack upon the Catholic Faith this last half century. Debilitating the status of Sister Lucia, demonstrating her new insignificance, was what Evaristo's walk into the enclave was all about. And make no mistake about it—every reader of these words is familiar with the hush that consumes even the most aggressive rock fan when he finds himself outside the dressing room of his favorite musician. In the history of human behavior there is no precedent that can explain Evaristo's charade other than this—the mastermind, working overtime to devalue anything Catholic in this world, orchestrated the vulgarization of chivalry displayed that morning. The sensation remaining explains the degree of their success: someone just wiped his shoes on your heart.

Despite the visit being officially agreed to by Mother Prioress, Father Gruner and Cardinal Padiyara were refused entry into the Carmel of Coimbra. And despite the chaplain of the convent saying that the last surviving seer of Fatima was ill, a half hour later Corazon Aquino and her party of nine met with Sister Lucia.

The chaplain added another ring to the circus of confusion by telling the daily newspaper *Journal de Noticias* that "He (Father Gruner) came to Coimbra to provoke this scene and nothing more." But he did not. The facts are clear. The agreement for this visit was given to Cardinal Padiyara, Bishop Michaelappa and Father Pacheco the day before. This is all witnessed by at least six people and cannot be denied.

Evaristo's sabotage of Father Gruner's interview with Sister Lucia is recalled by Mairead Clarke, an Apostolate employee who dealt with Carlos. She recounts that frustrating morning:

"I was present for the sequence of events. Carlos was to arrive early at our hotel at 7:00 a.m. so that the tail pipe of the car purchased for this Apostolate by a supporter could be repaired. A minor job of replacing a few brackets, which Carlos was aware of, but refused to do anything about, claiming that it was extremely difficult to get parts for foreign cars, which he had insisted we purchase as the only car worth having in Europe.

A supporter who was with us at the hotel had asked that the car be brought over early so that the exhaust could cool before using a wire hanger to effect the temporary repair. Any repairs were the responsibility of this Apostolate as we were the owners. (I say "were" as Carlos refused to turn the car over to us at the termination of his employment. He had changed the registration to his mother's name.)

However that Monday morning, Mina, Carlos' mother refused to wake him as "the boy needs his sleep". Yes I can quote her because I was the person who telephoned three times to his home to find out what was causing the delay. I finally told her that if Carlos did not arrive within the next few minutes I would personally come and get him out of bed. That last call was no more than an hour before the time of the meeting. Bishop Michaelappa had telephoned from his hotel to find out why Carlos had not already picked up Cardinal Padiyara and himself.

Father Gruner was very anxious to meet Sister Lucia. Finally Evaristo condescended to come to the phone and was strongly ordered to get the Apostolate vehicle over to the hotel immediately. He arrived at the hotel more than two hours late, with a dragging muffler that could not be repaired until the car cooled down."

The most dramatic meeting imaginable between two of the world's most devoted Fatima names never happened because Carlos Evaristo was "tired" and had a punctured muffler which he had been driving that way for months, including his trip just 1 day before up to Coimbra! Father Gruner and the Cardinal had been forced to call a cab! Yet Evaristo would dare to claim that Father Gruner missed his interview because he, not Evaristo, was late! Nevertheless, Evaristo miraculously was able to get to Coimbra himself in his "broken down" vehicle.

A few minutes after Father Gruner and the Cardinal had left the Convent, President Aquino and her entourage would arrive and immediately be escorted in to be received by Sister Lucia, who had miraculously recovered from the "illness" which had prevented a visit by Father Gruner and the Cardinal only a few moments before. Obviously Convent officials did not want the charade of the previous day to be subjected to the scrutiny of Father Kramer and Father Gruner together with the Cardinal.

§

Noon, Monday, October 12, 1992. The Paul VI Center in Fatima: At the end of the closing session of the First International Pastoral Conference at the Paul VI Center, Brother François de Marie des Anges confronts Monsignor Luciano Guerra regarding the apocryphal letters written on a word processor supposedly by Sister Lucia:

Brother François: Monsignor Rector, can you swear on the Gospel that you have not written the apocryphal letters of Sister Lucia?

Msgr. Guerra: No, I do not want to. I cannot do it now in these conditions ...

Brother François: Internal criticism of these letters show that they are fake.

Msgr. Guerra: I will not discuss with you. You have no heart ... you have no heart.

Brother François' trust in Sister Lucia stems from his simple faith in her upbringing: "Her sixty-five years of religious life and the many divine communications with which she has been favored can only give her a greater taste and esteem for the virtue and wisdom of her mother, Maria Rosa, who 'had never tolerated a lie from her children.'"

Furthermore, Heaven had prolonged the life of the eldest of the Fatima seers in the Carmel of Coimbra to the ripe age of 97, doubtless "... to repeat the message and doubtless to prevent it being stifled or falsified."

Furthermore, "When God has a great mission of charismatic order to be accomplished in history, He is wise and prudent enough to choose and prepare adequate instruments, and, without violating their freedom, to enable them to fulfill with His grace the essential mission for which He has destined them from all eternity."[149]

The undermining of the credibility of the last living Fatima seer and of the Fatima Apostolate other than the "official" Blue Army was just one in a series of steps seemingly aimed at relegating the Message of Fatima to that same dumping ground where so many treasures of the authentic Catholic Church had been discarded. Poorly trained clergy now in control of some Church bureaucracies feel obliged to constantly reinforce the myth that the Church began with Vatican II and that anything that came before is a cause for Catholics to apologize to the world at large.

Father Nicholas Gruner unmasks the salesmen of this new attitude with clear, concise accuracy:

"When it comes to Fatima, we have been sold a bill of goods, namely that Fatima is a private revelation and is not that important. But Fatima *is a public prophetic revelation*, not simply a private revelation.

"If one has a vision of Our Lady, in which Our Lady said, 'In order for you to save your soul you must say 15 decades of the Rosary every day', that would be a private revelation, and it would be imprudent for the individual not to pay attention to it.

"But any other person wouldn't have to believe it. Such a revelation is private to the one who receives it. It places no obligation on anyone else.

"But, at Fatima, Our Lady gave a message to the world and confirmed it by a public miracle before 70,000 people. That's not a private revelation. That's a public, prophetic message. It cannot be lumped in with private revelations.

"Saint Paul says in First Thessalonians, Chap. 5:19,20: 'Do not extinguish the spirit. Do not despise prophecy'. If we represent a certain public, prophetic revelation as something to which we need pay no attention then we can make the very serious mistake of despising prophecy.

"Miracles prove revelations. If God takes the trouble, by working the great Miracle of the Sun with first class miracles of cures, to make it evident that He has sent the Blessed Virgin Mary to give a message to mankind, then one does not have the option of despising that prophecy by terming it a private revelation to which we need give no attention.

"The second part of the passage in Colossians 2:20 says the Church is founded upon the foundation of the Apostles together with the prophets. The Holy Spirit spoke through a prophet of the Catholic Church and said, 'I want Saul set aside'. To set someone aside is to consecrate them to the service of God. The Holy Spirit said He wanted Saul set aside. The bishops understood and obeyed. They prayed, they fasted. Then they made Saul a bishop."

149 *The Catholic Counter-Reformation in the XXth Century*, Oct. 1992, p. 4.

Father Gruner then said: "The hierarchy has the obligation to test if the message comes from God. They have the right to test. They have an obligation to test. In fact, in that same passage of Sacred Scripture (1 Thess. 5: 21) St. Paul says, 'Test all things and hold fast to that which is good.' If it passes the test, then no one any longer has the right to say it is optional. They no longer can say I can ignore that. That is despising prophecy.

"We have a prophet in Sister Lucia, though she denies being a prophet out of humility. But God, through Our Lady, chose Lucia and this message cannot be despised. We despise it at the peril of our spiritual lives, of our eternal souls, even at risk of our physical lives.

"For priests to despise Fatima would be to do so at the peril of those lives and the souls entrusted to us priests. Maybe priests can be excused for mixing up their own lives, but ruining the lives of the faithful is not excusable. Priests must realize that Fatima imposes an obligation on them.

"However, any priest who tries to fulfill the demands placed on all of us by Our Lady of Fatima to work for the consecration of Russia becomes a target of that very bureaucracy that should be supporting priests in their work. Why? Once again we are brought back to the infamous Vatican-Moscow Agreement of 1962 when the Vatican made an agreement with Moscow to not denounce Communism. Besides being morally wrong, this is a fundamental error in geo-political strategy and bad for all of us."

Fingering his Rosary beads, Father Gruner continues: "I have denounced the Agreement as criminal, as being morally corrupt. It must not be sustained. Now, I am even going so far to say that the people who made the agreement back in '62 did it with good intentions. But it has been a disaster for the Church. Time has proven that I'm right. I'm prepared to say that in an open court of the Church.

"I do not stand alone in seeing the danger of dealing with Communists. Pope Pius XI and Pope Pius XII both saw the very real dangers that it poses to the world and to the Church.

"To be perfectly clear, Pope Pius XI, in his encyclical *The Divine Redeemer*, clearly taught 'Communism is intrinsically evil and no one who would save Christian civilization may collaborate with it in any undertaking whatsoever.'"[150]

Touching the Miraculous Medal around his neck, Father Gruner concluded: "The people responsible for the agreement are operating under the illusion that diplomacy can correct the errors of Russia. The Mother of God in Her messages at Fatima explicitly told us the only solution to avoiding the errors of Russia and not being a spiritual and physical victim of their killing errors, is exact obedience to Her message at Fatima. Does any faithful Catholic truly think that Her advice can be ignored?"

After the Sister Lucia "interview" there would surface a photo of Evaristo in Fatima proudly standing with Cardinal Casaroli, the Vatican Secretary of State, the "Great Architect" of *Ostpolitik*. Evaristo explained that Cardinal Casaroli had shown great interest in him. Might this interest explain his betrayal of the Apostolate and, indeed, Sister Lucia? One could hear the sound of certain pieces of a great puzzle snapping into place.

Yet Evaristo had become an even bigger embarrassment to the anti-Fatima forces than he had been to the Apostolate. The Evaristo pamphlet was a manifest absurdity which only helped the cause of Father Gruner's Apostolate by demonstrating the mendacity of its opponents. The anti-Fatima forces needed a definitive strategy for dealing with the "Gruner problem" in a way that would not explode in their faces. Soon they would reveal their new device.

---

150 Pope Pius XI, Encyclical Letter, *Divini Redemptoris*, Par. 58.

Chapter 12

The Incardination Game

In his opening speech to the Second Vatican Council, Pope John XXIII made the momentous announcement that with the advent of the Council the Church would cease dispensing Her traditional remedy for heresy, the anathema, because "[S]he prefers today to make use of the medicine of mercy, rather than of the arms of severity".[151] Henceforth, the Church would merely *explain* her doctrine in an amiable conversation with the world, "showing the validity of her teaching, rather than ... issuing condemnations."

This new approach to error could be viewed as an implicit criticism of Pope John's 259 predecessors on the Chair of Peter. In any case, His Holiness did not explain in this unprecedented speech how it could be an act of mercy to avoid condemning errors which lead souls into the eternal abyss of Hell.

Thus officially began the astounding process by which the Holy Catholic Church would be converted almost overnight from an impenetrable fortress against error into a veritable infirmary for the doctrinally diseased, who would soon be queuing up in large numbers to demand their daily dose of this new medicine of mercy, dispensed in a candy coating of "dialogue".

Within a few years of the Council's close the Church would throw down her "arms of severity": the Index of forbidden books would be abolished, along with the Oath Against Modernism prescribed by Pope St. Pius X. Gone would be the Councils of Vigilance that sainted Pope had ordered to be erected in every diocese in the world, as he had decreed in his monumental encyclical against the modernists, *Pascendi*.

Invigorated and emboldened by Pope John's amnesty, the heresiarchs who had been expelled from the seminaries and chanceries in keeping with the mandate of Pope St. Pius X's *Pascendi* would soon return in triumph, as prodigal sons who had *not* repented. Indeed, some had already returned in their new guise as *periti*—experts!—at Vatican II. Yesterday's heresy or proximate heresy would become today's "problem in theology", while the clear propositions of the past would soon recede in the endless palaver of the very modernists of whom St. Pius X had written in *Pascendi*:

> "They bowed their head for a moment, but it was soon uplifted more arrogantly than ever."[152]

Only this time, the head of modernism would be uplifted with the official toleration of many of the highest authorities in the Church.

The resulting resurgence of modernism, condemned by Pius X as "the synthesis of all heresies", would make the revolt of Henry VIII seem like a Catholic Restoration by comparison, as the perennial liturgy, priestly formation and catechesis of the Church were swept aside in a neo-modernist debacle of unthinkable magnitude. Soon the toleration of error would lead to the persecution of Truth by the very neo-modernists who would gain sway in the hierarchy, and strict adherence to Tradition would become the only condemned doctrine.

Yes, the Deposit of the Faith would remain intact through it all, as Our Lord had promised; but only a very diligent student of Tradition would be able to find it in the

151 Pope John XXIII, *opening speech* to the Second Vatican Council; also, Ralph M. Wiltgen S.V.D., *The Rhine Flows Into the Tiber*, p. 15.

152 Pope Pius X, Encyclical Letter, *Pascendi Dominici Gregis*, paragraph 3, promulgated July 3, 1907.

midst of the reigning confusion. For the rest of the faithful there was only a datum of daily experience in the light of which it would be difficult to disprove, to the average Catholic in the pew, the thesis that the Catholic Church had changed in substantial matters. No less than Cardinal Ratzinger himself would be forced to admit years later in his memoirs that the loss of appearances would make it impossible for many to find the substance of the Faith.

> "But if in the liturgy the communion of faith no longer appears, nor the universal unity of the Church and of her history, nor the mystery of the living Christ, where is it that the Church still appears in her spiritual substance?"[153]

In a Church which no longer wishes to condemn anyone or anything, but merely to explain itself to the world, how would it be possible to silence Father Nicholas Gruner? That he would have to be silenced was a foregone conclusion; his teaching and preaching of the undiluted message of Fatima had for too long been an intolerable irritant to the executors of *Ostpolitik* and the new ecumenism in the Vatican.

The mild-mannered priest from Canada was spoiling the global party by constantly pointing out in his vexatious magazine that the Pope is not the mascot of a New World Order of ecumenical brotherhood, but the Vicar of Christ, empowered by God Almighty to bring about the Kingship of Christ through the Reign of Mary, and with it *the end of all heresy*, by the means She had revealed at Fatima:

> "In the end, My Immaculate Heart will triumph. The Holy Father will consecrate Russia to Me. Russia will be converted, and a period of peace will be given to mankind ... If My requests are granted, many souls will be saved and there will be peace."

Such antiquated triumphalism was an embarrassing eyesore in the new post-conciliar landscape of religious liberty and world ecumenism. Who could speak seriously any longer of the Kingship of Christ and the Queenship of Mary, at a time when the Vatican was dispatching ambassadors to attend the gala opening of the first mosque in the city of Rome?[154]

But on what *grounds* could this meddlesome priest be silenced? After nearly 20 years of apostolic work, no Church authority had even suggested that Father Gruner had taught or believed anything contrary to faith and morals, much less that he had been guilty of immorality. It was certainly no canonical crime to do what Catholics had always done and to believe precisely what they had always believed. As for the Apostolate, there could be no question that under the 1983 Code of Canon Law, promulgated by Pope John Paul II himself, its activities were entirely permissible, indeed encouraged, and certainly in no need of any official "ecclesiastical approval" which could now conveniently be withdrawn.[155]

Besides, now that the Church had become thoroughly infested with openly heretical priests and laity and their innumerable heterodox associations, all of them operating with impunity under the same Code of Canon Law, any attempt to silence Father Gruner and his Marian Apostolate on doctrinal grounds would make the bureaucrats look ridiculous—they would lose their *bella figura*. What is worse, they would have to *prove* something in a canonical proceeding involving witnesses and documents, with a right of defense afforded to Father Gruner.

---

153 Josef Cardinal Ratzinger, the autobiography, *La Mia Vita*, April 1997; also, *The Wanderer*, May 8, 1997, p. 7.

154 *Latin Mass* magazine, Winter 1996, Vol. V, Issue 1, p. 6.

155 *1983 Code of Canon Law*, Cans. 212, 215, 216, 299.

No, that would not do. Yet there was one seemingly foolproof stratagem at the bureaucrats' disposal, and they would seize upon it with a vengeance: They would invoke the so-called "administrative law" of the Church, which regulates the status of priests through "extra-judicial" administrative "decrees" of bishops on such matters as where a priest will reside, what faculties he will be able to exercise in a given diocese, and what sort of "canonical mission" he will be given. In Father Gruner's case the ensuing administrative battle would revolve around a single word: incardination.

Canon 265 of the 1983 Code of Canon Law provides that:

> "Every cleric must be *incardinated* in a particular Church [the post-Vatican II term for diocese] ... unattached clergy are by no means to be allowed."

"Incardination" is a word derived from the Latin and literally means to be hinged or attached to something. As the Canon states, every priest must be "hinged" to a bishop so that there would be no unattached or "vagus" priests in the Church.

Father Gruner has never been a "vagus". Of course, like many other priests in the Church today, he had been given the right to live and work outside the diocese of his incardination. In fact, his permission had been given in the form of a binding, written decree, signed and sealed by the Bishop of Avellino. There was certainly no need for his services in the Diocese of Avellino, where his inability to speak the obscure local dialect precluded any parish assignment or other canonical mission. Thus, since 1978 Father Gruner had been conducting the Apostolate in Canada under the written permission to be outside the Diocese of Avellino, which permission was expressly to continue until such time as another bishop invited him to transfer to his diocese. At least three bishops would extend such an invitation to Father Gruner, but certain Vatican bureaucrats were not about to let a few benevolent bishops stand in their way.

For Father Gruner, a rather commonplace and perfectly legal arrangement with his bishop had become an Achilles' heel. *The Plan* to exploit it was quite simple: First, Father Gruner would be ordered to find another bishop to incardinate him; then the bureaucrats would block all offers of incardination by benevolent bishops in other dioceses; then they would cause the Bishop of Avellino to revoke the permission to live outside the diocese and order Father Gruner to return to Avellino, on grounds that he had "failed" to find another bishop.

If Father Gruner would not submit to exile in a foreign diocese, then he would be subjected to the ultimate penalties: suspension from the priesthood, followed by reduction to the lay state[156]—penalties which not even raving heretic priests are threatened with in the Church today. The destruction of Father Nicholas Gruner could thus be accomplished entirely in the realm of "administrative" decrees, without the slightest proof of any offense against faith or morals or any opportunity for Father Gruner to mount a defense. To be sure, *The Plan* would require the cooperation of the Bishop of Avellino, whose jurisdiction over a priest of his own diocese could not simply be usurped by Vatican bureaucrats. No matter: By judicious application of pressure from above, the bishop could be persuaded to go limp like a marionette and allow the bureaucrats to pull his strings. And while even an "administrative" decree must be founded on just cause and respect the natural rights of the priest, who would be looking over the bureaucrats' shoulders to make sure they had acted justly?

---

156 Can. 290 of the 1983 Code of Canon Law states, "After it has been validly received, sacred ordination never becomes invalid." A cleric can, however, lose the clerical state. This is not to say that the character of the priesthood is removed. *The Council of Trent*, Chap. 3, Can. 4, clearly teaches, "... If anyone says that no character is imprinted by ordination: or that he who was once a priest can become a layman again: let him be anathema."

In fact, the first attempt to implement *The Plan* had occurred back in May of 1989, when Father Gruner received a letter from the Bishop of Avellino warning of the "worried signals" he had been receiving from the Vatican "Secretary of State" and the "Congregation for the Clergy."[157] Thus the bishop was already being remote-controlled by "signals" from Vatican bureaucrats, broadcast on secret wavelengths to which Father Gruner would never be a party. Cardinal Innocenti would soon admit as much in his extraordinary July 1989 "intervention" referring to the secret "case" of Father Gruner which "arouses serious preoccupation on the part of the Holy See". (See Chapter 9.)

By November 1989 the bishop had responded to the "worried signals" of the bureaucrats by writing Father Gruner in broken English as follows: "In the meantime decide what to do: or you make you hing (i.e. 'hinge' or incardinate elsewhere) or you come back to Avellino."[158] But the bishop did not seem to have his heart in *The Plan*; he could not bring himself to carry out the unjust execution of his own priest.

In subsequent meetings and correspondence with Father Gruner and his friend, Father Paul Kramer, the bishop repeatedly reaffirmed Father Gruner's longstanding right to reside outside the diocese while seeking another bishop.[159] During one of those meetings, just before cooking a steak dinner for his guest from Canada, the bishop had declared: "Father Gruner, to suspend you would be a mortal sin. But if the Vatican tells me to do it, I will do it."[160]

He was never put to that test. In February 1993 a new bishop was installed in the Diocese of Avellino. Now *here* was a man who would quite eagerly play the marionette. This became apparent almost immediately: In July of 1993 Father Gruner received a written offer of incardination from the Bishop of the Diocese of Simla-Chandigarh, India, who was only too happy to sponsor Father Gruner and the Apostolate in his diocese.[161] It would have seemed to any objective observer that Father Gruner's administrative problem was over: He had been directed to find another bishop, so he had found another bishop. *Arrivederci* Avellino.

But the new Bishop of Avellino promptly took the unprecedented step of turning the offer of incardination over to the Congregation for the Clergy, waiting several months to advise Father Gruner that "the request for incardination has been passed to the Congregation and has (sic) put me in the condition of not being able to act. I await the instructions of Mons. Sepe [Secretary of the Congregation for the Clergy]."[162]

In other words, the new bishop had simply surrendered his jurisdiction over a priest of his own diocese to a Vatican Secretary who would now dispose of Father Gruner outside the proper channels of Canon Law.[163] While Father Gruner waited months to hear from the Bishop of Avellino, the Bishop of Simla-Chandigarh was reached in his remote diocese and "informed" by the bureaucrats of Father Gruner's "situation", and the offer of incardination was suddenly withdrawn. *The Plan* was proceeding to perfection.

On January 31, 1994, just as *The Plan* required, the Bishop of Avellino issued an "administrative decree" ordering Father Gruner to return to the Diocese of Avellino in

---

157 *A Canonical Recourse to The Sacred Congregation for the Clergy*, "The Fatima Crusader", Issue 53, Summer 1996, p. 21.

158 Ibid.

159 Ibid.

160 Ibid, p. 22.

161 Ibid, pp. 23-24.

162 Ibid, p. 24.

163 Can. 384 of the 1983 Code of Canon Law states that the bishop "is to have a special concern for the priests to whom he is to listen as his helpers and counselors. He is to defend their rights..."

30 days, after an approved absence of more than *sixteen years*.[164] Father Gruner was evidently expected to abandon his life's work, close up his residence, leave his personal affairs in disarray and immediately enter lifetime exile in a remote foreign diocese which had never supported him nor required his services since 1976!

The pretext for the decree was, of course, Father Gruner's pre-arranged "failure" to be incardinated in another diocese. But Father Gruner had met with the Bishop of Avellino only 18 days before to discuss, among other things, the offer of incardination from the Diocese of Simla-Chandigarh which the bishop *admitted* had been blocked by the bureaucrats. How in conscience could the bishop issue a decree only days later pretending that Father Gruner had culpably "failed" to find another diocese to accept him?

The bishop seemed to recognize that he needed a fig leaf to cover this atrocious fraud, as well as some pretext for the canonical "warning" contained in his January 31 decree. So he made reference also to unspecified "complaints" against Father Gruner. Yet during the meeting only 18 days before, the bishop had also admitted that *there were no complaints* against Father Gruner in his files, that Father Gruner was certainly a priest in good standing, and that it was only pressure from Vatican bureaucrats which was forcing the bishop's hand.[165] How in conscience could the bishop now issue a decree pretending there were "complaints" against Father Gruner?

And what was the evidence of these "complaints"? The decree mentioned nothing but an anonymous letter from 1978, regarding an unspecified complaint, *not from any Church authority*, but from someone within the Apostolate itself. The anonymous complaint apparently claimed that Father Gruner had somehow injured the Apostolate. Injured? Since 1978, the Apostolate had grown fifty-fold under Father Gruner's leadership, from a fledgling group of a few laypeople to one of the largest Fatima apostolates in the world.

During those sixteen years, the Apostolate had produced and distributed around the world several million books, magazines, pamphlets and tracts on the Message of Fatima; had broadcast thousands of hours of radio and television programs in North America; had sent over 20 mailings to every bishop in the world, including six books; and had staged a conference in *Vatican City itself*, and another conference in Fatima to which the entire world episcopate was invited. Yet in this vast record of teaching and preaching, in the entire life's work of Father Nicholas Gruner, the current Bishop of Avellino could dredge up only a *sixteen-year-old anonymous letter* containing unspecified charges as "grounds" for the recall to Avellino!

This lack of evidence was a major embarrassment to *The Plan*. Father Gruner had been conducting the Apostolate for the past 16 years without the slightest objection by three successive Bishops of Avellino. Apparently *The Plan* had no statute of limitations!

It was obvious that the strings of the marionette were being jerked very violently indeed, for *The Plan* needed to be accomplished, and quickly. Since the result was predetermined, the quality of the evidence hardly mattered—anything at all would do, even a sixteen-year-old complaint about nothing in particular. Curiously enough, never once in the working out of *The Plan* would the bureaucrats ever make reference to Father Gruner's preaching and teaching on the Message of Fatima. It was as if they were deathly afraid to mention the true objective of their actions.

Yet there remained a few more impediments to the destruction of Father Gruner and his work: there were other benevolent bishops willing to offer him sanctuary in

---

164 *A Canonical Recourse to The Sacred Congregation for the Clergy*, "The Fatima Crusader", Issue 53, Summer 1996, p. 24.

165 Ibid.

their dioceses. On May 29, 1994, the bishop of the Diocese of Anapolis, Brazil, offered Father Gruner incardination in his diocese, commencing July 16, 1994.[166]

Being mindful of the hostility of the bureaucrats, the bishop cautioned in his written offer that the incardination must remain confidential until its effective date. But it was not confidential enough. The bureaucrats soon contacted the bishop to "advise" him about Father Gruner's "case". After receiving this "advice", the bishop hastily withdrew his offer without explanation, telling Father Gruner only that he must "accept the decisions of the Congregation". Decisions? *What* decisions?

As Cardinal Innocenti had made clear in his 1989 intervention, a whole new mode of canonical procedure had been devised especially for Father Gruner: a secret "case" in the Congregation for the Clergy, culminating in secret "decisions" barring his incardination by benevolent bishops who would otherwise be happy to incardinate him in their dioceses.

The 1983 Code of Canon Law specifically guarantees the *right* of a priest to transfer to another diocese should he find a bishop who would make better use of his priestly services.[167] Yet Father Gruner would never be given even a glimpse of the secret proceedings by which this right was being denied him without due process. No mere law of the Church would take precedence over execution of *The Plan*.

Meanwhile, Father Gruner had made a canonical appeal from the Bishop of Avellino's order to return. *The Plan* had taken account of this contingency as well, however, for the appeal would have to pass before the Congregation for the Clergy, where the judges would be none other than two of the same bureaucrats who had been orchestrating *The Plan*, Cardinal Sanchez and Archbishop Sepe.

It was they, of course, who had issued "declarations" in the Vatican media urging the entire Church to shun the Apostolate's conference at Fatima, thereby effectively interdicting Father Gruner and the Apostolate without even a semblance of canonical due process. At the same time, of course, heretical associations were staging conferences and issuing impudent manifestos throughout the world without a peep from the Congregation for the Clergy.

It hardly required the gift of prophecy to predict that the same two bureaucrats would uphold the order to return to Avellino. In a perfunctory decree issued only days after Father Gruner's appeal was filed, they declared that the Bishop of Avellino had acted correctly in ordering his return—after all, Father Gruner had "failed" to find another bishop, had he not? *They* had seen to that. Thus was on display the marvel of "administrative law" in the Vatican bureaucracy: bureaucrats who had publicly condemned the accused without grounds or a hearing and had improperly interfered in his rights, were allowed to sit as judges on an appeal *from their own actions*.

On June 7, 1994 Father Gruner made further appeal to the Apostolic Signatura, the highest court in the Catholic Church, next to the Pope himself. Here the Incardination Game would continue, as the Prefect of the Signatura, Cardinal Agustoni, would issue a decree which teemed with factual and legal errors and embarrassingly strained to reach the desired result: permanent exile of Father Nicholas Gruner to a place where, it was hoped, he would never be heard from again.

More than two years would pass before Father Gruner received an official copy of the decree—he was literally the last to know. In the meantime, the Providential discovery

166 Ibid, pp. 24-25.

167 Cann. 270-271 of the 1983 Code of Canon Law details Church law regarding incardination and excardination.

of a "smoking gun" would ultimately force *The Plan* into the light of day. The canonical appeal process would reach a new level of complexity as the Incardination Game moved into its end-game sequence. But this is to anticipate. Only a few months after Father Gruner's appeal to the Signatura, there would be another Fatima conference: Mexico City, November 1994. What would the bureaucrats do about a second gathering of bishops to discuss the "forbidden" Message of Fatima?

In the foreground with white beard, Cardinal Padiyara, walking in procession from the concelebrated Mass on October 9, 1992. Father Gruner is following immediately behind to assist the frail Cardinal who was his guest at the Fatima Peace Conference. None of the shrine authorities objected, yet only a day later, on October 10, while again assisting the Cardinal, Father Gruner was attacked.

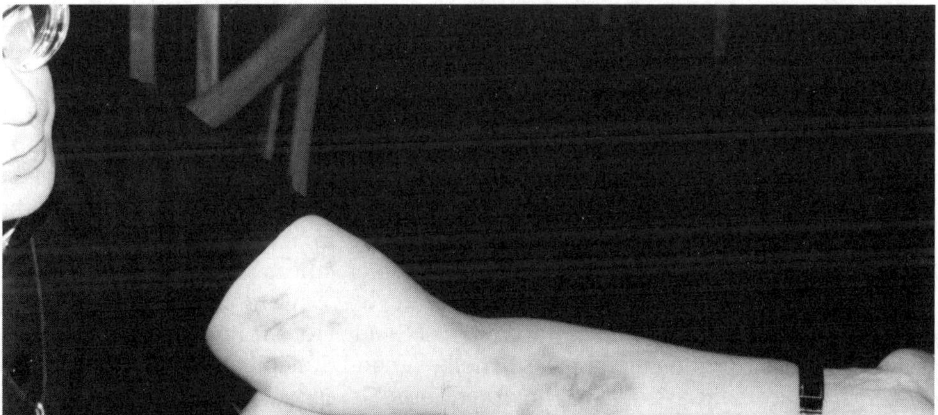

Photo of Father's injuries, shortly after being assaulted by two young men. One disappeared right after this attack; the other, not leaving quickly enough, was interrogated by Father Pacheco, who was also a lawyer who knew how to threaten this second assailant with the threat of penalties under Portuguese law, and under these circumstances he admitted to doing this attack under orders from Msgr. Guerra, Rector of the Shrine at Fatima at the time (1992).

Chapter 13

The Balamand Connection

In the offices of the Vatican Secretary of State there are exquisitely sensitive diplomatic alarms, attuned not to heresy, scandal or other threats to the Faith, but to the slightest breach at the perimeters of *Ostpolitik* and world ecumenism. In the spring of 1993, some 18 months before Father Gruner and the Apostolate would stage a second Fatima Conference in Mexico City, those alarms were tripped by an emergent situation in Romania and the Ukraine.

Now that the "former Soviet Union" had been "liberated", it seemed likely that a significant number of Russian and Romanian Orthodox clergy and laity would commit the diplomatic gaffe of simply resuming the practice of the Catholic Faith, picking up where their forebears had left off when the Communists seized their "uniate" Catholic parishes, arrested their priests and bishops and installed Orthodox clerics in their places, most of them KGB operatives.

In Russia, it was not an easy matter for the Soviets to create an Orthodox Church consisting essentially of KGB spies. It took awhile to wean the Russian Orthodox hierarchy of 50,000 priests down to a manageable 500 Soviet agents in clerical garb.[168] The Metropolitan of the newly constituted spy-church, Sergei Stragodorsky, was mysteriously released from prison in 1927 and announced to the world that the Russian Orthodox Church had not been persecuted.[169] He had apparently been persuaded to overlook the disappearance of 49,500 Orthodox priests.

The imminent recrudescence of Eastern Rite Catholicism should have been an occasion of great joy in the objective order of things, but for the schismatic Orthodox hierarchy, which had for so long enjoyed the use of Communist plunder, it was a grave emergency: several cathedrals and some 2,000 parish properties were already in dispute in Romania and the Ukraine, not to mention a potentially vast loss of forcibly-acquired adherents. The resulting hue and cry clearly posed a threat to the progress of *Ostpolitik* and world ecumenism in "the former Soviet Union."

A "fix" was not long in coming. In June 1993 Vatican representatives and representatives of the Russian and Romanian Orthodox Churches (among others) met in Balamand, Lebanon, to discuss the "crisis" at the "VIIth Plenary Session" of the "Joint International Commission for the Theological Dialogue between the Roman Catholic Church and the Orthodox Church." The chief Vatican representative, from the Second Section of the Vatican Secretariat of State, was Edward Cardinal Cassidy, who also carried the title, President of the Pontifical Council for the Promotion of Christian Unity. The result of the meeting was "The Balamand Statement". In this astounding document Cardinal Cassidy and the other Catholic representatives agreed that the Catholic Church would no longer seek either the conversion of the Orthodox or even their simple return to the Catholic faith of their forefathers:

> "[I]n the search for re-establishing unity *there is no question of conversion of people from one Church to the other in order to insure their salvation*." (¶ 15)
>
> "Pastoral activity in the Catholic Church, Latin as well as Eastern, *no longer*

---

168 Iain Colquhoun, *What Happened in 1929*, "The Fatima Crusader", Issue 47, Summer 1994, p. 29.

169 Ibid.

aims at having the faithful of one Church pass over to the other; that is to say, *it no longer aims at proselytizing among the Orthodox*. It aims at answering the spiritual needs of its own faithful and it has *no desire for expansion at the expense of the Orthodox Church*." (¶ 22)

"To pave the way for future relations between the two Churches, passing beyond *the out-dated ecclesiology of return to the Catholic Church connected with the problem which is the object of this document* [i.e. the "threat" of a mass return of Orthodox to Rome!], special attention will be given to the preparation of future priests ..." (¶ 30)

"By excluding for the future *all proselytization and all desire by Catholics for expansion at the expense of the Orthodox Church*, the commission hopes it has overcome the obstacles which impelled certain autocephalous Churches to suspend their participation in the theological dialogue ..." (¶ 35)[170]

At Fatima, Our Lady had prophesied that "In the end, My Immaculate Heart will triumph. The Holy Father will consecrate Russia to Me. *Russia will be converted*, and a period of peace will be given to mankind." Not if the Second Section[171] of the Vatican Secretariat of State had anything to say about it! After all, what did the Blessed Virgin Mary know about the exigencies of *Ostpolitik* and world ecumenism?

Consider: The Balamand Statement implicitly claims that when Our Lady spoke of the conversion of Russia, She, *and therefore Her Divine Son*, were espousing an "out-dated ecclesiology of return to the Catholic Church". Contrary to Our Lord and Our Lady, Balamand teaches that "in the search for re-establishing unity there is no question of *conversion* of people from one Church to the other in order to insure their salvation." Yet Our Lady of Fatima did speak unambiguously of the *conversion* of Russia to the Catholic faith, did She not? Was it therefore the position of Cardinal Cassidy and the Vatican Secretariat of State that Our Lord had allowed Our Lady to use the *wrong word* in the Message of Fatima? Did they suppose that Our Lady had not been advised by Her Son of future developments in the field of ecumenical relations which would render the term "conversion" rather quaint, and quite obsolete when applied to the adherents of Orthodoxy?

At Balamand, the bureaucrats had brought out a large rubber stamp and slammed it down on the Message of Fatima. And when the stamp was lifted the word "OVERRULED" appeared across the words of the Message. The Balamand Statement can only be seen as an insult to Our Lady of Fatima, and thus an infinitely graver insult to Her Divine Son, Whose message She had conveyed.

Yet one might at least find some solace in the fact that this arrant repudiation of the Message of Fatima lacked, and still lacks, formal papal approval. But this would be to ignore the reality of Church governance since the Second Vatican Council. Cardinal Cassidy's masterpiece of capitulation was promptly delivered to the Eastern Catholic primates by the Papal Nuncios, whose ascendancy as the Vatican's semi-secret diplomatic representatives began with the disastrous concordats of the Napoleonic era. With the Nuncial package came the implicit understanding that Balamand's "ecclesiological principles" and "practical rules" would, naturally, be implemented immediately—even though the Pope himself had not actually given such an order. Of course, a papal order

170 *Eastern Churches Journal*, Vol. 1, pp. 18-25.

171 The Second Section of the Secretariat of State has the particular job of forming and maintaining relations with civil governments. *The 1997 Annuario Pontifico*, p. 1814 describes the functions of the Second Section more indepth.

was a mere formality. After all, Cardinal Cassidy was head of a Pontifical Council; therefore he acted with papal authority, did he not? Not only that, the document had been delivered by a Papal Nuncio. Thus, it gave every *appearance* of being a papal order, even if it contained no actual order from the Pope.

One of the prelates who received the Balamand Statement *via* Nuncio was the Cardinal Archbishop of Lviv in the Ukraine, His Eminence Myroslav Lubachivsky. Cardinal Lubachivsky wrote to Cardinal Cassidy to assure him that:

> "I commit myself, my brother bishops, clergy and faithful, to applying the practical rules of the Balamand Document to the best of our ability. These include ... *not to seek the passage of faithful from one Church to another* ..." [172]

How distressing to note that on April 24, 1990, Cardinal Lubachivsky had written to Father Gruner to encourage his work in spreading awareness of the need for the Collegial Consecration of Russia, which he clearly agreed had not been effected in 1984 as the anti-Fatima forces were now claiming:

> "I want to thank you for all that you do for the Church and for continuing to spread the *full Fatima Message*; in particular for insisting on *the urgent need to have Russia consecrated by all the bishops of the Church in union with the Holy Father*. Be assured of my prayers and the prayers of the Ukrainian people *for all that you are doing to save Russia*."[173]

Only three years later, this same prelate would feel obliged to forget the conversion of Russia—on the strength of a non-binding statement by a theological commission meeting in Lebanon, negotiated by a Vatican bureaucrat of no greater hierarchical status than his own. And this despite the fact that it was atheistic Russia which had committed the genocide of 20 million of his own people and stolen their priests, bishops and churches from them. *Simply because a Nuncio had delivered a document from the Vatican apparatus*, this prince of the Church would immediately abandon any effort to exercise his Divine commission of promoting the return—yes, the *return*—of the Ukrainian Orthodox to the one true Church of Christ. Instead, he would now agree to view the perennial teaching of the Magisterium on the spiritual state of schismatics just as the Balamand Document said it should be viewed: "the outdated ecclesiology of a return to the Catholic Church."

And so a mere bureaucratic decree would become the policy of the Holy Catholic Church in Eastern Europe. It would soon come to pass that entire villages seeking to return to Rome would be told by Catholic bishops that a return was no longer necessary. No, they were to *remain* in the schismatic church in which their forefathers had been forcibly transplanted by Communist barbarians. The crisis was over. Mission accomplished. The world was safe for *Ostpolitik* and world ecumenism. Without the Collegial Consecration which would have made the conversion of Russia a certainty, the Balamand Document was all that was needed to keep it from happening.

The Balamand Statement recalls another tragic blunder of Vatican diplomacy in which defeat was snatched from the jaws of victory: Just as the *Cristeros* in the mid 1920's seemed to be turning the tide against the Masonic revolutionaries who were ravaging Mexico, U.S. Ambassador Morrow and Vatican representatives negotiated an agreement under which they would lay down their arms in exchange for paper

---

172 *Eastern Churches Journal*, op. cit., p. 34.

173 "The Fatima Crusader", Issue 33, Summer 1990, p. 11.

promises of amnesty and respect for the religious liberty of Catholics.[174] Following the orders of the Vatican, the *Cristeros* laid down their arms, only to be hunted down and butchered by the Masons.[175] The corpses of faithful priests and laity would festoon trees and telephone poles in Mexico for many years to come.

The Balamand debacle, like the betrayal in Mexico, shows how the Mystical Body has been pulled to the ground and immobilized by a thousand Lilliputian strings emanating from Vatican secretariats, councils and commissions which form no part of the divine constitution of the Church. It typifies the *modus operandi* by which the virtue of obedience in faithful clerics like Cardinal Lubachivsky is exploited by bureaucrats issuing documents which have the appearance of a command, but which in reality command nothing. These vaporous non-orders have acquired the power to negate Tradition, and even to overrule the plain words of the Mother of God.

It would be Father Gruner himself who unearthed another spectacular example of this phenomenon in May of 1995, at a public address by Alfons Cardinal Stickler on the subject of the Traditional Latin Mass. In response to Father Gruner's written question, the Cardinal revealed to the audience that in 1986 a group of nine Curial Cardinals assembled by Pope John Paul II himself, all with doctorates in Canon Law, had voted 8-1 in closed session that Pope Paul VI had never actually ordered the suppression of the Traditional Mass, and that its celebration had *never ceased to be entirely permissible* under Church law.[176] Incredibly, the Pope had been unable to determine just what his predecessor had ordered in promulgating the New Mass. In fact, the actual suppression of the Traditional Mass had been accomplished entirely through the decrees of Vatican congregations and commissions, and not by any explicit Magisterial act of Paul VI. As the vote of the Cardinals made clear, bureaucrats had obliterated the entire liturgical tradition of the Roman Rite without a single actual order of the Pope suppressing it!

Thus has the Catholic Church been governed for the past 30 years.

§

In the early summer of 1994, a year after Balamand, news of the Apostolate's plan for a Mexico conference on the Message of Fatima reached the bureaucrats of the Secretary of State, and the alarm bells rang once again: *What?*—a gathering of bishops to discuss the "conversion of Russia", after Vatican representatives had just negotiated an agreement promising not to convert the Russians? This was intolerable.

The first employees of the Secretary of State to be mobilized in any crisis are the Nuncios. Should the Nuncios be mobilized on a global scale against a lone Canadian priest and his Marian apostolate, they could present a formidable force which might well annihilate plans for the Mexican conference. Unthinkable? It should have been. Yet, that is exactly what happened in the summer and autumn months of 1994.

---

174 Solange Hertz, *Beyond Politics*, Santa Monica, California, 1995, p. 170.

175 Ibid.

176 *Catholic Family News*, August 1995, p. 13.

PART THREE

A Fatima Spirituality for the 21ST Century

Chapter 14

Terrible Words

The events which had unfolded since the Fatima conference of 1992, by any reckoning, would have annihilated most priests—especially one who was now being pressed in the vise of "administrative decrees" intended to crush the life out of his Apostolate by removing him from it, and who wished to speak with bishops in Mexico about the conversion of Russia which had just been bartered away at Balamand.

Nevertheless, while the Balamand Statement was being implemented, and the bizarre "Sister Lucia Interview" publicized by Carlos Evaristo was being taken as gospel by those who wanted apparitions with more ecumenical messages to replace Fatima's stern warnings, Father Gruner coolly moved forward to appeal once more to the bishops in the cause of Fatima.

The decision to hold a Second International Peace Conference in Mexico might seem like a suicide mission to most. But Father Nicholas Gruner saw it as providing a golden opportunity to penetrate even deeper into the compelling reasons for the collegial consecration of Russia. He could not forget that Our Lord's words to Sister Lucia at Rianjo conveyed one of the most terrifying prophecies and rebukes in a century of Marian apparitions:

In the August 1931 message, Our Lord in Rianjo, Spain, gave Sister Lucia of Fatima a very stern warning to pass on to the hierarchy when He said: "Make it known to My ministers, given that they follow the example of the King of France in delaying the execution of My command, they will follow him into misfortune".[177]

Our Lord is referring to the misfortune of King Louis XVI, who was the third king to reject Our Lord's plan given through St. Margaret Mary for the consecration of France to the Sacred Heart. Having failed to effect the consecration, Louis XVI was guillotined in 1793, by the French revolutionaries. Through Sister Lucia, Our Lord admonished the Pope and the bishops about the fate which awaits those who refuse to carry out the divinely mandated consecration of a nation.

The old "crock" on Father Gruner is that he is "disloyal" to the Pope. His critics have never bothered to explain how it could be loyalty for a subject to ignore a grave warning from a divine messenger that the life of his sovereign was in jeopardy. Our Lord had not predicted a great tea party when He told Sister Lucia at Rianjo that His ministers would follow in the footsteps of the beheaded Louis XVI should they fail to heed His commands at Fatima. If loyalty was lacking, it had to be on the part of the critics who continue to hide the warning of Our Lord from the Pope and the bishops.

What better place to remind the bishops than in the fast-beating heart of a country that has been the center of persecution of the Church throughout her long, tortured history—Mexico?

It is said that thirty million people live within whispering distance of one another in Mexico City. To descend by plane into the ocean of light this population generates at night is to experience the shock Cortes must have felt when he came through the high mountain pass of Popacatapetl and saw Montezuma's capital at his feet. Mexico is the center of a world apart. It was at the fast-pulsating heart of this endangered

177 Father Alonso, *Fatima Ante la Esfinge*, Madrid, Spain, 1979, p. 97; also, Frère François de Marie des Anges, *Fatima: The Only Way to World Peace*, p. 78.

world that the Second International Peace Conference for Bishops was scheduled for November of 1994.

In the months leading up to the Conference, invitations went out to the bishops of the world, announcements were sent to interested Church associations, 150,000 posters promoting the Conference were distributed and over 500,000 copies of a special issue of *The Fatima Crusader* were mailed to supporters.

To prepare for the Conference, the first undertaking in the spring of '94 was for Father Gruner to meet with Bishop Fuentes, the bishop of a small diocese in Mexico, whom he had met in Fatima in 1992. At first Bishop Fuentes appeared delighted with the proposal for a conference and most co-operative, going so far as to make introductions to the Mexican Bishops Conference, the CEM. Abbot Schullenberg, Rector of the Shrine of Guadalupe, encouraged Father Gruner to use the Aula Magna, the Great Hall at Lago de Guadalupe, which is owned by the CEM.

On May 2, the Secretary-General of the CEM, Bishop Ramon Godinez Flores, agreed to the rental of the Aula Magna conference facility,[178] the same facility where the Mexican Bishops hold their annual meetings. On May 5, the CEM accepted and deposited the check which had an endorsement clause typed on the back of the check indicating that endorsement and deposit of the check constituted an agreement to rent the Aula Magna conference facility. Everything seemed to be proceeding smoothly—too smoothly.

Under the relentless demands of producing the Conference, it was natural that the signs and signals of a determined opposition might slip by unnoticed or without being afforded the attention that may have been due. In the offices of the Vatican Secretary of State the opposition was forming its battalions, and they were ready to move into action.

October 2nd: A letter from Bishop Flores, dated a month earlier, arrived at Father Gruner's Canadian office. It contained the second of the checks initially sent to reserve additional rooms for the event, the text of the letter announcing that the reservations of the Aula Magna facilities had been canceled. The stunning words used were:

> "... this terminates the possibility of effecting the above-mentioned meeting."[179]

Not quite. Only five weeks remained to the opening speeches of the Conference, to which considerably over 100 bishops had committed to being present. Even so, no one panicked. After the letter of cancellation arrived, the immediate need was to find alternative facilities in Mexico City. It was done: God willing, the Second Fatima Peace Conference would take place instead at the Sheraton Maria Isabela Hotel on Paseo de la Reforma.

It was then that the Apostolate heard about the Big Lie. All the way from Rome to Mexico. At first it was just a whisper. Then a letter surfaced that had been sent to every bishop in the world *via* the global network of Papal Nuncios. Father Gruner began receiving notes from bishops who had been advised by the head of the Conference of Bishops in their own countries not to attend, on the strength of advice reaching them through the Apostolic Nunciature in each country. The letter from the Vatican was a recycled version of the same "declaration" published in *L'Osservatore Romano* and elsewhere by Cardinal Sanchez and Archbishop Sepe to derail the 1992 Conference in Fatima.[180]

178 Father Nicholas Gruner, *Special Report - Second International Bishops Peace Conference*, "The Fatima Crusader", Issue 48, Winter 1995, p. 20.

179 Ibid.

180 Ibid, pp. 20-21.

The letter referred once again to the old canard that Father Gruner did not have "permission of ecclesiastical authority" to hold the Conference in Mexico City. This in spite of the fact that it was manifest that bishops of the Catholic Church do not require the "permission" of Vatican bureaucrats to attend a private religious conference. To add to the absurdity, no official Vatican mechanism even exists for the "official authorization" of such private events. The "declaration" was demeaning, insulting to the bishops, and (as expected by its issuers) the cause of mass confusion and upset.

The letter was a prime specimen of the literally truthful lie: yes, there was no "ecclesiastical permission" for the conference, but *none was required in the first place*. By use of this literally truthful lie, the bureaucrats had hoped to create the impression that bishops—who by virtue of the divine constitution of the Church are the rulers of their own dioceses and answerable only to the Pope—were somehow subject to travel restrictions imposed by a pair of Vatican bureaucrats sitting in the Congregation for the Clergy!

The law of the Church is clear, and the law had not changed since the first Conference, when canon lawyers had emphatically stated what should have been a matter of common sense: Absolutely no "permission of ecclesiastical authority" is needed for any member of the faithful, much less a bishop, to be present at a private Marian conference. On the contrary, it would be a violation of the law of the Church to *require* such permission. The bureaucrats were, in fact, openly defying the present Code of Canon Law promulgated by Pope John Paul II—a Code which had by Providence made explicit the always-existent natural right of the faithful to form associations, conduct meetings and present their concerns about Church affairs to the sacred pastors.[180a] The modernists had been abusing this same natural right for thirty years, staging their motley assemblies and issuing their heretical manifestos with total impunity. Oddly enough, the bureaucrats had never seen fit to interdict any of these modernist gatherings with letters dispatched to the entire world episcopate through the Nuncios.

To give one example among many, in August 1995, the 25th Anniversary of the leftist *Campaign for Human Development* (CHD) was held in Chicago. At this event, twenty-five bishops, including three Cardinals, gathered with priests, nuns, ex-nuns, and laity. The conference promoted left-wing political actions, it sneered at "the religious right", promoted "anti-patriarchy" feminism and called for improvement for the lives of such "minorities" as gays and lesbians.

The Saturday afternoon CHD liturgy included pagan dance at the offertory by dancing girls in leotards and low-cut tops, and scandalous irreverence of the Blessed Sacrament after Communion when about ten lay "extraordinary ministers" gathered around the altar irreverently gulping down the consecrated Bread and Wine as if they were at a cocktail party, talking and chatting out loud with each other and friends all within arms reach of the 25 bishops who simply sat and watched.[180b]

Yet *not one* of the bishops participating in this event received even a slap on the wrist from Roman authorities for attending. But then, the modernists were not gathering to discuss and promote the "intolerable" Message of Fatima.

Although the Mexico Conference in no way offended Canon Law or general ecclesiastical practice, nevertheless a majority of the bishops who had planned to attend

---

180a The detailed case against these illegal maneuvers by a very small number of Vatican-based bureaucrats had been officially lodged with His Holiness Pope John Paul II, on November 20, 1996, in exact accordance with the provisions of Canon Law for cases like this one where a Church official grossly abuses his position of authority.

180b *Catholic Family News*, November 1996, p. 4.

cancelled after receipt of the Nuncial missive. Why the high casualty list? Because, without ever telling an explicit lie, the letter clearly implied two very false things: that Father Gruner was under some sort of ecclesiastical penalty, an outlaw; and that any bishop who attended the Conference would be engaging in an act of disobedience.

This was all couched in *studied ambiguity*. No specific offense was attributed to Father Gruner, nor any specific prohibition on attendance at the Conference—because there *was* no offense, and no prohibition. In the 18 years of his priesthood and work in the Apostolate, Father Gruner had never been charged with any offense whatsoever against the good of the Church, and neither had the Apostolate. The "declaration" was pure vapor. But the vapor had its effect.

To the outsider, the political maneuver from the clique of bureaucrats was nothing less than bizarre, and, with no little hangover from the '92 Conference, outright vindictive. Most priests would have been intimidated into abandoning the undertaking and seeking new winds to fill the mainsail. Yet that did not happen. Despite the withdrawal of many bishops, and the continuing interference of the same Vatican bureaucrats, Father Gruner persisted in completing plans for the Conference. His fixity of purpose was, as many watchers of his Apostolate now recognize, pure vintage Gruner.

Publicly, Bishop Flores made use of the Nuncios' letter to "justify" his cancellation of the Conference at the CEM facilities. As Bishop Flores proceeded to go about sweeping the whole thing under the carpet, and Father Gruner kept moving forward to meet his deadline, the serpent of old extended a second suffocating coil around the Conference plans.

From the Middle East came news that a bishop had been denied a visa on the grounds that the Conference was not approved by the Mexican Government. Incredibly, the Mexican government had indeed announced that they had not "authorized" the gathering.

October 21: An official communiqué from the Mexican Government revealed it was Bishop Flores himself who had gone to the Ministry of the Interior in Mexico City and condemned the Conference. On that same day, further confirmation of Bishop Flores' interference was received from the Consulate General of Mexico, in Toronto.

Officials of the Mexican Government found their hands tied. Under orders from the Ministry of the Interior they could not issue visas for people from other countries who wished to attend the Conference. Around the world, Mexican Consulates had been informed that those applying for visas for this purpose were not to receive them because the Secretary-General of the Bishops Conference in Mexico, Bishop Flores, had not given his *completely unnecessary* "authorization" for the Conference.

There were both physical and logistical hardships for the bishops who had seen through the vaporous letter from the Nuncios and managed to obtain visas (in most cases by not disclosing the exact purpose of their trip). Arrangements in some cases had been made many months in advance. Worse still, inconvenience to the guest lecturers scheduled to speak at the Conference mounted. Remunerative engagements turned down for the chance to address the bishops were lost.

All these obstacles caused Father Gruner to pause and consider whether there was really a way around the multiplying problems. But he remained convinced that he had a duty to proceed. Nor could he live with the pain of knowing that souls were being lost because the requests of Our Lady had been buried and forgotten in so many quarters of the Church:

"I believe in conscience that each day the Consecration of Russia as requested by Our Lady of Fatima is delayed, many, many people die in the state of unbelief and other mortal sins. Unless they miraculously convert on their deathbed, they will go to hell. Thus, due to each day's delay, many souls are lost for all eternity, and wars continue to erupt without abatement around the globe. Since 1984 alone, when the Consecration was supposedly done (according to the conjecture of the ill-informed), over 10 million people have died in new wars. If you consider the undeclared but very real war upon the unborn, since 1984 there have been, around the world, at least 600 million victims. Russia, since her supposed Consecration in 1984, has become the place where Polish Catholics go for their abortions. Is *this* the fruit of the Consecration which Our Lady promised would bring peace to the world? Please! Every day that we delay there are over 100,000 innocent victims in this war. It is a tragedy that the bishops of the world have the truth about Fatima hidden from them. Yet it is only through them that the wars and violence will stop as Our Lady of Fatima said, 'If My requests are granted, many souls will be saved and there will be peace.' This, after all, is why we work so hard at getting the consecration done.

"If I, like anyone else, do not do what I can to make the truth known, however small my effort, then each of us doing nothing will have complicity in this debacle, because we knew and did nothing."

And so the Conference would proceed. New arrangements to meet the bureaucratic offensive were being worked out in round-the-clock planning sessions back at the Apostolate. Coralie Graham recalls: "We were determined to provide in a dignified and gracious manner for the bishops who would attend. Thank God for the help of friends of the Apostolate like Ray Flores and Louis Acosta, whose fluency in Spanish was crucial to undoing the damage that had been done in Mexico City and to putting the Conference back on track."

November 8: Translators at the back of the Conference Hall in the Maria Isabela Hotel began their simultaneous translation of the opening speeches of the Second International Bishops' Conference. A moment of triumph for the cause of Our Lady of Fatima—and a day for savoring the irony in the October letter from Bishop Flores in which he had so confidently declared:

" ...this terminates the possibility of effecting the above-mentioned meeting."

The damage had been severe, but not terminal: Out of the 100-plus bishops who had committed to attending the Conference before the nunciatures applied their pressure, only a fraction would arrive in Mexico City. But their arrival was a testament to the inability of a few Vatican bureaucrats to negate entirely the divine constitution of the Church and the natural rights of the faithful. The curtain had been drawn back for a moment, and at least a few of the bishops had realized that like the Wizard of Oz, the bureaucrats were mere men, actuating the levers of a great machine which generated a lot of intimidating noise and smoke, but had no legitimate power over them. They realized that the only power these men exercised with their great apparatus was the power of fear; and they had overcome that fear.

Father Gruner felt deep sorrow that so many bishops were intimidated by the clique of bureaucrats in the Vatican, and did not attend. Father reflected on this tragedy.

"Although we very carefully conformed to all of the laws that the Church prescribes governing conferences, which are given in the 1983 Code of Canon

Law, promulgated by His Holiness, Pope John Paul II, the clique of Vatican bureaucrats still worked to prevent the conference. These officials were in clear defiance of the Code set up by His Holiness.

"Unfortunately, because of the vicious attacks by these bureaucrats, I have been made to look as though I am disloyal to His Holiness.

"On the contrary, I have a deep love and affection for His Holiness, and I regard myself as a 'loyal son of the Pope'. I am in opposition to some people around him today, because I am trying to warn the Pope that he is in grave danger. I cannot forget the dire warning directed to the hierarchy that Jesus gave Sister Lucia at Rianjo."

Father Gruner goes on: "As of yet, almost every prophecy given at Fatima has come to pass. The few that are left will happen in the near future. Francisco and Jacinta were both prophesied to die shortly after the apparitions, and they did die. Our Lady prophesied World War II, which would begin during the Pontificate of Pope Pius XI, and it happened as She said. Our Lady of Fatima prophesied a number of other world events which have also come to pass. Clearly, then, this prophecy which warns that the very lives of our Holy Father and the world's bishops are in danger, must be taken very seriously."

§

The Sheraton Maria Isabela on Paseo de la Reforma, in the very center of Mexico City, perfectly befitted the hosting of the Fathers of the Church. Throughout her history, the Church has never let danger or controversy intimidate it. The symbolism of veils, crosses, miters could not possibly go unrecorded in Mexico. Not too long ago, Catholic clergy could be shot for wearing clerical garb in this city, the way Father Pro and the *Cristeros* were shot during the Mexican Revolution—suddenly, without fanfare. International Masonry had tried awfully hard in the last two centuries to keep the Church out of Mexico. Now, under the mask of modernism, certain malevolent forces came close to succeeding once again, this time maneuvering from inside the Vatican itself.

The lesson was not lost on the bishops who appeared in the hotel lobby in the vestments of their office. In a country where pectoral crosses are rarer than passenger pigeons, the hotel employees, taxi drivers, street vendors, and passers-by stared awestruck at the colors of faith exposed so openly. They had reason to be awestruck—outside the hotel a statue of Gloria Liberty reminds anyone gazing out the Conference window that power in Mexico is in the same hands that once 'tilted the plank' on altar and crown in the France of Robespierre and Fouquier-Tinville.

The presence of these bishops in Mexico City was an eloquent gesture of licit resistance to Church bureaucrats who seem determined to suppress every element of Catholic Tradition. It seems that any bishop today is free to waltz with heretics and polka with infidels, flatter bizarre creeds, grovel before dissidents and allow a homosexual theologians' mafia to deform and disinform his seminarians. Yet, bishops had to struggle against fierce Vatican opposition to attend a conference devoted to Our Lady of Fatima. Had it been a conference of heretics, the journey to Mexico would have been unopposed.

For gatherings with heretics, there is freedom of speech and assembly. For conferences on the full message of Fatima, there is bureaucratic repression on a global scale. The disparity is a stunning example of how *Ostpolitik* is the one "dogma" that certain Vatican bureaucrats are willing to defend with stern measures.

In making the journey to Mexico, these bishops had reflected the fierce yet humble Catholic spirit of Mexico itself. Mexico is a culture and a world unique even among the many countries where the Church has suffered throughout the ages. For 100 years, priests and bishops in this profoundly Catholic nation had been at the head of an endangered species list. The survival of the Church in Mexico is the *history* of Mexico. Bishop Clement Kelley, one of the foremost historians on Mexico, wrote from the Mexican perspective on this ability of the Church always somehow to *survive*:

> "The historian is ever on the watch for her (the Church's) entrance upon any scene, always certain that, if She is not on the stage where the human drama of life is being played, She is somewhere in the wings, or perhaps, raising or dropping the curtain. She loves the peaceful and quiet parts, does not disdain even comedy, but tragedy is her very life."[181]

Next door to the Maria Isabela Hotel stands the American Embassy. For days to come, riot police would come and go from the streets, hoping to contain massive protests against California's Proposition 187. This too was fitting—Proposition 187 is all about keeping Mexican Catholics out of the United States. Mexico is peculiar that way. It is both a place from which Catholics seek to escape, and a haven in which the Catholic Faith has survived, despite the depredations of the Masons. Thus it seems that someone is always trying either to keep Catholics out of Mexico or forcibly to return them there.

Father Gruner believed the Conference had to proceed because the tragedy of Mexico's past could well mirror the tragedy awaiting the Church Universal if Our Lady of Fatima were not obeyed. A suggestion of the import of the meeting came at the airport terminal in Mexico City when Father Marcel Nault, a priest who always wears his cassock, was confronted by a man wanting to know if priests were now allowed to be seen in public in cassocks in Mexico. When Father Nault answered that yes, they were, the man asking the question gave him a look, which brought to mind the sight of dead *Cristeros* hanging from trees during the Mexican Revolution. Of course, the Revolution against the Church continues in every country in the world. That is why Our Lady came to Fatima. And that is why the bishops had come to Mexico City.

The opening Mass for the Conference started on time at the Shrine of Our Lady of Guadalupe. Ten million pilgrims a year come to pray before the Tilma of Our Lady on which Her miraculous image appears. All of the conflicts, crises, and struggles of the Church fade from mind as that small assembly of bishops lined up to concelebrate Mass. Then something happened. The bishops, upon entering, passed in single file before the image on the Tilma. Anyone who has seen it, passed by it, stood under it, gazed upon it, prayed before it, will tell you: *the image is alive*.

One looks upon it. It looks back. And the world changes. Those bishops who insisted on attending, gathered upon arrival to look up into the living eyes of God's Mother. She looked back at them. Millions have experienced Her glance. A living person looks out from the holy Tilma, subjecting Herself to the scrutiny of the curious for the sake of Her Son. She is indeed alive.

Perhaps it was there at the Shrine, before the Tilma, that the determination was made to go forward with the Conference as if numbers did not matter. From that moment on, the Conference unfolded with ease. As they concelebrated Mass before the Tilma, the bishops were serenaded by specially assembled Mexican musicians, the music of the Mexican people was a reminder that they were at the foot of Tepeyac Hill,

181 Bishop Francis Clement Kelley, *Blood Drenched Altars*, p. 102.

the very spot where Our Lady expressed to Juan Diego the will of Heaven itself with such eloquence She caused the great nation of Mexico to resound with Her praises throughout the centuries, regardless of opposition.

Not even the dreadful architecture of the new Shrine of Our Lady of Guadalupe could diminish the unquenchable Marian devotion of the Mexicans who flock there. Like much of the post-conciliar Church architecture, the new shrine is an incomprehensible clash of styles reflecting the conflict of ideologies clawing for supremacy in the Church today. It offers not one reflection of the glories of the Faith, the traditions of the past, the authority of the Church. Not even an echo of the glorious cathedral that was originally the home of the Holy Tilma is represented in the new shrine. It stands, a hollow, empty drum of cement, an appalling concrete tent pitched over the miraculous portrait of Guadalupe.

To the people of Mexico, the mammoth empty shell reflects none of their culture nor their faith which, from its inception, was nurtured by the Tabernacle of the Living Lord. As for the Tabernacle in the shrine, merely to locate it in this architectural wasteland could consume an entire Mexican holiday. Who could have been surprised, therefore, when Rector Schullenberg, who directed and oversaw its construction, was widely reported to have recently declared that Our Lady had never even appeared at Guadalupe.[182] The resulting public outcry would force his removal as rector—proving once again that sometimes the duty of maintaining the integrity of the Faith devolves to an angry laity, rising in righteous opposition to feckless clerics.

Nevertheless, amidst the coldness of the place, Bishop Salazar's warm words of gratitude and recognition during his first Mass at the Guadalupe Basilica touched the hearts of Father Gruner and his group: "I am here precisely because Our Lady called me through the continual invitation of Father Gruner and his group accompanying him. There is something precious here because what we are seeking is peace."

But no one gathered in the Shrine that day for the opening of the Conference could have foreseen that the Vatican bureaucracy's poison-pen letter was to bring to the floor of the Conference a voice that would cut like a two-edged sword, ripping apart the curtain concealing the forces which had tried to crush the Conference.

The dramatic moment came with the arrival on the Conference floor of the Vatican-based Archbishop Emmanuel Milingo. From this brother of Peter, Cardinal Sanchez and Archbishop Sepe received a fiery public reprimand. Also reprimanded was the Vatican Secretary of State's office, for its heavy-handed use of the Nuncios to browbeat bishops into shunning the conference. Archbishop Milingo issued a powerful testament that Truth cannot be imprisoned in a Nuncio's briefcase.

The deliberate undermining of his own personal and unshakeable loyalty to the Holy Father implied in the letter to the bishops triggered his dramatic statement to the stunned assembly. His ringing commentary was in the form of an authoritatively worded protest delivered not to the Conference but from him as a consecrated bishop of the Church of Rome to those forces that had tried to prevent him from attending.

Brandishing a letter from the Nuncio in Nigeria telling bishops not to attend the Conference, Archbishop Milingo electrified the delegates with an eloquent defense of the prerogatives of the episcopacy, which the bureaucrats seemed to have overlooked. He denounced the letter from the Nuncio as an illicit attempt to take away his freedom of conscience and his freedom to act on his own recognizance. He blasted the letter as

182 After Abbot Schullenberg, rector of the Guadalupe Shrine, on a radio broadcast in Mexico, expressed his disbelief in the reality of Our Lady's appearance at Guadalupe, a storm of protest broke out causing him to resign his post.

an abuse of authority, an insult and a humiliation to all the bishops who received it, and he noted, just for the record, the empty seats reflecting the number of less courageous prelates who had been intimidated into staying away.

Apparently, the much touted 'religious liberty' of Vatican II had been suspended at the hotel Maria Isabela, denied to the consecrated leaders of their own Church. The laity who had been preparing to speak to their pastors were to be denied freedom of speech on the very spot where Our Lady of Guadalupe had expressed the will of Heaven. To all this, Archbishop Milingo, a Church Father with six million followers, brought a crystal clear focus. Holding up the letter for all to see, he zeroed in on a major failing of the pastors and laity of the Church today with a litany for the episcopacy in our time: Why are we not making new disciples for Christ? Because the bishops are " ... shaking in their trousers!" he cried. Why are they shaking in their trousers? Because they don't have real authority.

Why don't they have real authority if they are consecrated bishops? Because a clique of bureaucrats in the Vatican, trading on the Church mystique, can, with unjustified letters, completely unchallenged and unchecked, dictate to bishops what they can and cannot do.

How can they get away with it?

Because bishops who resist them can find themselves removed to the backwoods, removed from benefits, reduced in every way imaginable! They are living on suspended authority, he proclaimed angrily. If the certain Vatican officials pull the plug then the bishop is retired. Under such conditions the episcopacy is merely a front for the games of unnamed and unseen bureaucrats.

The bureaucratization of the Holy See was harming the divine constitution of the Church, preventing the bishops from acting according to their conscience and denying the faithful their God-given right to petition the Holy Father for the Consecration of Russia:

> "I also have received thousands of letters that were addressed to the Pope for the Consecration of Russia to the Immaculate Heart of Mary. I myself have brought from my office directly to the Secretariat of State many, many, many of these letters since 1991 ... *I am quite certain that is where they stopped*. I really do not blame the bishops. If some resist, they are just a few. And letters like this will make some of the bishops have no courage."

But what of "obedience" to the "Holy See"? Should not the bishops comply with directives from the Secretariat of State? Archbishop Milingo reminded his brother bishops that Our Lord did not establish Vatican Secretariats to rule over the descendants of His Apostles, and that it was a false obedience which the anti-Fatima bureaucrats were promoting:

> "[T]his letter from the Nuncio telling us not to come to this Conference shows, as a matter of fact, how one can misunderstand obedience. This [letter] says to those who came here, you were disobedient because an official letter told you not to come. *Then people tremble in their trousers*. What a pity. It [The letter] is a humiliation to a human being who is an apostle—a humiliation intended to prevent him from fulfilling his duties according to his own personality and character... [Y]ou have got someone *suspending your authority* in carrying out your duties and fulfilling your responsibilities ... I am not one whose authority is suspended. Not at all. *I am an apostle*... If this letter represents their way to control us, it means that they don't trust the people to whom they have given

authority. And that doesn't do it at all. That is not at all correct. Therefore I am very happy to take this letter signed by the Papal Nuncio to the Holy Father ... I will explain about this, that I have been there [Mexico City], but I take full responsibility for coming here and I accept the consequences. *And I can assure you there will be no consequences*."[183]

Of course, Archbishop Milingo was right: There would be no consequences for his coming to Mexico City because, in truth, the Vatican bureaucrats had no authority to forbid or to punish his appearance. Where the descendants of the Apostles were concerned, the bureaucrats were in truth as powerless as the Wizard of Oz behind his flimsy curtain. If only his brother bishops would understand this, they could shake off the paralysis of fear which had gripped the Mystical Body of Christ since the Council:

"Not one of us will go to Heaven without holding a brother, a sister. Each and every one of us must step out of the crowd and stand on one's own feet strong enough to be a Christian ... We are acting as if the Catholic Faith were a private affair. That is not true at all. There is still a lot to be done even if the opening for the Consecration is not yet there ... The world must be saved and it must be saved through each one of us."[184]

The scenario Archbishop Milingo depicted in his fiery oration was indeed a bleak one. The Pope is dependent on his bishops. But the bishops have become subservient to the bureaucrats, whose agenda does not include the Message of Fatima. The Pope is therefore at the mercy of those same bureaucrats regarding the Collegial Consecration. The bureaucrats had decreed in Balamand that there would be no conversion of Russia, and the prelates who had endured Communist persecution in Eastern Europe obediently fell into line, somehow failing to notice that the piece of paper which commanded them to forget the Message of Fatima was in reality no command at all, but simply a piece of paper. It could not overrule the decree of Heaven at Fatima.

At the service of the bureaucrats are the Nuncios, transporting their demands and instructions from country to country, to the bishops of the world, as they had after Balamand. The Nuncio has become the henchman of the clique—thus have the words 'diplomacy' and 'diplomat' become ghosts of their former meaning, and the Nuncios mere couriers of an earthly enterprise.

The effect can be deep and long lasting. Consider that it is one thing for officials in Rome to pull the plug on a bishop, but how are they to dispense with priests? Simple. Even unsubstantiated fluff, passed from the hand of a Nuncio to a bishop, has the potential to irreparably damage a priest.

How then, in Archbishop Milingo's terms, can bishops make disciples of priests if the Nuncios have them "shaking in their trousers"? How then can priests make disciples out of the people if the priests are "shaking in their trousers"?

Is it any wonder the Church is wounded and limping? Under these conditions, a small, privileged clique, completely unthreatened by anyone in the Vatican regardless of what they do, can destroy anyone who stands in their way.[185]

This time, however, Father Gruner's refusal to cancel the conference had uncovered the less than savory practices of intimidation and coercion the Nuncios and their bosses around the world had been practicing. Their purpose being, in the words of Bishop

---

183 Archbishop Emmanuel Milingo, *Archbishop Milingo's Dramatic Speech*, "The Fatima Crusader", Issue 48, Winter 1995, p. 20.

184 Ibid.

185 Speech given by Archbishop Emmanuel Milingo, Nov. 13, 1994, in Mexico City, "The Fatima Crusader", Issue 48, p. 5.

Flores, to "terminate the possibility of effecting the above-mentioned meeting."

In mid-week of the Conference, the bishops concelebrated Mass in the Cathedral of Mexico, which once enshrined the image of Our Lady of Guadalupe. Few locations on earth more aptly mirror the state of the Church today. The building is propped up by scaffolding indicating a much-touted "restoration" and "renewal" that is supposedly under way. But anyone who understands scaffolding can tell at a glance that the cobwebs which cover it mean that the scaffolding is here to stay. The man-made structure it supports has already crumbled into dust; only the falling down remains. It would take a supernatural Hand to restore this once magnificent structure and remove the endless layers of artificial support.

To appreciate the reality of its decay, the bishops had only to walk to the center of the interior and see the pendulum hanging there. It is surely a most fitting symbol of the Church in our time. A gigantic plumb bob, suspended from the ceiling, hangs off kilter, pointing away from the perfect center of gravity. The Church is off her axis.

Yet, even in this collapsing Cathedral, nothing can prevent the faithful from adoring the Blessed Sacrament or walking on their knees to petition for favors. Confessions, a marriage, and baptism were occurring simultaneously amid huge crowds as the bishops entered and departed the Cathedral.

The power of Our Lady is demonstrated with overwhelming force just outside and behind the Cathedral walls. Here stand the fabled 'Halls of Montezuma', on the site of Montezuma's Great Temple where as many as 8,000 human victims a day had their hearts ripped out while they were still alive to appease a demonic force that had seized control of Aztec culture.

On this spot, where the tortured cultures victimized by the Aztecs may well have despaired of rescue, Cortes put an end to human sacrifice. Shortly after, in 1531, Our Lady appeared at Guadalupe. Within a few short years of Her appearance, nine million Mexicans were baptized into the Catholic Faith, replacing within the Church the number of Catholics the arch-heretic Luther had led out of it, in Europe. But the intersecting lessons of Fatima and Mexico do not end there.

Thirty miles north of the city, the pyramids of Teotihuacan stand, as they have since long before those same Aztecs came to central Mexico. History has allotted these structures the names of the Pyramid of the Sun, the Pyramid of the Moon, and joining them, the Avenue of the Dead. It was indeed a sobering moment when the bishops were guided toward a ledge from which they could look down into the enclosure where the demonic priests of that bloodthirsty culture performed human sacrifices.

This is a city of death. It is also a metaphor in stone for our own times, when the ravenous god of progress demands daily flesh and blood from once-Catholic cultures. Suzanne M. Rini, in writing on current-day eugenic experimentation, states the parallel with horrifying clarity:

> "... the human preborn baby (especially prized by eugenics researchers) is, through the power, will and imagination of the scientist, 'elevated' to the status of a live human sacrifice in return for the demonic reward of the secret knowledge regarding human life itself."[186]

We ought to take a moment to allow the overwhelming nature of this parallel to impress itself upon our hearts. Can there be a more poignant example in the whole history of this century of the effect of the errors of atheistic Russia than the way that

---

186 *Catholic Family News*, January 1995, p. 7.

evil empire's "legalized" sacrifice of the unborn has spread, as Mary predicted at Fatima, throughout the world—all the more so since the alleged "consecration" of 1984? The Aztec warrior-priest at least indulged in his sacrifice to appease the demands of an imaginary god. Today, the innocent child is slaughtered to appease the demands of a credit-card vacation or a car payment.

The whole truth about Fatima is that Our Lady promised to turn all this around. She laid out simply and clearly how it would be done. The conversion of Russia would come when the Pope and the bishops of the world together consecrated Russia—Russia!—to Her Immaculate Heart. Yet that is the only thing that has *not* been done in the era of *Ostpolitik* and world ecumenism.

So much for pretending Fatima is over and done with. So much for the word-processed "letters of Sister Lucia", proclaiming the very opposite of what she had said in her own handwriting so many times before. So much for creating the illusion that the consecration of Russia has been done and there remains nothing more at stake in the Fatima story. Clearly the stakes are as high as ever. The few bishops who had attended the Conference in Mexico City knew this well.

In reality, it appears as if the Mexico agenda had proven to be the greatest challenge to the Vatican bureaucracy since the Vatican-Moscow Agreement and the Balamand Statement provided the Russian Orthodox hierarchy and the KGB a foolproof impediment to the Consecration of Russia.

§

One of the trademarks of secret societies is that nobody knows where the order comes from. This time, however, an Archbishop had dragged into the light of day in Mexico City the men behind the campaign to silence one lone priest—a priest who in himself could not have caused them the slightest concern, if not for the content of his message.

Within the closeted precincts where appalling agreements have been forged which betray the mission of the Church, there lays an offspring coiled and ready to poison any movement toward fulfillment of the Fatima requests. It was spawned from the illicit union of atheistic Communism and the chaperones of the Bride of Christ. Nothing reveals its character more than the tactics it employed in attempting to derail the Mexico Conference: Intimidation; denial of the freedoms to assemble and to speak openly without fear; humiliation of the rightful heirs of authority; and always the veiled threat of reprisal.

We have seen these tactics before. They are the currency of the Communist State, whose crown jewel is Russia, where the citizens of Poland today take weekend sojourns to obtain their abortions—15 years after the supposed "consecration" of Russia in 1984.

Communism was founded on lies. It was coached by the "father of lies". It lied its way into the Vatican just before the Second Council. And it cannot stop lying.

On a trip to the Pyramid of the Sun during the Conference, so near to one of the greatest victories of Our Lady in history, Her conquest of the hearts of Mexico, a reprise of the Fatima Message was inevitable. It was to Louis XIV, who called himself The Sun King, that Our Lord sent Margaret Mary Alacoque, on June 17, 1689, with the request that France be consecrated to the Sacred Heart, with the promise that He would save France by this means. The Sun King did not fulfill the request. One hundred years later to the day, his grandson, Louis XVI, was stripped of power and France convulsed under the forces that brought about the French Revolution.

Louis XVI studied clocks. His hobby was assembling them. Louis might be called the Time King. The sound of his clockwork ticking in the old Templar Fortress as he awaited his coach ride to the guillotine must surely be one of the most horrifying sounds in history. The ticking clock of history could be heard again when Our Lord said to Sister Lucia at Rianjo that the Ministers of the Church are following the example of the King of France in delaying the execution of Heaven's command, and that "they will also follow him into misfortune."

Watching these brave bishops from around the world contemplate the pyramids with this message in mind, one thought of Bishop Francis Clement Kelley's great work on the conversion of Mexico, *Blood Drenched Altars*, which enshrines the words of Christopher Hollis on the faith of Saint Thomas More:

> "It is the mark of a Christian ... that he possesses the imagination to jump back across a thousand or two thousand years of history. His whole life is lived under an excitement similar to that of the first disciples when they heard the tomb was empty. To him the news is so amazing that he never forgets to be surprised at it. And ... the news, if true, is so important, that it is mere madness to give one's mind to any other business ..."[187]

Today, certain bureaucrats in Rome are telling us that Catholics must apologize for their past, their present, their future. This means apologizing also for the Message of Fatima, because the Message of Fatima tells us that Christ must be King and Mary His Queen. The world will not tolerate this Message today; we must, therefore, stop proclaiming it, and start apologizing for it. That is why the Message of Fatima must be suppressed wherever it might be spoken loudly enough for the world to hear.

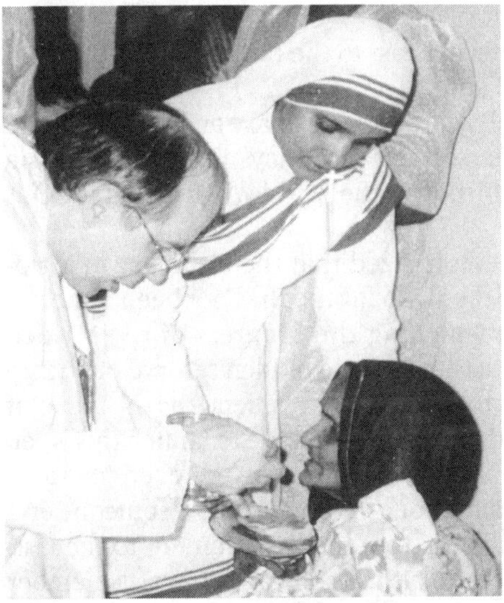

November 1991 - The Sisters of Mother Teresa welcome the Pilgrim Virgin statue into various convents and houses of charity where their great love and devotion is most edifying. Mother Teresa, herself, promised to pray for Father Gruner.

[187] Bishop Francis Clement Kelley, *Blood Drenched Altars*, p. 103.

Chapter 15

Fourteen Fabulous Footsteps Forward to Our Lady

When we opened our eyes in the 20th Century to the horror of war, the war that killed St. Pius X, the war throughout which Benedict XV struggled so hard to keep the Church neutral, we were opening our eyes to the horrors of which man is really capable. Our Lady of Fatima imprinted on our souls the words reparation, consecration, and the word "Russia". Is this consecration done? Is it not done? If it is done or not done, what do we do about it? If the Holy Father in 1984, and on a previous occasion, chose to omit the word "Russia", what does that mean? A Canadian teenager, who wishes to remain anonymous, in a Wednesday evening study class on encyclicals came to a conclusion.

"I have a solution", he said. "In *Quas Primas*, Pius XI reviewed why specific and great devotions had been inaugurated throughout Church history. When Pius XI discussed the Sacred Heart, he said, 'The feast of the burning love of the Sacred Heart was inaugurated to warm men's hearts that had grown cold for lack of love, lack of faith.' And he instituted the Feast of Christ the King and the processional of Christ the King, so that Christ would get the acknowledgement of His Divine Kingship as He deserves."

So this teenager said, "The solution is simple—institute a Feast of the Immaculate Heart."

He had to be told that Pius XII had instituted a Feast to the Immaculate Heart and that Paul VI instituted a Feast to Our Lady of Fatima.

The teenager did not give up. He said, "Well, why don't they make an act of gratitude for all that Our Lady has done for us, every year, on this same day? Consecrate Russia every year on that day. Sooner or later, every bishop in the world will take part as Our Lady wants."

In his fiery address, Archbishop Milingo emphasized that the bishops would co-operate if the Pope made specific demands of them. So far that has not been done.

There could be no doubt, among those watching the progress of the Mexico Conference, that Father Nicholas Gruner has access to some hidden reserve of energy and determination. He, himself, merely refers to his uncanny resiliency as the result of 'undeserved grace'. Knowing the obstacles that had to be overcome to launch this week of bishops' talks, one would have expected him to be sidelined by the need for some peace and quiet, even perhaps to take the first day as one of rest and allow someone else to open that day's sessions. But he was at the helm from the first moment to the last, never at a loss for co-ordinating the interests of the bishops on hand. It was a member of the laity who placed the whole conference in perspective for the average Catholic in pews around the globe.

> "Since Vatican II, the modern Church has been playing down the Message of Fatima," said New York delegate Jean Fioretti. "When I was in school, I had 12 years of Dominican teachers. Every year we heard the Message of Fatima. The Message of Fatima through the '50's was very important. We spent the '50's waiting for the Secret to be opened in 1960. Then it never happened.

"There's been a great loss of faith since then. Catholicism is 'easy' now. People have become, in fact, lazy. We don't hear anything anymore about sacrifice, only about celebration and mercy. Of course, the mercy of God is ever available, but you no longer hear about the penance God asks for to win His mercy.

"My generation was raised to listen to the priest and the nuns, to listen to the Church. After Vatican II we were told we had to 'start thinking for ourselves', as if we hadn't been doing that all along. It became very hard to disregard what the priest was saying.

"Our Church with its modern look is very sterile. They forget that we're human and humans have to have things appeal to their senses—music, flowers, candles. One can pray anywhere but oh, how helpful it is to have the beautiful."

One of the great sources of beauty for the faithful in this century was the whole Fatima story; from beginning to end it had beauty, warmth, love, hope, and it was peopled by characters whose personalities stayed with you all your life.

Regarding the conference, Jean Fioretti remarked: "The first few days, there was a natural reticence—nobody wanted to say too much or make any waves. But all were very receptive to the Fatima focus. It was successful because we don't have these things being said anywhere else in the establishment Church. Being human, we know all these things but we forget them.

"It's so important to know there are others out there who believe as we do. Again, being human, it's a kind of fearful thing to feel so alone. You think, is there something wrong with me? Why am I the only one who still says my Rosary?"

The opportunity to answer that need for the laity worldwide was at hand, front and center of the conference hall. Father Gruner took full advantage of it. It was his skill in drawing upon the best in all the personalities present in the room that allowed this small beleaguered representation of the world's episcopacy to hammer out a veritable catechism of Fatima. Under his chairmanship, the bishops crafted fourteen unique resolutions for the purpose of advancing the cause of Our Lady of Fatima. These Fourteen Resolutions, represent a new treasure for Our Lady, diamonds for Her crown, crystallized under colossal pressure. They read as follows:

The 14 Fatima Resolutions

I/We hereby agree to the Resolutions drafted and agreed to by the bishops, priests and laypeople at the Second Bishops Conference for World Peace held in Mexico City on November 8-14, 1994 as indicated below. I, the undersigned, in my personal capacity, responding to the inspiration of Our Lady of Fatima to work for peace, have read the resolutions that I have signed and agree with each one's doctrinal content and personally undertake to see that the truth contained in each resolution be lived and any undertaking stated therein I shall personally do.

In order to bring about peace and proper ordering of man to God as individuals, in society and in the Church, I hereby make the following resolutions and encourage men and women of good will around the world to join us.

1. We the undersigned individual laypeople, priests, bishops, in our personal capacity, hereby profess our loyalty to the Holy Roman Catholic Magisterium and the august person of His Holiness Pope John Paul II and above all to the Catholic Faith as handed down by the dogmatic councils, tradition, and the approved creeds, not limited to but including the Apostle's Creed, the Nicene Creed, the Athanasian Creed, the Creed of the First Vatican Council and the Credo of the people of God of Pope Paul VI and those doctrines taught Magisterially by the Second Vatican Council.

"Magisterially"—That is, those doctrines that are taught infallibly by the Ordinary and Universal Magisterium of the Church in Vatican II documents.

2. We, as loyal Roman Catholics, as expressed above in resolution number one, also believe that world peace will not be brought about except through obedience to the full meaning and message of Our Lady of Fatima.

3. We undertake to do what we can and we believe it is part of our duty of state to bring about the Triumph of the Immaculate Heart through the specific plans and requests She made to us in the public and prophetic Message of Fatima.

4. It is our duty according to our state to do all we can and tell those we can to thereby make the full message of Our Lady of Fatima known as Jesus Himself has commanded, despite any difficulties.

5. We the undersigned, mindful of Our Lady of Fatima's request, undertake to personally pray the Rosary every day and to strongly promote this devotion to Our Lady, to those around us.

6. We the undersigned, mindful of Our Lady of Fatima's request that we, each of us, wear the Brown Scapular of Mount Carmel, undertake to personally wear the Scapular and to promote the Brown Scapular among the faithful and men of goodwill that God puts on our path.

7. We the undersigned, recognizing that Our Lady of Fatima and God Himself want to establish devotion in the world to the Immaculate Heart of Mary; and further recognizing that Our Lady and Our Lord especially want us to embrace this devotion; we therefore, personally undertake to make the personal act of consecration to Our Lady's Immaculate Heart. We will also promote it to those God puts on our path.

8. Since Jesus and Mary have so ardently desired the practice of the Five First Saturdays and Communions of Reparation to the Immaculate Heart of Mary, we personally undertake to do these Five First Saturdays as requested and explained by Our Lady of Fatima and Jesus Himself. We also undertake to promote the Five First Saturdays to the faithful Catholics God puts on our path.

9. Since Our Lady of Fatima wants the Third Secret to be published to the world, we the undersigned, until it is officially revealed, will endeavor to read, study and distribute knowledge of the Third Secret—from the best sources available.

10. We also respectfully petition for the release of the actual words of Our Lady's Third Secret according to Her instructions.

11. Since Jesus and Mary in the Fatima Message make it clear that it is only by means of the solemn and public Consecration of specifically RUSSIA, RUSSIA to the Immaculate Heart of Mary by all the Catholic bishops together with the Holy Father on the same day at the same hour, that true peace will be given to the world: we the undersigned undertake to bring about the long desired Act of Consecration. Such actions (to cause this Act of Consecration) are not limited to, but may include: Prayers; Rosaries; Sacrifices offered to Jesus and Mary for this intention; to attend seminars, symposiums, conferences; to hold such conferences to promote this Consecration; to circulate books, videos, audio tapes to laypeople, priests and bishops to promote this Consecration.

12. We the undersigned, will strive to make known those prophecies that as far as we can ascertain, contain parts of the Third Secret which are found in Sacred Scripture and in Church approved apparitions, as Cardinal Ratzinger indicated in his interview with Vittorio Messori, published in November 1984 *Jesus* magazine.

13. Inasmuch as God wants all men to be saved and come to the knowledge of the truth, and inasmuch as in an approved apparition of Our Lady of 1838—Our Lady revealed the Green Scapular of the Immaculate Heart of Mary—especially for the preservation among Catholics and the spread of the Catholic Faith to non-Catholics; and inasmuch as God wants to establish devotion to the Immaculate Heart throughout the world; we the undersigned resolve when opportune to propagate as widely as possible among men, women and children of the world, the Green Scapular and encourage others to do the same and to pray the prayer indicated therein for the conversion of all non-Catholics and the preservation of all Catholics in the Catholic Faith which is so necessary in order to save one's soul.

14. That in the light of our desire to please Our Lady, that the Consecration of Russia be renewed on the Feast of the Immaculate Conception—December 8th, each year by the Pope and all the Catholic bishops of the world; we the undersigned, respectfully ask for this Consecration of Russia to be done on the above date.

§

On the final day of the Conference, as its Fourteen Resolutions were printed up and distributed for all to see, there was a trace in the air of music—festive, familiar, a sound the bishops had encountered after leaving the shrine of Guadalupe to climb Tepeyac Hill—a mariachi marimba band, from somewhere within the hotel. The Virgin of Guadalupe, it seemed, was coming to them.

Before the closing of the Conference, Father Gruner was presented with a life-sized crucifix purchased on the Shrine grounds. Looking up into Christ's eyes on this crucifix gave one a small taste of His Agony and Passion: exquisitely painted, not skimping on the Blood as most modern-day artists do; transparent tears fill His eyes and spill down over His cheeks; His eyes conveying an intense plea for our repentance.

The magnificent Crucifix was presented to Father Gruner with few but very meaningful words: "You have carried many crosses, Father; we felt you would not mind one more." Perhaps Father Gruner and the Apostolate had participated in some small way in the Passion of Christ, as all Catholics are called upon to do. When he returned to Canada, Father Gruner had the Crucifix erected in the Fatima Center Chapel, literally cutting a hole in the roof to accommodate its magnificent presence.

Opposition to Our Lady throughout the Church today is formidable; but the Virgin's defenders deflect the blows gladly, because they know the blows are really aimed at Her. Yet always the question remains—how much punishment can a man absorb? Surely after Mexico anyone would decamp and rest. Take a strategic retreat. Yes, Father Gruner and the members of the Apostolate would do that. And when they were rested, then what? Surely not another campaign ...

Chapter 16

Window on the Arena

Rome, July 3, 1995. 6:30 a.m. The Bridge of Angels has carried countless armies across the Tiber over the centuries. They have strolled, strutted and goose-stepped onto the cobblestones before Castel St. Angelo with remarkable frequency, carrying onto the north bank of the river all manner of ferocious determination. But it is doubtful if even one of their number did not sense a dent in his resolve when the ancient street beneath his feet deposited him on the edge of St. Peter's Square. The vision in marble staring back at him represents the most awesome power on earth, the dome of the Fisherman, the incomparable St. Peter's, the earthly intersection of Time and Eternity.

To comprehend the character of Father Nicholas Gruner, one can do no better than to see him, alone, an army of one, stepping off the Bridge of Angels, and contemplating the dome before him. It cannot be said that he too is not intimidated. No one born of woman could resist recognizing his smallness before this treasured dome rising above the very center of all Christendom. The old Borgo that once obliterated the view of the dome from the Bridge of Angels is no longer there. Today the Via Della Conciliazione, designed at Mussolini's request in response to Pius XI signing the Lateran Pact of 1929, gives a clear view of the breathtaking outline of the historical center of Christianity. Bramanti, Michelangelo, Della Porta knew how to intimidate.

Rome has been civilization's center of gravity for so long that, should it cease to exist, civilization would be knocked off its axis. Countless intersecting prophecies of the end times do predict the earth being knocked off its axis. Some interpreters of the Fatima phenomenon read the Miracle of the Sun as a depiction of that coming catastrophe, when order will be restored to the globe through the intercession of the Virgin.

This July morning, the rising sun warms the dome with a golden stroke of the brush. In ancient days, the Romans watched the sun pass overhead on its way to slumbering the night away in Lusitania. Today, the sun watches Romans pass from Christianity back to a long-slumbering paganism. The Church has been knocked off its axis and is rolling crazily out of orbit. Only Christ can save her. When He comes to do so, as He promised He would, He will come from the East, like a flash of sunlight. That is why throughout its history, churches were built facing eastward, for Christ was their hope. Then modern liturgists turned everything around. Now, when Christ returns, the priests will not see Him coming. They will have their backs turned, paying tribute to "the dignity of man"; for according to what can be glimpsed through the modernist theologians' fantasy threshold, man—not God—is the new hope.

The neo-modernist debacle of the past 35 years reminds us of the warning given by Pope Pius XII in light of the Message of Fatima:

> "Suppose, dear friend, that Communism [Russia and Russia's errors, in Fatima terms] was only the most visible of the instruments of subversion to be used against the Church and the traditions of Divine Revelation. *I am worried by the Blessed Virgin's messages to Lucia of Fatima* ... A day will come when the civilized world will deny its God, when the Church will doubt as Peter doubted. She will be tempted to

believe that man has become God."[188]

Father Nicholas Gruner is not shaken at the prospect of being in this city of cities. He lived here during his early seminary days and afterward; he knows the sounds, the smells, the pace of the streets. He knows also that the Church was put in the hands of Italians, among other reasons, because of their unrelenting ability to endure the vicissitudes of time.

This day Father Gruner shares a goodly portion of that patience. He has come to Rome on a mission as bold as any he has ever pursued since the day he first offered himself to Our Lady of Fatima. He moves through the streets as one who knows he has no time to lose. That, of course, is the ultimate reality—there is no time left. Not for the world, not for Rome itself.

Christ promised that when He returned, it would be terrible, with all the power and might of Heaven armed for battle, more terrifying than the sun falling from the sky at the Cova da Iria. Mankind has this escape—the Virgin. Just as at Fatima, when the sun obeyed Her command, the Virgin in the end will bring us to safety. For She and She alone is our threshold to Christ.

All of Father Gruner's efforts over the years in promoting the consecration of Russia had brought to bear on his life and his Apostolate the full weight of the bureaucracy that plans and labors in the offices and corridors and meeting rooms circling the great piazza of St. Peter's. For centuries the famous obelisk now standing in the center of that piazza marked the spot where St. Peter was crucified upside down in A.D. 67 in the area where now stands the sacristy. Then it was moved to center stage of the new St. Peter's landscape, carved out of Vatican Hill in the 16th Century.

Today the obelisk makes of the cobblestone surface of the piazza a great sundial. Upon the rising of the sun, the shadow of the obelisk points directly at the balcony from which the reigning Pontiff has delivered his New Year's blessing *Urbi et Orbi* for the last four hundred years. Atop the obelisk stands a cross which contains a sizable portion of the True Cross brought back from Jerusalem by St. Helena. Each day, the shadow of the True Cross is drawn over the cobblestones by the passing overhead of the sun. Many a penitent pilgrim has deliberately positioned himself motionless in prayer in the piazza where the shadow of the True Cross would roll ever-so-slowly over his legs, arms, shoulders, bowed head.

When the shadow of the True Cross leans exactly north-northwest it points directly at the window of the Papal apartment, known simply as "the Pope's window"—second from the end on the top floor. Each Sunday, the Holy Father stands in full view of the pilgrims gathered below and leads them in the Angelus from that window. The daily shadow on the window reminds us that inside is a man to whom Christ said: "Whatsoever you bind on earth shall be bound in Heaven; whatsoever you loose on earth shall be loosed in Heaven."[189] For, yes, that man is Peter.

If the man behind that window were the only man on earth who could bind and loose, all men who understood the nature of sin would come to this piazza and never again leave it. Alas, in today's Church the true nature of sin is scarcely understood by a large number of its members. Still, the man who resides behind the window remains the earthly head of legions of men to whom Christ, through Holy Orders, extended the same power to bind and loose in the Confessional that He had given to Peter. Father

188 Msgr. Roche, *Pie XII devant l'histoire*, pp. 52-53; also, *Inside the Vatican*, Jan. 1997, pp. 6-7.

189 Matthew 16:19.

Nicholas Gruner is but one of them; but there in the shadow of the obelisk, he is as much at home as any priest who has walked these cobblestones over the centuries, looking up at that window.

During World War II, Pius XII looked out the window at a city in the grip of Nazi rule. On February 11, 1929, Pius XI looked out the window on the anniversary of the first appearance of the Immaculate Conception at Lourdes, toward the Lateran Palace where Mussolini and the Pope's envoy, Cardinal Gaspari, were signing the Lateran Pact which ended the Roman Question, the relationship between the government of Italy and the Holy See, and sixty years of the Pope being a "prisoner of the Vatican". But that piece of paper did not end the phenomenon of the Pope as prisoner.

Many Catholics today [1998] believe that the current Pope is a "prisoner of Vatican II". The commitments made to *Ostpolitik* and world ecumenism by his predecessors and their bureaucrats have trapped him in a never ending round of concession-making to non-Catholic and non-Christian peoples. Catholics may differ in their view of the ecumenical venture of John Paul II, but what is not in dispute is the present-day crisis of faith around the world.

This much was admitted without ambiguity by the Cardinal Prefect of the Holy Office, which is now called the Congregation for the Doctrine of the Faith. In 1985, for the first time in the history of the Church, the man in charge of defending Her doctrine for the Pope published a book explicitly and repeatedly stating that the faith of Catholics is under severe attack and is weakening around the world. *The Ratzinger Report* was published in a number of languages and sold over 1 million copies. No one in the know has refuted Ratzinger's thesis. According to Father Alonso and Frère Michel this crisis of faith is the main subject of the Third Secret of Fatima. It is certain that many Catholics agree that the looming crisis in the Church and the world is the direct result of not fulfilling the precise requirements of Our Lady.

Even so, for Father Nicholas Gruner, there has always been hope that his efforts on Her behalf, however small, will help bring the desperately needed about-face. After all, Our Lord did not say His Church would last until the Age of Aquarius and then be given away by resident aquarians. He said it would last until the end of time.

It was directly below the Pope's window, on May 13, 1981, just a little east of north by northwest, that John Paul II felt Mehmet Ali Agca's bullet tear into his body. That bullet, taken from the abdomen of John Paul II, now rests in the crown of the statue of Our Lady of Fatima standing at the Capelinha in the Cova da Iria on the exact spot She hallowed with Her presence in 1917. What greater verification could the faithful need that the Message of Fatima and the crisis in the Church intersect in time and space?

On July 3, 1995, as Father Nicholas Gruner moves through Rome on a private mission, the shadow of the True Cross on the obelisk in the piazza pointed at the Pope's window:12:30 noon. Father Gruner is very aware on this day that the Congregation for the Clergy in the Vatican, a few paces from the obelisk, has been charged with the duty to uphold the rights of priests against the abuse of ecclesiastical power. And yet an abuse of power had emanated from that very Congregation against him. Not once, but at least six times. What are Diocesan priests to do when it is the bureaucrats in that same Congregation who persecute them? It is in the defense of priests whose rights are not defended, that Father Gruner goes on this mission.

A brisk fifteen minutes' walk from the obelisk, across the Bridge joining Via St. Pius X, down the Corso Vittorio, is the Piazza della Cancelleria. There, the Apostolic

Signatura meets to consider appeals from the Congregation for the Clergy. There Father Gruner had made his appeal from the self-affirming decree of Cardinal Sanchez and Archbishop Sepe. What he did not know on that day in July 1995 was that the Signatura had already implemented the next phase of *The Plan* for his destruction: the punishment for his proclamation of the Heavenly Message which had been "overruled" by the theological negotiators at Balamand.

The decree of the Apostolic Signatura, dated May 15, 1995, would soon be leaked to the anti-Fatima forces. It would appear in *Soul* magazine, the publication of an organization once known as The Blue Army, but which had recently taken to calling itself "The World Apostolate of Fatima", as if to hide its embarrassment over once having been a part of the outdated Church Militant. *Soul*, now duly "approved" by "ecclesiastical authority", had become the mouthpiece of the forces which had produced the Vatican-Moscow Agreement and the sell-out at Balamand. *Soul* was delighted to announce that the Signatura had agreed with Cardinal Sanchez and Archbishop Sepe: there was indeed "just cause" to consign Father Gruner to oblivion in the Diocese of Avellino. He had, after all, "failed" to find another bishop to accept him. No matter that the "failure" had been orchestrated by Cardinal Sanchez and Archbishop Sepe themselves, in an arrogant suspension of proper canonical procedure. *Soul* was not interested in the justice of the matter. The important thing was to declare Father Gruner a non-person, so that the New Fatima, the "Fatima Lite" of the Carlos Evaristo pamphlet, could be peddled to a narcoticized public in place of the real thing.

The decree of the Signatura would not be the end of Father Gruner—not yet. His case would return to the Signatura on new grounds.

And there would be further complications to *The Plan*. Those complications would lead to further canonical appeals which could not be so easily disposed of. It would seem as though Our Lady were politely tripping Father Gruner's pursuers, sending them sprawling to the ground each time they were about to lay hold of their prey.

Long ago, at the crossroads in old Jerusalem where the thoroughfare coming in through the Damascus gate goes toward the marketplace, and intersects with the Via Dolorosa, Our Lord met His Mother. There Mary gave the future priesthood of the Church a gift of Her own will and action to keep them free of doubt for all time. She went up the hill to Calvary with Him. There's only one way for today's priest to know for sure which way to go in today's Church. Stay with Mary. She has no doubts about which way to go. And stay close to those priests who visibly and openly serve Her. Father Gruner was in Rome in Her service.

On the lower floors below the Pope's window, behind the Bronze Doors, lay the Vatican Secretariat of State which had long ago taken notice of the Canadian priest with the worldwide following. This day its power seemed even more overwhelming, because on this day the Pope was out of town. It is always unsettling to know that the Pope is out of town. There is about the papacy a sense that Peter should always be here, where the Church of Christ on Vatican Hill rises from the spot where the blood of Peter soaked the soil of Nero's Circus. The Pontiff will return for the Wednesday General Audience, but his momentary absence prompts the question, "What is a Pontiff?"

"A bridge builder," wrote Anne O'Hare McCormick in her *Vatican Journals*. "For he comes from farther back in time and sees farther into the future than other leaders", at the service of what she calls, "...the only unbroken tradition left in the world."

This bridge builder, John Paul II, knew that he had not yet fulfilled the command to consecrate Russia. On March 25, 1984, after he consecrated the world to the Immaculate Heart, the Holy Father said twice to Our Lady and to thousands of the faithful that, *although* he had consecrated the world, still he had not done what Our Lady of Fatima commanded to be done. This was openly repeated on the 26th of March in the official Vatican newspaper, *L'Osservatore Romano.** It was this fact, more than the injustice of his particular case, which had brought Father Gruner to Rome for the job he had to do.

Not only by personal observation and reflection, but also by reliable reports of the Pope's own words, Father Gruner is convinced that the Pope feels he needs more support from the Catholic bishops of the world before he can actually consecrate Russia as Our Lady asked at Fatima. For this reason, Father Gruner had sought and received confirmations from more than 1500 bishops that they supported Our Lady's command. If the Pope gave the order to consecrate Russia, these bishops would obey, of that Father Gruner was certain. It was the bureaucrats, the technicians of Balamand and the Vatican-Moscow Agreement, who were striving to keep from the bishops the whole truth about Fatima; it was they who had convinced the Holy Father that his bishops would not obey. How does one penetrate this phalanx of bureaucrats to tell the Pope that his bishops will obey him?

Father Gruner reached a print shop within walking distance of the Vatican and made his way to the back rooms where layout and design are finalized. He spread out, before the workers, the text of the letter he had carried to Rome. He had picked them especially for their skill and professionalism, and their ability with languages, for this letter was intended for His Holiness, John Paul II himself. It was not intended for mailing. It would appear as "An Open Letter To The Pope" in a two-page spread in Rome's largest daily newspaper, *Il Messaggero*. And the deadline was fast approaching.

To catapult over the heads of the bureaucracy surrounding the Pope has been a fantasy engaged in by many a priest over the centuries. Few have ever succeeded. Father Nicholas Gruner knew that he must, for he was all too aware that he represented not only the membership in his Apostolate, but the entire beleaguered priesthood of the Catholic Church. The Open Letter would serve not only his mission, but countless priests who were being ground up in the bureaucrats' inexorable machinery of intimidation and reprisal.

Father Gruner was not daunted by the gamble. A priest, he always insists, is within his rights to demand that the law be upheld. So too are the laity. Two ecumenical councils of the Church have indeed defined as a doctrine of the Faith the right to petition the Pope for redress of just grievances in the Church.[190] But how does one exercise this God-given right when the Pope is immured in layers of bureaucracy which filter out the pleas of the faithful? The Open Letter seems the only way.

And so, on a hot July day in Rome, the leverage of the press is about to be employed to plead a case to "the final judge". No one, not even His Holiness, could overlook a request so public, though the format of the appeal was bound to trod on the feet of nearly everyone in the Secretariat of State, the Congregation for the Clergy and the Apostolic Signatura.

Father Gruner's right to do so has never been in doubt. "It is Catholic dogma that

---

* See photographic reproduction of this article on page 290.

190 The Second Council of Lyons (1274 A.D.) teaches, "Anyone who is aggrieved may appeal to it (the Holy Roman Church) in matters pertaining to the ecclesiastical court; and in all cases that require ecclesiastical investigation, one may have recourse to its judgement", Denzinger, thirtieth edition, paragraph 466; also, Vatican Council I (1870 A.D.) says, "And because, by the Divine right of Apostolic primacy the Roman Pontiff is at the head of the whole Church, we also teach and declare that he is the supreme judge of the Faithful and that one can have recourse to his judgement in all cases pertaining to ecclesiastical jurisdiction", Denzinger, thirtieth edition, paragraphs 1830-1831; also, see 1983 Code of Canon Law, Cann. 221; 1405 No. 1.

Catholic priests are members of the hierarchy and our God-given rights in the Natural Law cannot be morally or legally taken away by anyone, not even by a bishop's decree."

Nor would the false "obedience" to ecclesial bureaucrats which had surrendered Romania and the Ukraine to the dictates of the Balamand Statement prevent Father Gruner from petitioning his Pope in this way. He would later explain that his belief in the right, and duty, of licit resistance to abuse of authority in the Church had been formed in him during his days at seminary:

> "A Monsignor doing his doctorate in philosophy talked about how the situation in the Church could be turned around. He explained, 'all it would take is one medium-sized diocese, five pastors or so, to say: "We will not go along. We will not have Communion in the hand. We're going to preach Catholic doctrine." If just *five* of them took a united stand the bishop would find it very hard to touch them. He could move one around, punish him, but *five* of them standing united?' The persecution of five parish priests who are standing up for the Magisterium would be manifested very clearly. If several dioceses did the same thing, there would build a will to resist corruption. But too many priests today make a virtue out of weakness, citing 'obedience', 'humility' and 'docility' as excuses for not standing up for God and His truth. David, in the Scriptures, says: '*be angry* and sin not'. There is a time for holy anger. Anger not for ourselves but for God. If priests realized that, they would stand up and do their duty...
>
> "...Their duty to the common good is greater than the average person's. They are members of the hierarchy and have an obligation to not be silent like dogs, an obligation to speak out and not worry that certain people find it politically incorrect."

Throughout the day Father Gruner comes and goes from the back room, studying proofs, giving them a meticulous scanning. A day is consumed by attention to minuscule details: translating, re-translating, spell-checks, leaving not one punctuation mark to chance. The Open Letter is finally put to bed. It is late evening. Daylight lingers late in the sky over Rome. Time to walk where saints and apostles have walked.

§

St. Paul Outside-the-Walls, Rome. Midnight. For centuries this location defended Rome from attacks from the sea. It perfectly befits, therefore, the site for the massive enclosure named after the Apostle to the Gentiles. In the distinctive Roman moonlight, the hooded statue of St. Paul stares directly at the silhouette of a cassocked priest at the gate. Slivers of moonglow outline the two edges of St. Paul's upright broadsword.

Two thousand years of efforts by dissenters from the True Faith have failed to imprint on men's minds the image of St. Paul as an opponent of Peter's. Other religions have tried to adopt Paul as their very own; Protestant efforts to make him their Peter have consistently come to naught. The unshakable integrity of Saul of Tarsus resists all attempts to paint him as disloyal. When he challenged Peter, it was out of love for the purity of the faith, not in opposition to it.

St. Paul Outside-the-Walls is a fitting place for Father Nicholas Gruner to contemplate his priesthood, his past as a seminarian, his present as a promoter of the Fatima Message, and the future that he will have to endure, now that the 'Open Letter to the Pope' has gone to press. He, too, has had his loyalty to the Pope impugned by his critics. He directs those critics to examine his record. He readily admits that, so long as God permits, there will be one unalterable purpose to his Apostolate—the collegial consecration of

Russia to the Immaculate Heart of Mary. In spite of endless criticism, and the risk of losing his audience, he has continued for two decades his repetition of the words "the consecration of Russia", hoping to keep that divine imperative before the minds of the faithful and the hierarchy.

His choice of approach has been misconstrued as an "attack" on the Holy Father. There are reasons to believe that John Paul II did not see it that way at all. There are reasons to believe that Father Gruner has been surreptitiously targeted by the bureaucracy for extinction *precisely because* the Holy Father harbored sympathy for the work of Father Nicholas Gruner. Father Gruner explained it this way:

> "We are on a collision course, the Apostolate of Our Lady of Fatima and the bureaucracy. Either the Apostolate will back down and cease proclaiming the Fatima Message or the Secretary of State will stop promoting the Vatican-Moscow Agreement and the betrayal at Balamand."

The Vatican-Moscow Agreement and the Balamand Statement have given the most voracious hunter in history an open field in which to pursue the hunted. Men of blood, atheistic power mongers, seek to victimize and control the whole of the world. Abortion, socialism, liquidation of the middle class, God excluded from public affairs, immorality, immodesty.

A new world order with a one world religion is the goal of these internationalists. They are dead of soul, and work to impose their godlessness, their coldness, their emptiness on all of us. In their language, they want to proclaim the world "God-free". What they really want is to tyrannize the rest of us, but as long as we have God, we have our God-given rights. If they succeed in taking faith in God away from us, then they succeed in enslaving us. The number one bastion of defense, the Catholic Church, has suffered insidious attacks by infiltrators, as St. Jude warns in his Epistle. Those interlopers have lowered the drawbridges, drained the moats and left the flock very vulnerable.

Whether the hunter will succeed in capturing and killing all but a remnant of the prey will, of course, depend finally upon the correspondence of the man in the pew with the graces he is given. In any other century but this one, perhaps, that might have been a reliable ingredient in the equation. But the man in the pew is no longer encouraged to be Roman Catholic. He is being told that he must apologize for 2,000 years of Catholic history, learn to have more respect for Martin Luther, forget his liturgical heritage, assume personal responsibility for the holocausts of madmen, and stop speaking of conversion to the one true religion. That he is expected to continue to believe in and remain loyal to a Church which could have insisted upon such disastrous reversals as these, surely ranks as one of the great enigmas in recorded time.

As Sister Lucia said: "The devil is in the mood for engaging in a decisive battle against the Virgin. And a decisive battle is the final battle where one side will be victorious and the other side will suffer defeat." Each man must choose sides. If he chooses the side of God, his weapons have already been issued to him. The Rosary. The Scapular of Mt. Carmel. Daily sacrifices. The Five First Saturdays. But the climate in today's Church is not conducive to the promotion of devotions such as these. Some Cardinals, bishops, priests shun anything that smacks of pre-1960 piety. That the Rosary, daily sacrifices and the Five First Saturdays are uniquely Roman Catholic practices makes them totally unwelcome in certain quarters of the Church. In today's ecumenical Disney park, anything goes as long as it is not Roman Catholic.

Bureaucratic anger at the placing of the ad in *Il Messaggero* would be ignited because it had provided John Paul II with an opportunity to intervene and settle one of the most contentious battles raging in the Church today. And therein lies the cause of so much of the bureaucratic opposition to Father Nicholas Gruner: such a show of authority by John Paul II would cure, at one stroke, the ecclesiastical paralysis resulting from the fatally flawed principle of collegiality operating through bureaucracy.

Retaliation for the printing of the Open Letter will surely be aimed hot and heavy at Father Gruner by the unseen bureaucrats in the Vatican. They will go as far as they can, as long as they don't risk losing their anonymity.

"In the end, Our Lady will triumph," Father Nicholas Gruner repeats again and again. "But enough people must be on the right side. If you are not on Jesus and Mary's side, you are on the side of the Evil One and his earthly allies."

Down along the embankment from the grilled entrance to the courtyard of St. Paul Outside-the-Walls, several cars of midnight revelers enjoy the late night and one another's company. As Father Gruner walks back to his car, eyes pick up his cassocked figure walking through the moonlight. For a brief moment he stands motionless, an icon of the besieged priesthood of Our Lady in today's tormented Church. The cassock bridges the centuries linking together those countless men who have exhausted their lives in the order of Melchisedech. He is just one in the long line of those who undertook untold risks to serve their Master, and spread His precious Word.

Saint Isaac Jogues, a veritable mirror reflecting the daring character of St. Paul himself, gave his life for the baptism of native Americans. Nothing could deter him from returning to his Indians again and again, even though they despised him so much that he was made to curl up and sleep with their dogs. Even while Father Jogues was in North America, it was known throughout Europe that his Indian captors had chewed his fingers off. They would chew down to one knuckle, let it heal, then chew down to another. Rescued by Protestant Dutch merchants, he made his way back to France. Upon being received in the foyer of his former Jesuit residence, he was bundled up against the cold, arms held tight under cover for warmth. Upon hearing that a missionary had returned from America and was in the foyer, the Superior came running into the room and cried aloud asking if the stranger had any news to relate about Isaac Jogues. Father Jogues did not answer. He merely unfolded his arms and extended toward the Superior the stumps of his fingers. The Superior fell on his knees, kissing the mangled hands, and showered the priest with his tears. Shortly after, Father Jogues returned to his Indians and to his martyrdom.

There is no happiness in today's world for the priests of Mary. She did not promise them any. Bitten off little by little each day in this era of the "dignity of man" is the dignity of God's ordained. Nowhere in today's world can the Marian priest be sure of a welcome. Not even in the Church they serve. That is all part of the "persecution of the Church" that was spoken of at Fatima in 1917. No one who truly understands the Fatima Message should be surprised at it. Persecution from within would not have occurred to anyone before 1960. But after the last thirty-five years of turmoil, lies and betrayal, no one any longer looks exclusively outside the Church for the enemy.

From St. Paul Outside-the-Walls to St. Cecilia's in Trastevere is a short drive that leads through the ruins left behind when the Church of Christ conquered pagan Rome. Outside the gate of St. Cecilia's, the sounds of Trastevere remind the tourist that there is a Left Bank in every city that has a "soul". How perfect that the great Saint who was martyred here should be the Church's patron of music.

Here in this church is where it really all began for Father Nicholas Gruner. It was here that his father, Malcolm, was instantly converted to Catholicism so many decades ago, and it was here that St. Cecilia was sealed inside a steam room to suffocate, or so the persecutors of the faithful virgin hoped. When the door was unsealed to ascertain her fate, there she sat, breathing freely, a mystery memorialized by artists who so often place a calliope in her hands. So she was beheaded. But she survived the first two strokes of the axe, living for two days during which she dictated her spiritual and legal legacy. Then she died. Sculptors depict her prone, offering her throat to the blade yet one more time.

For nearly six years, Father Gruner had survived the steam room in which the bureaucrats had placed him. Now that the Open Letter was about to be published, the question remained: Would he be able to survive the axe blade the anti-Fatima bureaucrats were sharpening in the Vatican?

1968: Nicholas Gruner (left with a beard) kneels for Padre Pio's blessing. Padre Pio, at 81, is pushed in a wheelchair towards his room as he greets the pilgrims. While he worked nearby, Nicholas resided for seven months in San Giovanni Rotondo to be near Padre Pio and to receive the help of his powerful prayers and counsel.

1980 - Father Gruner holding the Rosary blessed by His Holiness, Pope John Paul II, personally given to him inside the Vatican by the Pope's secretary, Father John Magee, in February 1980. This picture appeared in the *Catholic Register*, the Canadian Catholic paper.

Chapter 17

The Letter

On the morning of July 12, 1995, readers in Italy of *Il Messaggero*, the largest daily in Rome, are stunned to open their newspaper and see:

OPEN LETTER TO POPE JOHN PAUL II
and to all Catholics and to all peace-loving men

Most Holy Father . . .

One year ago, planning began for a great Conference of Catholic bishops to be held in November 1994 in Mexico City, Mexico. The purpose of this Conference was to privately bring together our Church leaders to discuss the Message of Our Lady of Fatima and its unique Heaven-ordained role in the search for peace in our troubled world. As Our Lady said at Fatima, "If My requests are granted, many souls will be saved and there will be peace."

As organizers of this Conference, we were guided first and foremost by the teachings of our Holy Mother, the Church, especially those contained in documents of the Second Vatican Council pertaining to the rights and obligations of the laity. As Your Holiness knows, the Dogmatic Constitution on the Church enjoins the faithful to "disclose their needs and desires" to their pastors and states that "by reason of the knowledge, competence or pre-eminence which they have, the laity are empowered—indeed sometimes obliged—to manifest their opinion on those things which pertain to the good of the Church." (*Lumen Gentium* IV.37; see also the New Code of Canon Law, 212.)

Your Own Advice, Holy Father

Moreover, in all our planning, Holiness, we were constantly mindful of the advice you yourself had offered in the presence of Cardinal Wyszynski in 1980 that those seeking the fulfillment of Our Lady's Fatima requests (especially the Consecration of Russia as a condition of world peace) should go to the bishops first and seek their support and assistance. From 1983 to 1993 we have written all the Catholic bishops numerous times about this matter; as well, we called and met with a number of bishops, particularly at our first Bishops Conference at Fatima in 1992.

As a result of all these efforts we have obtained the support of 700 Catholic bishops from every part of the world for the consecration of specifically Russia to the Immaculate Heart of Mary. But still it seemed we had not done enough.

And so, in the spring and early summer of 1994, in a pious and humble spirit, we wrote again to all the bishops of the world and invited them to come together in a private setting near the Shrine of Our Lady of Guadalupe in Mexico to openly and freely discuss the Message of Fatima. Through the generosity of many thousands of faithful souls committed to the goals of this Conference, we were also able to offer the bishops the full financial assistance they needed to travel and stay in Mexico.

Your Holiness should know that, prior to sending this invitation, we had consulted in person with His Excellency, Bishop Ramon Godinez-Flores, Secretary-General of the Mexican Conference of Bishops, and informed him of our intentions. In May 1994, Bishop Flores gave his enthusiastic approval to the Conference and went so far as to offer us the rental of the Mexican bishops' own official headquarters as a site for the Conference. We gladly accepted and provided His Excellency with an immediate deposit for the facility.

The Bishops Respond Enthusiastically!

Over the course of the next few months, we received many cordial replies from bishops around the world, indicating their intention to attend the Conference and warmly commending the notion of such an event. It is clear that the bishops have both an obligation and a right to know (as completely as possible) the full Message of Fatima, and they rejoiced at the opportunity. From the early and enthusiastic responses we received, we estimated that as many as 300 bishops would attend the Conference, representing close to *10 percent* of the entire Catholic Episcopate worldwide! A tremendous accomplishment considering the private nature of the gathering and the logistical and travel difficulties involved.

It was at this time, Holy Father, that we began to receive disturbing reports of letters and phone calls being made by some few bureaucrats of the Holy See to various bishops and nuncios in a direct effort to discourage and even forbid participation in our Conference. At first, we could hardly believe these reports, not understanding why Vatican bureaucrats would or could object to a private gathering of Catholic bishops and priests whose *only* purpose was to freely discuss the plan for peace that God's Mother gave the world at Fatima!

A Campaign of Deception and Lies

Sadly, upon further investigation and with the assistance of sympathetic bishops, we discovered that indeed such letters had been sent from a few Vatican bureaucrats to chancelleries around the world. Incredibly, at a time when you yourself were forcefully speaking out publicly on the need for peace, these letters from your own subordinates suggested that our Conference was somehow inappropriate or out-of-order. To make matters worse, these letters contained outright lies and egregious libels concerning the prime organizer of the gathering, Father Nicholas Gruner. With no regard for the truth, Father Gruner's status as a priest-in-good-standing was called into serious question as well as his proven loyalty and dedication to Your Holiness' person and high office.

These unfounded charges and outrageous accusations were especially painful in the face of Father Gruner's long and tireless efforts (even at the expense of his own health) on behalf of Our Lady and Her Fatima Message. In the last 20 years, despite constant opposition from radical modernists and anti-Marian forces within the Church, he has succeeded in creating one of the largest lay Apostolates in the world, bringing together nearly 500,000 individuals in a community of prayer and sacrifice dedicated to promoting the full and complete Message of Fatima. Through magazines, radio and television programs and in public appearances in many countries, Father Gruner has brought the Mother of God's Fatima words to tens of millions of souls around the world ... and all in perfect accordance with the teaching and traditions of the Holy Magisterium. Father Nicholas Gruner's current status as priest-in-good-standing is unquestionable and dramatically verified by the testimonial you yourself issued on February 1, 1993, honoring his 16 years of priestly service and personally congratulating him on his work for Our Lady of Fatima.

No Word of Warning or Protest

Your Holiness, it is an understatement to say that we were dumbfounded when we first read the outrageous statement contained in these "official" letters. The Conference had been public news for many months, yet in all that time not a single Church official had even once contacted us with objections. More than 4,000 formal invitations had been sent to bishops, including yourself, and not a single word of protest had been received from any ecclesiastical authority. Now, only weeks before the Conference was due to commence, we found ourselves fighting against unseen enemies spreading false information and outright lies.

Despite our best efforts to counter this campaign of deception and lies by providing the true facts of the case, many bishops felt obliged to withdraw their support of the Conference out of fear and simple confusion. It soon became plainly obvious to us that spreading just this kind of dissension and confusion amongst the bishops was the underlying intention of this campaign in the first place! Adding insult to injury, not long before the event, we received a letter from Bishop Flores canceling our agreement for accommodation and withdrawing his official sanction. His Excellency cited comments made by an official of the Secretariat of State as being responsible for his decision.

Holy Father, we are sure you will understand that we were deeply discouraged and disheartened by these events. We debated long and hard whether we should move, postpone or cancel the Conference outright. In the end, we turned to Our Lord and Our Lady in prayer and, confident of Their guidance and protection, chose to continue our plans as originally announced. Even though time was critically short, by God's Grace, we were successful in obtaining (albeit at considerable financial cost) new meeting facilities and sleeping accommodations for the bishops. Through His Mercy, we were also able to overcome the last-minute legal and political impediments that Bishop Flores had engineered through the Mexican government (in clear violation of both God's law and civil law) to prevent the issuance of travel visas to bishops who wished to attend our Conference. Blessed be God. Blessed be His Holy Name!

The Conference is Held!

On November 8, 1994, "the Conference on World Peace and the Immaculate Heart of Mary" was formally convened in Mexico City in the presence of bishops from every continent in the world as well as honored guests and members of the Catholic and secular press.

Over the next week, in a series of plenary sessions that were extraordinary for their seriousness and piety, the participants freely and openly discussed Our Lady's Fatima Message and its special role in the Church's effort to bring peace to our nations, to our families and to the world.

Your Holiness, while the number of bishops in attendance was far short of our original expectations, we were nevertheless deeply gratified that those who did attend represented a so diverse and honored cross-section of the Episcopacy. In prelates like Archbishop Accogli, Archbishop Capucci and Archbishop Milingo, we truly witnessed men who were worthy and noble successors to the Apostles themselves! We will forever be thankful for the courage and dedication that they and their colleagues showed in attending our Conference.

In the end, despite the sinister machinations of Our Lady's enemies, the assembled delegates came together to produce an historic document that we believe represents a new treasure for the Church. Consisting of 14 Resolutions, this document reaffirms Our Lady of Fatima's crucial role in the process towards true peace and in the mystery of our salvation itself.

Archbishop Milingo Accuses the Bureaucrats!

Holy Father, it was left to a member of your own sacred Curia to deliver the most dramatic address of the Conference. Archbishop Emmanuel Milingo, formerly Ordinary of Lusaka and now Special Delegate of the Pontifical Council for the Pastoral Care of Migrants and Itinerants, rose and delivered an electrifying condemnation of those who had attempted to prevent this gathering of bishops from occurring.

Speaking to his fellow bishops and to the entire Catholic world, His Excellency deplored the efforts of a few Vatican bureaucrats to suspend the lawful authority of the Episcopacy and prevent the bishops from carrying out their duties and fulfilling their responsibilities. Holding a copy of the letter that had been sent to the bishops of Nigeria, Archbishop Milingo stated:

"What a pity! It is a humiliation to a human being, who is an apostle, a humiliation—intended to prevent him from fulfilling his duties according to his own personality and character ... It is sad. It is humiliating. It lowers the dignity of a human being to have a letter like this going around that actually prevents someone from coming to a conference for Our Lady. ... If this letter represents their way to control us, it means that they don't trust the people to whom they have given authority."

Archbishop Milingo concluded his address by forcefully encouraging all those who truly believe in peace to persevere in our efforts to bring the *full* Fatima Message to the faithful and to the world. As His Excellency said, "I think we can go very, very far if we can make each and every one of our Catholics concerned with the whole welfare of the world." And, indeed, it is just in that spirit of Christian charity and with utmost respect and humility that we are publishing this Open Letter.

Holy Father, World Peace is in Your Hands!

The Blessed Mother of God came to Fatima to give the world the way to achieve true and lasting peace. She entrusted the means to this end to the Church, through you, the Vicar of Christ, in union with the bishops of the world. It has now been 78 years since Our Lady first appeared at Fatima. In that time, we have witnessed millions of lives destroyed through violence and war. Today, we continue to watch as millions of children are murdered in their own mothers' wombs and tens of thousands of more lives are lost each year in bloody conflicts around the globe. The Queen of Peace has offered us an end to this tragic cycle of death and misery *if* we will but obey Her requests for prayer, reparation and consecration.

Your Holiness, we intend to continue to do our part to encourage all Catholics and others of good will to place their trust in the Sacred and Immaculate Hearts of Jesus and Mary. With all respect and love, we also intend to continue our efforts to bring Our Lady's *full* Fatima Message to the Church, particularly to you and your fellow bishops. Our campaign for the Consecration of Russia to the Immaculate Heart (as commanded at Fatima) will continue unimpeded. We and the other 5,000,000 souls who have signed petitions to you asking for this act to be accomplished (and the millions more who await it) shall not be frightened or intimidated into silence by mere bureaucrats in pursuit of a private agenda.

The history of our Holy Church and the lives of our holy saints teaches us that we must resist evil from wherever it arises. Our hearts remain indissolubly united with yours, Holy Father, but we fear that you are being deceived and misled by those in whom you have placed your trust. The facts we have presented in this Open Letter combined with private information from Episcopal sources lead us inevitably to the conclusion that a small handful of Vatican bureaucrats are *deliberately* and *maliciously* withholding information from you and acting without proper authority in your august name. We respectfully urge you to take this opportunity to investigate the actions of those officials who—in clear violation of Canon Law and the Constitution of the Church—attempted to sabotage our recent Conference and blacken the name of a pious and humble priest who has sacrificed so greatly for the sake of Our Lady and the glory of Holy Mother Church.

We Appeal to You, Holy Father!

Your Holiness, at the time of our first Bishops' Conference in Fatima in 1992, we were appalled by the manifestly unjust statements made by certain Vatican bureaucrats who opposed the gathering. Nevertheless, we held our tongues, hoping and praying for Christian charity to prevail. We fully expected that, following the event, the magnitude of their error would be so obvious that these officials would publish an immediate retraction. At worst, we assumed that these illegal and unjust efforts to prevent us from promoting the Fatima Message would stop.

Now, following the events described in this Open Letter, it is manifestly clear that our patience and silence was taken by these individuals as a license for even more bold and unjust action against our attempts to bring Our Lady's Message to the bishops and to the world. After the bitter experiences of the last two Conferences, it now seems undeniable that there exists a small group of Vatican officials who have become so confident of their unbridled power that they will use *any* means (including lies, slander and libel) to silence anyone promoting the *full* Fatima Message. Thus, Holy Father, we are obliged to appeal to you directly in this public letter, trusting as always in your probity and fairness.

A New Conference is Announced!

At the Mexico City Conference in November, we were encouraged by the bishops and others in attendance to undertake yet another meeting of bishops to discuss the Message of Fatima and its role in the peace of the world. Several bishops specifically urged us to hold this next conference in Rome under your protection and guidance.

Lest we be accused of planning in secret or not seeking proper authorization, we here and now—in this public forum—announce that we shall yet for a 3RD time invite every bishop in the world (whether friend or foe of Fatima) to join together in Rome for a Conference on Peace and the Immaculate Heart of Mary, dates and times to be announced by formal letter and publication.

Holy Father, we pray that you will bestow your Papal Blessing on this meeting and, if possible, attend one or more of its sessions. No Pope has ever spoken as movingly as you have of the urgent need for peace nor given so much respect to the Message of Fatima. We believe it is therefore most fitting and proper that your name come first in the list of those in support of this historic event.

Submitted in all respect and love to Your Holiness and in the names of Our Lord and Savior, Jesus Christ and His Blessed Mother, Mary.

§

The Open Letter was signed by an archbishop, a bishop, many priests and religious as well as more than 9,000 lay supporters.

Spread across two full pages of the largest daily in Rome, the ad was a calm and articulate presentation to His Holiness John Paul II of everything that Father Gruner and the members of the Apostolate had yearned to say to their Pope over the past three years. The Open Letter was both a plea and chronicle: In tones both reverent and frank, a plea for the Collegial Consecration, and a chronicle of the systematic abuse of power by the anti-Fatima forces in the Vatican bureaucracy, who had acted as if they thought themselves above reproach and beyond the strictures of Canon Law.

Avoiding harsh polemics, while according the bureaucrats in question the dignity of anonymity, the Open Letter had vaulted the concerns of the 9,000 faithful Catholics who had signed it over a phalanx of papal advisors and into the full view of His Holiness.

Opponents of the Apostolate would call it a "scandal", but the careful reader could see that the signatories of the Open Letter believed they were expressing true loyalty to the Pope in this, the Age of Fatima. They had launched a respectful but fearless entreaty to the Vicar of Christ—precisely because he *is* the Vicar of Christ—to bring about the triumph of the Immaculate Heart of Mary, and with it world peace and the Reign of Christ the King, by the means entrusted exclusively to the Pope at Fatima. Not the peace of an earthly Utopia, but the Reign of Christ the King, and Mary His Queen Mother. Not the grotesque accommodation of an ecumenical brotherhood between the adherents of contradictory and warring creeds, but the unity of *one Lord, one Faith, one Baptism* in a Catholic social order embracing the globe. The very globe beneath Our Lady's feet, as depicted in the Miraculous Medal whose design She Herself had specified in Her apparition to St. Catherine Labouré.

Yes, the signers of the Open Letter had advocated triumphalism, pure and simple. For triumph is the destiny of Christ from all Eternity, and the mission of His Holy Catholic Church is to secure that Triumph and nothing less than that Triumph, or we should be unfaithful to His unalterable commission: "Make disciples *of all nations*, baptizing them in the name of the Father, the Son and the Holy Ghost; teaching them to observe all things whatsoever I have commanded you." *All things whatsoever*, including the necessity of joining the one true Church; and the necessity, too, of the Catholic Church obeying the Message of Fatima which "imposes an *obligation* on the Church" as the Holy Father himself had declared at Fatima on May 13, 1982.

In a Church which had been seething with open heresy and scandal for the past 35 years, the bureaucrats' global campaign against a cassock-wearing Marian priest from small-town Canada had been without precedent. Fittingly, so was this response by the thousands of rank-and-file Catholics who had supported Father Gruner's work over the years. To be sure, since the issuance of *Humanae Vitae* dissidents of all stripes had resorted to the forums of public opinion, even open letters in newspapers, to vent their splenetic fury against some detested article of the Faith. But never had loyal Catholics so clearly in awe of the power of the papacy ever ventured to approach the Holy Father in this way: "Our hearts remain indissolubly united with yours, Holy Father, but we fear that you are being deceived and misled by those in whom you have placed your trust." The Open Letter was an act of love, born of necessity. There was nothing else to do.

§

"No comment" was the Vatican's official reaction to the two-page "Open Letter" to the Pope which appeared in Rome's largest daily paper *Il Messaggero* on July 12, 1995. The ad, entitled an Open Letter to His Holiness, Pope John Paul II, was paid for by the free-will offerings of nearly 10,000 Catholics from around the world.

The Italian news media, including the major news agencies, devoted extensive coverage to the Open Letter after it appeared in Rome. The Venice-based *Il Gazzettino* spoke slightingly of "hardened traditionalists who do not realize that Russia has changed" and erroneously noted that "it is not the first time that Catholic groups from America buy full pages of European papers to publicize ideas and initiatives." *L'Indipendente* described the ad as an "awkward form of correspondence," whereas Milan's *Il Giorno* report called it "articulate" and an "unusual initiative from which the Vatican distances itself by saying 'there is nothing to say'." This was followed, several days later, by a full-page interview with the papal advisor and Fatima expert, the Slovak bishop Pavao Maria Hnilica, who described the Open Letter as "undoubtedly significant" since it was published by a Marian movement that is "widespread throughout the world."

There would soon be a talk show, the staple of Italian television, revolving around the "Open Letter". In the crossfire of the participants, Father Rene Laurentin would finally be forced to admit, despite everything he had said before, that the Collegial Consecration of Russia requested by Our Lady of Fatima had never actually been done in the manner requested.[191]

Completely overlooked by the media was the appearance of another (this time, anonymous) ad in *Il Giornale* on July 14, headlined "July 13, 1917: Third Meeting with Our Lady". July 13 is the anniversary of the third apparition of Fatima, a date scarcely noted by the media in their coverage of the Open Letter's publication. This anniversary coincided with one of the most horrific events in the ongoing Balkan conflict: the fall of Sbrenicia. The ensuing massacres, rapes and mass displacements featured prominently on the front pages of all the newspapers, were a terrible (if unconscious) reminder of the great chastisement of war that forms so integral a part of the Fatima Message.

At offices of *Il Messaggero* itself, which curiously ran no story about the Open Letter, the phones rang incessantly the day after publication, until they were taken off the hook. It was reported that more than one of the callers was a furious Vatican bureaucrat demanding to know how this could have happened. One can well imagine the commotion in the Vatican offices of those who had devoted their ecclesiastical careers to such "triumphs" as the Vatican-Moscow Agreement and the surrender at Balamand. Above all else, the Open Letter was a reminder that Heaven has ordained that real, lasting peace will never come through negotiations with the powers of the world. It will come through the Mother of God, mediating to men the non-negotiable and irresistible *fiat* of Christ the King.

The Mother of God does not lie. It is *only* through Her that Russia will be converted—*converted*—and peace granted to the world. The Open Letter had pleaded with the Pope and the world to address what is manifest: that the Consecration has not been done. Certainly the errors of Russia have spread across the planet. No one with eyes to see could genuinely claim that those errors have undergone a contraction since the putative consecration of 1984. Rather, they have only deepened and intensified, finding new and more evil ramifications by the day. Unless the Holy Father commands all the bishops of the world to join him in the act of consecration, the errors of Russia will most certainly enslave the world.

Hence the Open Letter, whatever the consequences it might bring to Father Gruner and the Apostolate.

§

St. Peter's Square, evening: Father Gruner responds to a request to bless a rosary.

---

191 Father Laurentin made this statement on the Italian television talk show "FORMAT-MISTERI," after Paolo Apolito challenged him on the topic; Giovanni Minoli, director; Lorenza Roschini, interviewer; Autumn 1995.

It is for a grandmother who is a "fervent Catholic". The young California woman holding the rosary out to be blessed is well spoken, beautifully respectful and totally self-composed. She volunteers that she herself is not a Catholic. She listens courteously and with genuine interest as Father Gruner commences with ease to instruct her and her companion. She could have had no way of knowing that the priest leading her into considerations of the Faith is arguably the most controversial priest in the Church today.

Father Nicholas Gruner has been at the center of one controversy or another his entire priestly life. But he has never claimed to be anything other than a priest promoting the Message of Our Lady of Fatima. As such, he has attracted the animosity, envy, and hatred of his adversaries, plus the regular censorship of those "Untouchables" in the Catholic Press who feign righteous horror at his tactics. What he is and what he does is known worldwide. Yet there is about his priesthood an aspect that draws intense fire from those who would like to see his traditional style of priesthood vanish.

In conjunction with the Open Letter, Father Gruner brought 40,000 petitions from Catholics around the world, in addition to the hundreds of thousands of petitions he had already delivered. All of the petitions pleaded with the Holy Father to consecrate Russia according to the exact specifications of the Virgin—pleaded with His Holiness because it is manifest that something is wrong. In the nine years which followed the apparition of Our Lady of Guadalupe, nine million souls, an entire nation, climbed out of the abyss of pagan idolatry and human sacrifice and into the sanctuaries of Catholic churches, baptized and converted. But now [in 1998] it is 14 years since the putative consecration of Russia in 1984—in which the bishops had not participated and only the world, not Russia, had been mentioned. In those 14 years, the most optimistic reports indicated around one hundred thousand conversions in a nation of two hundred and fifty million people, including the Ukraine.

Indeed, the conversion of Russia had incredibly, been *forbidden* by the Vatican bureaucrats whose capitulation at Balamand would bar as "outdated" the return of the Russian Orthodox to the Holy Catholic Church.

Having been forbidden to convert, Russia had become even more corrupted by her errors, while the world had continued its ever-accelerating descent down that declivity whose terminus is Hell. None of this could have come to pass if Our Lady's Message had been fulfilled. For Our Lady does not lie. Her designs of peace had been thwarted by men.

The size of the constituency represented in the Open Letter is staggering for those who have not followed the Apostolate's ups and downs. But would that constituency and the Apostolate remain intact during the events of the coming year, as the conference in Rome approached and the bureaucratic thrusts aimed at the heart of Father Gruner's priesthood seemed near to striking the mark? Perhaps the answer would lie in the decree of yet another benevolent prelate who would come forward in the cause of Our Lady of Fatima.

Chapter 18

End Game

"Remember, O Most Gracious Virgin Mary, that never was it known that anyone who implored Thy help or sought Thy intercession was left unaided."

Some four months after publication of the Open Letter, Father Nicholas Gruner knew that he had not been left unaided by Her to Whom he had devoted his entire priesthood. On November 4, 1995, His Excellency Saminini Arulappa, the Archbishop of Hyderabad, India, handed Father Gruner a formal decree incardinating him into his Archdiocese.[192] The two men were standing in St. Mary's Church. It was the First Saturday of the month. And not ten feet away was the Apostolate's Pilgrim Virgin statue, blessed by Pope Paul VI, of which Father Gruner had been the curator for nearly 20 years of travels in the cause of Our Lady of Fatima.

It was, appropriately, a Marian pilgrimage which had brought Father Gruner on this day to the teeming precincts of Hyderabad and St. Mary's Church. Over the years Father Gruner had made several pilgrimages to India, where hundreds of thousands of the Indian faithful had gathered to see the statue, to receive rosaries and scapulars and to hear Father Gruner preach in his quiet way on the Message of Fatima.

In Hyderabad, the Apostolate supports an orphanage which has the care of fifty [in 1998] little souls. The welfare of these children is one of the many things at stake in the canonical struggle which began when the bureaucrats pulled the strings of their marionette, and the Bishop of Avellino suddenly recalled Father Gruner after an approved absence of more than 16 years.

The Plan for Father Gruner's virtual imprisonment in Avellino had depended, of course, entirely on the pretense that since Father Gruner had "failed" to find another diocese to accept him, he must return to the Diocese of Avellino. Yet here was the *third* benevolent bishop in succession to offer Father Gruner incardination outside Avellino. The bureaucrats had "persuaded" the first two bishops to withdraw their offers easily enough; the Nuncios had done their job of back-channel influence. This time, however, no less than an Archbishop of 25 years standing had gone so far as to issue a formal decree of incardination to Father Gruner, on the record, before the bureaucrats had been able to get to him.

But the Archbishop had done more than simply incardinate Father Gruner in his Archdiocese. With the full authority of his office, the prelate had extended his protection to the whole Apostolate and had condemned the bureaucrats who were trying to destroy it:

> "I grant you all the faculties you need for continuing your God-given mission on earth. *Evil forces have conspired to destroy your work of love*. But you go ahead trusting in the Lord. His love is steadfast and He will never fail, though you may be subject to many a trial and even persecution ... *Bureaucratic forces cannot stifle God's work*. It is my prayer that you continue in your God-given mission in spite of great opposition."[193]

The Archbishop's decree was a canonical bombshell. At the very moment their

---

192 Christopher A. Ferrara, Esq, *Archbishop Shows: "There is a Conspiracy Against This Priest"*, "The Fatima Crusader", Issue 54, Winter 1997, pp. 73-74.

193 Ibid, pp. 74-75.

carefully prepared circumvention of the Code of Canon Law had nearly succeeded in neutralizing its target, the Archbishop had rescued him with the stroke of a pen. To make matters worse, the Archbishop had just provided objective confirmation in an official ecclesiastical document that "bureaucratic forces" were engaging in illicit maneuvers against Father Gruner.

The Plan was at a standstill. Father Gruner could not very well be ordered back to Avellino for having "failed" to find another bishop, when an Archbishop had just incardinated him with a formal decree the bureaucrats would not be able to countermand. They had absolutely no power under the Code of Canon Law, much less the Divine Constitution of the Church, to dictate an Archbishop's decision about whom he could incardinate in his own Archdiocese; and they knew it. But they did have one tool at their disposal: fear.

The unexpected visit of a Papal Nuncio can intimidate even an Archbishop. When the clasps on a nuncial briefcase snap open, it would only be natural to cringe in apprehension over what might be inside. Sometime in January 1996 the Papal Nuncio to India, Archbishop Zur Giorgio, got aboard an airplane and flew from Delhi to Hyderabad—a most unusual expenditure of time and money for a Vatican ambassador with many pressing duties of state. The Nuncio's only purpose in making this extraordinary trip was to meet with Archbishop Arulappa concerning Father Nicholas Gruner. This was a most urgent meeting—so urgent it could not even wait for the Archbishop to recover from the heart surgery he had just undergone. When the meeting was over, the Archbishop had begun to view the matter of Father Gruner's incardination somewhat differently. He was afraid. And who could blame him? He had not seen behind the curtain of the Wizard of Oz.

On January 31, 1996, Father Gruner received a letter from the Archbishop: Did Father Gruner have a decree of "excardination" from the Diocese of Avellino, releasing him from the jurisdiction of its bishop?[194] This was indeed a technical requirement for the transfer. But as Providence would have it, the Bishop of Avellino had issued just such a decree to Father Gruner in 1989, before the bureaucrats began tugging on the strings of his more compliant successor. Father Gruner still had the document in his files. He had the decree of excardination hand delivered to Hyderabad. The technical requirements were complete. He was now a priest of the Archdiocese of Hyderabad—or at least he was according to the Code of Canon Law. For any other priest in the world, the matter would have ended there. But for Father Nicholas Gruner the Code of Canon Law was no longer operative, it had been suspended in his case.

The Open Letter to the Pope and the benevolent intervention of the Archbishop of Hyderabad had shown the hunters that their prey was not without resources. Father Gruner would not simply lie down and die. Something was keeping this priest on his feet and moving forward. The prey, then, would simply have to be crushed to death, rather less elegantly than anticipated, by the vast apparatus at their command. Of course, this would require further actions outside the normal channels of canon law, but *The Plan* could not otherwise be fulfilled. The law of the Church would not serve the hunters, so it would have to be discarded. Nevertheless, the appearance of following the law would be maintained as the "front end" of their operation. They must maintain their *bella figura*.

What followed over the next six months was a coordinated international campaign

---

194 January 10, 1996 letter from Archbishop Arulappa is filed with Father Gruner's personal records.

of punitive actions the like of which no priest in living memory had ever been subjected to—including the heretics and homosexuals who contentedly infest seminaries and parishes of North America without the slightest disturbance from Rome.

January 1996. The Papal Nuncios carry a new "declaration" from Archbishop Sepe, Secretary of the Congregation for the Clergy, to every bishop in the world. It concerns the Apostolate's upcoming Fatima Conference in Rome, which had been announced in the Open Letter. Sepe's decree is an incredible travesty of canon law: the interdiction throughout the entire Catholic Church of a priest who had done nothing wrong:

> *"The Gruner case has a long history and consequently there are volumes of dossiers in the archives of this Congregation."*

What exactly was "the Gruner case"? And what was contained in the "volumes of dossiers" at the Congregation for the Clergy? Sepe does not say. Better to create the false impression that there must be *something* pretty terrible in those records.

> *"Also this conference [in Rome] includes plans for a number of activities which the Reverend Gruner has developed without any ecclesiastical permission ..."*

What "ecclesiastical permission" is needed to hold a conference on Fatima? None, of course, but Sepe does not mention this. The Literally Truthful Lie is launched around the world again. In a Church teeming with conferences and workshops—none of them with "ecclesiastical permission", and many conducted by fulminating heretics—only one gathering consumes the attention of Archbishop Sepe and his fellow Vatican bureaucrats: a conference in Rome devoted to the Message of Fatima.

> *"So that this priest might not continue his harmful activities, the Bishop of Avellino, on January 31, 1994, called upon him to return to the diocese within one month."*

What "harmful activities" was Father Gruner guilty of? Archbishop Sepe has no particulars to offer. And neither did the Bishop of Avellino in his order recalling Father Gruner—the very order Archbishop Sepe himself had orchestrated by blocking Father Gruner's incardination in any other diocese but Avellino.

> "At this point in time there is nothing to do but to ask ... the bishops of your country not to accept the invitation of Father Gruner, and to avoid doing anything in this regrettable situation to make matters worse."[195]

Why exactly is the situation "regrettable"? What would happen to any bishop who made "matters worse" by showing support for Father Gruner? Better to leave that threat *sub rosa*. End of letter.

What had Father Nicholas Gruner actually *done* to merit this unprecedented communication to every Catholic bishop in the world? Even a cursory reading of Archbishop Sepe's letter would reveal the answer: *nothing*. That is, nothing which the Archbishop could safely mention. For it simply would not do to admit that the "harmful activity" in which Father Gruner had been engaged for his entire priestly life was nothing more or less than teaching and preaching the Heaven-sent Message of Fatima—especially its now-intolerable claim that Russia must be *consecrated* to the Immaculate Heart and converted to the one true religion, so that the world would be saved from Russia's errors.

January 26, 1996. The Bishop of Avellino issues an "admonition" to Father Gruner that he must return there because "idle had been the various written interventions of

---

[195] Quoted from the letter of Archbishop Carlo Curis, Apostolic Pro-Nuncio of Canada, Protocol No. 8007/95, taken from original letter from Archbishop Sepe.

my predecessors ... with which you were invited to look for another bishop."[196] Father Gruner sends two letters in February, pointing out that he has been incardinated in the Archdiocese of Hyderabad, has therefore *found* another bishop, and is no longer bound to return to Avellino. The bishop offers no reply. He is clearly awaiting further orders about what to say regarding Hyderabad.

February 1996. A copy of the decree of the Apostolic Signatura upholding the first order to return to Avellino is published in *Soul* magazine, organ of the "World Apostolate of Fatima"—the new "Fatima Lite" version of the once-militant Blue Army, which now has direct ties to the Vatican anti-Fatima bureaucrats. Oddly enough, Father Gruner himself had not yet received a copy of the decree, although the "World Apostolate of Fatima" has obtained it from the Canadian Bishops' Conference. The decree is accompanied by a libelous error-filled "exposé" by E. William Sockey III, which portrays Father Gruner as a disobedient, schismatic cleric without priestly faculties.[197] In the same month, a local affiliate of the "World Apostolate of Fatima" publishes the same decree, but includes a fabricated paragraph condemning Father Gruner which is nowhere to be found in the original document.[198]

March 1996. The bureaucrats attack the Hyderabad problem: Archbishop Arulappa receives a letter from Cardinal Sanchez advising him not to incardinate Father Gruner, even though he has already done so. The letter mysteriously lacks a protocol number which would place it in numerical sequence with the official documents of the Congregation[199] —evidently because it is *unofficial* and quite outside the proper channels of canon law. Cardinal Sanchez has absolutely no authority to forbid an Archbishop to incardinate a validly ordained priest. He does so anyway. Who will stop him? Three months later the beleaguered Archbishop would write to Father Gruner: "I request you to understand my predicament in the present circumstances. I do hope, God willing, a satisfactory solution will be found."[200] He would also disclose through his assistant that he had been placed in fear of reprisals against his whole Archdiocese because of his support of Father Gruner.[201] Still, the Archbishop would never actually withdraw the decree of incardination. There would have to be grounds to do so, and a hearing at which Father Gruner could present a defense.

§

By mid-spring of 1996, with the Rome Conference only six months away, the bureaucrats were ready to implement the final phase of *The Plan*. It commenced on May 16, 1996. On that date the Bishop of Avellino issued a further decree advising Father Gruner that unless he returned to the Diocese of Avellino in 29 days he would be suspended from the sacred priesthood.[202] The decree claimed that the matter had been decided the day before at a "hearing" to which Father Gruner had not been invited. Actually, it had been decided years before in the offices of certain Vatican bureaucrats.

Yes, but what about Father Gruner's incardination in the Archdiocese of Hyderabad? Did it not place him beyond the jurisdiction of the Bishop of Avellino? The May 16 decree

196 The January 26, 1996 statement from the Bishop of Avellino to Father Gruner is filed with Father Gruner's personal records.

197 *Soul* magazine, Vol. 47, No. 1.

198 Father Zweber of the local chapter of St. Paul, Minneapolis, Blue Army newsletter.

199 Christopher A. Ferrara, Esq, op. cit., p. 75.

200 The letter of Archbishop Arulappa to Father Gruner is filed with Father Gruner's personal records.

201 Christopher A. Ferrara, Esq, op. cit., p. 76.

202 Ibid.

revealed the stratagem on which the bureaucrats had settled to deal with that particular problem: the incardination in Hyderabad was declared *tanquam non existens*—it was non-existent! Poof.

But on what basis had the incardination in Hyderabad been declared non-existent? According to the May 16 decree, Father Gruner was not "canonically set free" to be incardinated there. And why was he not "canonically set free"? Because he had been ordered to return to Avellino. But why had he been ordered to return to Avellino? Because he had not found another bishop. But was not the Archbishop of Hyderabad another bishop? Yes, but his incardination of Father Gruner was non-existent. The classic circular argument. Crude. Ridiculous. But it would do until something better came along. The main thing was to achieve, at last, the objective of *The Plan*: the exile or defrocking of Father Nicholas Gruner, preacher of the unacceptable Message of Fatima.

Father Gruner would appeal the preposterous decree of May 16 to the Congregation for the Clergy. There, once again, Cardinal Sanchez and Archbishop Sepe, his executioners, would also be his judges. This time, however, Father Gruner would request their recusal. Perhaps even they would recognize the absurdity, if not the injustice, of sitting as judges in a case they had been stage-managing behind the scenes for years. To Father Gruner's request for recusal, the judges had a ready reply: "The request for disqualification cannot be taken into consideration because it is not foreseen in the legislation."[203] In other words, Father Gruner had no right to an impartial judge! But the right to an impartial judge is foreseen in "the legislation", namely, Canon 1449. Also, natural law, common sense and basic decency all dictate that a man cannot judge a case in which he is an adverse party. But Canon 1449, natural law, common sense and basic decency were impediments to *The Plan*. The bureaucrats simply heaved them overboard.

On September 20, 1996, with the Rome Conference two months away, Cardinal Sanchez and Archbishop Sepe upheld the May 16 decree of the Bishop of Avellino. That is, they upheld their own manipulation of the marionette whose strings they had been pulling since at least January 1994.

The End Game was now down to a few rooks and pawns on the board, and the pieces left were heavily weighted in favor of his opponents. The remaining moves seemed few, and too easily calculable for the other side, but Father Gruner would force them to make every move until checkmate. He would do so not out of any perverse stubbornness, but for the cause of Our Lady of Fatima, and because it was not in his nature to allow the truth to be subjugated to the crooked rules of a rigged game. He would later explain:

> "If it were merely the question of my own personal ruin, there might be no need for such resistance. But they are not interested in ruining me for its own sake. What they really seek is to silence a message they do not want to hear, and do not want others to hear: the Message of Fatima in all of its political incorrectness. The suppression of *the truth*, that is the only reason they are interested in silencing me. In the entire record of the so-called 'Father Gruner case' referred to by Archbishop Sepe in his letter to every bishop in the world, you will find nothing which states exactly what it is I am supposed to have done to justify actions against me which not even the worst heretics in the Church today are subjected to. How can they mention that it is the truth which so offends them? It is the truth which is at stake. And so I must resist, with all the means the law of the Church gives to me."

---

203 The Sept. 20, 1996 decree of the Congregation for the Clergy, signed by Archbishop Sepe and Cardinal Sanchez, Protocol No. 96002499, p. 11.

On November 15, 1996, the very day he boarded the plane for Rome, Father Gruner would appeal the Congregation's decision to the Apostolic Signatura. Not even the bureaucrats could do anything to alter the basic norm of Canon Law, that the appeal prevented the operation of all threatened penalties. Thus, there would be no suspension from the priesthood, nor any obligation to return to Avellino. When he arrived in Rome to address the Apostolate's Third Fatima Conference, Father Nicholas Gruner would be, as he had always been, a priest in good standing.

And when he arrived he would have with him a document as unprecedented as the illicit global campaign against him by the bureaucrats, yet a document expressly authorized by the Code of Canon Law Pope John Paul II himself had promulgated. That document, together with the appeal to the Signatura, would bring new complications to the End Game, prolonging it in ways his opponents had never anticipated.

§

November 18, 1996. Rome. The Apostolate's Third Fatima Conference begins. Across Piazza Euclide from the hotel where the Conference is being held is an impressive parish church in the Greco-Roman style. On its curved stone facade is an inscription in Latin: *In Honorem Immaculati Cordis B. V. Mariae Reginae Pacis*—"In Honor of the Immaculate Heart of Mary, Queen of Peace." At a conference entitled "World Peace and the Immaculate Heart of Mary", the inscription is one of those signposts on the byways of Providence which encourage a weary traveler.

By now the bureaucrats' strange preoccupation with the Canadian priest and his Marian apostolate had become almost laughable. Ten months earlier the Nuncios had delivered the urgent missive of Archbishop Sepe to every bishop in the world, stating that the Conference was "without permission of ecclesiastical authority." A week before the Conference began the Nuncios delivered yet another priority bulletin to the entire world episcopate. This one was from Cardinal Gantin, Prefect of the Congregation for the Bishops, who conveyed the alarming news that:

> "Father Gruner has convened the Third International Conference on 'World Peace and the Immaculate Heart of Mary' to be held in Rome 18-23 November 1996; it is absolutely without approval of ecclesiastical authority."

The Literally Truthful Lie had been given added emphasis in the latest communiqué: the Conference was *absolutely* without the "approval of ecclesiastical authority". Since it was *absolutely* without approval, no bishop should go to Rome to discuss World Peace and the Immaculate Heart of Mary. But since no ecclesiastical approval was required in the first place, why *exactly* should the bishops stay away? Why, because of Father Gruner's "situation" and "activities", the communiqué suggested. *What* "situation", and *what* "activities"?

The bureaucrats had already seen what happens to bishops who are provided with the full Message of Fatima: *they listen*. And once they listen, they tend to become supporters of the Apostolate's work in making known to all the faithful the urgent nature of the Message in its entirety, despite the negative implications of that Message for the grand human scheme embraced by the Vatican-Moscow Agreement, *Ostpolitik* and the Balamand Statement.

At the 1992 Conference in Fatima 60 bishops had politely insisted that the Bishop of Fatima give his approval to the conference. After Father Gruner was assaulted in the sacristy of the Fatima Shrine by thugs in the employ of its rector, two prelates who had attended the Conference vowed to petition the Pope for the retirement of the Bishop of Fatima, who had clearly lost control of the Shrine. Three months later the Bishop of Fatima was retired. Had the Apostolate been heard, with sympathy, by the Pope?

At the Mexico conference in 1994, the assembled bishops had drafted and approved 14 Resolutions which constitute a veritable charter for promulgation of the Fatima Message in its entirety, including the Consecration of Russia and disclosure of the Third Secret. The Resolutions were a statement of uncompromising Catholic militancy in an era of ecclesial accommodation and retreat. These 14 Resolutions were published in Rome on July 12, 1995, as part of the Open Letter to the Pope. Had not the Holy Father become aware of the consensus of these bishops?

By autumn of 1996 the bureaucrats could not have failed to notice that the Conferences and related activities of the Apostolate had marshaled the support of some 1400 bishops, about 33% of the total world episcopate, for the collegial Consecration of Russia. The Conference in Rome could not be interdicted by any *legitimate* means, because nothing about it was doctrinally, canonically or morally objectionable—nor could the bureaucrats credibly claim otherwise. But it would not do to have an end run of bishops, priests and laity around the Vatican-Moscow Agreement, *Ostpolitik* and the Balamand Statement, which the bureaucrats evidently considered better policies than the words of the Queen of Heaven. Thus, the Third Bishops' Conference obviously loomed large in the bureaucratic radar: the full Message of Fatima was going to be discussed again. *With bishops*. Once again, therefore, measures had to be taken.

As with the Mexico conference, the nuncial apparatus had managed to block the issuance of visas to many of the bishops who had committed to being in Rome. But, as in Mexico, a few determined prelates avoided diplomatic confinement and made their way to the Conference. One of these was His Excellency Benedict To Varpin, Archbishop of Madang, Papua New Guinea. He had made the journey despite a seemingly endless series of phone calls, faxes and letters from the Nuncio pressuring him not to go.[204] On the ride from Leonardo da Vinci Airport to Piazza Euclide, Archbishop To Varpin explained that he had seen enough carnage among the warring factions of his own island nation to recognize that the promises of Our Lady of Fatima could not possibly have been fulfilled. He had come to Rome to find out why. Over the next few days he would know the answer.

And so they came for a third time: bishops, priests and laity from around the world. A modest group, really, but large enough to cause the mobilization of a worldwide apparatus against the gathering. Most curious. Or rather not so curious when one considered that the list of topics to be covered by the speakers at the Conference read like an Index of Forbidden Subjects in the Church today:

> "Heaven's Request for the Consecration of Russia to the Immaculate Heart"
>
> "The Fatima Message Imposes an Obligation on the Church"
>
> "The Third Secret of Fatima and the War Against the Church"
>
> "Has Russia Been Converted?"
>
> "The World As It Will Look Under the Reign of Mary"
>
> "Outside the Church there is No Salvation"
>
> "The Plot to Silence Our Lady"
>
> "Divine Impatience"

204 Archbishop Benedict To Varpin, *Welcome to Fatima 2000*, "The Fatima Crusader", Issue 54, Winter 1997, p. 32.

"The Five First Saturdays"

"How to Avoid Hell and Shorten Purgatory"

"The New Paganism and Globalism versus the Principles of a Catholic Nation"

"One World Church Expected Next Year"

"The Perestroika Deception"

Throughout the world today conferences, congresses and "workshops" devoted to undermining the Holy Catholic Church convene and spread their errors with impunity: women priests, the end of priestly celibacy, the 'coming out' of homosexual clergy, changes in the teaching on marriage and procreation, celebration of the 'gay and lesbian communities', inclusive language, goddess worship, Wicca, popular election of the Pope, use of polls and petitions to determine Catholic doctrine—the heresies and absurdities freely discussed, diffused and demanded are uncountable.

This unprecedented situation in the Church suggested a thought-experiment to more than one of those who had come to Piazza Euclide that week in November: Suppose they had gathered, not to discuss the Message of Fatima, but to revel at yet another festival of heretics. What would the world's Nuncios have done to stop them? The results of the experiment registered almost instantly in the mind: Why, the Nuncios would have done nothing! For there would have been no communiqués from the Vatican Congregations to deliver to every bishop in the world; nor would the Nuncios have been ordered to engage in the arduous work of denying travel visas to descendants of the Apostles. The slumber of the bureaucrats in the face of ecclesial chaos would have continued serenely.

Since 1965 [at least until 1997 when this book was first published] exactly *one* Catholic has been excommunicated by the Vatican for heresy: an obscure and laughably clumsy "theologian" in Sri Lanka. The *subtle* heretics, who pose the real threat to the faith, have remained ensconced in seminaries and universities throughout the Church. Meanwhile, at a bookstore only a few paces from the perimeter of Vatican City, one can purchase theological texts propounding any number of propositions that were once condemned. Adoring crowds wave to the Pope on his various motorcades, but when they go home they ignore his teaching on contraception or divorce and remarriage. The pollsters who interview papal fans when the outdoor Masses in the football stadiums are over, find that most of them "disagree" with the Pope on other matters of the Faith as well.

In the 33 years since the Bronze Doors closed on Vatican II the clamor of dissent from both clergy and laity has become the baseline; a constant "white noise" like static on a television set when a station has gone off the air. As anyone who has fallen asleep with that noise in the background would know, it is a very soothing noise to sleep by. Today it would seem that only a confluence of the zealously orthodox is capable of producing a sound to rise above the static and waken a bureaucrat or two in the Vatican. For a *zealous* orthodoxy is not content to attribute the crisis in the Church merely to Original Sin, and to inquire no further. Those who love their Church with a fierce love will tend to ask questions about what has gone wrong; and those questions will invariably lead them to Fatima, and then to Rome.

The clergy and laity assembling at Piazza Euclide had come, therefore, to ponder embarrassing questions: *Why* had the Church descended into this fugue state of chaos? *Why*, eighty years after the Virgin appeared at Cova da Iria, had the promises of Our Lady of Fatima not been realized? Why had those promises instead been allowed by the sacred pastors to recede beyond the memory of nearly everyone, while the world succumbed to an ever-expanding holocaust of the unborn and a violent disintegration of nations which the Church seems powerless to arrest—no matter how many papal trips are made to the areas of distress.

There was something else these Catholics had come to Rome to consider; a matter which caused perhaps the greatest agitation among the bureaucrats who had tried to keep the bishops from attending:

Some forty years earlier the auxiliary bishop of Fatima held a sealed envelope up to the light and tried to discern the writing inside. He counted 25 handwritten lines on a piece of paper which he could not read: the Third Secret of Fatima. Those 25 lines had been written by Sister Lucia after three months of being terrified to commit them to paper. Only after January 2, 1944, when the Virgin had appeared again to tell her that it was Heaven's will, was Sister Lucia finally able to write the Secret down and deliver it in a sealed envelope to the Bishop of Fatima.

The Third Secret was to have been revealed to the world not later than 1960. Sister Lucia had explained that by then the meaning of the Secret "would be more clear." The Secret was delivered to the Vatican under seal in April 1957, and the faithful of the world waited. In February 1960, Pope John XXIII, having read the Secret, caused worldwide dismay by announcing through an anonymous press release, which no one took responsibility for, that the Secret would not be released that year and possibly not ever. Pope Paul VI, Pope John Paul II and Pope Benedict XVI have since read the Secret, along with several other current members of the hierarchy, but none of them has divulged its contents.*

By those who have read the Secret we have been told, in turns, that it is not sensational, and that is sensational; that it is not apocalyptic, and that it concerns what is already revealed in the Book of the Apocalypse; that it does not predict a world catastrophe, and that it predicts the sudden loss of millions of lives. The one thing we have not been told—as we have in the case of every other Marian warning of the past century, no matter how dire—is what the Third Secret actually *says*.

It is a common perception among Catholics that the world began to come apart in earnest around 1960. It is the year that seems in retrospect to mark a great divide beyond which the exhausted remnants of Christendom lost their remaining power to restrain evil, and all that had been unthinkable quickly became commonplace. The year before, Pope John had convened his Council with the promise that it would mark the opening of the Church to the "modern world". He illustrated his intention in a famous incident: a reporter had asked what His Holiness hoped to accomplish at the Council, whereupon the Pontiff strode across the room and threw open a window. Yes, that musty old Catholic Church needed some fresh air.

On June 30, 1972, thirteen years after Pope John opened his window, Pope Paul VI would lament that "from somewhere or other the smoke of Satan has entered the Church."[205] Pope Paul too had read the Third Secret. He would die wearing a hair shirt, it is said, having wept over the establishment of an abortion mill in Rome. Like the others who have read the Secret, Pope Paul would not disclose its contents; but who could doubt that his terrifying and wholly unprecedented remark about the state of

* **Editor's Note:** In the year 2000 (on June 26), they revealed what they claimed was the whole Third Secret—but, in fact, it was not. This is explained in great detail in the books *The Secret Still Hidden* (published in 2008) and *The Devil's Final Battle* (2nd edition, 2010).

205 Pope Paul VI, discourse of June 29, 1972; also Frère François de Marie des Anges, *Fatima: Tragedy and Triumph*, p. 273.

the Church reflected something in those 25 lines in the handwriting of Sister Lucia. Sister Lucia had said that the meaning of the Secret would be clearer in 1960. Many Catholics who attended the Conference, and millions more around the world, had long suspected that they knew why: *Because the Secret predicted an unprecedented debacle in the Catholic Church beginning around that year.*

In the decades before the Council a line of Pope Pius had warned us of the shoals ahead which threatened the barque of Peter. After 1960 every one of those warnings would be forgotten:

- In his encyclical *Quanta Cura* and his *Syllabus of the Errors of the Modern World,* Pius IX had condemned the modern notion of "religious liberty" as a right proper to every man and essential to a just society. After the Council that very notion would be embraced by much of the Vatican hierarchy.
- In *Pascendi,* Pius X condemned modernism as "the synthesis of all heresies", prescribing the Oath Against Modernism for all priests and theologians. After the Council, the Oath was abandoned and modernists took key positions throughout the Church.
- In *Mortalium animos,* Pius XI condemned the fledgling "ecumenical movement" as a threat to the very foundations of the Catholic faith, and forbade any Catholic participation in it. After the Council, many Vatican bureaucrats would embrace the ecumenical movement.
- In *Mediator Dei,* Pius XII condemned the innovators who sought to revise drastically and render in the vernacular, the "august Sacrifice of the Mass." After the Council, the ancient Latin liturgy of the Roman Rite was abandoned overnight in favor of an unprecedented new rite of Mass—entirely in the vernacular.
- In his Christmas message for 1957 Pius XII had repeated the constant teaching of the Church that "dialogue" with Communism is impossible because it does not share a common language with Christianity, and he maintained the excommunication for any Catholic voting for or joining the Communist Party. In 1962 Cardinal Tisserant dialogued with Communist prelate Nikodim of the Orthodox Church, a KGB agent, and committed the Catholic Church to the Vatican-Moscow Agreement, promising that at the upcoming Council there would be no denunciation of Communism. After the Council began, Pope John XXIII, in *Pacem in Terris,* suggested that one could be a member of the Communist *movement* as an evolving historical phenomenon without necessarily embracing condemned principles.

While none of these reversals of Church policy compromised directly the Deposit of the Faith or negated the charism of papal infallibility, never had the constant judgement of so many popes in so many matters been in practice so completely reversed. *Every reversal occurred within a few years of 1960.*

If the Third Secret of Fatima does indeed speak to the post-Conciliar period—to the unprecedented destruction of the Roman liturgy, the universal collapse of Church discipline, the pandemic of dissent, the softening of the Church's obdurate opposition to Communism—then its disclosure would be nothing less than the unsealing of a heavenly indictment of the governance of the Church since Vatican II. That indictment would implicate some of the very bureaucrats who had tried to interdict the Conference. It would condemn what had been wrought by the architects of the Vatican-Moscow Agreement, *Ostpolitik*, and Balamand who still walked the corridors of the Vatican. Those implicated in the indictment would naturally do everything in their power to prevent it from being unsealed.

Here, then, lies the beating heart of the bureaucrats' constant opposition to the work of Father Nicholas Gruner; for nothing else about this mild-mannered priest could explain the concentration of forces against him. The heart of the matter is simply this: *To view the crisis in the Church from the perspective of Fatima is inevitably to realize that the crisis is a failure of the upper hierarchy.*[206] To stand in the Cova da Iria and look toward Rome in 1996 is to see that the premonition of Pius XII, spoken at the edge of that great divide of 1960, was a true prophecy:

> "I am worried by the Blessed Virgin's messages to Lucia of Fatima ... A day will come when the civilized world will deny its God, *when the Church will doubt as Peter doubted*. She will be tempted to believe that man has become God."[207]

November 20, 1996. Paul VI Audience Hall. If one walks down the Via Aurelia, along the south wall of Vatican City, one will see something quite startling jutting above the wall: a huge concrete shell with a drooping roof line, and set in its wall a great squashed ovoid of a window, the modern notion of a clerestory, its concrete muntins describing counterpoised ripples which meet in the center and cancel out. You will have found Nervi's Paul VI Audience Hall, a Vatican tribute to that great age of architectural renewal: the Sixties.

The participants in the Conference would go to the audience hall on this day to see their Pope. Once they were inside they would be appalled; because the place is indeed appalling. The vast sterile space is oriented *downward* toward the stage on which the Vicar of Christ appears for his Wednesday general audience. The holder of the Keys to the Kingdom of Heaven will be looking up at the spectators as they look down upon him. The enormous expanse of concrete floor is studded with thousands of steel pedestals on which thousands of small, armless seats are perched like mushrooms. Beneath each seat is something very curious: a metal drain grate. Is the Papal audience hall *hosed* clean?

After the hall was completed in 1971 papal audiences would no longer be held in St. Peter's Basilica. The audience hall of the Vicar of Christ in this post-conciliar era is devoid of any sign of the Catholic Faith. It is a sparsely furnished living room for a conversation with the world, designed neither to offend nor to awe any non-Catholic guest.

And then there is The Thing. At the rear of the audience hall's enormous stage, spanning most of its great width, sits a mass of twisted shards of metal, resembling a giant thorn bush; and in the midst of the thorn bush, the huge figure of an emaciated man, limbs and torso grotesquely attenuated, hair gathered in an undulating rope which streams off to its left, as if the figure were being sucked into a vacuum located offstage. The Thing is horrifying. The Thing is Pericle Fazzini's "Resurrection of Christ."

Soon the Pope will enter from stage right, sit in front of this embarrassing monstrosity, and deliver his weekly audience talk. But first the prelates who have come to see the Pope will be given seats on the stage. Among them are two attending the Conference

---

206 Amerio, *Iota Unum*, Sarto House, Kansas City, Missouri (1996), p. 6. First published in Italy, 1985.

207 Msgr. Roche, *Pie XII devant l'histoire*, pp. 52-55; also, *Inside the Vatican*, January 1997, p. 7.

at Piazza Euclide: Archbishop To Varpin and Bishop José Alfonso Ribeiro.

The Pope arrives on the stage, and it is clear that the Holy Father is terribly ill. He shuffles when he walks, and his posture is severely stooped. His face shows little expression. His limbs appear rigid, so much so that he must fall backward into the papal chair. His left hand trembles uncontrollably, and his speech is slurred. One can barely make out the words of his brief address. The Vatican has ceased denying that the Pope has Parkinson's disease, and indeed the standard medical description of the progress of the disease is a description of the man on the stage:

> The disease begins with a 4-to-8-hz 'pill rolling tremor' of one hand. The tremor is maximal at rest ... The hands, arms and legs usually are most affected, in that order. Progressive rigidity, slowness and poverty of movement and difficulty in initiating movement follow ... The face becomes mask-like and open-mouthed, with diminished blinking ... The posture becomes stooped ... Patients find it difficult to start walking; the gait becomes shuffling with short steps, and the arms are held flexed to the waist and fail to swing with the stride ... [*Merck Manual,* 16th Edition, p. 1496]

Throughout 1996 the Pope had seemed to be moving in his audience addresses toward an infallible definition of Mary as Mediatrix of All Graces and Co-redemptrix. In audience address after audience address the Holy Father had been explaining the virtues of Mary, as if to instruct the faithful in preparation for a definitive pronouncement on Her role in the economy of salvation. The preparation would have to be extensive indeed, for the infallible definition of this Marian dogma might trigger a storm of protest from the forces of world ecumenism which would make the worldwide dissent from *Humanae Vitae* seem like papal allegiance by comparison.

Were the Pope to proclaim that Mary is Mediatrix and Co-redemptrix he would remind the world that the Catholic Church is different in *essence*, not merely in appearance, from any other organization on earth which calls itself a church. No human institution could possess such countercultural audacity. Ironically, he would also be bringing to a screeching halt the very "ecumenical venture" to which he had wedded his pontificate.

But such surprises are not uncommon in the history of the Church, given the influence of the Holy Spirit on her course. The world was surprised and outraged when Pope Paul VI, acting against his own advisors, affirmed the constant teaching of the Magisterium against the contraceptive act. Similar outrage greeted Pius IX's *Syllabus of Errors*, written by the once-liberal pontiff after he had been driven from the Quirinal palace in 1848 by Mazzini's Masonic army, fleeing for his life in disguise after his personal secretary had been shot to death. Through such surprises does the Holy Spirit govern the Church in times of gravest crisis.

There were no doubt bureaucrats in the Pope's retinue of advisors who vigorously opposed the Marian definition: "Holy Father, it would not be opportune. The consequences for ecumenism would be disastrous. We urge you to wait, Holy Father." Many of those who were attending the conference, including Father Gruner himself, could well envision the same advice being given by the same advisors regarding the Collegial Consecration of Russia. On May 18, 1936, Sister Lucia related to Father José Bernardo Gonçalves, S.J., her spiritual advisor, an intimate conversation with Our Lord in which He had said: "Pray very much for the Holy Father. He will do it (the Collegial Consecration of Russia) but it will be late." On November 20, 1996, in the Paul VI Audience Hall, it was very late indeed, yet still not too late.

Were the Pope to proclaim this Marian dogma infallibly he would surely roll back many of the gains of the post-conciliar revolutionaries. But if he were to insist upon the Consecration of Russia as well, he would annihilate the Revolution completely and bring on the Reign of Mary, as She had promised at Fatima on the authority of Her Divine Son. He would put to an end the dark time prophesied by Pius XII and likely also predicted in the Third Secret; the time when "the Church herself would doubt as Peter had doubted." The consecration of Russia was the fervent hope of those who had come to Rome for the Third International Fatima Conference; it was their prayer for an ailing Pope.

The papal audience moved toward its conclusion, with various groups, including some Texas Baptists, leaping to their feet and waving, singing or whooping when their names were read from a list of attendees. In an age when the Pope is viewed as a celebrity, rather than the anointed Vicar of the King of the Universe, papal audiences had come to resemble high school pep rallies. But then, what would one expect to see in a place that resembled nothing so much as an outsized high school auditorium?

As the audience concluded, however, something happened which reminded the spectators at the pep rally, for a moment at least, of that ancient unity of divine worship which had been destroyed by the post-conciliar "reforms": the Our Father was prayed in Latin. Many in the vast crowd still remembered, and the majestic words rose up into the hall and toward Heaven: *advéniat regnum tuum: fiat voluntas tua, sicut in caelo, et in terra.*[208] There would be no Hail Mary, lest the Protestants in the audience be offended, but for that moment there was *Catholic* worship in the unity of Faith. There was also a sense of loss for what had been toppled over and shattered by the violent winds blowing into the Church through Pope John's open window.

The members of the Conference had come to see their Pope, but they had come to do something else. They had come to exercise a God-given right, infallibly defined as such by two Ecumenical Councils: the right of the faithful to petition the Supreme Pontiff for redress of just grievances in the Church.

At the end of the audience a line of prelates and disabled people moved past the Pope on the stage to receive his personal greeting. When Archbishop To Varpin and Bishop Ribeiro reached the Pope they each handed him a document. (See appendix in Volume II of this book.) A companion document was handed to the Pope by Joseph Cain, a worker for the Apostolate who was pushing Ed Reczak, a disabled lay member of the Conference confined to a wheelchair.

The document the Pope had just received was specifically authorized by Canons 1389 and 1405 of the 1983 Code of Canon Law, promulgated by John Paul II himself. The document was a *libellus*, a canonical lawsuit. The defendants were Cardinal Sanchez, Archbishop Sepe and all those who had collaborated with them in the attempted destruction of Father Nicholas Gruner and the Apostolate. The plaintiffs were Father Gruner and several lay directors of the Apostolate, who had devoted their lives to its work.

The *libellus* set forth in painstaking detail the proof of what Canon 1389, enacted by their Pope, was designed to punish: the abuse of ecclesiastical power by high-ranking prelates in the Church. It detailed the illicit execution of *The Plan*; the unprecedented interference with the rights and jurisdiction of the benevolent bishops who had wished to incardinate Father Gruner or attend the Fatima Conferences; the outrageous attempt to interdict throughout the entire Church a Marian priest, and a Marian apostolate of

---

208 Thy Kingdom come, Thy Will be done on earth, as it is in Heaven.

faithful clergy and laity, who had done nothing wrong. And, finally, the *libellus* pleaded for relief from all the actions of those who had abused the authority of their high ecclesiastical offices to crush that priest and that Apostolate, while heresy and scandal run riot in the Church.

Under Canon 1405 this case was reserved exclusively to the Roman Pontiff. Only Pope John Paul II could hear it. And now the Pontiff had received the case from the hands of an Archbishop, a bishop and a humble young man pushing a wheelchair. The case was before the First See; there would be no biased judges passing judgment upon the validity of their own illicit acts. The judge would be the Pope—judge of the judges in the Church. In a most righteous sense, then, the hunters had become the hunted.

Before the Pope received it, Father Gruner presented a copy of the *libellus* to a distinguished Monsignor residing in Rome, a holy cleric of great learning who had found a niche in which to weather the post-conciliar storm. The Monsignor had been involved in the drafting of Canon 1405. As he read the *libellus* he smiled. Yes, it was for the redress of grievances such as these that Canon 1405 had been written, he confirmed. Father Gruner had understood well, and had proceeded correctly.

§

In three days the Third International Fatima Conference would end with a blessing by the bishops in attendance. Replicas of the Pilgrim statue would be distributed and the *Memorare* recited. The participants in the Conference would return to their homes and their dioceses around the world, renewed in their commitment to keep alive the Message of Fatima. The Message would not die with them.

Father Gruner would return twice more to Rome in the next six months to search for canon lawyers who were not afraid to assist him in resisting *The Plan*. Several had seemed interested but had hastily backed away after consulting with certain bureaucrats at the Vatican tribunals.

Before Father Gruner returned to Canada to await the outcome of the End Game he would have another surprise for his opponents across the board. He had found the proverbial "smoking gun". Civil litigation in Canada had uncovered in the files of the Archbishop of Toronto a most interesting letter, dated October 27, 1989, from Cardinal Agustoni, Prefect of the Apostolic Signatura, who in 1989 was Secretary of the Congregation for the Clergy. The letter was addressed to the Bishop of Avellino. Entirely in Italian the letter secretly instructed the bishop to revoke Father Gruner's permission to live outside the diocese, recall him to Avellino, threaten him with suspension, and if necessary to silence him, reduce him to the lay state. The letter cautioned that the bishop was to act as though these measures had been his own idea and not the Cardinal's. *The very judge who was about to decide Father Gruner's case in the Apostolic Signatura had been the one to devise "The Plan."*

The Code of Canon Law requires that any request for recusal of a Cardinal from judging a matter in a Church tribunal be made directly to the Pope.[209] Father Gruner would dispatch to the Pope from a Roman post office a copy of Cardinal Agustoni's 1989 letter and implore His Holiness to remove the Cardinal from his case. The smell was too putrid for even the bureaucrats to hide. It was announced several days later that Cardinal Agustoni had stepped down, marking the first time in the history of the

209 The recusal request for a Cardinal must be referred to the Pope himself under Can. 1449 according to the authentic interpretation of that Canon. (CF. Response of the PCIV/67-84, 01-07-1976, AAS 68 [1976] 635; CLD8 [1973-1977] 1091-1092.)

Apostolic Signatura that its Cardinal Prefect had been recused. Another unprecedented turn in the unprecedented case of Father Nicholas Gruner.

The Signatura, minus Cardinal Agustoni, would now decide the two appeals which Father Gruner had placed before it: The first was an appeal from the original decree of the Signatura upholding the 1994 order to return to Avellino, which decree Father Gruner had finally received. The second was an appeal from the 1996 order to return to Avellino, which order had simply ignored Father Gruner's incardination by the Archbishop of Hyderabad. And then there was the canonical lawsuit now before the Pope. The End Game had become vastly more complicated than the opponents had imagined it would be. One could hope that Our Lady of Fatima was smiling down upon the chess board.

Father Gruner had done all that was humanly possible within the law of the Church. It was time for him to go home. To wait. To work. Above all, to pray.

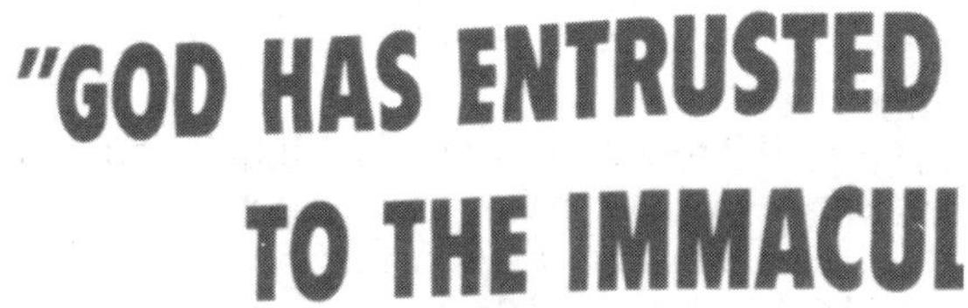

Bishop Pestana addressing the First Bishops Conference. At every bishops conference at least one bishop addressed the whole assembly of bishops.

Archbishops Toppo and Sobrinho, and some of the over 60 bishops who attended the First Bishops Conference in Fatima.

Chapter 19

The Great Amnesia

Revolutionaries throughout human history have always sought to bury the past. For a people which forgets its past is a people with no conception of its present or its future. The victims of revolution, like the victims of amnesia, are compelled to accept a new present and a new future which are not of their choosing. What else can they do, having lost the memory of where they came from?

Is it possible that the Church, a society both human and divine, could suffer the amnesia borne of revolution? That the Church can never teach error is a certainty secured by Our Lord's promise of His divine assistance until the consummation of the world. But Our Lord never promised us that the human members of His Church would not forget, if only for a brief time in history, what they were charged to remember and pass on. From such forgetfulness arose Peter's doubt and betrayal of Christ, the spread of the Arian heresy throughout the Church in the reign of Pope Liberius, and the other crises great and small in Church history.

St. Thomas Aquinas, the greatest of the doctors of the Catholic Church, taught in his *Summa Theologica* that throughout salvation history God has sent prophets to His people in times of forgetfulness, "not to give a new doctrine, but to remind the faithful of what they must do to save their souls."[210] For this reason did St. Paul counsel us: "Despise not prophecy; hold fast to that which is good."[211] And so, in 1917, God sent His Blessed Mother to Fatima to remind forgetful "modern man" what he must do to save his soul:

> "You have seen hell, where the souls of poor sinners go. *To save them*, God wishes to establish in the world devotion to My Immaculate Heart. If what I say to you is done, *many souls will be saved* and there will be peace ... In the end, My Immaculate Heart will triumph. The Holy Father will consecrate Russia to Me, which *will be converted*, and a period of peace will be granted to the world ..."[212]

For a time the faithful listened, even if the Consecration of Russia was not performed by the hierarchy. Devotion to the Immaculate Heart of Mary grew as never before in Church history, and the harvest of converts grew also—until the critical year of 1960.

In 1960 the whole Catholic world awaited disclosure of the Third Secret of Fatima. Yet in February of that year Pope John XXIII consigned the text of the Secret to a locked desk drawer in his papal apartments, privately dismissing it as irrelevant to his pontificate. Turning away from Fatima (of which he said almost nothing publicly), Pope John looked out upon the vast audience of assembled bishops who had gathered in the great *aula* of St. Peter's Basilica for the first day of the Council that no one had expected him to call. And then the Great Amnesia began.

Four years after the Council's conclusion, Pope Paul VI made a stunning announcement: The ancient Latin liturgy of the Roman Rite, descended from the Apostles themselves and regarded as sacrosanct by every Pope for more than 1,900 years, was to be junked in a matter of weeks to make way for a new rite of Mass in the vernacular, concocted by a committee which had solicited the advice of six Protestant ministers.[213] In his

210 St. Thomas Aquinas, *Summa Theologica*, II, II, Q 174 art. 6.

211 1 Thess. 5:20, 21.

212 *Fatima in Lucia's Own Words* (Sister Lucia's Memoirs), Fatima, 1976, p. 162.

213 Davies, Michael. *Pope Paul's New Mass*, Angelus Press, Kansas City, p. 585.

unprecedented audience address of November 26, 1969, Pope Paul, speaking as no pope had ever spoken before, insisted that the Church literally forget her own liturgical past:

> *A new rite of Mass: a change in the venerable tradition that has gone on for centuries.* This is something that affects *our hereditary religious patrimony*, which seemed to enjoy the privilege of being *untouchable and settled* ... No longer Latin, but the spoken language will be the principal language of the Mass ... *We are parting with the speech of the Christian centuries;* we are becoming like *profane intruders* (!) in the literary preserve of sacred utterance ... What can we put in the place of that language of the angels? *We are giving up something of priceless worth* ...[214]

It cannot be said that Pope Paul was a conscious revolutionary. No man on earth may judge the interior disposition of the Roman Pontiff. Yet the Pope's own words objectively declared a revolutionary aim, whatever his subjective intention might have been. Within a few years of Pope Paul's inexplicable demand that the faithful abandon the very form of their divine worship down through the centuries, a plague of forgetfulness would sweep across the entire Church. In June of 1972 Pope Paul surveyed the devastation and uttered his famous lament: "(F)rom somewhere or other the smoke of Satan has entered the temple of God ..."[215] From somewhere or other.

By the time Pope Paul had passed from this world in 1978, much of what comprised the Church's greatness as a visible institution had already vanished into that incredible memory-hole known as "the renewal of Vatican II." Sent forth by the Pope himself, amazingly rash men had entered the house of God while we were sleeping and carried off nearly all the furnishings, replacing the divine patrimony of the ages with their own crude tinkerings. And when we awoke to find out what had happened, we were told that we must rejoice in the loss of every precious possession, and celebrate the "renewal" of our home.

The Catholics who attended the apostolate's Third Fatima Conference in that November of 1996 had come to draw a line (at least for themselves) at the edge of the still-swirling vortex of post-conciliar "reform", which had most recently disgorged the appalling spectacle of girls in pigtails assisting at the altar of God. Among the faithful who had gathered at Piazza Euclide one could almost sense the constant whisper of a common thought: "Not Fatima. No, not Fatima." They had come to Rome to cling to the memory of Our Lady of Fatima with all their might, to keep Her, too, from disappearing down into the memory-hole.

After all, it was only eighty years ago that Our Lady appeared at the Cova da Iria to deliver a divine message for our time, authenticated by a prodigious public miracle the likes of which had never been seen in the history of the world. The Miracle of the Sun was not some pious legend of Catholic antiquity, but a brilliant historical fact of the 20th Century which even Hollywood had been compelled to acknowledge in a popular motion picture. The events at Fatima had occurred, moreover, within the lifetime of nearly every bishop who attended the Second Vatican Council.

The Message of Fatima was delivered and authenticated by a miracle to remind the world, in a time of unprecedented peril for souls, that Christ had founded His Church to *save* souls from the fires of Hell through the intercession of His Immaculate Mother. But today it seems the Vatican no longer remembers how to speak as Our Lady spoke at

---

214 Audience address of Pope Paul VI, November 26, 1969.

215 Speech of June 30, 1972, quoted by Romano Amerio, *Iota Unum*, Sarto House, Kansas City, 1996, p. 6.

Fatima, only 45 years before Vatican II got underway. Not only the traditional externals of the Faith, but many of the words by which the Faith is expressed have been forgotten. The simple Catholic words Our Lady spoke at Fatima—"hell", "the souls of poor sinners", "Immaculate Heart", "to save them", "souls will be saved"—have disappeared from the texts of post-conciliar Vatican pronouncements. In their place strange new words have been substituted: "ecumenism", "dialogue", "collegiality". In less than a generation these new words, completely unknown in the Church before 1960, became the governing notions of post-conciliar thought, despite the alarming fact that no one really knows exactly what they mean.

Father Gruner is only one of millions of Catholics who have noticed something terribly amiss in the language of the post-conciliar Church: it no longer speaks to the world of death, judgment, heaven, hell, purgatory. The Last Things, which had comprised the very core of the Church's evangelism and catechesis for nearly 2,000 years before the Council, are no longer mentioned by the generality of post-conciliar churchmen. Today, preaching on the Last Things is found almost entirely on the pages of spiritual books published before Vatican II and distributed by a few private Catholic apostolates, like the one headed by Father Gruner.

In 1994 the Italian journalist Vittorio Messori submitted a series of written questions to Pope John Paul II, who provided written answers. The resulting "interview" was published under the Pope's name as a best-seller entitled *Crossing the Threshold of Hope*. One of Messori's questions to the Pope related to this mysterious and unparalleled silence of the post-conciliar Church about the Last Things:

> Recently in the Church, words have multiplied. It seems that in the last twenty years more 'documents' have been produced at every level of the Church than in the entire preceding twenty centuries. *Yet to some it has seemed that this very loquacious Church is silent about what is most essential: eternal life* ... Why do so many churchmen comment interminably on topical issues, *but hardly ever speak to us about eternity*, about that ultimate union with God that, as faith teaches, remains man's vocation, man's destiny, and ultimate end? [216]

In response to this grave accusation in the form of a question, the Pope rather wistfully recalled the pre-conciliar teaching of the Church on the Last Things. His Holiness wrote in the past tense, as if this most basic element of Church teaching were some sort of heirloom that had been lost and could not be recovered, not even by the Pope:

> Let's remember that not so long ago, in sermons during retreats or missions, the Last Things—death, judgment, heaven, hell, purgatory—were always a standard part of the program of meditation, and preachers knew how to speak on them in an effective and evocative way. How many people were drawn to conversion and confession by these sermons on the Last Things!
>
> Furthermore, we have to recognize that this pastoral style was profoundly personal: 'Remember that at the end you will present yourself before God with your entire life. Before His judgment seat you will be responsible for all your actions, you will be judged not only on your actions and on your words but also on your thoughts, even the most secret.' ... It could be said that these sermons, which correspond perfectly to the content of Revelation in the Old and New Testaments, went to the very heart of man's inner world. They stirred his conscience, they threw him to his knees, they led him to the screen of the

216 *Crossing the Threshold of Hope*, Alfred A. Knopf, New York, 1994, p. 178.

confessional, they had a profound saving effect all their own.[217]

Having noted what is self-evident, that the traditional teaching on the Last Things converted many souls, the Pope conceded to Messori that "*one no longer speaks of these things* in evangelization, in catechesis, and in homilies ..." That is to say, the Church no longer speaks of them at all. Yet the Pope did not seem to recognize in this amazing development any sort of emergency for the Church, but only a change of her "pastoral style."

But if the Church's "pastoral style" is no longer "profoundly personal", if after 2,000 years she has suddenly ceased speaking to each person about the realities of death, judgment, Heaven, hell and purgatory, then what *does* she teach men today that they might save their souls? The Pope's remark to Messori is as enigmatic as it is disturbing:

> It can be said that until recently (i.e., for the first 1,962 years of Church history) the Church's catechesis and preaching centered upon an individual eschatology, one, for that matter, which is profoundly rooted in Divine Revelation. The vision proposed by the Council, however, was that of an eschatology of the Church and of the world.[218]

What are the faithful to make of this? If the teaching on the Last Things is "profoundly rooted in Divine Revelation", then why was it suddenly replaced with a "vision proposed by the Council"? Or *was* it replaced? Does the Council's "eschatology of the Church and of the world"[219] exclude the traditional teaching on the Last Things? If it does not, then why would the Pope cite the Council's "vision" to explain to Messori why the teaching on the Last Things has vanished from the post-conciliar Church?

And what does this "eschatology of the Church and of the world" really mean to the individual man, who must still turn away from mortal sin and live a life of supernatural faith in order to be saved? Is the Council's eschatological vision anything more than a beguiling abstraction which causes pastors to ignore the jeopardy of souls? As the Pope conceded to Messori, that is exactly what it is:

> We can ask ourselves if man, with his individual life, his responsibility, his destiny, his personal eschatological future, *his heaven or hell*, does not end up getting lost in this cosmic dimension. Recognizing the good reasons which led to your question, it is necessary to respond honestly by saying *yes*. *To a certain degree man does get lost*; so too, do preachers, catechists, teachers; and as a result, they no longer have the courage to preach the threat of hell ... (emphasis added)[220]

Despite these explosively disturbing admissions, the Pope clearly views the Council's "vision" as a good thing. But is it a good thing? Or is it possible that this unprecedented loss of focus on the eternal destiny of the individual soul is the very calamity foretold in the Third Secret of Fatima? Sister Lucia spoke of a "diabolical disorientation" in the post-conciliar Church.[221] Could there be a more diabolical disorientation than for the sacred pastors to lose sight of death, judgment, Heaven, hell and purgatory?

Messori's question to the Pope had only touched upon a great and terrible truth which can be seen in shadow behind the painted facade of "the great renewal of Vatican II." There are still many Catholics who have not forgotten the state of the Church before

217 Ibid, pp. 179-180.

218 Ibid, p. 180.

219 Ibid, p. 181.

220 Ibid, p. 183.

221 *The Whole Truth About Fatima*, Vol. III, *The Third Secret*, Frère Michel de la Sainte Trinité, p. 755, Buffalo, 1990.

the Council. Like Father Gruner, they remember full seminaries and convents, a majestic liturgy, parish churches packed to capacity every Sunday. No, they do not remember an ecclesial paradise in which every member of the Church had the fervor of a saint. But they do remember that the Church as a whole had vigor; that her preachers had "the courage to preach the threat of hell"; and that her members believed in hell and kept the moral law, if only with the imperfect contrition borne of a fear of hell. And they remember that this once vigorous Church made many converts. Until 1960. Until the Third Secret of Fatima was locked away in Pope John's desk drawer, instead of being revealed to the faithful as Sister Lucia's superiors had promised her it would be.

The Catholics who remember what the Church was only fifty-three years ago are not prepared to consign the entire pre-conciliar past to the memory-hole, with a nod to the Council's vague new vision and a fond recollection of the Church's former "pastoral style." What the Church was before the Council, she must be again. The Catholics who still remember have passed that memory on to their children; and their children have grown to have children of their own. Three generations of Catholics now on the face of this earth still carry the memory with them, even if they comprise a tiny minority of those who call themselves Catholics today.

Those who still remember, including Father Nicholas Gruner, ask the same question Messori asked the Pope—the question certain Vatican bureaucrats find intolerably embarrassing. They want to know how it has come to pass that a Church divinely commissioned to save souls from hell no longer *mentions* hell. They want to know, quite simply, why the Church has forgotten how to speak as Our Lady spoke at Fatima.

§

From the eternal perspective of the Holy Catholic Church there is no "modernity" to speak of; no age in which the Church has been obliged to recognize that man has finally "progressed" to the point where there is something truly new about him which the Church must learn and assimilate into her teaching. Man can never progress one iota beyond what the Church has always known about his nature. For human nature does not change, and what the Church knows of man has been revealed to her by God. Can the creature that God fashioned from a lump of clay tell God something new about its constitution?

The age-old attitude of the Church toward man's pretentious claims of "modernity" is only a reflection of God's eternal attitude. Throughout salvation history men have presented their Towers of Babel to their Creator, impudently demanded recognition of their great achievements, and watched them crumble under the hammer-blows of divine wrath. So what else is new?

In 1864, only seventy-five years after the French Revolution, the current version of the Tower of Babel was already beginning to rise in the world. "Modern man" was announcing everywhere, even in Catholic countries, his final emancipation from God and His Church. In response, Blessed Pope Pius IX promulgated his *Syllabus of Errors*, declaring his intention to "unveil and condemn all those heresies and errors ... averse to the eternal salvation of man (which) the most bitter enemies of our religion, deceiving the people and maliciously lying, disseminate ... by means of pestilential books, pamphlets and newspapers dispersed over the whole world." His Holiness condemned an entire list of the false propositions which are the very foundation stones of "modern civilization"—everything from unrestrained "liberty of worship" for false sects, to "liberty of conscience", to "freedom of the press", to the abolition of the Church's indirect power over temporal affairs.[222]

In #80 of the *Syllabus*, Pope Pius specifically condemned as error the proposition that "The Roman Pontiff can, and ought to, reconcile himself and come to terms with progress, liberalism and modern civilization." In this he merely echoed every one of his predecessors. For why should the Vicar of Christ pay tribute to the latest version of the Tower of Babel, when God will sooner or later reduce it to a pile of rubble?

There is no mere human haughtiness at work in the Church's perennial disdain for the claims of "modern civilization." The ephemera of modernity have always been transparent to the Church; in every age she looks through them to see the very same thing: a world full of fallen men in danger of hellfire. Our Lady said as much at Fatima, at the dawn of the 20th Century: "You have seen hell, where the souls of poor sinners go. To save them, God wishes to establish in the world devotion to My Immaculate Heart."

But in 1960 the Third Secret of Fatima was locked in a papal desk drawer. And then came Vatican II.

The Conciliar document *Gaudium et spes* bears the disturbing subtitle "Pastoral Constitution on the Church in the *Modern* World." For the first time in Church history a Council had deigned to regard a particular era as *modern* in distinction to all the previous eras of human history. The very phrase "Church in the *modern* world" was an implicit concession to the 20th Century *Zeitgest*, which insisted that "modern man" had finally come of age, and that the Church was obliged to view him, his "rights" and his "modern world" with a new respect. No less than Cardinal Ratzinger [the future Pope Benedict XVI] would confirm that this was the very tenor of *Gaudium et spes*:

> "The feeling that now, at last, the world had to be, and could be, changed, improved and humanized—this feeling had quite obviously taken hold of them (the Council Fathers) in a way *that was not to be resisted* ... (T)here reigned at once a feeling of euphoria and frustration. Euphoria, because it seemed that nothing was impossible for this Council which had *the strength to break with attitudes that had been deeply rooted for centuries*; frustration, because all that had thus far been done *did not count for mankind* and only increased *the longing for freedom, for openness, for what was totally different.*[223]

The Council, then, "breaking with attitudes that had been deeply rooted for centuries", yearning to satisfy "modern man's" desire for something "totally different", decided to celebrate man and his great accomplishments, to admire his technology and his recently discovered "rights." The Council would declare that "Man is on the road to a more thorough development of his personality, and to a growing vindication of *his own rights*."[224] This "new age" of man was not to be condemned for its abominable offenses against God's law, including Communism and abortion, but rather was to be admired: "(W)e can speak of a new age in human history ... (W)e are witnesses of the birth of a new humanism, one in which man is defined first of all by his responsibility toward his brothers and toward history."[225] The Council would even declare, in an almost giddy embrace of imprecision, that "the human race has passed from a rather static concept of reality to a more dynamic and evolutionary one."[226]

222 *Quanta cura*, nn.1, 6; *Syllabus of Errors* of Pius IX.

223 Joseph Cardinal Ratzinger, *Principles of Catholic Theology*, Ignatius Press, 1987, p. 380.

224 *Gaudium et spes*, n. 41.

225 Ibid, n. 54.

226 Ibid, n. 5.

These were stunningly naive opinions in view of the horrors of this century raging outside the *aula* of St. Peter's. The Message of Fatima is that the "modern world" must listen to the Church, beg forgiveness and do penance for its incomparable sins, so that a worldwide chastisement might be avoided. But the message of *Gaudium et spes* is that the Church must listen to the "modern world", and make up for having been so insensitive to its needs for so long. To that end, the document declares that priests and bishops "should fit themselves to do their part in establishing *dialogue with the world* and with men of all shades of opinion."[227] And what precisely was meant by "establishing dialogue with the world"? Had the Bride of Christ been mute for the previous 2,000 years? Was the Church just now, at Vatican II, learning how to speak to man?

This much is clear: After the promulgation of *Gaudium et spes* the Church which had always been known as *mater et magister*—mother and teacher—would suddenly and mysteriously cease speaking to the world with the authority of a divinely founded institution to which the world must listen. Now *she* would listen, most attentively, to all of the very important things "modern man" had to tell her.

Perhaps the most striking example of the Council's willingness to sit at the feet of the world and listen, is the opinion in *Gaudium et spes* that "In pastoral care, sufficient use must be made not only of theological principles, but also of the findings of the secular sciences, especially of psychology and sociology, so that the faithful may be brought to a more adequate and mature life of faith."[228] More adequate and mature? Was it really the Council's teaching that the faith of Catholics for twenty centuries—a faith nourished by the seven Sacraments, the prayers of the saints, and the blood of the martyrs—was less adequate and mature than it could have been with the help of *psychology and sociology*? Were the faithful really expected to believe that the Church established by God Himself now needed to consult the practitioners of recently invented pseudo-sciences which view man as a subject with no immortal soul or eternal destiny? What did the likes of Sigmund Freud and Margaret Mead have to say to the Bride of Christ about the life of Faith? And which of the many conflicting schools of psychology and sociology would the Council have the sacred pastors consult in their care of souls? The Council offered no definite advice. Nor did it have the slightest competence to do so, for Our Lord did not commission the Church as a referral network for psychologists and sociologists. The divine commission is to preach the Gospel and administer the Sacraments, which God has given men as the only truly effective balm for their wounded souls.

The Council would acknowledge the "problems" of the "modern world" in the course of extolling its supposed progress. Yet *Gaudium et spes* would say nothing about the gravest of those problems: world Communism, whose adepts were killing, torturing and imprisoning Catholics at the very moment the document was being promulgated. The Vatican-Moscow Agreement had insured that the Council which purported to address the state of "the modern world" would, absurdly, neglect to condemn or even mention the greatest threat to the world's survival.

All in all, as Cardinal Ratzinger has noted, in *Gaudium et spes* "the attitude of critical reserve toward the forces that have left their imprint on the modern world is to be replaced by a resolute *coming to terms* with their movement."[229] But what of #80 of Pius IX's *Syllabus*, which had condemned the very notion that the Church ought to "*come to*

---

227 Ibid, n. 18.

228 Ibid, n. 12.

229 Ratzinger, *op. cit.*, p. 380.

terms with progress, liberalism and modern civilization"? Like the Roman liturgy and the teaching on the Last Things, the *Syllabus* would be forgotten in the Great Amnesia. As Ratzinger explains:

> If it is desirable to offer a diagnosis of the text as a whole, we might say that (in conjunction with the texts on religious liberty and world religions) it (*Gaudium et spes*) is *a revision of the Syllabus of Pius IX, a kind of counter-syllabus* ... Let us be content to say here that the text serves as a *counter syllabus* and, as such, represents, on the part of the Church, an attempt at *an official reconciliation with the new era inaugurated in 1789* ...[230]

So what Pius IX had solemnly condemned as error was officially accepted by the "counter-syllabus" (!) of *Gaudium et spes*. Pope was pitted against Council, and the teaching of the Pope was "revised" to reconcile the Church to "the new era inaugurated in 1789"—an era which began when Robespierre and Marat filled barges with priests and nuns, mothers and children and sank them in the Loire, on their way to butchering a million Catholics in the French Revolution.

How could the Church attempt an "official reconciliation" with an era which had begun with the genocide of Catholics in France and was continuing with the genocide of Catholics in the Soviet Union? How could the Church have "a resolute coming to terms" with a civilization in which every vital link between Church and State had been severed, and even Catholic states had embraced the very error Pius IX condemned in the *Syllabus*: "In the present day it is no longer expedient that the Catholic religion be held as the only religion of the State, to the exclusion of all other forms of worship."[231]

These questions lead to an ultimate question about the Council itself: If *Gaudium et spes* "revised" the solemn condemnations in the *Syllabus*, was it not the case that the Church had contradicted her own prior teaching? Has the Church herself, then, failed? The answer, of course, is no. For the Council itself had declared that "In view of the pastoral purpose of the present Council, this sacred Synod defines matters of faith and morals as binding on the Church *only* when the Synod openly declares so."[232] Vatican II was the first Council in Church history to issue a disclaimer on the weight of its own documents. This was no small relief to many of the Council Fathers, who were troubled by the strange ambiguities and novel attitudes which permeated *Gaudium et spes* and other conciliar texts. The Irish bishop Thomas Morris, for one, would confide to a reporter shortly before his death that "I was relieved when we were told that this Council was not aiming at defining or giving final statements on doctrine, because a statement of doctrine has to be very carefully formulated and I would have regarded the Council documents as *tentative and liable to be reformed*."[233]

Nowhere in *Gaudium et spes* did the Council "openly declare" that it was defining any doctrine to bind the faithful, or that it was actually overruling the *Syllabus*. What the Council had ventured (as Ratzinger noted) was a mere "attempt" to reconcile the Church with "the new era inaugurated in 1789." An attempt is not a doctrine, and *Gaudium et spes* was manifestly not a doctrinal pronouncement, but an exercise in sociological commentary by bishops who were not commissioned to teach sociology. There is really no contradiction, then, between what the authentic Magisterium has always taught and

230 Ibid, p. 382.

231 *Syllabus of Errors* of Pius IX, n. 77.

232 Theological Note to *Lumen gentium*, November 16, 1964.

233 Interview of Bishop Morris by Kieron Wood, *Catholic World News*, September 27, 1997, at http:\\www.cwnews.com\news\viewrec.cfm?RefNum=4091.

what the Council "attempted" in *Gaudium et spes* because an "attempt" is not a *teaching*. And the constant *teaching* of the authentic magisterium has never contradicted itself. No Catholic is bound to follow an "attempt" or an "attempted" teaching.

And yet this non-doctrinal *excursis* on modernity, like the other documents of this pastoral Council, has somehow attained the appearance of dogma in the post-conciliar amnesia, obliterating the memory of all the truly doctrinal teaching that had come before. Just as the conciliar "vision" of *Lumen gentium* has eclipsed the traditional teaching on the Last Things, so has *Gaudium et spes* eclipsed the traditional opposition of the Church to the "modern world" with its modern "liberties." Even Cardinal Ratzinger, the Pope's own defender of doctrine, felt obliged to make a public protest against this fraudulent exaggeration of the Council's importance in the history of the Church:

> "The Second Vatican Council has not been treated as part of the entire living tradition of the Church, *but as an end of Tradition, a new start from zero*. The truth is that this particular Council defined no dogma at all, but deliberately chose to remain on a modest level, as a merely pastoral council; and yet many treat it as though it had made itself into a sort of super dogma which takes away the importance of all the rest."[234]

So it is not a defect of doctrine which has led to the current crisis, but a loss of memory which has caused the Council to be regarded as "an end of Tradition, a new start from zero." Perhaps it is this development which brought to Fatima no less a prophet than the Mother of God. Our Lady came to Fatima knowing what was to happen in the Church during the lifetimes of the children who would become the bishops of Vatican II. She came to remind them of the simple things they must teach the world in order that men might save their souls. For what did the Second Vatican Council really need to say to the "modern world" that Our Lady had not already said at Fatima? Repent. Do penance. Make the communions of Reparation. Make sacrifices. Consecrate Russia and establish devotion in the world to My Immaculate Heart. Do these things to prevent the annihilation of nations.

Yet the Council Fathers had made no mention of these things. They issued instead a document which exhorts us to "scrutinize the signs of the times",[235] while ignoring the great sign of Fatima and the great evil Our Lady predicted would spread throughout the "modern world" if Her requests at Fatima were not heeded.

And so it seems that the dazzling "modern world" of science and technology tempts even churchmen to behave as if the Faith of the 20th Century cannot really be so simple as those three primitive shepherd children from Portugal made it out to be. Surely, in this enlightened age of psychology and sociology, ecumenism and "interreligious dialogue", salvation is a much more complicated affair than simply praying for the intercession of the Immaculate Heart of Mary to save "poor souls" from the "fires of hell". Surely, once we have finished pondering all the recently developed *nuances* on the question of salvation, taking into consideration the elaborate psychological excuses men have lately discovered to justify their sins, we can safely place the Message of Fatima into the category of a pious exaggeration.

The "modern world" ridicules such "exaggerated" notions as souls burning forever in the fires of hell. The modern world says: "Hell is a violation of the rights of man. Who is this God who coerces us to believe with threats of hellfire? We will not hear of Him."

234 Speech in July 1988 in Santiago, Chile; quoted in *Latin Mass* magazine, Spring 1998, p. 23.

235 *Gaudium et spes*, n. 4.

Modern churchmen, who have "established dialogue" with the world and no longer teach with authority, find they cannot bring themselves to say any longer that God will damn to hell everyone who dies in a state of mortal sin. They have "lost the courage to preach the threat of hell," as the Pope himself concedes. And what will the Vatican do about this loss of courage in the Church? The answer is not clear, for there has yet to be any talk of hell from the post-conciliar Vatican itself.

§

The annals of this century are filled with babble about "human rights"—the right to this and the right to that, declared in numberless treaties, charters, declarations and speeches by the movers and shakers of the incomparably pretentious "modern world." Since Our Lady appeared at Fatima in 1917, the men who ignore Her heavenly message have been regaling themselves with an earthly symphony of "human rights." The symphony has built to a deafening crescendo, while the noise from the orchestra pit has drowned out the cries and muffled screams of hundreds of millions of victims being led to slaughter in the gulags and abortuaries which are the monuments to this age of unrivaled human depravity.

Even the Fathers of the Second Vatican Council were impressed by all this modern noise about "human rights," having declared in *Gaudium et spes* that "man is on the road to a more thorough development of his personality, and to a growing vindication of his own rights ..."[236] The mad orchestra plays on, the musicians delight in their loud but lifeless music, and even the members of the Church applaud.

Not so long ago men commonly understood that "human rights" have no meaning unless they originate with an omnipotent and avenging God, Whom men must obey under pain of eternal damnation. For once the notion of "human rights" becomes detached from God as the author of life and the ultimate judge of all wrongs, on what ground can one stand to say that there is a "right" to anything—even a right to life? Can one stand on "the dignity of the human person"? What does "human dignity" mean without God? Nothing more than what men agree that it means. Without God there are no true rights, but only agreements. And whenever the agreements become inconvenient, the doors to the gulags and the abortuaries swing open.

Who is this God Who gives us our rights and secures them with His divine authority? He is the God Who hung on the Cross and died for our sins. He is Christ the King:

> He humbled himself, becoming obedient unto death, even to the death of the cross. For which cause God also hath exalted him, and have given him a name which is above all names: That in the name of Jesus every knee should bend, of those that are in heaven, on earth, or under the earth: And that every tongue should confess that the Lord Jesus Christ is in the glory of God the Father. (*Phil.* 2: 8-11)

Here one encounters yet another sector of the Great Amnesia: the Church's constant teaching before the Council on the Social Kingship of Jesus Christ. Father Gruner is one of the dwindling number of the faithful who still remember that on December 11, 1925, His Holiness Pope Pius XI proclaimed the Feast of Christ the King in the encyclical *Quas primas*. The date was only eight years after Our Lady's final apparition at Fatima, and literally one day after Our Lord came to Pontevedra to ask for the Five First Saturdays of Reparation for the sacrileges against His Mother's Immaculate Heart.

236 Ibid, n. 41.

It was also a mere thirty-seven years before the first session of Vatican II. Yet this great 20th Century encyclical would seem centuries removed in the amazing time-warp of the post-conciliar period.

In *Quas primas* Pius XI warned the world that "human society was tottering to its fall" because it had rejected the Social Kingship of Christ over all men and all nations. His Holiness declared to the world's rulers that if they "wish to preserve their authority, to promote and increase the prosperity of their people, they will not neglect *the public duty* of reverence and obedience to the rule of Christ."[237] His Holiness was affirming the teaching of all his predecessors,[238] who in turn were affirming what Our Lord Himself had declared just before His Ascension into Heaven:

> All power is given to Me in heaven *and in earth*. Going, therefore, teach ye *all nations*, baptizing them in the name of the Father, and of the Son and of the Holy Ghost; teaching them to observe all things whatsoever I have commanded you ... (*Matt*. 28:18-20)

What the Church has always taught about the Social Kingship of Christ is, like all the rest of her teaching, completely consonant with common sense. For if Christ be God, then reason itself demonstrates that not only individuals, but the societies they form, owe duties to Christ the King. To hold that individual men ought to be Catholic, but not their societies, is nothing less than an insult to God, who is the Author of both man and society. This is why Pope Leo XIII did not hesitate to declare to "the modern world" what the Church has always believed about her rightful place in the social order:

> Since, then, *the profession of one religion is necessary in the State, that religion must be professed which alone is true*, and which can be recognized without difficulty, especially in Catholic states, because the marks of truth are, as it were, engraven upon it.[239]

It was to remind all nations of their public duty to obey and reverence Christ that Pius XI composed an act of Consecration of the whole human race to the Sacred Heart, ordering that it be included in the Roman Missal and performed in every parish church annually on the new feast day. The words of that Consecration evince all of the fearless Catholicity of the pre-Conciliar Vatican:

> Be Thou King, O Lord, not only of the faithful who have never forsaken Thee, but also of the prodigal children who have abandoned Thee ... Be Thou King of all those who are still involved in the darkness of idolatry and Islamism, and refuse not to draw them into the light and kingdom of God. Turn Thine eyes of mercy toward the children of that race, once Thy chosen people. Of old they called down upon themselves the Blood of the Savior, may it now descend upon them a laver of redemption and life.[240]

But the "modern world" has become ever so much more modern since the bronze doors closed on Vatican II. Eighty-eight years after the promulgation of *Quas primas*, men all over the world are putting the finishing touches on that great global ant-heap known as the New World Order. When it is finished, it will be modern man's greatest achievement: a global economy controlled by a global government which knows no national boundaries. Of course, the new order will not be Catholic, or even nominally

237 *Quas primas*, n. 18.

238 Leo XIII, *Annum sacrum*, *Libertas humana*, *Immortale Dei*; St. Pius X, *Vehementer nos*; Gregory XVI, *Mirari vos*; Pius XI, *Adeo nota*, and many others.

239 *Libertas humana*.

240 *Quas primas*, appended act of Consecration.

Christian. It will be utterly godless in its laws and institutions.

One of the reasons Father Gruner has been in the cross hairs of certain Vatican bureaucrats for so long is that the apostolate (unlike the neutralized Blue Army) has been willing to publish the truth about the Vatican's response to the emergence of the New World Order. And the terrible truth is this: The Vatican supports it in principle, and has supported it since the Council. To be sure, there are Vatican statements from time to time condemning the new order's universal regime of abortion and contraception, and cautioning against the creation of "inequalities" in the new global economy. But the *idea* of a New World Order—a one-world government, economy, and system of justice—meets with no objection from the post-conciliar Vatican. On the contrary, Vatican bureaucrats are assisting in its formation.

This comes as no surprise to anyone who has studied *Gaudium et spes* and the pertinent pronouncements of the post-conciliar popes. *Gaudium et spes* is, in fact, a virtual charter for Church support of the emerging world government. In one of its many opinions outside the realm of faith and morals, the document declares that the "outlawing" of war:

> " ... *undoubtedly requires the establishment of some universal public authority* ... endowed with an effective power *to* safeguard, on the behalf of all, security, regard for justice and respect for rights".[241]

It did not seem to concern the Council that any such "universal public authority" would not be Catholic in its principles, but would be controlled at all its key points by atheists or non-Christians who reject Christ and His Church. The Council did not address the obvious problem. But Paul VI did.

On October 4, 1965, during the Council's final session, Pope Paul went to New York City to pay tribute to the emerging "universal public authority" at its very center: the United Nations. To the delight of the U.N. delegates, the Vicar of Christ praised their 20th Century Tower of Babel as "this lofty institution" and the "last great hope for concord and peace."[242] *The last great hope*? What, then, of the Holy Catholic Church, founded by none other than the Prince of Peace Himself to bring peace on earth to men of good will? And what of the Message of Fatima, Heaven's own plan for peace in this epoch, delivered personally to the world by the Mother of God within the lifetime of Paul VI? Paul VI did not speak of Fatima that day at the United Nations. Instead, to the thunderous applause of the General Assembly, he placed the Vatican's seal of approval on a godless world government to be administered from the glass and steel temple of the New World Order:

"Let unanimous trust in this institution grow, ***let its authority increase*** ..."[243]

And so it has. Ever since the Council the Vatican has been a permanent observer to the United Nations. The same Vatican bureaucrats who administer *Ostpolitik* have negotiated the Vatican's signature to a number of U.N. treaties, including the deplorable Beijing Conference agreements and the "U.N. Convention on the Rights of the Child," which makes no mention of the right of the child to be born. The Vatican signs these humanistic manifestoes with certain "reservations"; but sign them it does, thereby legitimating the awful notion that the U.N. is a valid moral body which ought to exert authority over the whole of mankind.

---

241 *Gaudium et spes*, n. 82.

242 Address of Paul VI to the United Nations, October 4, 1965.

243 Ibid.

The further Our Lady's warnings at Fatima recede from the memory of the Vatican, the firmer its embrace of the structure (if not the moral excesses) of the New World Order. Thirty years after Paul VI paid homage to the U.N., Pope John Paul II took his turn. Addressing the General Assembly on October 5, 1995, he proclaimed the "*esteem* of the Apostolic See and of the *Catholic Church* for this institution" and pronounced the U.N.—worldwide promoter of abortion, contraception and godless humanism —"a great instrument for harmonizing and coordinating (!) international life."[244] To which an average member of the faithful might instinctively reply: "God forbid!"

As Father Gruner's apostolate has noted, the United Nations, rather than promoting a "qualitative leap in international life", is subsidizing a worldwide regime of abortion and contraception, foisting population control programs upon even the Catholic peoples of Bolivia and the Philippines. Father Paul Marx, the founder of Human Life International, had also been fearless in his condemnation of the U.N.: "By far—with the sole exception of Satan himself—the single biggest threat to the sanctity of human life and the family today is the emerging agenda of the United Nations/World government ... the United Nations is already laying the groundwork for worldwide population control through any means possible."[245] Even Cardinal Ratzinger, in the twilight of his career, would break ranks with his Vatican confrères and publicly admit the simple truth that Father Gruner and the apostolate had been publishing all along: The United Nations is an evil organization with an evil agenda. In his prologue to a book entitled *The Gospel in the Face of World Disorder*, Ratzinger warned that the U.N. is promoting "a new world order", "a new man", "a new world" and "a new anthropology". And what is so dangerous about the U.N., observed Ratzinger, is that its agenda is not some utopian dream but a nightmare which could easily become reality: "(T)he Marxist dream was utopian. This philosophy (of the U.N.), on the contrary, is very realistic."[246]

Why two Popes would express such high esteem for an institution which is promoting worldwide genocide in the womb remains a matter of considerable mystery—a mystery the apostolate has not been unwilling to explore. Perhaps the conciliar popes have supported the U.N. because their advisors in the Vatican Secretariat of State have convinced them that papal influence could somehow turn an evil institution to the good. In like manner, Cardinal Casaroli convinced Paul VI that he should abandon the Church's fierce opposition to Communism in favor of *Ostpolitik*, even though Paul was reportedly torn by that decision.[247] Yet the notion that the members of the Church should participate in evil organizations to make them "better" was the very notion condemned by Pius XI in his encyclical *Divini Redemptoris*. Recognizing that a bad tree will never produce good fruit but will only poison those who partake of it, His Holiness forbade any Catholic participation in the seemingly benign social movements spawned by Communists:

"Under various names that do not suggest Communism ... (t)hey invite Catholics to collaborate with them in the realm of so-called humanitarianism and charity; and at times make proposals that are in perfect harmony with the Christian spirit and the doctrine of the Church ... See to it, Venerable Brethren, that the Faithful do not allow themselves to be deceived! Communism is intrinsically wrong, and no one who would

244 Address of John Paul II to the United Nations, October 5, 1995.

245 *L'Osservatore Romano*, May 28, 1997, p. 11.

246 See Vatican web site at http://www.vatican.va

247 Catholic World News Report, November 24, 1997, http://www.cwnews.com\news\viewrec.cfm?RefNum=6363.

save Christain civilization may collaborate with it in any undertaking whatsoever."[248]

Like Communism, the U.N. is an incomparably bad tree, irremovably rooted in the secular humanist soil of 20th Century civilization. Yet the Vatican's pursuit of a "civilization of love" under its branches seems to have become relentless. Vatican representatives chase the illusion not only at the U.N., but at innumerable Vatican-sponsored conferences and prayer meetings with what it now calls "the respected leaders of the world's religions."[249]

Father Gruner is hardly the only one who has noticed that the post-conciliar Vatican no longer speaks to the world of the Social Kingship of Christ over the whole human race, including Muslims and Jews. Whereas Pius XI decried Islam as darkness from which souls needed to be rescued by the light of Christ, some 72 years later the "Pontifical Council on Interreligious Dialogue" would declare in 1997 that Catholics and Muslims must "share their faith" and that the "Call to Islam" and "Christian Mission" should be conducted "in a spirit of collaboration (!), and as a service to mankind." The faithful could be forgiven for asking how a religion of darkness, whose errors the Church had been battling for thirteen centuries, had suddenly become a "service to mankind" with which Catholics must now collaborate.

Father Gruner and the apostolate have not hesitated to point out the alarming development that the consecration of humanity to the Sacred Heart of Jesus has disappeared from the Vatican's agenda, along with the Consecration of Russia to the Immaculate Heart of Mary. The Hearts of Jesus and Mary are not among the talking points of the Vatican emissaries who travel the gleaming byways of the New World Order and walk the halls of the U.N. Today the main items for discussion are "human rights", "dialogue", and something called "the civilization of love."

The Vatican's new approach to the world is strikingly evident in a keyword search of the Vatican Internet archive: one will find no fewer than 52,000 entries on "dialogue", 2,000 on "human rights" and 1,000 on "the civilization of love"—but not a single entry on the Kingship of Christ, or, for that matter, the Consecration of Russia to the Immaculate Heart.[250] There is no longer any mention in Vatican pronouncements of the divine imperative "that in the name of Jesus every knee should bend (and) every tongue should confess that the Lord Jesus Christ is in the glory of God the Father." That teaching has vanished without a trace. The new vocabulary has completely obliterated the old.

The "civilization of love" is a phrase reputedly coined by Paul VI. In practice this notion appears to involve a U.N.-administered utopia in which people of all religions, and no religion at all, somehow reach agreement through "dialogue" to respect "human rights" and "the dignity of the human person." This universal flowering of selfless humanitarianism is evidently supposed to occur without the supernatural grace of conversion to the Catholic Faith or any recognition by societies of the reign of Christ the King. Pope John Paul II summed up the new notion in his 1995 address to the United Nations:

> The United Nations has the historic, even momentous task of promoting this qualitative leap in international life ... by fostering values, attitudes and concrete initiatives of solidarity ... The answer to the fear which darkens human existence at the end of the 20th Century is the common effort to build the civilization of

248 *Divini Redemptoris.*

249 *The Wanderer*, June 18, 1998, p. 3.

250 See Vatican web site at http://www.vatican.va

love, founded on universal values of peace, solidarity, justice and liberty ..."[251]

At the "World Day of Prayer for Peace" at Assisi in 1986 Catholics witnessed perhaps the most ambitious of the Vatican's post-conciliar attempts to manifest a non-existent "unity" between the members of the Mystical Body and the adherents of false religions—the same religions deplored by Pius XI in his consecration of the world to the Sacred Heart of Jesus. Hewing perfectly to the Vatican's new agenda, Cardinal Arinze, head of the Vatican Secretariat for Non-Christian Religions, declared that "for building world peace *we need the United Nations*." Cardinal Arinze praised the Pope's "unprecedented step" in calling "leaders of all world religions, Christian and otherwise, to Assisi to pray for peace in the world."[252] The Cardinal did not explain what sort of "peace" he hoped to obtain through the prayers of "religions" which condone the very sins that bring down God's wrath upon the world. War is a punishment for sin, Our Lady told the three children at Fatima. But the New World Order promotes sin while claiming it is for peace. Today it is no longer even suggested by the Vatican that these "leaders" of the "world religions" are false shepherds who preach abortion, contraception, divorce, polygamy, the ordination of women as "priests", the reincarnation of humans as animals, the worship of idols, and innumerable other lies, superstitions and abominations in the sight of God. Instead of warning men to flee false shepherds, the Vatican invited as many of them as it could find to "pray for peace" at Assisi.

Toward the conclusion of the scandalous events at the "World Day of Prayer for Peace", the Pope, holding a potted plant, stood in a kind of chorus line with Protestants, Muslims, Jews, Buddhists, Hindus, Animists, Amerindians, Confucians, Shintoists, and Zoroastrians, all arrayed in a great semicircle outside the Basilica of St. Francis. The Vicar of Christ was depicted for the cameras as just one of many "respected representatives of the world's religions" on equal footing before God in the "search for peace". Eleven years later the Basilica was rocked by three earthquakes, which collapsed the dome of the Basilica and crushed its altar. For those who do not suffer from the Great Amnesia, the crushed altar was a sign easily understood.

When the empty gestures of Assisi were done with, the "respected representatives of the world's religions" returned to their own nations and promptly resumed their age-old opposition to the Reign of Christ the King. In India, Hindu fanatics have been killing priests and nuns almost every year since the "World Day of Prayer for Peace", while Muslim militants of Pakistan shoot Christians on sight. When the Hindu nationalist government of India exploded three atomic bombs underground, people in New Delhi danced in the streets, shouting praise to their Hindu gods.[253] (Perhaps at Assisi the "respected representatives" of the Hindu religion were praying to Shiva, the Hindu god of destruction.) A few days later Pakistan exploded its own atomic bombs, announcing an arms race with India. Meanwhile, in Israel, Jews are still routinely stripped of their citizenship for the "crime" of becoming Christians.

And so goes "the civilization of love." Yet anyone who remembers the teaching of Pope St. Pius X on such notions could have predicted the failure of this dismal modern substitute for the Kingship of Christ. It was St. Pius X who condemned in a fiery apostolic letter the very idea of a brotherhood of the different religions, calling it "a miserable effluent of the great movement of *apostasy* being organized in every country *for the*

251 Address of John Paul II to the United Nations, October 5, 1995.

252 *Assisi: World Day of Prayer for Peace*, Pontifical Commission, Justitia et Pax, Vatican City, 1987, p. 137.

253 Ibid, p. 39.

establishment of a One-World Church ..." And it was he, the only canonized pope in the past 450 years, whose body lies incorrupt in St. Peter's Basilica, who forcefully reminded the world of an essential fact of history which the Vatican of today seems to have forgotten: that the only "civilization of love" the world will ever know "is Christian civilization, it is *the Catholic City*."[254]

How could it be otherwise? For it was Our Lord Himself who told us that He had come to bring not peace, but the sword. The sword of Christendom would mark out an ineradicable dividing line across the world and down the ages between those who would follow Him and those who would not. Being deprived of the grace of Holy Baptism (or having rejected it once received), the men who will not follow Him inevitably destroy the peace of the world through their malice or indifference to Christ the King: "He who is not with Me is against Me; and he who is against Me *scattereth*." This is why Pius XI declared in his encyclical *Ubi Arcano Dei* that "Because men have forsaken God and Jesus Christ, they have sunk to the depths of evil ... The *only remedy* for such a state of affairs is the peace of Christ since the peace of Christ is the peace of God, which could not exist if it did not enjoin respect for law, order and the rights of authority."

In light of Fatima and the constant teaching of the Church before the Council, a few obvious questions will present themselves to any Catholic who ponders the current Vatican program: How could there be a "civilization of love" without the Social Kingship of Christ and obedience to the teaching authority of His Church? As the Council of Trent defined infallibly: "If anyone says that Jesus Christ was given by God to men, as a Redeemer in Whom to trust, and not also as a legislator Whom to obey; let him be anathema."[255] And how could this civilization possibly arise without the triumph of the Immaculate Heart of Mary and the conversion of Russia? Without the grace of baptism, and the supernatural virtues of faith, hope and charity which are the gifts of Christ through His Holy Church, how could men be good for any length of time, much less good enough for long enough to build a "civilization of love"? After all, if men could build a "civilization of love" without the grace of Christ and membership in His Church, then what need was there for Him to hang upon that wretched cross?

But men cannot live in true justice and peace except through the grace of God won for us on Calvary by Jesus Christ's death on the cross. Against the semi-Pelagian heresy of goodness without Christ's grace, Trent infallibly decreed: "If anyone saith that the grace of God through Jesus Christ is given only for this, that man may be able more easily to live justly and to merit eternal life, as if by free will without grace he were able to do both though hardly indeed and with difficulty; let him be anathema."

What should have been obvious all along to the proponents of the new agenda is that without Christ and His Church, the "civilization of love" can only devolve into the very "culture of death" decried by the Pope. The "civilization of love" and the "culture of death" are, in fact, *one and the same thing*, no matter how mightily Pope John Paul II had tried to separate them. A civilization which refuses to submit to Christ and the Church is a civilization which has insured its own death.

Catholics who raise these points in private communications to the Vatican receive no answer. Their inquiries are shunted aside with a polite acknowledgment of receipt, forwarded to a different Vatican office or simply ignored. In the face of the Vatican's monolithic silence, Father Gruner and the apostolate have raised the same questions

254 *Our Apostolic Mandate Against the Sillon*, Section II, Pope St. Pius X, 1910.

255 Council of Trent, Canons on justification, Session 6, Canon 21.

publicly. They too receive no direct answers. But the implicit reply of the Vatican bureaucrats who oppose Father Gruner and his work is this: You and your apostolate will be silenced.

§

Fifty-three years after the Kingship of Christ was replaced by the "civilization of love", certain conclusions suggest themselves: Is the post-conciliar Vatican apparatus embarrassed to tell the world any longer that poor souls are saved from hell through the intercession of Mary's Immaculate Heart, and that without Her intercession souls will be lost forever? Has the Vatican become *ashamed* of the childlike piety of the Message of Fatima in all its sheer Catholicity? Is the story of Fatima to be put away on a shelf like a child's bedtime book, no longer to be read aloud to the adults of "the modern world" exactly as it was written, lest our modern churchmen appear ridiculous?

To the "modern world" and the churchmen who pay it human respect, Fatima may indeed seem a thing for children. And so it is. For every man is a child before God, and all of salvation history tells us that God's children suffer dire consequences whenever they begin to fancy themselves adults—most especially in "the modern world". For this reason did Our Lord teach us that Heaven is a place reserved to those who understand precisely that they *are* children, who must accept with a child's humility the simple, unalterable language of Heaven: "Amen I say to you, whosoever shall not receive the kingdom of God as a little child, shall not enter into it." (Mark 10:15) For this reason, too, was the Message of Fatima confided to children for the edification of adults.

The three little children who knelt by the holm-oak tree at the Cova da Iria that summer, not so long before Vatican II, received from Mary Immaculate nothing less than immaculate simplicity—the simplicity of the Faith Our Lady knew would soon be obscured in an age whose hallmark is a false and deadly sophistication. The great irony of our age will be that its legions of sophisticates, believing themselves to have achieved the adulthood of mankind, were not even children but only squalling babies who pushed away the spiritual nourishment of Holy Mother Church.

This much Father Nicholas Gruner has always understood about Fatima. In its heavenly economy of words, the Fatima message is a summation of everything that has been forgotten in The Great Amnesia: the Roman liturgy, which enshrined the reparatory Sacrifice of the Mass offered on the First Saturdays; the Last Things, which reminded men of their eternal destiny; the divine right of the Church to teach the world with the peremptory authority of God Himself; the Social Kingship of Christ; the triumph of the Immaculate Heart of Mary in a Catholic civilization.

Father Gruner is not alone in understanding what has been lost with the loss of Fatima. Around the world there remain bishops, priests and laity who have not subscribed to the reigning sophistication, who have not succumbed to The Great Amnesia. Yet their number is alarmingly small, for the post-conciliar revolution has claimed many millions of victims. In 2013 the number of priests in the world is 50,000 smaller than it was *53 years earlier*, despite a huge growth in world population. The seminaries and convents have nearly emptied.[256] For the great majority of those who still call themselves Catholic, the teachings of the Magisterium on marriage and procreation are now regarded as nothing more than "the Pope's opinion", and the rate of abortion and divorce among nominal Catholics is the same as that for Protestants and Jews. The people no longer

256 *New York Times*, May 17, 1998, Sec. 4, p. 1.

seem to fear the hellfire which many in the Church no longer mention. But Lucia, Jacinta and Francisco saw the fires of hell for a few moments at Fatima—moments of holy terror which made them into saints. And now the world which ignores hell, which is no longer reminded of hell even by the Vatican itself, is clearly entering into the final arrangements for its own destruction.

As Sister Lucia of Fatima said: "Father ... my mission is to indicate to everyone the imminent danger we are in of losing our souls for all eternity if we remain obstinate in sin. Father, we should not wait for an appeal to the world to come from Rome on the part of the Holy Father, to do penance. Nor should we wait for the call to penance to come from our bishops in our diocese, nor from the religious congregations. No! Our Lord has already very often used these means and the world has not paid attention. That is why now, it is necessary for each one of us to begin to reform himself spiritually. Each person must not only save his own soul but also all the souls that God has placed on our path."[257]

These are the facts which impel Father Gruner to continue shouldering an apostolate that has brought down unending persecution on him and those who have the hardihood to support his work. He remembers. And because he remembers, he is an enemy of the Revolution whose aim is the obliteration of memory and the making of a new future—a future uninformed by the substance of the past. A future without Fatima.

A painting depicting the apparition of the Child Jesus and the Immaculate Heart of Mary, Who, with Her hand resting on Sister Lucia's shoulder, promises salvation to those Catholics who practice the Five First Saturday devotions.

257 For the text of this interview of Sister Lucia with Father Fuentes at Coimbra, see *La Verdad Sobre el Secreto de Fàtima*, page 107. Most Reverend Sanchez, Archbishop of Veracruz, gave the imprimatur for the above interview of Dec. 26, 1957. Also, see Frère François de Marie des Anges, *Fatima: Tragedy and Triumph*, pp. 26-32; also, Frère Michel de la Sainte Trinité, *The Whole Truth About Fatima*, Vol. III, *The Third Secret*, pp. 504-509.

Chapter 20

Court of Mirrors

For the past fifty-three years Vatican emissaries have lectured the world on the need to respect "human rights" in the "civilization of love." But what of the Vatican's own tribunals? Even the aridly humanistic Universal Declaration of Rights, adopted by the U.N. General Assembly in 1948, recognizes that "Everyone is entitled in full equity to a fair and public hearing by an independent and impartial tribunal, in the determination of his rights and obligations ..." [258] John Paul II has hailed the Declaration as "one of the highest expressions of the human conscience of our time."

Yet it appeared that the judges of the Vatican tribunals considered themselves exempt from the standard of justice the Vatican preaches to other men. Even godless civil tribunals recognize the right to an impartial judge; the right to a specification of charges; the right to a fair and open hearing; the right to confront witnesses; the right to appeal an unjust decision to an impartial appellate court. For Father Nicholas Gruner, however, none of these rights seemed to be operative in the chambers of the Congregation for the Clergy and the Apostolic Signatura. How many other disfavored priests had been sucked into this human-rights vacuum, and then ejected with their reputations and priestly status in shreds?

In the documents he had filed in the Congregation and the Signatura, Father Gruner had provided incontrovertible evidence that the canonical proceedings against him were an utter sham: that the orders recalling him to Avellino were not the bishop's orders, but those of Cardinal Agustoni, Prefect of the Apostolic Signatura; Cardinal Sanchez, Prefect of the Congregation for the Clergy; and Archbishop Sepe, the Congregation's Secretary—all of them secretly dictating the result in the very case in which they were sitting as judges.

Father Gruner had pointed out that such interference in the jurisdiction of a bishop over his own diocese was unprecedented in the annals of canon law, for the Church has always taught that the bishop is the monarch of his own diocese. That Agustoni, Sanchez and Sepe were Vatican prelates of higher rank than the Bishop of Avellino was beside the point. They had no right to tamper with the divine constitution of the Church by commandeering the Diocese of Avellino and turning its bishop into their puppet. On the contrary, their functions as members of Vatican tribunals was supposed to be the correction of abuses of power by bishops, not using a bishop to commit abuses themselves.

Father Gruner's proofs had even included a copy of the providentially uncovered 1989 letter from Cardinal Agustoni to the Bishop of Avellino, directing the bishop to recall Father Gruner and pretend that it was all the bishop's idea. The discovery of that "smoking gun" had finally forced the removal of Agustoni from further consideration of Father Gruner's case in January of 1997—the first time in the history of the Signatura that its Prefect had been forced to step down on grounds of bias. Yet Agustoni had already rendered his adverse decision of May 1995 upholding the Bishop of Avellino's first order to return—the very order Agustoni himself had secretly directed the bishop to issue.

Father Gruner had presented enough evidence of gross judicial misconduct to

258 Universal Declaration of Human Rights (1948), Article 7.

reverse any verdict in a secular, civil tribunal. But the judges of the Church tribunals who were executing *the Plan* for Father Gruner's demise were evidently unmoved by any sense that the justice of the Church should exceed that of the scribes and pharisees of the secular judiciary. No, *the Plan* would proceed unimpeded by the notions of "justice and solidarity" which the Vatican prescribed for the hypothetical "civilization of love."

In July 1997, some eight months after the Third Fatima Conference in Rome, Father Gruner would receive the Apostolic Signatura's decree on his recourse from the first order to return to Avellino. It was no surprise that the removal of Cardinal Agustoni had not altered the predetermined result. The matter had simply been turned over to Agustoni's right-hand man, Archbishop Zenon Grochelewski, Secretary of the Signatura, who rejected the recourse with the terse Latin phrase *manifeste caret quolibet fundamento*—manifestly without any foundation whatsoever. It was the Latinate way of saying: "We refuse to hear your case."

Archbishop Grochelewski was another biased gatekeeper standing at the gateway of the tribunal. Several months before Archbishop Grochelewski's decree, Father Gruner had conferred in Rome with canonist Franco Ligi about taking his case. Ligi is an eminent attorney who practices in both the Vatican tribunals and the Supreme Court of Italy's civil judicial system. After speaking with Grochelewski at the offices of the Signatura, Ligi had declined to take the case. Ligi told Father Gruner that Archbishop Grochelewski had audaciously admitted that the case was really not about Father Gruner's incardination in this or that diocese, but about "what he says. He causes division." Division in what sense? Was there anything false in what Father Gruner said? Or was the "division" Grochelewski complained of the result of a priest speaking the truth about Christ the King and the triumph of His Queen Mother, in an epoch in which those subjects had become intensely embarrassing to the Vatican? Was it not the very division Our Lord Himself had predicted would arise from the preaching of the Gospel, as summed up with heavenly conciseness in the Message of Fatima?

Ligi had readily agreed with Father Gruner that if the case was really about what Father Gruner said, then it should be transferred to the Congregation for the Doctrine of the Faith, where Father Gruner could defend his preaching and teaching on their merits. That would never happen, of course. A doctrinal examination of Father Gruner's work was the last thing Grochelewski and his fellow executors of *the Plan* wanted to see, for it would only lead to an acquittal of their target. The case would remain in the Signatura. And now it was in the hands of Archbishop Grochelewski, who had openly admitted to Ligi that the entire proceeding was a pretext for suppressing an apostolate that could not otherwise be suppressed.

Grochelewski's decree stated that Father Gruner's recourse had been rejected on the technical ground that it was not filed within fifteen days of Cardinal Agustoni's 1995 decision upholding the first order to return to Avellino. Yet Father Gruner had never received a copy of that decision from the offices of the Signatura in the first place, so how could he have known there was a decision to appeal? The answer given in the decree was that Father Gruner's canon lawyer had received a copy. But the aged canonist was so gravely ill that he had failed to notify Father Gruner of the decision for nearly seventeen months after it was issued, and Father Gruner had not even known of the decision until it was published months later by the Blue Army in *Soul* magazine. Too bad. *Manifeste caret quolibet fundamento*.

But even civil courts administered by unbelievers allow blameless litigants to reopen cases which are "defaulted" through a lawyer's illness or negligence. Surely a tribunal of the Catholic Church would be at least as just as godless civil tribunals in similar circumstances. Not so. *Manifeste caret quolibet fundamento*.

Yes, but seriously, how could Father Gruner be expected to appeal in fifteen days a decision of which he had no knowledge until its contents appeared, many months later, in the Blue Army's magazine? Most unfortunate. *Manifeste caret quolibet fundamento*.

Well, then, what about the intolerable injustice of the whole affair? Father Gruner had discovered and presented to the Signatura conclusive proof that it was Cardinal Agustoni who secretly instigated the order to return to Avellino, counseling the Bishop of Avellino to pretend that it was the bishop's own idea. If Cardinal Agustoni was forced to step down now because of this discovery, should he not have stepped down *before* he had rendered his decision against Father Gruner? How could Agustoni be allowed to get away with the ruse of sitting in judgment on an appeal from what were, in essence, his own actions, falsely posing as an impartial judge of the "bishop's" order to return? Was not Agustoni's 1995 decree null and void as a fraud upon Father Gruner? Sorry, too late. *Manifeste caret quolibet fundamento.*

What, then, of Father Gruner's right to his good name? Father Gruner had pointed out that Cardinal Agustoni's self-serving decision was laden with easily demonstrable falsehoods, including the suggestion that Father Gruner was a "vagus" (wandering) priest, when in truth he had written permission from the Bishop of Avellino to reside in Canada. Was not Father Gruner entitled to repair the damage to his reputation which resulted when Agustoni's "confidential" decree was leaked to *Soul* magazine, where it was published throughout North America? No, not at all. *Manifeste caret quolibet fundamento.*

Thus did Grochelewski's three-page decree dispose of the entire life's work and good name of a Catholic priest who had committed no offense against either faith or morals. The contrast with cases of real priestly misconduct was astonishing: Pedophile and pederast priests are moved from parish to parish by their bishops for years, until someone in their train of victims files criminal charges or a multimillion dollar civil suit.[259] Preachers of the most outrageous heresy are left alone, or simply reassigned to another pulpit on belated orders from the Vatican, while remaining priests in good standing.[260] But for Father Nicholas Gruner the wheels of Vatican justice were grinding away with a remarkable and remorseless efficiency which seemed to suggest that, as to him at least, the judicial machine was conscious, vigilant and determined to reach a final result.

And yet the case was not entirely over. There remained to be decided Father Gruner's second recourse to the Signatura, against the Bishop of Avellino's second order to return. It was this order which (unlike the first) carried an actual threat of suspension from the priesthood if Father Gruner did not agree to incarcerate himself forever in Avellino. Squarely at issue in the second recourse was Father Gruner's incardination by the Archbishop of Hyderabad, the second prelate in less than three years who had offered in writing to sponsor Father Gruner's work in a friendly diocese. Cardinal Sanchez and Archbishop Sepe, in the Congregation for the Clergy, had already declared the

259 Among hundreds of examples: The Diocese of Stockton, California was subjected to a verdict of $23 million for harboring a pedophile priest by shuttling him from parish to parish in response to complaints from victims and their parents. The jury was persuaded to award the damages by the evasive testimony of Cardinal Roger Mahony, who failed to explain why, when he was Bishop of Stockton, he had approved the continual reassignment of a known pedophile. The Diocese of Dallas, Texas was subjected to a liability verdict of $123,000,000 under virtually identical circumstances.

260 Richard Owen, London Times Foreign News Service, March 26, 1998.

incardination in Hyderabad to be "non-existent." What would the Signatura say about this unprecedented canonical magic of the vanishing incardination?

As Father Gruner awaited the answer, the tide was beginning to turn in another forum: the forum of public opinion. When the executors of *the Plan* had leaked Agustoni's decree in the first recourse to the Catholic press, it was evidently expected that Father Gruner's apostolate would be mortally wounded by the mere disclosure in *Soul* magazine that "the Church's highest court" (i.e., Cardinal Agustoni) had "ruled" that Father Gruner was a "vagus" who had "failed" to find a bishop to incardinate him, and that he was "disobedient" in failing to return to Avellino. Of course, *Soul* had not disclosed that the only reason Father Gruner had "failed" to find another bishop is that Agustoni, *et al.* had systematically prevented him from doing so.

But the resort to public opinion would prove to be a costly mistake. Publication of the decree in *Soul* had opened the door to a public reply by Father Gruner and the apostolate in *The Fatima Crusader* magazine and elsewhere. As the people learned the details of *the Plan*, a groundswell of outrage began to build on the part of bishops, priests and laity who had seen enough of the double-standard which sheltered pedophiles and pederasts and heretics while mercilessly hounding a Marian priest.

Anticipating the inevitable decision in the second recourse, in mid-1997 the apostolate began circulating for signature a second Open Letter to John Paul II for publication in the Italian press, pleading once again for the Pope's intercession in Father Gruner's case. The response was galvanic: over several months, twenty-seven bishops—including ten archbishops—1,500 priests and nuns and more than 15,000 members of the laity had signed the letter. The number of bishops willing to sign had increased more than thirteen-fold since the first Open Letter in 1995.

The bureaucrats' campaign to consign Father Gruner to oblivion was suddenly losing ground rather dramatically; the press leaks of the Signatura's decrees had only exposed *the Plan* to withering public scrutiny. Viewed in the public forum they had chosen to enter, the maneuverings of Sanchez, Sepe and Agustoni enjoyed no more respectability than any other abuse of power.

By early February 1998 Father Gruner had received the reply to his second recourse, containing the expected result. The Signatura's latest decree (issued by Archbishop Grochelewski in the absence of Agustoni) advised Father Gruner that his recourse would not even be admitted for discussion to the judges of the tribunal. The recourse had been stopped again on Grochelewski's desk with the same peremptory Latin phrase: *Manifeste caret quolibet fundamento*. This time, however, the executors of *the Plan* had felt constrained to drape their doings with a bit of window-dressing, in light of the unfavorable publicity they had brought down upon themselves. Enter the "promoter of justice."

In canon law the "promoter of justice" is ostensibly a neutral third-party who assesses the facts and law of a case and renders an independent opinion on how it ought to be decided. In this case, not surprisingly, the "promoter of justice" would serve as the Promoter of the Predetermined Result—the result which had already been ordained in the secret missive of Cardinal Agustoni to the Bishop of Avellino.

Unknown to Father Gruner the "promoter of justice" had issued "findings" of fact and law in Latin even before Grochelewski's decree was issued. Father Gruner's new advocate, Sandro Gherro, was supposed to answer the document and forward a copy to Father Gruner in accordance with the terms of his written mandate. In an astounding repetition of the former advocate's dereliction, Gherro simply filed the document away, offered no reply whatsoever and failed even to advise Father Gruner that the document existed. This was malpractice of the grossest sort—rather like a civil lawyer accepting delivery of papers in a lawsuit against his client, failing to answer the suit in time, and then saying nothing to the client until after a default judgment is entered for millions of dollars. In Father Gruner's case, however, the matter at stake—the exercise of his sacred priesthood—was worth infinitely more than any sum of money. A "default judgment" in this case could have spiritual consequences beyond all human calculation. The "promoter of justice" had issued his report on November 22, 1997—the feast day of St. Cecilia, who was killed on that date by the repeated blows of an axe. Soon Father Gruner would learn that the first axe-blow had fallen on him.

In fourteen pages of tortured reasoning the "promoter of justice"—completely unopposed by Gherro—had "found" that it was perfectly just and proper that a priest of twenty years' standing, who had done nothing wrong, and who, moreover, had found three benevolent bishops willing to accept him in their dioceses, should be subjected to the following measures: (a) return to Avellino on 29 days' notice, after having resided in Canada without objection for more than 16 years; (b) immediate destruction of his entire life's work with the apostolate, even though three bishops were perfectly willing to foster it in their dioceses; (c) dismissal of the apostolate's 150 employees; (d) an end to subsidies for the orphanage caring for over 50 children which the apostolate's funds were supporting; (e) abandonment of his residence, his relatives and his personal affairs in Canada, and (f) virtual life imprisonment, under threat of suspension from the priesthood, in a foreign diocese whose bishop had not requested his services since 1978!

And why would this horror be a "just" result, according to the "promoter of justice"? The document had not even attempted to develop a canonical rationale for treating a morally upright priest with vastly greater harshness than the roving pedophiles and pederasts and public heretics who were afflicting the post-conciliar Church with near-impunity. All the "promoter of justice" could offer was the naked conclusion that "There were grave reasons for denying a letter of excardination" from Avellino, so that Father Gruner could be incardinated in Hyderabad. And what were these "grave reasons" for denying excardination? Why, they were "the same grave reasons for recalling Father Gruner to the diocese." Alright, then: What were the grave reasons for recalling Father Gruner to the diocese? Moving on to the next paragraph, the "promoter of justice" had simply left the question unanswered. But the answer was understood implicitly, not only by the "promoter of justice" but by everyone else who was collaborating in the execution of *the Plan*: The "grave reasons" for recalling Father Nicholas Gruner to the Diocese of Avellino, and preventing him from finding a home in any other diocese in the world, were these: First, Father Gruner had been far too effective, for far too long, in promoting the Message of Fatima. Second, the Message of Fatima was an intolerably embarrassing reminder that the interdenominational "civilization of love" being promoted by Vatican emissaries was not exactly the triumph of the Immaculate Heart which Our Lady had proclaimed at Fatima. Nor was the current agenda what Pope Pius XI had envisioned when he proclaimed the Feast of Christ the King and prayed before the whole world that God would rescue idolaters, Muslims and Jews from their darkness and bring them into the one true Church.

In short, Father Gruner and the apostolate were an annoyingly persistent reminder of the teaching of all the Popes before 1960 on the Social Kingship of Christ and the

Queenship of Mary. But that teaching had been replaced by the "Spirit of Vatican II", by *Ostpolitik* and world ecumenism, by "dialogue", "human rights" and the "civilization of love." The new vocabulary could not be at home with the old. All the antiquated pre-conciliar talk of kings and queens, and every knee bending before the Lord, and Russia converting, and the triumph of the Immaculate Heart—all of it was hopelessly out of place in the new arrangements Vatican emissaries had forged with the powers of the world, and most especially the United Nations. It was necessary, then, that Father Gruner and the apostolate be silenced, but not in a way which would call any attention to the underlying questions.

The "promoter of justice" had been called upon to do more than merely affix his stamp of approval to *the Plan*. For *the Plan* had fared disastrously in the court of public opinion, and its executors surely knew that the second Open Letter was circulating for signatures among clergy around the world, with publication in Rome imminent. Since early 1994, when the first order to return was issued, Agustoni, Sanchez and Sepe had counted on the "incardination game" to force a checkmate that would exile Father Gruner to Avellino or subject him to suspension if he declined exile. But now the situation was drastically different: Over the past six months a growing number of the apostolate's supporters, including twenty righteously angry bishops, were demanding to know why, in a Church ridden with unchecked scandal and heresy, a perfectly sound priest was being blocked by the Vatican itself from finding a friendly bishop to incardinate him. What in heaven's name was going on here?

The executors of *the Plan* were now confronted with their own failure to give any substantive grounds for all of their unprecedented actions against this one priest. After all, if Father Gruner hadn't actually *done* anything contrary to faith or morals, a reasonable observer could only wonder why his pursuers would not just leave the man alone and let him find another bishop—like all the other priests who transfer routinely from diocese to diocese throughout the Church without any objection from the Vatican, including the pedophiles, pederasts and public heretics.

The "promoter of justice" had attempted to fix this lingering problem for his superiors: His "findings" asserted that Father Gruner had indeed done something wrong which justified his harsh treatment: Why, he had perpetrated a "fraud" on the Archbishop of Hyderabad in order to obtain incardination there. And what exactly was this "fraud"? According to the promoter, in November 1995 Father Gruner had "acted fraudulently" with the Archbishop by presenting him with the 1978 document issued by the Bishop of Avellino, which gave him permission to be incardinated in any diocese that would accept him. And why was this a "fraud"? Because the 1978 document "was already destitute of all juridic value", according to the promoter.

But the claim of "fraud" was obviously false: In the first place, Father Gruner had not presented the 1978 document to the Archbishop of Hyderabad at the time of his incardination, nor was there any evidence to suggest that he had. The "promoter of justice" had simply "promoted" a non-existent event into a "fact". Furthermore, even if Father Gruner had presented the 1978 document to the Archbishop in 1995, it could not possibly have been "destitute of all juridic value" at that time, because the opinion that it was "destitute of all juridic value" was not expressed by the "promoter of justice" until November of 1997, more than two years later. In essence, the "promoter of justice" had accused Father Gruner of "fraud" for failing to see into the future!

In an effort to make sense of his absurd accusation, the promoter further claimed that Father Gruner should have known the 1978 document was "destitute of all juridic value" because it had been "revoked" when the Bishop of Avellino issued his first order to return on January 31, 1994. But the first order to return did not even mention the 1978 document, let alone revoke it. Thus, despite the order to return, Father Gruner would have been free to find another bishop to accept him under the original terms of the 1978 document. He had indeed found another bishop in the Archbishop of Hyderabad. What is more, under canon law a priest has the right to transfer to another diocese whenever it would be in his best interest. It was clearly in Father Gruner's best interest to transfer from a diocese whose bishop was manifestly hostile, to a diocese where a benevolent bishop had offered to accept him.

All of this was evidently understood by the Bishop of Avellino: When Father Gruner informed him in writing (in early 1996) that he had achieved incardination in Hyderabad and need not return to Avellino, the bishop had offered no objection to the incardination for months.

In attempting to explain away these facts, the promoter had made some remarkable disclosures in his "findings": Sometime in March of 1996, about four months after Father Gruner's incardination in the Archdiocese of Hyderabad by Archbishop Arulappa, the Bishop of Avellino had sought "clarification" of Father Gruner's status from Cardinal Sanchez of the Congregation for the Clergy. This was a very odd request indeed, since Cardinal Sanchez would soon be required to serve as the "impartial" judge of Father Gruner's appeal from the bishop's second order to return to Avellino. How could Sanchez legitimately confer in private with the very bishop whose order was about to be appealed to Sanchez by Father Gruner? What about the requirement of neutrality on the part of an appellate judge?

The promoter also disclosed that Sanchez had thereafter (on March 18, 1996) issued a quite unprecedented letter to Archbishop Arulappa—a letter whose text Father Gruner had yet to see, but whose existence the promoter was now confirming. In this letter Sanchez had "advised" the Archbishop that Father Gruner's incardination in Hyderabad was "*tanquam non existens*"—non-existent. According to the promoter, Sanchez's letter had also related how Sanchez "explained" to the Bishop of Avellino that when the bishop issued his decree of January 31, 1994, recalling Father Gruner to Avellino for the first time, he had intended by that same decree to "revoke" Father Gruner's 1978 permission to be incardinated in another diocese—even though the decree did not actually say so! Since the bishop himself had not given this interpretation to his own decree, Sanchez had "clarified the situation" for him. In other words, the Bishop of Avellino was privately instructed by Sanchez that he was to "intend" whatever Sanchez told him to intend, even if it was after the fact. Thus, not only the Bishop of Avellino's authority over his own diocese, but his very thought processes had been commandeered by *the Plan*.

So the "promoter of justice" had done justice in spite of himself. His disclosure of the Sanchez letter uncovered the second "smoking gun" in the proceedings, and it explained a great deal: After having failed to object to Father Gruner's incardination in Hyderabad for several months, the Bishop of Avellino had suddenly issued his decree of May 16, 1996, declaring that Father Gruner's incardination in Hyderabad was "tanquam non existens"—precisely the same language which appeared in Sanchez's letter to the Archbishop of Hyderabad. Some five months after the promoter's disclosure of its existence, Father Gruner would finally receive a copy of the Sanchez letter from Archbishop Arulappa, in April of 1998. Only then would Father Gruner notice that not only the telltale phrase "*tanquam non existens*", but an entire paragraph had been lifted from the Sanchez letter and placed bodily into the Bishop of Avellino's May 16, 1996, decree, containing the second order to return to Avellino. The words of the Bishop's decree had literally been dictated to him by Sanchez.

Thus, the appellate judge, Cardinal Sanchez, had told the lower court, the Bishop of Avellino, exactly how to rule on the case even before Father Gruner's appeal from that ruling had come before Sanchez. The whole appellate process in the Congregation for the Clergy had been a fraud.

It had already been proven that it was Cardinal Agustoni who secretly initiated the first order to return to Avellino, pretending it was all the bishop's idea when Father Gruner's appeal from that order came before Agustoni in the Signatura. Now it had just been established beyond doubt that it was Cardinal Sanchez who initiated the second order to return, even supplying its precise wording, only to pretend to be reviewing "the bishop's intervention" (as Sanchez called it) when Father Gruner's second recourse came to him in the Congregation for the Clergy, on its way to the Signatura.

Twice in the same case, therefore, judges of Vatican tribunals had engaged in the outrageous charade of "reviewing" the propriety of an order they themselves secretly had instructed the Bishop of Avellino to issue. And now the "promoter of justice" was defending that charade as perfectly fair and just.

The "promoter of justice" would end his "findings" with the amazing conclusion that "the Bishop of Avellino acted according to law when he (!) threatened the penalty of suspension" in the second order to return. Not once in his fourteen pages of "findings", however, did the "promoter of justice" even hint at the glaring truth: the Bishop of Avellino's every action in the case from beginning to end had been orchestrated from "on high" by Cardinal Agustoni, Cardinal Sanchez and Archbishop Sepe. The "findings" of the "promoter of justice" had been nothing more than a paper construct to cover over what was really going on beneath the surface of the case.

Since Sandro Gherro had failed to offer any reply to the "promoter of justice", it had been a simple matter for Archbishop Grochelewski to reject Father Gruner's recourse from the second order to return, based on the "facts" as determined by the promoter—to which "facts", Grochelewski pointedly noted, "the advocate (Gherro) for the recurrent (Father Gruner) did not respond." When Gherro was confronted with this debacle, he would react in a manner which by now seemed rather typical of legal representation in the Roman tribunals of the Church: He sent a letter declaring that he intended to renounce his representation of Father Gruner unless Father Gruner expressed complete satisfaction with his "services", agreed not to question the legitimacy of any further proceedings in the Signatura, no matter what the outcome, and paid him $5,000 in additional fees immediately.

Within a few days Father Gruner flew to Rome and secured the services of another canonist: Alan Kershaw, an American living in Italy, and the only American regularly practicing in the Vatican tribunals. Kershaw evinced a keen intelligence in his immediate penetration to the heart of the matter: There had been a gross abuse of power which had been hidden from effective review by a series of peremptory rulings—issued by the perpetrators of the abuse themselves—that Father Gruner's recourses were "manifestly without foundation" (*manifeste quolibet caret fundamentum*). Father Gruner's case had been declared lacking any foundation even though he had yet to receive a hearing of his claims.

In addition to intelligence and an evident willingness to fight for his client, as opposed to rolling over and playing dead, Kershaw had the merit of being an American. As such, he had neither penetrated, nor been captured by, the network of obsequiously deferential "old line" Roman advocates of the Signatura—men who seemed to think their function was to provide a rather terse canonical burial service for their clients, in suitably dignified Latin, for which they expected to be paid rather large sums of money.

Kershaw had noticed something else about the case, one of those facts so obvious that it can easily be overlooked: The order to return to Avellino was a blatant violation of Italian immigration law. Since Father Gruner had never been a citizen or permanent resident of Italy, the Bishop of Avellino had no legal right in the first place to order him to take up permanent residence in Italy! In fact, Kershaw was familiar with the cases of non-Italian priests and nuns who had been expelled from Italy precisely for attempting to take up permanent residence without the proper immigration status. Father Gruner could literally be arrested at the airport and deported back to Canada for attempting to "obey" the order to return. So *the Plan* was not only a violation of canon law, but also Italian civil law—a point the executors of *the Plan* had never even bothered to consider. But Kershaw was about to bring it to their attention.

With only a few days remaining to meet the deadline for a final appeal, Kershaw and his assistant, Andrea Fuligni, agreed to accept the case during an emergency meeting at the Hotel Michelangelo, a few hundred feet from the Vatican walls. Kershaw's strategy was simple: If the matter could only be gotten past Grochelewski and placed before all the judges of the Signatura for a full hearing, there was a chance that justice would result. Perhaps one or more of the judges would be repelled by the spectacle of the proceedings to date, and sway some of the other judges. Or perhaps the Pope would take action on the still-pending canonical lawsuit he had received during the third Fatima conference in Rome—assuming he had ever been allowed to read it.

To have any chance of succeeding, Kershaw knew that he would have to risk embarrassing the Signatura with the almost unbelievable malfeasance of its own functionaries—something that he, unlike the previous "advocates", was not afraid to do. He moved swiftly to file the necessary pleadings.

On March 28, 1998, Kershaw would submit his appeal to the Plenaria, the Latin term for the full bank of judges in the Signatura. In essence, Kershaw would ask all of the judges to examine the case themselves for the first time in the proceedings, instead of relying upon the "advice" of Grochelewski and the now-recused Cardinal Agustoni. This document would be followed by a petition for *restitutione in integrum*—an extraordinary plea to set aside all previous decrees in the case on grounds of newly discovered evidence. That evidence was the actual text of the letter of Cardinal Sanchez to the Archbishop of Hyderabad, which Father Gruner had just received from the Archbishop. This new evidence demonstrated (if any doubt remained) that the entire canonical process so far had been a sham in which the Bishop of Avellino was reduced to a helpless puppet whose decrees were the void products of coercion from above, rather than his own decisions in the matter.

The appeal to the Plenaria included a statement by Father Gruner raising two simple questions he hoped the tribunal would finally answer:

> Will the highest Tribunal of the Holy Catholic Church tolerate a proceeding in which the judges are allowed to act secretly as adverse parties against the very priest they are judging, preventing him from carrying out the very order they

> convict him of disobeying, while the nominal promoter of justice turns a blind eye to what they are doing?
>
> Will this tribunal allow to stand clearly erroneous findings of fact and law which have resulted in part from the failure of two of its own certified advocates to perform their most basic duty?

§

Five days after Kershaw had lodged the appeal to the Signatura, the Second Open Letter to the Pope appeared in the major Roman daily *Il Messaggero*. The first of the twenty bishops whose signatures appeared in support of Father Gruner was that of Archbishop Saminini Arulappa, the Archbishop of Hyderabad. Two months later the Archbishop would write to praise Father Gruner for his help in building the orphanage the apostolate was subsidizing, and to express his good wishes to both Father Gruner and the apostolate. It did not appear that the Archbishop considered himself to have been "defrauded" by Father Gruner, as the "promoter of justice" had speciously asserted in his "findings of fact." One could imagine the promoter's reddened face as he viewed the Archbishop's signature in *Il Messaggero*, or on the 2,000 posters of the Open Letter on display around the Vatican—every poster putting the lie to his concocted accusation. What would the judges of the Signatura make of this? Only time would tell.

The Open Letter expressed with firmness and respect the signers' plea to their Pope for even-handedness, at last, in the case of Father Gruner:

> Your Holiness, Father Gruner has given voice to the concerns of many of these loyal Catholics, including all of us. Can we not be heard in a matter which concerns the good of the Church and the salvation of souls? Or will it really be the case that the ever-multiplying voices of dissent continue to be tolerated, while Father Gruner is mercilessly hounded, exiled and silenced for preaching the Message of Fatima?

The signers' reference to the invidious double-standard of justice in the post-conciliar Church was borne out with exquisite timing by none other than Cardinal Angelo Sodano, the Vatican Secretary of State. Only a week before the Open Letter was published, Sodano had delivered a heavily publicized address in which he praised the writings of Hans Kung, the most notorious dissident "theologian" of this century. The address was delivered at the Lateran, the official cathedral church of the City of Rome and a site of immense importance in Catholic history. The choice of venue was clearly no accident.

Kung has questioned every Catholic doctrine from the divinity of Christ to the Real Presence, and has called for women priests and Church approval of divorce and contraception. Yet Kung has remained a priest in good standing—even though, in addition to his public heresies, he has condemned John Paul II for "rigid, stagnating and despotic rule in the spirit of the Inquisition."[261] While the Pope, acting through Cardinal Ratzinger, had declared in 1979 that Küng could no longer claim to be a Catholic theologian, Sodano had pointedly described Küng in his address as "the Swiss theologian" who has written "beautiful pages dedicated to the Christian mystery." It was as if Sodano regarded the Pope as already dead and buried, and was jockeying for access to the papal throne with his conspicuous appearance at the Lateran. That indeed is how the press would "spin" Sodano's brazen public tribute to the Pope's avowed enemy:

261 Richard Owen, London Times Foreign News Service, March 26, 1998.

POPE'S RIGHT-HAND MAN STAKES HIS CLAIM TO THRONE

London Times Foreign News Service

> The Pope's right-hand man yesterday attempted to emerge from the shadow of the ailing pontiff and raise his profile as a potential successor by declaring that the Roman Catholic Church needed urgent and continuous reform under a strong papacy for the new millennium. Cardinal Angelo Sodano, the Vatican Secretary of State, astonished Vatican-watchers by praising Hans Küng, the Swiss theologian and the fiercest liberal critic of the Pope ... Küng's views are anathema to the Pope ...[262]

A renegade priest from Switzerland, who denies dogmas of the Faith and condemns the Pope as a despot, had not only retained his good standing as a priest but had received lavish public praise from the Vatican Secretary of State. Yet an orthodox Catholic priest from Canada, devoted to the Blessed Virgin Mary, had been ordered into permanent exile under threat of suspension from the priesthood. Sodano had confirmed everything the Open Letter would say about the state of the Church today.

This second Open Letter aroused even greater interest in the Italian press than the first, not least because 27 bishops had subscribed to it. But the aim of the second Open Letter, like the first, was not publicity for its own sake or a public exchange with the Vatican. The aim was to convey an urgent message to the Pope in the only forum left open to the apostolate and its supporters. Perhaps, this time, the message would bear fruit. Perhaps, just once, a group of faithful orthodox Catholics would be able to obtain redress by the same sort of public entreaty the liberals had been using so effectively since the Council to pressure the Vatican for everything from Communion in the hand to altar girls, with the Vatican caving in every time.

Only a few months before the second Open Letter appeared in *Il Messaggero*, public protests by liberals in the diocese of Chur, Switzerland had resulted in the Vatican ordering the transfer of its conservative bishop, whose principal "offense" was to rid the diocese of its plethora of women "ministers" and lay "preachers".[263] And only two months after the Open Letter was published, the leader of Austria's "We Are Church" movement would be invited to sit in the V.I.P. section at the outdoor papal Mass, next to the Pope himself. The dissident would impudently reject the offer because the Pope had not yet agreed to change Church teaching in accordance with his demands. Yet Austria's Cardinal Schoenborn had extended the invitation as part of his effort "to make peace in Austria's church by engaging in dialogue with Catholic dissidents."[264]

There had been no peace overtures in the war against Father Nicholas Gruner and the apostolate, nor any offer of "dialogue." The double-standard decried in the Open Letter was alive and well. For it was evident that what Father Gruner and the apostolate were promoting was far more disturbing to certain members of the Vatican apparatus than the heresy and apostasy flourishing throughout the Church. What Father Gruner and the apostolate were promoting was a teaching that simply could not exist in "the civilization of love"; the teaching Our Lady had given to three peasant children standing before a holm oak tree at Fatima:

> "You have seen Hell, where the souls of poor sinners go. To save them, God

262 Ibid.

263 Reuters News Service report, December 21, 1997.

264 *New York Times*, June 22, 1998, p. A-11.

> wishes to establish in the world devotion to My Immaculate Heart ... In the end, My Immaculate Heart will triumph. The Holy Father will consecrate Russia to Me, which will be converted, and a period of peace will be granted to the world ..."

In the "civilization of love" there was no longer to be any talk of poor sinners going to hell, or souls being saved from hell through the intercession of the Virgin Mary, or the conversion of nations, or the triumph of the Immaculate Heart throughout the world. None of this had any place in the negotiations and endless concessions by Vatican diplomats to men who reject the one true religion—a process that had begun with *Ostpolitik* and was continuing now with the emergence of the New World Order.

Three months after his public praise of Hans Küng, Cardinal Sodano would meet privately at the Vatican with U.N. General Secretary General Koffi Anan.[265] The topic of their discussion was the creation of an International Criminal Court (ICC) under the auspices of the United Nations. The ICC was to have the power to indict the citizens of any nation for various "crimes against humanity." It was a safe bet that the list of "crimes against humanity" would never include the holocaust of abortion, which the U.N. subsidizes throughout the world.

Curiously enough, the ICC conference was being held in Rome. Sodano's apparatus had already expressed its enthusiastic support for this newest expansion of U.N. authority: Archbishop Martino, the Vatican's permanent observer at the United Nations, declared in *L'Osservatore Romano* that "the creation of an International Criminal Court is a very important initiative which will touch upon the rights and lives of nations and communities ... May almighty God bless *our efforts* so that future generations will look upon this Court as a substantial contribution to respect for law and for the rights of all men and women in the world ..."[266] On July 12, 1998, the ICC treaty was approved by the overwhelming majority of the nations represented at the conference, including the Vatican City-State. The United States, however, rejected the treaty as a threat to national sovereignty. The Vatican hailed the monster it had helped to create as "an historic step" that would afford "ever greater protection and wider expansion of human rights."[267] It was far from apparent how "human rights" could be protected and expanded by an international version of the same godless courts which had already "legalized" genocide of the unborn in every nation. Nor was it apparent why the U.N., which was promoting that genocide throughout the world, should be looked upon by the Vatican as a trustworthy guardian of human rights.

The feminist proponents of the ICC had demanded that any effort to restrict abortion be prosecuted by the new super-court as a form of "enforced pregnancy." The Vatican was pleased to announce, however, that after intense negotiations the term "enforced pregnancy" would be limited to rape. At least for now.[268] It is diplomatic "victories" like this for which the Vatican settles today; the pruning of a twig or two from the bad tree of the New World Order. More than twelve hundred years ago, St. Boniface picked up an axe and struck the "Tree of Thor" again and again. When the oak totem crashed to the ground the conversion of Germany began. Today, Vatican representatives clamber about in the branches of a vastly larger bad tree, looking for twigs to remove. It does not seem to occur to them that the tree itself must be toppled in the name of Christ the

265 "U.N. Chief Seeks Help for International Court", EWTN news report, June 16, 1998.

266 *L'Osservatore Romano*, June 17, 1998.

267 "Vatican Greets International Court", EWTN Vatican Update, July 20, 1998.

268 Ibid.

King. The Kingship of Christ which sounded out in every blow of the axe wielded by St. Boniface has been replaced by the timid snip-snip of the Vatican's pruning shears.

Here again it seemed that the Vatican's representatives had overlooked questions which would have been obvious to pre-conciliar churchmen:

If the civil judicial systems of the various nations had already created what John Paul II decries as a "culture of death", including abortion and mercy-killing, how could the cause of "human rights" be advanced by erecting an international super-court staffed by the same godless judges?

When this super-court inevitably expanded its jurisdiction to add such things as "hate crimes" against homosexuals or pro-life activism to the list of "crimes against humanity", how was the Vatican going to protect the rights of Catholics who might be unjustly accused of these newly-minted "crimes"? Would Vatican bureaucrats be able to prevent the arrest of Catholics in their homes, and their deportation for a trial at the Hague or wherever else the super-court directs?

In America, for example, pro-life protesters are convicted of "racketeering" in federal lawsuits brought by abortionists who kill children for a living. What guarantees was the Vatican prepared to give that such suits would not find their way into the new super-courts? What protection would the Vatican be able to offer Catholics indicted in such cases? Could the Vatican be counted on even to issue a statement deploring the unjust prosecution by the very court the Vatican helped to create?

And what of the Church's constant teaching on the Catholic principle of "subsidiarity" in such encyclicals as *Quadragesimo anno* by Pius IX? Subsidiarity requires that governmental functions be conducted at the *lowest* possible level, not the highest, in order to decentralize power, prevent injustice and to secure the right of appeal. What had possessed the Vatican to abandon this principle and support a godless, international super-court from which there would be no appeal?

The Vatican's support for the ICC was yet another symptom of the Great Amnesia documented so extensively in the apostolate's publications. Surely it was no coincidence that the same Vatican Secretariat of State which helped give birth to the ICC was also the source of the "worried signals" first received by the Bishop of Avellino in 1989, when *the Plan* to neutralize Father Gruner and his apostolate was first divulged by Cardinal Agustoni. At that time the Vatican Secretary of State was Cardinal Casaroli, the great architect of *Ostpolitik*, but he had turned the reins over to Cardinal Sodano in 1991. Casaroli would not live to see the latest triumph of Vatican diplomacy: A month before the ICC treaty was approved and the Vatican was committed to supporting a godless international criminal court, Casaroli would die of unexpected complications from minor surgery.[269] A glowing obituary in the *New York Times* would note approvingly that "Casaroli signed a concordat in 1984 under which *Roman Catholicism ceased to be the state religion of Italy*."[270]

Even in Italy, the Social Kingship of Christ was no longer acceptable to the Vatican bureaucracy. Neither, obviously, was the triumph of the Immaculate Heart prophesied at Fatima. Nor could there be any acceptance in the current scheme of things for any priest or apostolate whose work stood as a constant reminder that the Church of Our Lady of Fatima was not the Church of the "civilization of love".

§

269 *New York Times*, June 10, 1998, p. B10.

270 Ibid.

By the time the ICC had become a reality, Father Gruner had returned to Canada. The canonical strategy for his final appeal had been decided, the papers filed, the second Open Letter published. Once again, there was nothing more for him to do but pray and wait.

At the Piazza della Cancelleria, in their offices above the courtyard of the Apostolic Palace, the executors of *the Plan* pondered their next move. They sat, as always, in their figurative Court of Mirrors—mirrors facing mirrors, in an infinite regression of images. And in the mirrors could be seen the faces of the accusing witnesses, the adverse parties, the judges, the jury and the executioners in the case of Father Nicholas Gruner. But the faces were all *their* faces. The executors of *the Plan* were looking only at themselves.

The next few days, or months, would tell whether the door to this Court of Mirrors could be opened, so that the truth of Father Gruner's case could at last escape into the light of day outside the chamber where it had been imprisoned for so long. But for now there was only prayer and waiting.

In Canada, the sun descended beneath the edge of the Niagara escarpment as Father Gruner prayed the Divine Office in Latin, fulfilling one of the duties of the state to which God had called him more than twenty years before. Those who have opposed Father Gruner's work for so long know that the grace of his priesthood sustains him. When the sun that had descended on Niagara rose in Rome, the battle over Father Gruner's priesthood would continue.

This picture was taken at Fatima, on Sunday, October 11, 1992, at 5:30 in the afternoon in the main hall of the Paul VI Pastoral Center, at the end of the conference given by Father Fox. Frére François at the microphone denounces, in the presence of Father Kondor (seated at far right) and Father Fox (seated left), the five bogus letters (including the fake Noelker letter quoted by Cardinal Bertone) which had circulated from August 1989 to August 1992 and which had been attributed to Sister Lucia. These fake letters—which all speak about the Act of Consecration of March 25, 1984—had been circulated and published by Father Fox and Father Kondor.

Frére Francois denounces these letters in their presence and says: "These letters are fake. I have already published the demonstration of it, and my demonstration has not been refuted. I am ready to justify my accusations and, if necessary, to retract them if my criticisms are refuted in a decisive manner." The next day, October 12, Abbé Rene Laurentin will express a certain astonishment upon learning that neither Father Fox nor Father Kondor gave any answer to Frére François. Instead, the session simply was swiftly closed because both Father Fox and Father Kondor simply got up from their chairs and left without speaking one word.

Chapter 21

Signs of the Times

In *Gaudium et spes* the Second Vatican Council declared that "At all times the Church carries the responsibility of reading the signs of the times and of interpreting them in the light of the Gospel, if it is to carry out its task." There have been few signs in the history of the world as unmistakable as the one given by Heaven itself at Fatima on October 13, 1917, only 45 years before the Council began.

More than a few of the bishops who attended the Council had been old enough to read about the Miracle of the Sun in the secular press which had recognized it as a world event. The Church had long since pronounced the Message of Fatima worthy of belief. Indeed, many of the Council Fathers had been consecrated bishops by Pius XII, who was known as "the Pope of Fatima."

At Fatima the Church was given nothing less than a sign to govern the course of her mission in this age of human history. Yet, since the Council, it was this very sign which had been almost universally ignored by churchmen. As a consequence, the Church is now witness to other signs—signs which show that the tragedy of Fatima continues, because the triumph of Fatima has been postponed. One need look no further than the headlines of the secular newspapers:

YELTSIN'S CHOICE EASILY RATIFIED;
A SHIFT TO THE LEFT

The New York Times —September 12, 1998

"Yvegenny Primakov handily won confirmation as Prime Minister from the Russian Parliament today, and signaled a sharp shift toward a more socialist economic model by endorsing two of the Communist Party's hand-picked candidates for top posts."

MUSICAL CHAIRS IN MOSCOW

The New York Times—September 11, 1998

"The choice of Mr. Primakov was dictated by parliamentary opposition to Mr. Yeltsin's first choice ... Mr. Yeltsin turned to a man who was acceptable to the Communist-dominated body."

ON EVE OF NATIONWIDE STRIKE,
RUSSIAN PREMIER URGES CALM

The New York Times—October 7, 1998

"With prices soaring, the ruble sagging, and a mountain of wages due, the Communists are flexing their muscles ... The Communists have already placed allies at the head of the central bank and at the head of the government's economic policy."

VATICAN PROTESTS
NEW RUSSIAN RELIGION LAW

Catholic World News—September 26, 1997

"A Vatican official has expressed 'bitter regret' at the passage of a new law restricting religious freedom in Russia ... Cardinal Ratzinger went a step further in condemning the new law, saying that it ... 'complicated the situation for the Catholic Church in Russia ...'"

LOCAL AUTHORITIES THREATEN CATHOLIC PARISH IN SOUTHERN RUSSIA

EWTN News Brief—February 10, 1998

"Local authorities in Russia's Karbardino-Balkaria Republic ... have ordered a Catholic parish in the town of Prokhladny to immediately apply for a brand new registration—even though the parish is already registered—a move which Catholic sources in Moscow believe is a pretext for restriction of the parish's activities ...

"Such an application might be rejected under Russia's restrictive new law on church-state relations, leaving the parish with no legal basis to function ..."

NEW RUSSIAN RULES IMPEDE CATHOLIC PRIESTS

Keston News Service—July 20, 1998

"The Russian government is ready to implement a new visa system that could prevent the Catholic Church from bringing foreign priests into the country ... [The rules] allow visas for only three-month periods. Unlike foreign athletes or businessmen, [priests] are not given the right to extend their stays in Russia or to apply for multiple-entry visas."

CATHOLICS BARRED FROM CHURCH NEAR MOSCOW

Keston News Service—May 28, 1997

"[L]ocal authorities ... continue to withhold registration of the Catholic Church on the pretext that the parish is a 'foreign' religious organization ... [T]he authorities plan to turn the church building, now under repair, into a Russian Orthodox museum..."

BELARUS PRIEST REMOVED FOR RESISTING STATE DESIGNS ON CHURCH

EWTN News Brief—December 22, 1997

"The Catholic bishops of Belarus have bowed to pressure from the government of the former Soviet Republic and removed a priest from his parish for leading protests against plans to turn the historic church, at least partially, into a museum ..."

CATHOLICS IN CHINA, FACING CRACKDOWN, RETURN TO THE UNDERGROUND

The New York Times—January 27, 1997

"The new wave of religious repression in China seems in largest measure the product of President Jiang Zemin's policy to shore up 'the socialist spiritual civilization'..."

NEW REPORT SAYS DOZENS OF CHINESE PRIESTS, BISHOPS DETAINED

Catholic World News—February 3, 1998

"A US businessman working in China said on Tuesday that scores of Catholic priests and bishops have been detained by the Chinese government in the last four years because of their continuing allegiance to the universal Catholic Church."

POLISH EX-COMMUNISTS BLASTED BY CARDINAL

CWN—May 30, 1997

"Cardinal Josef Glemp told 20,000 worshipers in a Corpus Christi procession that although Communism ended in 1989, the same people remain in power... '[T]he spirit of Marxism is rising over different fields of endeavor'."

October 13, 1998—81st anniversary of the Miracle of the Sun.

To read the headlines from the perspective of Fatima is to recognize that a Heavenly promise has not yet been fulfilled. The lack of fulfillment is not, of course, the fault of Heaven: "Russia will be converted" the Virgin said at Fatima, and the Virgin does not lie. The fault can only be with men. The earthly plans of men militate against the Message of Fatima.

Eighty-one years ago, Our Lady of Fatima appeared at the Cova da Iria to deliver a message from God, authenticated by a public miracle the like of which has never been seen in the history of the world:

> "The Holy Father will consecrate Russia to Me and she will be converted, and a period of peace will be granted to the world...If people do what I ask, many souls will be saved and there will be peace."[271]

The Message of Fatima is not only a promise but a warning. The promise has not been fulfilled because the warning has not been heeded:

> "If My requests are not granted, Russia will spread its errors throughout the world, raising up wars and persecutions against the Church, the good will be martyred, the Holy Father will have much to suffer and various nations will be annihilated."[272]

In Canada, Father Gruner reads the headlines from Russia and China and ponders "the fall of Communism"—a "fall" which is looking more and more like a very skillful reorganization. He takes no pleasure in the news which confirms what he and the apostolate have been saying for so long: that Russia has yet to be consecrated to the Immaculate Heart of Mary in accordance with Heaven's command. In Russia the Communists are resurgent, and a new law discriminates against the Catholic Church and in favor of Russian Orthodoxy, Judaism, Islam and Buddhism. Catholic parishes are now required to register annually as if they were foreign sects, and the registrations can be revoked at will by any local bureaucrat in a bad mood. The Russian Orthodox are told by Catholic bishops that they need no longer return to Rome, and a Catholic parish becomes a Russian Orthodox museum. Russia has not converted.

Poland today is ruled by atheists. They are Communists by a different name. Since

271 *Fatima in Lucia's Own Words* (Sister Lucia's Memoirs), Fatima, 1976, p. 162.

272 Ibid.

the "fall" of Communism, religious instruction in kindergarten classes has been replaced by sex-education. In response, Cardinal Glemp had asked: "Who can be opposed to little childrens' natural inclination toward God?" The answer is that men who hate God can be, and are, opposed to it. They are the same men who "liberalized" Poland's abortion law in 1993. During his trip to Poland in June of 1997, the Holy Father addressed his people as a father addresses his errant children, pleading with them to turn away from the soul-destroying materialism they have embraced since the "fall" of Communism. "A nation which kills its own children is a nation without hope", he warned them. But even the Pope's own people have not listened to him. Later in that year Poland's liberal abortion law was pared back, but not repealed. Abortion is still "legal" in Poland, and sex-education is now mandatory in Poland's public schools.[273]

In China, Catholics have been driven underground, and priests and bishops are routinely arrested for the "crime" of being Catholics in union with Rome. In Europe, nations that were once Christian are being merged into a European Union of abortion on demand, universal contraception, divorce and homosexual "rights." Throughout the world the sins which demand divine retribution are hailed as "the rights of man." Russia has not converted, and the world becomes ever more deeply infected by its errors. The world, in fact, is dying.

Our Lady of Fatima said that "Russia is the instrument of chastisement chosen by Heaven to punish the whole world (for its sins) if we do not obtain, beforehand, the conversion of that poor nation."[274] And how was that conversion to be obtained? Only "by this means", She said: the Consecration of Russia to Her Immaculate Heart by the Pope and all the Catholic bishops of the world, on the same day and at the same hour.[275] And what if this request were not obeyed? Or what if some other ceremony were substituted—one less offensive to the Russian people, one more in keeping with current Vatican policies? Our Lady's warning about the consequences of such disobedience was quite clear: "various nations will be annihilated"[276] and "Russia will overcome the whole world."[277]

For the past thirty years the purveyors of "Fatima Lite", now allied with the anti-Fatima forces in the Vatican, have been promoting the delusion that the Pope consecrated Russia to the Immaculate Heart of Mary in the Orwellian year of 1984. Oddly enough, the Pope himself had never publicly said so, although they constantly invoke his authority for their claim. Indeed, the Pope has said quite the opposite on the front page of *L'Osservatore Romano*.[278] Yet the anti-Fatima forces persist in saying that Fatima is finished. As they peddle a Message of Fatima stripped of its divine warnings and reduced to a generic pietism, the world moves ever closer to that great chastisement of which the Virgin has warned us again and again in this age of apostasy.

In 1951, Pope Pius XII declared that "the world today is worse than before the flood."[279] But in 1951 abortion had not even been legalized—except, of course, in

273 "Solidarity Loses Polish Parliament Vote on Sex Education in School," *CWN*, December 31, 1997.

274 Interview of Sister Lucia by Father Fuentes, Dec. 26, 1957. Quoted in *Fatima: Tragedy and Triumph*, p. 27, by Frère François de Marie des Anges.

275 *Fátima Ante La Esfinge*, by Father Joaquin María Alonso, p. 107; also, *The Fatima Crusader*, Issue 50, p. 14; also in the article written by Abbé Pierre Caillon, Issue 16, p. 23. Both authors quote the communication of Jesus to Sister Lucia in May of 1936.

276 *Fatima in Lucia's Own Words* (Sister Lucia's Memoirs), Fatima, 1976, p. 162.

277 Ibid.

278 *L'Osservatore Romano*, March 26-27, 1984, pp. 1, 6, reporting on the remarks of the Holy Father made on March 25.

279 The encyclical *Evangelii praecones*.

the Soviet Union and Red China. Since then, Russia has spread her errors, including abortion, throughout the world, just as Our Lady predicted at Fatima. Since 1984 alone, more than 600,000,000 children have been exterminated (up until 1998) in the abortion holocaust. Yet 1984 was the very year "Consecration Lite" was introduced to the public by the merchants of "Fatima Lite"—a consecration of Russia which did not even *mention* Russia, and which most of the world's bishops did not join in any case. The blood of every child aborted since the introduction of "Consecration Lite" cries out to Heaven for vengeance, as Sacred Scripture confirms. But the merchants of "Fatima Lite" continue to peddle their fraudulent products, ignoring the divine warning that stares them in the face.

It is the warning of Fatima which most concerns Father Gruner today. The time for conversion and repentance promised by the Virgin if men cooperated with Her requests must nearly have expired, and the annihilation of nations must nearly be upon us. For many Catholics, there is a palpable sense that this is true. But for too many others, there is denial. "To whom shall I speak? And to whom shall I testify that he may hear? Their ears are uncircumcised and they cannot hear...And they healed the breach of the daughter of my people disgracefully, *saying 'Peace, peace', when there is no peace...*"[280] Thus declared the prophet Jeremiah against the false prophets of Jerusalem, who had made themselves deaf to the warnings of Heaven. In 1998 the false prophets had made their ears deaf to the Message of Fatima. "Peace, peace", they say, when there is no peace.

Father Nicholas Gruner does not claim to be a Jeremiah. He has never claimed to be anything but a Catholic priest who can see what is manifest: that the promises of Our Lady have not come to pass, and that the fault cannot be Hers. He will not say 'peace, peace,' when he can see there is no peace. He will not commit that sin. He resolves to go on with what he is doing until God no longer permits it. He will pray for the strength to do so.

Introibo ad altare Dei. I will go unto the altar of God. The prayer of the Mass ascends to Heaven in the private chapel of Father Gruner's modest dwelling. Anyone who has seen Father Gruner offer Mass will be reminded that he is, before all things, a priest. He offers Mass as he always does, in the ancient Latin rite of the Catholic Church. Here, too, the words of Jeremiah may be recalled: "Stand ye on the ways, and see, and ask for the *old* paths, which is the good way, and walk ye in it, and you will find refreshment for your souls..."[281]

Early in 1997, while Father Gruner was in Rome seeking a canon lawyer to defend him, Cardinal Ratzinger gave a press conference at which he introduced his newly-published memoirs. In those memoirs, the Cardinal concedes what had been obvious all along: The drastic reforms of the Mass in 1969 had caused "extremely serious damage" to the Church[282], and the suppression of the "old Mass" was a "break in the history of the liturgy, the consequences of which could only be tragic."[283] And most significant in light of the Third Secret, which the Cardinal has read: "I am convinced that the ecclesial crisis in which we find ourselves today depends in great part on the collapse of the liturgy."[284]

For nearly 30 years the post-conciliar revolutionaries and their active and passive

280 Jer. 6:14.

281 Jer. 6:16.

282 *La Mia Vita* (The Memoirs of Cardinal Ratzinger) as quoted in *Latin Mass* magazine, Summer 1997, p. 8 in the article entitled "Aid and Comfort from Ratzinger".

283 Ibid.

284 Ibid.

collaborators had mocked and marginalized "traditionalist" Catholics as "disobedient" and "disloyal" to the Pope, for saying the very things now being said by the Prefect of the Congregation for the Doctrine of the Faith. Cardinal Ratzinger was known to be the closest advisor to the Pope—the same Pope in whose hands Father Gruner's *libellus*[285] had been placed nearly two years before by a pair of bishops and a young man pushing a wheelchair. As 1998 drew to a close, there was no word on Father Gruner's final appeals to the Apostolic Signatura, nor any word on the *libellus* which had been lodged with the Pope. Yet Father Gruner found some small measure of relief and hope in what the Cardinal had said in his memoirs. The tide was perhaps beginning to turn, not merely for him but for the whole Church. The Message of Fatima might yet be heeded; the new Jerusalem might yet avoid the fate of the old.

After Mass in the private chapel, there would, as always, be many additional prayers at the altar. Father Gruner would kneel serenely for nearly half an hour on a solid wood kneeler which would cause others to squirm in pain in a few moments. Later there would be the Divine Office, and always the Rosary. Some three hours that day, and every day, would be consumed by prayer. Mass after Mass, Rosary after Rosary, would be offered for the Consecration of Russia and the Apostolate devoted to its promulgation.

As the priest prays, his prayers are joined by those of bishops, priests, religious and laity around the world who have stood by him and supported his work despite all the controversy it has engendered. Why do they do so? The answer to that question cannot be found in any mere attachment to the man. The man is no more important than other men. The answer is found in what he *says*. For what he says is only what Our Lady said at Fatima.

The priest on his knees in the little chapel understands that the Message of Fatima is the urgent plea of a Mother to Her children, at a time of unprecedented peril for a world which grows more rebellious by the hour: "Only I can help you," She said at Fatima. By the grace of God obtained through the intercession of the Blessed Virgin Mary, the priest believes this as a child believes it—literally, and with his whole heart. So, by that same grace, do many others. But not enough.

On a stage far vaster than the distance between Canada and Rome, the drama of Fatima moves swiftly toward its conclusion. In the fading light of a secluded chapel, Father Gruner prays. On the left side of the altar where he has just offered the Holy Sacrifice of the Mass is a statue of the Pilgrim Virgin, blessed at Fatima by the very Pope who proclaimed that Mary is Mother of the Church as well as Mother of God. The Pilgrim Virgin smiles down upon the kneeling priest, as She has throughout the twenty years of their travels together.

The Apostolate goes on, and the man they call "Fatima Priest" continues to guide dissemination of the Message of Fatima to millions. To the bewilderment of the anti-Fatima forces, the Apostolate continues to gather support for the cause of Our Lady of Fatima from Catholics around the world. In the end, it can only be explained by the priest's unwavering adherence to a Message which is not his, or any mere man's, but Hers. The many Catholics who support Father Gruner and his work bear witness, therefore, that his survival despite all opposition is owing to nothing more or less than this: He tells the truth.

285 Rome, Nov. 20, 1996, "A Canonical Petition to His Holiness John Paul II", Appen. VII, *Fatima Priest*, first edition, p. 328.

Chapter 22

A Law for One Man

Many people have opinions about the priestly standing of Father Nicholas Gruner, but very few of them know the facts. This chapter sets forth in a compelling narrative the unprecedented interventions by Vatican bureaucrats against a priest who has violated no law of the Church nor committed any offense against faith or morals.

Father Gruner's persecution is attested to by the Archbishop of Hyderabad, who has incardinated Father Gruner in his archdiocese and praises and supports his Fatima apostolate. In his formal decree incardinating Father Gruner, the Archbishop declared: "Evil forces have conspired to destroy your work of love ... Bureaucratic forces cannot stifle God's work."

Father Gruner's one "offense" has been his insistent preaching and teaching of the Message of Fatima over the past 36 years, including his call (in which millions of Catholics have joined) for the Vatican's release of the Third Secret.

Now that Pope John Paul II has ordered publication of the Secret after 40 years of Vatican silence, those who have disparaged Father Gruner and his apostolate as "kooky" or "irrelevant" will be forced to confront the continued vitality of the Fatima Message to which this priest has dedicated his life. They will also have to contend with the Pope's own evident dedication to Our Lady of Fatima as Heaven's prophet for our age.

As St. Thomas Aquinas teaches in his *Summa Theologica*, human law is useless and unjust unless it provides a common standard on which all the members of a community can rely in governing their conduct: "For if there were as many rules or measures as there are things measured or ruled, they would cease to be of use, since their use consists in being applicable to many things. Hence law would be of no use if it did not extend further than to one single act."

A practical example suffices to demonstrate the truth of St. Thomas' teaching on human law: Imagine a highway with a posted speed limit of 55 miles per hour. A motorist driving at 50 miles per hour is stopped by a police officer, who issues him a ticket for speeding. "But officer, I was only doing fifty!", protests the motorist. "Yes, I know," replies the officer, "but I have decided that for *you* the speed limit should be forty." A speed limit which applied to only one motorist would obviously not be a law, but an abuse of authority pretending to be law; and any court which sustained a conviction for speeding in such circumstances would also be acting lawlessly.

Law, if it be law, must apply to all. Even God Himself is bound by this axiom of justice: On Judgment Day the Lord will not announce to some poor soul that he had failed to abide by an *eleventh* commandment, never before revealed, which did not apply to the rest of humanity.

Yet, for the past five years, Father Gruner had found himself in the ecclesiastical equivalent of the situation faced by the hypothetical motorist. Thousands of other priests could live and work outside the dioceses in which they had been incardinated in perfect conformity with the Code of Canon Law, but not Father Gruner. Permissions and arrangements completely commonplace for priests on every continent, were deemed illegal in his case. For him, and him alone, the speed limit was 40, not 55.

October 14, 1998, Fort Erie, Canada. Father Gruner receives word from his advocate, Alan Kershaw, that the process of fashioning a law for one man was continuing. A new Promoter of Justice, Frans Daneels, O. Praem, had been assigned to the case and had just a few days earlier issued a 40-page document purporting to set forth additional facts to justify the actions taken against Father Gruner.

The "Promoter of Justice" had taken almost five months to prepare his "votum", a supposedly impartial summary of Father Gruner's case. It was soon obvious that the document, and its author, were not impartial at all, but that Daneels was acting as a partisan of Father Gruner's adversaries.

There was also a 12-page Latin document prepared by Carlo Martino, who had been retained by the Congregation for the Clergy as the "patron" or advocate to defend the positions taken by the Congregation.

Kershaw advised Father Gruner that the two documents had been issued under a restriction: Father Gruner could not have copies of the documents unless he first signed a written oath to keep them secret! At first Father Gruner could not believe the Signatura was serious, but the requirement of secrecy was confirmed in a letter from the Signatura, signed by none other than Promoter Daneels—who was also acting as secretary of the Signatura! The Promoter of Justice was supposed to be a neutral party in the case, yet here he was signing letters on behalf of the tribunal. This was akin to the prosecutor in a criminal court simultaneously serving as the judge's law clerk. In any secular court such a blatant conflict of interest would be prohibited, but in the Vatican tribunals it was just another day at the office.

Daneels had even written out the oath for Father Gruner to take, which included the promise that "I will not in any way make known said information to third parties." Father Gruner promptly declined to take the oath, especially considering that the Signatura had already allowed its 1995 decree against Father Gruner to be published to the whole world in *Soul Magazine*. Why should secrecy be a one-way street? Not even a secular criminal court would require the accused to swear secrecy before he could have a copy of the complaint against him. What were Daneels and the Signatura trying to hide?

The Signatura could hardly claim that the requirement of secrecy was for Father Gruner's benefit, given that its prior decree had been published to the world. The inescapable conclusion, therefore, was that the Signatura was seeking only to protect itself, that there was something about these documents it considered highly embarrassing to the tribunal. Father Gruner would soon learn that the Signatura had good reason to fear embarrassment.

Since he was unwilling to swear an oath which would bind him but not the Signatura, Father Gruner was reduced to reading the documents in the presence of his advocate, without keeping copies for himself. This meant that Kershaw would have to travel 6,000 miles from Rome to Canada, exhibit the documents to Father Gruner long enough for him to make notes, and then whisk them back to Italy, where they would presumably be kept under lock and key. By the time Kershaw could rearrange his affairs and travel to Canada, only a few days remained to translate, digest and respond to 50 pages of Latin text from Daneels and Martino.

Martino's document posed little difficulty, since it consisted of nothing more than twelve pages of unsubstantiated invective bordering on the hysterical, including the following: "All the bishops who are knowledgeable of the operations of Father Gruner with one voice say that Father Gruner should be cast forth from the bosom of the Catholic priesthood!" All of the bishops? With one voice? And what of the three bishops who had offered Father Gruner incardination in their dioceses, including the Archbishop of Hyderabad, who had said of Father Gruner's work:

"Evil forces have conspired to destroy your work of love ... Bureaucratic forces cannot stifle God's work." Contrary to Martino's denunciation, the bishops most knowledgeable of Father Gruner's "operations" were precisely the ones who wished to incardinate him—in the bosom of the priesthood.

In keeping with the general tenor of the proceedings against Father Gruner, Martino had not bothered to state exactly why Father Gruner should be "cast forth." Meanwhile, the "bosom of the priesthood" harbored innumerable open heretics, homosexuals and child-molesters who had neither been "cast forth" nor even reprimanded for their crimes.

So much for Martino. But why had the Signatura allowed such an embarrassingly inept document to be filed in defense of "ecclesiastical authority"? The answer probably lay in the fact that Martino was none other than the brother of Archbishop Renato Martino, the Vatican Secretariat of State's observer at the United Nations. It had been "worried signals" from the Secretary of State in 1989 (and pressure from Cardinals Innocenti and Agustoni) which first provoked the Bishop of Avellino to apply pressure to Father Gruner. Over the years since then, Father Gruner and the apostolate had been reporting constantly on the dangers of the New World Order steadily emerging under UN auspices, including the International Criminal Court (ICC) created with the assistance of none other than the Vatican Secretary of State.

It was Archbishop Martino who had publicly praised the new super-court as a great advancement for human rights, even though it would have the power to arrest and try Catholics of any nation for vague offenses yet to be defined in its statutes. Since Father Gruner's return to Canada after further meetings with Kershaw, the drafters of the ICC statutes had already proposed that priests be compelled to violate the seal of the confessional in ICC investigations of "crimes against humanity." It had also been announced that the ICC would be headed by the U.N.'s "High Commissioner of Human Rights", Mary Robinson, the pro-abortion former President of Ireland. The ICC was hardly shaping up as the human rights haven extolled by Archbishop Martino.

Alarming developments such as these had prompted the apostolate to criticize the Vatican's whole involvement with the United Nations and its one-world agenda. That criticism inevitably focused on the Vatican Secretary of State and the work of Archbishop Martino at the UN. The assignment of Archbishop Martino's brother to defend "ecclesiastical authority" did not appear to be a coincidence.

The document of Promoter Daneels would be far more difficult to answer quickly simply because of its length. Daneels had managed to churn out 40 pages of wandering, convoluted reasoning in Latin, which drifted almost aimlessly from one point to another, and then back to the same points all over again. This document represented the first effort by "ecclesiastical authority" to provide the appearance of a substantive case against Father Gruner. On close examination, however, the "case" was nothing but a large collection of trivia and hearsay unsupported by any evidence, combined with outright errors of fact. For example, Daneels suggested that Father Gruner had dishonestly published in his magazine a certificate of good standing from the Bishop of Avellino when he already knew that the bishop (under pressure from the Congregation) had requested that the certificate be returned. In truth, the issue of the magazine in question had been published prior to the bishop requesting the certificate's return, and before Father Gruner had received the bishop's request in the mail. Moreover, no reason had been given for demanding the return of the certificate other than Father Gruner's publication of it to prove his good standing. It was hardly improper to use a certificate of good standing to prove one's good standing.

In another example, the Promoter referred to an alleged request by the Papal Nuncio to the bishops of Canada for "information" about Father Gruner, as if to suggest that the bishops had evidence of wrongdoing. And what "information" was provided? Apparently none, since the Promoter's document failed to mention any particulars. The Promoter did allege, however, that the bishops had requested that Father Gruner stop "his insane and damaging activities." Not surprisingly, the Promoter failed to specify what was "insane" or "damaging" about the work of the apostolate. On the other hand, the Canadian bishops had plenty of truly insane and damaging activities to handle in their own dioceses, where pedophile and pederasty priest scandals were erupting with almost metronomic regularity.

The Promoter's document did make two important admissions: The first was that the previous Promoter of Justice had erred when he accused Father Gruner of "defrauding" Archbishop Arulappa by exhibiting the 1978 decree of Bishop Venezia at the time of his incardination in Hyderabad. It was now admitted that this "fraud" could not have occurred, because Father Gruner had no way of knowing that the Congregation would later declare the document to have been revoked before the incardination in Hyderabad. Besides, Father Gruner had not shown the document to the Archbishop in the first place.

The Promoter had made an even more important admission: In attempting to buttress his case the Promoter identified at least ten private interventions by the Congregation and other Vatican officials, which had been taken without notice to Father Gruner and did not allow him to exercise his right of appeal. These included secret directives imposing restrictions on Father Gruner's incardination which would have required him to abandon his apostolate (and in particular *The Fatima Crusader* magazine) before any other bishop could accept him. There was also mention of a secret "resolution" with another Vatican congregation, that was never reported to Father Gruner or otherwise officially disclosed in Church records. The Promoter did not specify the exact nature of this mysterious "resolution." Also mentioned for the first time was a letter sent by the Congregation to the Nuncio of Canada on January 3, 1989, containing the absurd and libelous accusation (unsupported by any facts) that Father Gruner had "extorted ordination to the sacred priesthood."

As the Promoter had revealed, the process of secret decisions and denunciations was even more extensive than Father Gruner had suspected. He wrote immediately to the Signatura and the Congregation, requesting copies of the various letters and other documents the Promoter had disclosed. They would never be provided.

On the whole, the Promoter's rambling collection of irrelevancies had little to do with the rather simple matter at hand: the Congregation's unprecedented interference in Father Gruner's basic priestly right to attach himself to a benevolent bishop, and (like any other member of the Church) to participate in a private apostolate without the formality of episcopal approval. In four years of proceedings that were little more than a sham designed to give the appearance of due process, "ecclesiastical authority" had not provided a single concrete reason why Father Gruner could not do what other priests were doing routinely around the world. Neither had the Promoter. Nevertheless, Daneels had to be answered, lest it be declared that Father Gruner had admitted his allegations.

Working around the clock for nearly two weeks, Father Gruner and at least two typists were able to prepare a 100-page typewritten reply to the Promoter's document and transmit it to Kershaw in Rome, who filed it on December 10, 1998, literally 30 minutes before the deadline expired.

Father Gruner's reply meticulously refuted every one of the Promoter's allegations (as well as those he reported coming from others) and pointed out that the Promoter had failed even to make a proper accusation against Father Gruner in due canonical form, specifying which law of the Church Father Gruner was supposed to have violated. The reply amply demonstrated that the Promoter's document was factually unfounded and legally vacuous.

After Father Gruner's reply was delivered, the document of Promoter Daneels would never again be mentioned by the Signatura. Although the Signatura had demanded Father Gruner reply to Daneels in a matter of days, it would take nearly nine months for the Signatura to prepare its next pronouncement.

§

Nine months after Father Gruner's reply to Daneels was filed, the apostolate had nearly completed preparations for its fourth international bishops' conference to be held in Hamilton, Ontario, from October 11-17, 1999. In a few days, Archbishops, bishops, priests and laity from around the world would assemble to consider the Message of Fatima in relation to a world whose decomposition had only accelerated since the third Fatima conference in Rome in 1996.

In the fall of 1999 Catholics were being slaughtered in East Timor by Muslim fanatics, missionaries were being murdered by Hindu nationalists in India, and Russia had not only failed to show any signs of conversion, but had continued its rapid material and spiritual decline (while its military might continued to increase). Since 1996 it had become all the more apparent that the pan-religious "civilization of love" promoted by Vatican functionaries was nothing more than that same pan-religious utopia Saint Pius X had condemned in *Notre charge apostolique* as a delusion which undermines the integrity of the Catholic Faith. Yet the Vatican was proceeding with its plans for another World Day of Prayer for Peace with the "representatives of the world's great religions" in late October. This time the prayer meeting would take place at the Vatican itself, followed by a pan-religious bus caravan to earthquake-ravaged Assisi, the site of the original World Day of Prayer for Peace.

On October 1, 1999, two weeks before the bishops' conference in Hamilton, the Synod of European Bishops got underway in Rome with the publication of a "working document." The Synod's candid admissions would have been condemned as doomsaying and "bishop-bashing" had they been stated in an article in *The Fatima Crusader*. The Synod recognized that the seemingly encouraging events since the "fall of Communism", including the demolition of the Berlin Wall, had proven to be only "weak hopes and disappointments." As one commentator observed, the Synod was now confronted with the reality that the moral conscience of post-communist Europe had "crumbled in the East and the West, giving way to consumerism, violence, loss of meaning … while *the Church grew ever more timid, abstract or sentimental in her words and in her witness*." [Zenit news agency report, September 3, 1999]

But the Synod's proposed solution for this belatedly admitted crisis was just another large dollop of the same abstract and sentimental mush the Synod itself was decrying: "To overcome 'a widening separation between private conscience and public values', which is emptying the existence of the European individual and the witness of the Church, the working document proposes ... personalism, in its relation with the community; family; youth; solidarity."

Personalism? Solidarity? What about that ancient prescription for social decline, commonly known as the Catholic Faith? What about the simple truth that violation of God's law through personal mortal sin, not a lack of "solidarity", was the principal cause of Europe's terminal decline? What about the restoration of Christendom? What about Fatima?

The European Synod had only demonstrated why there had to be a Fatima conference in Hamilton, and conferences like it all over the world: the Church was losing her witness because too many of her prelates had forgotten the very vocabulary of the Faith. This is precisely why Our Lady had conducted Her heavenly tutorial at Fatima.

It was, of course, completely predictable that only days before the October 1999 conference in Hamilton, Father Gruner would receive in the mail what appeared to be the Signatura's final decree in his case. Nor was there any surprise in reading, yet again, that the case had been refused admission for a discussion by all the judges of the tribunal. At the end of the document appeared the same dismissive Latin phrase which appeared at the end of all the Signatura's decrees in the proceedings: *manifeste quolibet caret fundamento*. "Manifestly without any foundation whatsoever." Oddly enough, the Signatura had required 26 pages of dense Latin to explain why there was absolutely no merit to Father Gruner's claims.

The decree had been signed by five prelates, including Archbishop Zenon Grochelewski, who had replaced Cardinal Agustoni as Prefect of the Signatura. This was the same Archbishop Grochelewski who had freely admitted to canonist Franco Ligi two years earlier that Father Gruner's case really had nothing to do with his incardination in this or that diocese, but rather with "what he says; he causes division." In other words, the Prefect of the very tribunal considering Father Gruner's case had admitted that the proceedings were nothing but a pretext for the desired result: the silencing of a priest who could not otherwise be silenced. What did the particular facts and circumstances matter if the proceedings were a mere pretext? Father Gruner was going to be sent back to Avellino in order to shut him up, and that was that. There was no need for a hearing by the full tribunal, because that hearing could not possibly alter the preordained result.

Amazingly enough, in this latest decree the Signatura openly conceded its indifference to the facts and even the ostensible reasons on which the decisions against Father Gruner had been based:

> "It must be carefully distinguished between the impugned decisions and the reasons brought forth. *Even if there should be errors* in the exposition of the facts or the motives [reasons], the decision can nevertheless be just and legitimate."

In other words, the decisions against Father Gruner were "just and legitimate" even if they were based on errors of fact and reasoning! All that mattered was the result. So declared the five members of the Signatura—"having only God before their eyes", as the decree exclaimed just above the signatures.

This statement was an implicit admission that the Congregation's facts were wrong, as Father Gruner had shown in his various recourses. Now the Signatura was declaring that the Congregation's decisions would stand despite these errors because, in effect, it did not care about the facts but only the result.

But how could a decision be just and legitimate if it was not based on the true facts? The application of the law always turns upon correct factual determinations; if a judge errs in his fact-finding, an erroneous decision will necessarily follow. The Signatura's statement was akin to saying that a conviction for speeding at 80 miles per hour would be "just and legitimate" even if the evidence showed that the convicted motorist was traveling only 40 miles per hour.

Furthermore, if the administration of justice in the Church did not depend on the true facts of a case, what need was there for tribunals in the first place? Some prelate could simply issue a decree based on his sense of what the "just and legitimate" result should be, without any reference to the facts. That is precisely what had happened to Father Gruner, although the pretense of due deliberation and consideration of the facts had at least been maintained until now.

Since the Signatura was no longer interested in factual accuracy in Father Gruner's case, it had also dispensed with any consideration of the matters raised by the Promoter of Justice:

> "This definitive decree deliberately deals only with all those matters which strictly pertain to the matter itself. Regarding the matters not dealt with in this decree, it certainly would not follow that the opinion of the Reverend Gruner on those matters left out are confirmed by silence."

Here the Signatura was referring obliquely to Father Gruner's 100-page reply to Daneels'. The tribunal had suddenly decided that the matters addressed in the reply did not "strictly pertain" to the case. If that were so, then why had the Signatura engaged Daneels in the first place to write forty pages of Latin on precisely the same matters?

The Signatura clearly did not wish to step into the quagmire of an attempted defense of Daneels' document. Yet the tribunal refused to concede that Father Gruner had refuted Daneels: " ... it certainly would not follow that the opinion of the Reverend Gruner on those matters left out are confirmed by silence." Rather than addressing the allegations its own "promoter of justice" had raised, only to be soundly refuted, the Signatura had resorted to a lame general denial that Father Gruner could possibly be right about anything.

In a secular court, the accuser has the burden of proving that his accusations are true. If the accused demonstrates that the evidence produced against him is false, then the accuser cannot simply remain silent. He must come forward with a rebuttal, or else his accusations must be dismissed. But the judges of the Signatura evidently did not feel themselves bound by this basic norm of justice.

Confronted with proof that Daneels' accusations against Father Gruner were false, the Signatura would remain silent, offer no rebuttal, and then assert that its silence did not mean that Father Gruner had been vindicated. Even in a secular court this would be viewed as a dereliction of judicial duty. In the highest tribunal of the Catholic Church it was inexcusable.

Having dispensed with any real analysis of the facts, the Signatura now proposed a minimalist version of the case against Father Gruner: the sole grounds for Father Gruner's return to Avellino after an approved absence of sixteen years was the need to correct his "*condicio irregularis*", a portentous Latin phrase meaning "irregular condition." This "irregular condition" consisted of Father Gruner residing outside the diocese of his incardination while conducting an apostolate—an arrangement no different from that enjoyed by priests around the world.

After years of proceedings, and thousands of wasted hours, this claim of an "irregular condition" was all that remained of the case against Father Gruner. Daneels' totally discredited allegations had been abandoned. Also abandoned were the vague and never specified allegations of "scandals" and "outrages" upon which the Bishop of Avellino had supposedly based his original decree of January 31, 1994, ordering Father Gruner back to Avellino for the first time. The Signatura now tacitly conceded that "ecclesiastical authority" never had any evidence of "scandals or outrages" in the first place. The charge was but an empty pretext for recalling Father Gruner to Avellino.

What, then, of Father Gruner's alleged "irregular condition"—whatever that meant?

In the first place, the law of the Church contains no reference to the supposed offense of having an "*irregular condition*." The phrase does not even appear in any of the canons governing the rights and duties of the clerical state. While a priest might incur a particular *irregularity* due to a proven grave offense against faith and morals—for example, that the priest had attempted marriage after ordination—no such offense could be charged to Father Gruner, whose moral and doctrinal probity had never even been questioned. A priest is either guilty of a particular offense against Church law or he is not. The phrase "irregular condition" was canonically meaningless. It made no more sense than charging a motorist with "irregular driving" when he has not violated any traffic law.

The proper inquiry in Father Gruner's case, therefore, was not whether his "condition" was "irregular", but whether he had actually violated any law of the Church by residing in Canada while conducting an apostolate. Under the laws which applied to every other priest in the Catholic Church, the answer had to be in the negative.

First of all, the 1983 Code of Canon Law promulgated by Pope John Paul II made it quite clear that priests could reside outside the dioceses of their incardination so long as they had their bishop's permission:

> Canon 283 § 1: "Clerics ... are not to be absent from their diocese for a considerable period of time, to be determined by particular law, *without at least the presumed permission of their proper ordinary*."

Father Gruner had not only the presumed permission of his bishop to reside outside the Diocese of Avellino, but also formal written permission by way of Bishop Venezia's 1978 decree. In fact, the Bishop of Avellino had denied any canonical parish mission to Father Gruner because he could not speak the obscure local Italian dialect. Due to the language barrier, he had not been allowed to hear confessions or even to deliver a sermon unless it was written out and approved in advance. The only reason Father Gruner had been ordained in Avellino in the first place was to enter the English-speaking Franciscan community in Frigento, Italy. When that community did not materialize as he had expected, he was unable (despite a diligent search) to find an English-speaking Franciscan community which would afford a Marian apostolate. Among the other problems he encountered was that none of the Franciscan communities he investigated could ensure that he would not be compelled to distribute the Blessed Sacrament in the hand—a practice he was bound in conscience to regard as a sacrilege.

Under these circumstances, Bishop Venezia had been only too happy to allow Father Gruner to reside outside the Diocese of Avellino, at no cost to the diocese. Thus, Father Gruner had not violated Canon 283 by residing in Canada; on the contrary, the canon permitted the arrangement.

What about Father Gruner's involvement in the apostolate? Wasn't this "irregular"? Hardly. John Paul II's Code of Canon Law was equally clear that every member of the faithful has a natural right—that is, a right endowed by God—to form private associations with other Catholics for various apostolic works:

Canon 299

> Canon 299, §1. By *private agreement among themselves*, Christ's faithful *have the right* to constitute associations for the purposes mentioned in can. 298 . . .

Canon 298

> §1 ... In these associations, Christ's faithful, *whether clerics or laity or clerics and laity together*, strive with a common effort to... promote public worship or christian (sic) teaching. They *may* also devote themselves to other works of the apostolate, such as initiatives for evangelization, works of piety or charity, and those which animate the temporal order with the christian (sic) spirit.

Furthermore, while these private associations of the faithful *may* be approved by ecclesiastical authority, such approval is not required, because the natural right to associate with others comes from God, not from the permission of bishops:

> Canon 299, §2. Associations of this kind, even though they *may* be praised by ecclesiastical authority, are called *private associations*.

Do priests have the same right as the laity to be involved in private associations? The Code of Canon Law leaves no doubt of it:

Canon 278

> Secular priests have *the right of association with others* for the achievement of purposes befitting the clerical state.

A "secular priest" means a diocesan priest or other priest who lives in the world and is not bound by a special vow of obedience to the superior of a religious order, such as the Dominicans or the Franciscans (which Father Gruner had legitimately declined to join). Priests who belong to orders voluntarily surrender their natural right of association with groups outside the order, and must receive special permission for such associations. But Father Gruner did not belong to any religious order. He was undeniably a "secular priest" who retained the same rights as any other secular priest, including the natural right to establish or join private associations of the faithful.

What is more, Father Gruner's participation in the apostolate had been on the recommendation of a Catholic Eastern Rite bishop, who was the spiritual advisor to the apostolate and who told its Board of Directors that a priest should be placed on the Board. In fact, upon his election to the apostolate's Board, Father Gruner received written congratulations and a blessing from none other than Pope John Paul II's personal secretary. This had been followed by two apostolic benedictions (in 1990 and 1993) from the Pope himself! The Signatura would dismiss these as mere empty gratuities.

Thus it was manifest that there was nothing "irregular" about Father Gruner's "condition" in any legal sense: he had his bishop's permission to reside in Canada as well as a natural right to engage in a private association of the faithful without episcopal approval. Under the actual facts and the law, the Signatura's charge of "irregular condition" was—to use the Signatura's own phraseology—manifestly without any foundation whatsoever.

But this was to assume that the Signatura would accept the facts and the law as they were. In the Signatura's latest decree, however, the facts and the law had been amended to fit the preordained result.

Addressing Father Gruner's permission to reside outside the Diocese of Avellino, the Signatura had now decided—for the first time in the entire proceedings—that Bishop Venezia's 1978 decree "does not by any means say [Father Gruner] was given permission to reside outside the Diocese of Avellino, regarding it, the bishop did not intend anything except '*ad experimentum*' to receive an order of incardination." In other words, the Signatura was now claiming that the bishop had given Father Gruner permission to reside in Canada *only* if another bishop had first accepted him *ad experimentum* (as an experiment) or had formally incardinated him.

This amazing claim had never occurred to Bishop Venezia himself—or, for that matter, to anyone else in the 21 years since the decree had been issued. Not even the Congregation for the Clergy, in its relentless pursuit of Father Gruner, had taken this position. Now, in its final decree from which there could be no further appeal, the Signatura had conveniently adopted an entirely new position to which Father Gruner would be unable to respond. An examination of Bishop Venezia's decree showed that the Signatura's new reading of it was a pure invention:

> If Bishop Paul Reding *does not have the possibility of consenting to your request* [for incardination in the Diocese of Hamilton] you can *always* present my letter to *another bishop* who, according the Code of Canon Law in effect, can accept you in his diocese ... I hope that this decision of mine will meet with your satisfaction and can definitively resolve your situation in my diocese of Avellino.

Nowhere does the decree even suggest that Father Gruner's permission to live outside the Diocese of Avellino was conditional upon some bishop first accepting him. On the contrary, the decree specifically acknowledges that Bishop Reding had *not* accepted Father Gruner and quite possibly might never accept him, but that some other bishop might do so in *the indefinite future*. Meanwhile, Father Gruner could "always present" the decree to obtain incardination and would obviously be allowed to remain in Canada, where the decree had been mailed to him from Avellino. Another small but telling fact became apparent upon a reading of the 1978 decree: although Bishop Reding was the Bishop of Hamilton, Ontario, the decree had been mailed to Father Gruner in Montreal, Quebec, where Father Gruner had gone with permission. This fact alone negated the claim that Father Gruner had been given permission to reside only where a Canadian bishop had already accepted him.

Since the Signatura had now dispensed with the requirement of getting the facts right before issuing a judgment, the latest decree failed to note (among many other crucial facts) a letter to Father Gruner from Bishop Venezia's successor, Bishop Pierro, dated November 11, 1989. This letter refers to "*the permission to stay in Canada* that my predecessor Mons. Pasquale Venezia gave you" and threatens to revoke the permission unless Father Gruner found another bishop—the very directive which the Congregation for the Clergy had made it impossible for Father Gruner to obey by secretly pressuring benevolent bishops to withdraw their offers of incardination.

The "permission to stay in Canada" acknowledged by Bishop Pierro was also reflected throughout the sixteen years of written correspondence as well as personal conversations between Father Gruner and the Bishop of Avellino, none of which was mentioned in the Signatura's latest decree.

So, while in 1989 the Bishop of Avellino expressly referred to Father Gruner's longstanding permission to stay in Canada, in 1999 the Signatura was suddenly claiming that the Bishop had never given such permission. In so doing, the Signatura was not only contradicting all the evidence, but also what *the Signatura itself* had stated before. In its decree of January 20, 1998, denying Father Gruner's recourse from the first order to return to Avellino, the Signatura conceded that Father Gruner had permission to reside in Canada since 1978, but claimed that the permission was revoked in November 1989, "renewed" on April 8, 1990, and then finally revoked again on July 18, 1990. This finding was also false (there was no attempt to revoke the permission until January 31, 1994), yet it did at least recognize that the permission to reside in Canada had existed in the first place, and had continued to exist for more than ten years.

Thus, the Signatura of 1998 said Father Gruner had permission to reside in Canada between June 5, 1978, and November 15, 1989, and again between April 8, 1990, and July 18, 1990, but the Signatura of 1999 said there was no such permission. The Signatura had blatantly contradicted its own official version of the facts.

A close student of the case would notice something very suspicious in this contradiction: if the Signatura had simply continued to maintain that Father Gruner's permission to reside in Canada was "revoked" in July 1990, then its 1999 decree would have been consistent with its 1998 decree. Why had it gone further in the later decree, claiming there was never any permission in the first place? *What did the Signatura have to gain from a self-contradiction that was not even necessary to reach the result it desired?* The answer to the question would only be apparent to someone familiar with recent developments in a certain litigation in Canada.

Back in June of 1990 the Vice Chancellor of the Archdiocese of Toronto, Msgr. A. McCormack, published a "clarification" in the archdiocesan bulletin which stated (among other things) that Father Gruner's "status is irregular"—a phrase remarkably similar to the one now being used by the Signatura—and that no Catholic should make donations to the apostolate. Yet only two months before, the Bishop of Avellino had sent Father Gruner, in Canada, a certificate attesting to his good standing as a priest. McCormack's accusation of "irregular status" was therefore demonstrably false. "Irregular" priests do not receive certificates of good standing from their bishops. McCormack's "clarification" had been circulated in the secular press throughout North America, shaking donor confidence and causing severe damage to the apostolate. When McCormack refused to make a retraction of his patently false statements, the apostolate's directors authorized the filing of a libel suit to protect the apostolate's good name—an action fully in keeping with Catholic moral theology in the case of a calumniator who refuses to retract.

In August of 1999 Father Gruner testified under oath at a deposition in the suit. By this time McCormack had been rewarded with a promotion to the Vatican. Father Gruner testified that as of June 1990 (the date of McCormack's "clarification") his status could not possibly have been "irregular" because he had Bishop Venezia's permission to reside in Canada and the bishop's successor had given him a certificate of priestly good standing as recently as April 1990. After Father Gruner's deposition it was clear that McCormack was at serious risk of a judgment against him for libel.

From these facts, certain conclusions seemed highly probable: McCormack (or someone else in the Vatican) had read the transcript of Father Gruner's deposition and realized that Father Gruner was likely to prevail in the libel litigation. Therefore, in order to protect McCormack, who was now a Vatican functionary, Father Gruner's status in 1990 would somehow have to be declared "irregular" by the Signatura. This could be accomplished by holding that Father Gruner never really had permission to live in Canada, so that his presence there had been "irregular" from the start. Then McCormack could claim—nine years after the fact—that his libelous accusation of an "irregular status" in 1990 was "true" after all, because the Church's highest court had just said so.

This would explain the appearance of the novel and canonically meaningless concept of "irregular condition" in the Signatura's latest decree; the language mimicked McCormack's phrase, "irregular status." It would also explain why the decree was dated in July even though it was not issued until September: If the decree had been given a September date, it would have been all too apparent that it had been written with a view to helping McCormack overcome Father Gruner's deposition testimony in August. So the decree was backdated to July, before the deposition took place.

None of this is to suggest that all five of the prelates who signed the decree knowingly engaged in such a deception. It was entirely possible that they signed a decree prepared for them by someone else (perhaps Grochelewski) without reading it very carefully, following the Signatura's newly-enunciated principle that the accuracy of the facts does not matter so long as the result is "just and legitimate."

Now that the Signatura had revised the facts to dispense with Father Gruner's 1978 permission to reside in Canada, what would it say about his involvement in the apostolate?

While not denying that Canon 278 guaranteed the natural right of secular priests like Father Gruner to associate with others in private apostolates, the Signatura cited Canon 278, §3, which states that "Clerics are to refrain from establishing or joining associations whose purpose or activity cannot be reconciled with the obligations proper to the clerical state." How could an apostolate devoted to Our Lady of Fatima possibly be irreconcilable with the obligations of the priesthood? The Signatura offered no explanation. On the contrary, for the first time in the entire proceedings, the Signatura had actually conceded that the apostolate itself was legitimate:

> "For reasons of clarity it is to be noted that here *we are not dealing with the legitimacy of the private association* but only regarding the condition of Reverend Gruner himself."

If the legitimacy of the apostolate was conceded, if it was conceded that the Church did not require permission for it, then how could Father Gruner's involvement in the apostolate be inconsistent with the priestly state? More to the point: How could a priest's legitimate apostolic work constitute an "irregular condition"?

Here the Signatura offered a further non-answer: "The Second Vatican Council teaches that priests... are collaborators of the bishop in the service of Christ... Incardination since the Second Vatican Council is especially understood as incorporation into a particular church (diocese) and its presbytery (priesthood) with the service of the same church under the leadership of its pastor ..." Yes, and so what? All of this was equally true before the Council, but it was also true that priests have the natural right to engage in apostolates without episcopal permission, and that the Signatura *did not even question* the legitimacy of Father Gruner's apostolate.

The Signatura had avoided these obvious objections, resting on its mere *ipse dixit* that an admittedly legitimate apostolate was somehow inconsistent with incardination "since the Second Vatican Council." Yet it was the Pope, not the Signatura, who had the authority to interpret and implement Vatican II's purported teaching on incardination. The Pope had exercised this authority by promulgating Canon 278, which guarantees the right of secular priests to establish and join private associations of the faithful—all the more so, associations conceded to be legitimate!

As if this were not enough to sustain Father Gruner's position, three different bishops had offered to incardinate Father Gruner with permission to continue his work in Canada, precisely because they deemed it a service to their own particular churches. In fact, Father Gruner was already serving the "particular church" of Hyderabad by building an orphanage and supporting the orphans with the apostolate's resources, and by conducting Marian pilgrimages which had attracted tens of thousands of potential Hindu converts, drawn by devotion to the Virgin Mary as fostered by the apostolate's papally blessed Pilgrim Virgin statue. These were among the reasons which led Archbishop Arulappa to issue Father Gruner a decree of incardination for the continuation of what the Archbishop himself had called "God's work." The same Archbishop had been the first signatory on the Open Letter to the Holy Father, protesting Father Gruner's mistreatment. Clearly Archbishop Arulappa recognized in Father Gruner precisely the sort of "collaborator" his diocese needed, in keeping with "the teaching of Vatican II" on incardination.

If no fewer than three bishops viewed the apostolate as consistent with Father Gruner's priestly obligations, on what basis could the Signatura say otherwise? Yet another non-answer: "Leaving aside the question by which the bishop in India or Brazil could permit a priest incardinated in his diocese to reside in Canada and be active in a private apostolate"—leaving aside, that is the very crux of the matter!—"it is clear that, hypothetically, in no manner would this have rectified Reverend Gruner's condition." And why was that? If the Signatura did not question the apostolate's legitimacy; if the apostolate was already performing major corporal and spiritual works in the Archdiocese of Hyderabad; if the Archbishop of Hyderabad considered it "God's work"—if all this was true, then why would incardination in Hyderabad not rectify Father Gruner's alleged "irregular condition"?

These facts had not impressed the Signatura. Evidently, the members of the tribunal had concluded—having only God before their eyes—that building orphanages and feeding orphans in a poverty-stricken Third World diocese did not constitute a service to the local church. No, it was all very "irregular." As the Signatura would have it, Father Gruner had much more important works to perform in the Diocese of Avellino: the work of keeping quiet about the Message of Fatima; and, of course, the work of curing his "irregular condition" by remaining in Avellino for the rest of his life, doing nothing. The orphans would have to find another benefactor.

Throughout its discussion of Father Gruner's status, the Signatura had completely ignored a basic norm of canonical interpretation, most recently expressed in Canon 17 of the 1983 Code: *favorabilia amplianda, odios restrigenda*—rights and privileges are broadly interpreted, while restrictions on rights and privileges are narrowly interpreted. In other words, the presumption in canon law is in favor of proper liberty and against the undue restriction of liberty. In Father Gruner's case, however, the Signatura had given the narrowest possible interpretation of Father Gruner's liberty to engage in an apostolate under Canon 278 §1, and the broadest possible interpretation of the restrictive phrase "cannot be reconciled with the obligations of the clerical state" in Canon 278 §2. That is, the Signatura had turned the law on its head, taking a narrow view of rights and a broad view of restrictions in the Code.

The Signatura maintained the same upside-down approach to the law in addressing the related question of the Congregation's unprecedented directive that the Bishop of Avellino deny excardination to Father Gruner, so that his incardination in the Archdiocese of Hyderabad could be blocked.

Canon 270 states that:

> Excardination can be lawfully granted only for a just reason, such as the advantage of the Church or the good of the cleric. *It may not, however, be refused unless grave reasons exist ...*

This canon reflects the truth that when a priest is incardinated in a particular diocese he does not become an indentured servant for life to his original bishop, but rather has the right to transfer to another diocese where his talents and particular priestly charisms would be better used—not only for the good of the Church but for his own personal good. In short, priests are not chattel slaves, but human beings like everyone else. This is why Canon 270 provides that a priest may not be refused excardination to another diocese without "grave reasons."

What exactly were the "grave reasons" for denying Father Gruner excardination from Avellino, where he could not speak the dialect and had never been given a canonical mission in the first place? The only reason now given by the Signatura was Father Gruner's "irregular condition." But the "irregular condition" consisted of nothing more than engaging in the very apostolate which the Archbishop of Hyderabad (not to mention two other bishops) was happy to sponsor. It was only the intervention of the Congregation, not any "grave reason", which was at work here. The Signatura had never denied that the Bishop of Avellino admitted to Father Gruner that he himself had no cause to deny excardination.

In short, there were no grave reasons to deny excardination. In fact, there were no reasons at all, only the determination of the Congregation and the Signatura that Father Gruner must be confined forever to the Diocese of Avellino.

But the travesty would grow even deeper. The Signatura still had to address the matter of the Congregation's deliberate interference in offers of incardination by three successive bishops, as well as the request for excardination from Avellino.

Throughout the proceedings thus far, the Congregation for the Clergy and the Signatura had taken the position that the Congregation was merely *advising* the bishops on what to do, and merely upholding the Bishop of Avellino's own decrees against Father Gruner. In the latest decree, however, the Signatura had finally abandoned this pretense. It now asserted that all along the Congregation had been acting directly against Father Gruner "in the name of the Supreme Pontiff with ordinary executive *vicariate power* ... as the *hierarchical superior* of the bishops." This might explain why the Promoter of Justice had disclosed the existence of numerous written and oral interventions by the Congregation against Father Gruner with the bishops of Anapolis, Simla-Changidarh and Hyderabad. These interventions no longer had to be hidden, because under the new theory of the case they were only routine exercises of the Congregation's vicarious papal authority as the "hierarchical superior" of every Catholic bishop in the world.

The problem with this breathtaking claim is that the Congregation itself had never mentioned it. All of its prior decrees were cast entirely in terms of merely upholding decrees of the Bishop of Avellino. In fact, the Congregation had passed over in silence Father Gruner's objections to its interference in his excardination and incardination, never once claiming that it had the right to interfere in the name of the Pope.

To this the Signatura replied that in July of 1989 the Congregation did indeed openly assert its supposed vicarious papal authority when Cardinal Innocenti (then Prefect of the Congregation for the Clergy) issued his letter ordering Father Gruner to return to the Diocese of Avellino by September 30, 1989, if he had not found another bishop. But the Signatura failed to mention that Father Gruner had immediately appealed this directive both to the Congregation and the Pope himself on grounds that it was clearly outside the Congregation's authority, since the Bishop of Avellino had never given any such order himself and the Congregation did not have the right to run his diocese. The Signatura also failed to mention that after Father Gruner's appeal to the Congregation and the Pope, neither Innocenti nor the Congregation itself ever mentioned the 1989 directive again, nor is there a single reference to it in any of the Congregation's subsequent decrees or announcements against Father Gruner over the next ten years. The Congregation's silence spoke volumes.

To this the Signatura could only reply that "the argument from silence proves nothing." On the contrary, it proved everything. For if Cardinal Innocenti's 1989 intervention had been a valid exercise of the Congregation's alleged vicarious papal authority, the Congregation would certainly have relied upon it in declaring Father Gruner "disobedient" to "ecclesiastical authority"—indeed, the "vicarious" authority of the Pope himself! But the Congregation had said nothing about the decree from August 21, 1989 to the present. Nor had the Congregation ever responded to Father Gruner's 1989 appeal against the decree. The Congregation having received the appeal, its ten-year silence could mean only one thing: that the Congregation knew it had acted outside its authority and that Father Gruner had been correct in asserting the illegality of its action.

The Congregation's total retreat from the 1989 intervention demonstrated (better than any argument) that the Congregation knew it was not the "hierarchical superior" of the Bishop of Avellino (or, for that matter, any other bishop) and had no right to issue orders to Father Gruner without the bishop's approval. This was precisely why, in his subsequent letter of October 28, 1989, Cardinal Agustoni (with Cardinal Innocenti as co-signer) merely *requested* that the Bishop of Avellino recall Father Gruner to the diocese, while pretending that it was the bishop's own idea. Meanwhile, having been forced to retreat after Father Gruner's appeal to the Pope, Cardinal Innocenti let it be known that the name of Father Gruner was never to be mentioned in his presence again—hardly the behavior one would expect from a man who thought he was acting with the Pope's own authority.

It did not take a very deep knowledge of Catholic teaching to recognize that the Signatura's newly expansive view of the Congregation's authority would wreak havoc with the divine constitution of the Church. As the First Vatican Council solemnly defined, the primacy of Peter in no way detracted from "that power of *ordinary and immediate episcopal jurisdiction* by which the bishops, who 'placed by the Holy Spirit', have succeeded to the place of the Apostles as true shepherds, individually feed *and rule* the individual flocks assigned to them..." As the Council further declared, the local sovereignty of bishops "is asserted, confirmed and vindicated by the universal shepherd ..." And what of *Pastor bonus*, John Paul II's apostolic constitution defining the authority of the Congregation for the Clergy, which states that the Congregation was formed "*without prejudice* to the right of bishops ..."?

While the Pope can (and, indeed, must) delegate certain limited functions to the congregations which make up the Roman Curia in order to be able to govern a vast Church, even the Pope must respect the "ordinary and immediate episcopal jurisdiction" of local bishops as successors of the Apostles, as Vatican I solemnly teaches. By what right, then, did the Congregation for the Clergy dictate to the Bishop of Avellino whom he would excardinate, or to the Archbishop of Hyderabad whom he would *in*cardinate?—especially when the Congregation had no reason for its interventions beyond "worried signals" from the Vatican Secretary of State?

When he was ordained a priest Father Gruner had made a promise of obedience to his bishop, not to the Congregation for the Clergy. Yet the Signatura had now effectively declared that the Congregation acts as a kind of super-bishop or junior pope, exercising *original papal jurisdiction* over every priest in the world, *even if there was no recourse before it*. And this is why, according to the Signatura's newly announced theory, the Congregation had the right to "order" Father Gruner to return to Avellino on its own initiative in 1989, even if the Bishop of Avellino had never given such an order himself.

If the Congregation for the Clergy could issue direct orders to priests on such matters as where they would reside and which apostolates they could conduct, and priests had no choice but to obey these orders, what was left of the ordinary power of episcopal jurisdiction over dioceses? Clearly, it would become an empty formality. The bishops in each diocese would be merely caretakers of their respective territories whose judgments could be overruled by the Congregation whenever the Congregation deemed it expedient.

The Signatura contended that its expansive interpretation of the power of the Congregation "would not mean that the bishops are mere delegates to the Congregation or that the Congregation can act arbitrarily." Given that the Signatura acknowledged that the Congregation could not act arbitrarily, how could the Signatura uphold the following sequence of actions: (1) ordering a priest to find another bishop to incardinate him, then (2) ordering any interested bishop not to incardinate the priest, then (3) ordering the original bishop not to *ex*cardinate the priest, and then (4) declaring that the priest is "disobedient" because he had "failed" to find another bishop. Did the Congregation's alleged "vicarious papal authority" include the right to engage in such shamelessly tyrannical maneuvers? If such actions were not arbitrary, then what would be?

Thus it seemed that even the Divine Constitution of the Church would have to be adjusted to allow for the disposal of Father Nicholas Gruner. Naturally, the Signatura had concluded that the Congregation "rightly carried out the office commissioned to it by the Supreme Pontiff" when it employed secret interventions, levelled false accusations and browbeat bishops in order to prevent Father Gruner's incardination in any diocese in the world except Avellino. And why was this whirlwind of global activity necessary to prevent the otherwise routine incardination of one priest? Because the bishops should not be allowed to confirm "*de facto* his [Father Gruner's] irregular condition." In a Church convulsed by crisis and scandal in so many dioceses throughout the world, the one thing bishops could *not* be allowed to do was confirm Father Gruner's "*de facto* irregular condition." The Congregation simply had to act in this emergency! In the name of the Pope, of course.

The phrase "*de facto* irregular condition" was yet another novelty which seemed to have been coined especially for Father Gruner's case. There is a distinction in jurisprudence between matters *de facto* and matters *de jure*. Matters *de facto* are matters of fact; matters *de jure* are matters of law. Violation of the law is a matter *de jure*, not *de facto*. For example, one cannot be a *de facto* speeder. One has either violated the speed limit or he has not. To say, then, that Father Gruner was guilty of only a "*de facto* irregular condition" was to admit that he had not actually violated any law of the Church, and that as far as the law of the Church was concerned, his "condicio" was perfectly legal and thus certainly not "irregular". The charge made no more sense than a summons for *de facto* speeding.

In sum, the Congregation for the Clergy had spent ten years under three successive Cardinals, engaging in and upholding utterly unprecedented interventions to address the situation of one priest whose situation was not even illegal to begin with, in order to put a stop to an apostolate whose legitimacy was not even denied. This had to rank as one of the greatest puzzles in the annals of canon law. Or rather, it was no puzzle at all: The apostolate was, of course, at the very heart of the matter, but the Signatura could never admit this. Nor could the Congregation. For how could it be admitted that all of these factual and legal contrivances had been aimed at destroying promotion of the Message of Fatima by the only priest who was doing it effectively on a worldwide basis? To admit this would be to open the door to a hearing on what the case was really about: the fundamental opposition between the Message of Fatima and the current agenda of the Vatican bureaucracy, which was heir to the Vatican-Moscow Agreement and the entire post-conciliar "opening to the world"—an enterprise whose failure had been nothing short of catastrophic.

All that remained now were a few loose ends. There was the matter of Father Gruner not being an Italian citizen. How could he be expected to take up permanent residence in Italy after an absence of more than twenty years? The bishop's order to return was legally impossible to fulfill. Illegal aliens are expelled from Italy just as they are from Canada or the United States.

Undeterred by this legal reality, the Signatura simply observed that many foreign-born priests live and work in Italy, without mentioning that these priests have proper immigration status and cannot be expelled. Since 1994 the Bishop of Avellino had taken no steps to obtain the proper visa for Father Gruner, which would require that the bishop give the Italian consulate in Canada written guarantees of Father Gruner's financial support and medical coverage. Acting under coercion from the Congregation, the bishop had simply issued orders to return without any thought to the legalities involved.

But while the Signatura evinced no concern about Father Gruner's immigration status in Italy, its own prior decree in 1997 cited supposed problems with Indian immigration law as just reason to deny incardination in the Diocese of Hyderabad. So, when it came to Father Gruner's incardination in Hyderabad, immigration laws were a major impediment, but when it came to incardination in Avellino (after an absence of more than 20 years), immigration laws were no problem at all. Straining to reach the preordained result, the Signatura had contradicted itself again.

But the fact remained that without the Bishop of Avellino's guarantees of financial support and medical coverage, Father Gruner could not obtain the necessary visa for a permanent return to Italy. Yet, incredibly, the Signatura had declared in the same decree that Father Gruner was not entitled to these very things: "The conditions were not fulfilled according to which Father Gruner would have merited remuneration for his ministry or social assistance in case of infirmity or old age." So, according to the Signatura, Father Gruner was supposed to return to Italy immediately without a proper visa, without salary, without medical coverage, and without any provision for his old age. Presumably, Father Gruner, now almost sixty [in 2013, now over 70], could spend five years or so in the Diocese of Avellino as an illegal alien harbored by the bishop (a period just long enough to ensure the total destruction of the apostolate, not to mention Father Gruner's personal estate), after which it would not matter if he was arrested by the Italian police and deported to Canada in the condition of a pauper.

The Signatura turned, finally, to Father Gruner's objection that he had never received a hearing before an impartial tribunal because the very members of the Congregation who were blocking his excardination to another diocese were acting as the judges of his recourse from the denial of excardination. Shifting ground yet again, the Signatura announced that Father Gruner was not entitled to an impartial judge in the Congregation because *the Congregation is not a tribunal*. Rather, it was the "hierarchical superior" of all bishops and priests in the Catholic Church.

But the Congregation itself had never denied that it was acting as a tribunal in Father Gruner's case, nor had it ever claimed that it was acting as Father Gruner's hierarchical superior. Rather, the Congregation had declared that the right to an impartial judge in "administrative proceedings" in the Congregation was "not foreseen by legislation", and the Signatura had upheld that position in one of its earlier decrees. The Signatura had contradicted itself yet again.

To conclude this point, the Signatura declared that, in any event, Father Gruner *had* received a hearing before an impartial tribunal—none other than the Apostolic Signatura! But the Signatura had yet to grant Father Gruner a hearing, having decided at every juncture of the proceedings that Father Gruner's case was not worthy of discussion—"manifestly without any foundation whatever."

As the Signatura's final decree had made clear, for Father Gruner an "irregular condition" meant any condition in which he would be able to engage in his apostolate, while a "regular" condition meant only one thing: permanent confinement in Avellino as a virtual pauper and slave of the bishop with no prospect of excardination to any other diocese. And this preposterously restrictive view of incardination had been presented in all seriousness as nothing more than the teaching of Vatican II—the most liberalizing council in Church history!

Merely to summarize the Signatura's final decree against Father Gruner was to demonstrate the shameless injustice of the entire proceeding against him:

1. While the law of the Church states that priests can live outside their dioceses with merely presumed permission, Father Gruner could not do so even with *written* permission repeatedly affirmed over 16 years by three successive bishops of Avellino.

2. While the law of the Church (as well as natural law) states that priests can engage in private apostolates without episcopal approval, Father Gruner could not do so even *with* episcopal approval (from no less than three bishops), even though his apostolate is admittedly legitimate, supports orphans and is considered God's work by an Archbishop of more than 27 years' standing.

3. While excardination cannot be denied except for a grave reason, Father Gruner's excardination could be denied without *any* reason, besides an "irregular condition" consisting of nothing more than conduct which the Code of Canon Law not only does not prohibit, but positively allows.

4. While Italian immigration law prohibited Father Gruner's permanent residence in Italy, Father Gruner must still return after an absence of 20 years—without a proper visa, without salary, without medical insurance, without provision for his old age. This he was expected to do even though under Canon Law (Can. 22) the Church agreed to be bound by Italian Civil Law on immigration, and even though Father Gruner could be arrested and jailed as an illegal alien on Italian soil.

5. While claiming that Father Gruner had been given an "impartial" hearing in the Signatura, Grochelewski had refused to admit the case for discussion by the judges of that same tribunal.

For Father Gruner only, Vatican II and the Code of Canon Law comprised a straitjacket no other priest in the Church was wearing. Meanwhile, priests truly in need of straitjackets were roaming the Church out of control, demanding, and getting, freedom for all kinds of private undertakings, many of them openly inimical to the Church's teaching on faith and morals. Knowledgeable Catholics were well familiar with the cases of globetrotting dissident priests and nuns who were allowed to inflict incalculable damage on the Church for years and even decades without the slightest disciplinary action being taken against them by the Vatican: the Boffs, the Küngs, the Foxes and the Currans of the post-conciliar Church had the whole world at their disposal, including the mass media, for the spreading of their poison. Not one of them had ever been threatened with the suspension from priestly orders about to be imposed on a priest from Canada whose only offense was to conduct a legitimate Fatima apostolate rather too effectively for the Vatican Secretary of State.

As the Signatura's final decree against Father Gruner was being readied in the summer of 1999, the supposed "resolution" of the case of Father Robert Nugent and Sister Jeannine Gramick provided an apt example of the invidious double-standard at work in Father Gruner's case.

Since 1977 Nugent and Gramick had traveled the globe under the auspices of their so-called "apostolate", New Ways Ministry, openly contradicting the Church's settled teaching on the intrinsically disordered nature of the homosexual condition. It took *seven years* for the Congregation for Institutes of Consecrated Life and Societies of Apostolic Life to order Nugent and Gramick to sever their ties with this "apostolate", whereupon they simply resigned as officers but continued their involvement in the organization in open defiance of the Vatican's order. Another *four* years elapsed before the Vatican established a commission to "study" the teaching of Nugent and Gramick. Another *six* years went by before the commission issued its 1994 "findings" that Nugent and Gramick's "ministry", while exhibiting "positive aspects", had "serious deficiencies" which were "incompatible with the fullness of Christian morality." In other words, Gramick and Nugent were spreading immoral teaching throughout the Catholic Church.

Having received the Vatican Commission's findings, the Congregation for Institutes of Consecrated Life and Societies of Apostolic Life "recommended" disciplinary measures, including "some sort of notification"—some sort of notification, after *seventeen years* of open disobedience and contradiction of Church doctrine.

Then the Congregation discovered, to its great surprise, that Nugent's and Gramick's false teachings involved doctrinal matters which should be considered by the Congregation for the Doctrine of the Faith (CDF). It promptly turned the whole matter over to the CDF, having failed to impose any discipline whatsoever on Nugent or Gramick.

In 1996—after *nineteen years* of spreading error in the Church— Gramick and Nugent were asked by the CDF to answer questions about their erroneous views and to affirm the Catholic teaching. The CDF deemed their responses "not sufficiently clear", at which point it opened—opened!—a doctrinal investigation of the two, after a mere *nineteen years* of complaints about them.

Another year went by before the CDF announced what has been known from the beginning, that Nugent's and Gramick's teachings were "erroneous and dangerous." Instead of imposing discipline, however, the CDF asked them both to *respond* to the CDF's conclusions.

Still another year passed before the CDF received Gramick and Nugent's responses, which it deemed "unacceptable." But still no discipline. Instead, in 1998—*after 21 years of false teaching and disobedience*—Nugent and Gramick were asked to *formulate declarations* expressing their agreement with Catholic teaching! They sent in their statements, but neither declaration was acceptable.

Finally, on July 14, 1999—*twenty-two years* after Nugent and Gramick began their career of dissension from Church teaching—the CDF announced that their false doctrine had caused "confusion among the Catholic people and harmed the community of the Church." And what was to be the penalty for all the 22 years of confusion and harm they had caused to souls? No suspension or reduction to the lay state for either, but merely an order that they cease ministering to homosexuals or holding offices in their respective religious institutes! They were not ordered to cease preaching their errors against the Faith, which had been published in two books, or even to retract their errors. And this was all the Vatican was willing to do to remedy nearly a quarter century of serious damage to the Church.

The comparison with Father Gruner's case was nothing short of sickening. Unlike Father Gruner, Gramick and Nugent were never even threatened with suspension or reduction to the lay state. Unlike Father Gruner, Gramick and Nugent did not suffer any interference in their basic canonical rights on the theory that the pertinent Congregation was acting in place of the pope with direct authority over their immediate superiors. Unlike Father Gruner, Gramick and Nugent were not subjected to secret interventions, secret letters, or secret "resolutions"; they had been notified of every step in the proceedings and given opportunity to respond. Indeed, throughout the Nugent and Gramick affair obsequious deference was shown to their rights. After 22 years of brazen disobedience and heterodox teaching, they suffered minimal punishments and remained, respectively, a priest and a nun in good standing, free to continue undermining Catholic moral teaching on the grave disorder of the homosexual condition—with untold damage to the faith and morals of Catholics, especially the young.

Yet Father Gruner, a morally upright and orthodox priest, had been summarily pronounced "disobedient" and subject to suspension from the sacred priesthood without ever having been shown to be in violation of any law of the Church, much less a basic moral teaching. As Cardinal Agustoni had stated in his letter to the Bishop of Avellino in 1989, Father Gruner would even be defrocked and reduced to the lay state if he would not agree to be silenced. *Defrocked* for preaching the Message of Fatima, while public heretics received a slap on the wrist after decades of dancing with the Vatican.

The conclusion was inescapable: There are two standards for the administration of justice in the post-conciliar Church. The first standard is for those who preach heresy and violate Church law. These are given every available procedural right before any sort of minimal penalty is imposed, if indeed there is ever a penalty at all. The second standard is for those who incur the wrath of certain Vatican functionaries by too successfully promoting some element of traditional Catholicism. These are deprived of due process and subjected to an absurdly strict and unjust interpretation of the law.

The net result was an intolerable paradox in the post-conciliar Church: Those who violate the law are given the benefit of the law, while those who obey the law are deprived of its benefit.

And so the triumph of Father Gruner's opponents in the Vatican Secretariat of State would appear to be complete. Five members of the Apostolic Signatura had signed a "definitive decree" which contradicted not only the law and the facts, but the Signatura's own prior pronouncements. Never mind that this final decree had changed the rules of the game and shifted ground to entirely new arguments that Father Gruner would have no opportunity to answer. Although the proceedings had been a travesty, the preordained result had finally been obtained. Now it would simply be a matter of announcing to the world that Father Gruner had been "suspended" for his "disobedience".

But it would not be so simple as that, after all. For there was yet another surprise in store for Father Gruner's canonical executioners—another gift, perhaps, from Our Lady of Fatima. It would come once again from the Archdiocese of Hyderabad.

Some four months before the date of the Signatura's final decree, Archbishop Arulappa had sent to Father Gruner his own decree in the matter of Father Gruner's incardination in Hyderabad. The Archbishop's decree was a forthright rejection of the Congregation's arbitrary declaration that the incardination of Father Gruner in Hyderabad in 1995 was "non-existent":

> "Having reviewed the documents of Father Nicholas Gruner, including the letter from the Diocese of Avellino, dated August 4, 1989, I am satisfied that my decree of November 4, 1995, incardinating Father Gruner into the Archdiocese of Hyderabad is valid and effective, and he is validly incardinated as a priest of the Archdiocese of Hyderabad from that date ... After due discernment, I am convinced that I am acting correctly *though I was partly misled by influential people*. I strongly feel that the good work he is doing in spreading devotion to the Immaculate Heart of Mary should not be hampered for the present, especially through *undue canonical or juridical pressures*. May Jesus Christ be Praised!"

The Archbishop had taken a stand against the corruption of justice in the Church, again giving objective confirmation to the reality of Father Gruner's persecution.

The Archbishop's decree had been forwarded to the Bishop of Avellino in August of 1999, and the bishop had yet to reply. Would the Congregation exercise its newly-acquired "vicarious" papal authority, issuing a "papal" order nullifying an Archbishop's decree? Or would it concede that it had no authority to do so and remain silent, as it did after the 1989 intervention? If so, how could it be claimed that Father Gruner had been "suspended" for "disobeying" the Bishop of Avellino, when an Archbishop in India had decreed that Father Gruner was a priest of *his* Archdiocese, not Avellino?

The Congregation and the Signatura had embarked upon a travesty with their first unprecedented decrees against Father Gruner in 1994 and 1995. Now the travesty had acquired a dimension they could not have anticipated when they first began to interfere in the rightful jurisdiction of bishops.

For years Father Gruner had been made the victim of a law written for just one man. The Archbishop of Hyderabad had recognized the divine truth that a law for one man is no law at all, but lawlessness. Since Vatican II the Church has been plagued by lawlessness and scandal in places high and low. But here, now, in the case of this priest, the laws of the Church—laws which applied to *all* the faithful—were being upheld by a prelate who would not tolerate their corruption any longer, not even by his fellow prelates in the Vatican.

The case of Father Nicholas Gruner has not yet been closed. Nor has the cause of Our Lady of Fatima been ended, for Heaven will not allow it to end until Her promise has been fulfilled. "In the end, My Immaculate Heart will triumph".

PART FOUR

A New Day for Fatima

Chapter 23

2000: The Vision of a "Bishop Dressed in White"

For every capital sin there is an opposing capital virtue. In opposition to the capital sin of sloth or laziness is the capital virtue of diligence or perseverance. And this virtue of perseverance has yielded great fruit in the priestly labors of Father Nicholas Gruner, particularly in the dozen years that have passed since the last edition of this work appeared. Father Gruner's thirty-five years in this battle for souls and for Our Lady's honor had led, by the year 2012, to a veritable new day for the cause of Fatima, despite the best efforts of the Vatican Secretary of State to consign the Fatima event to the eternal night of forgotten history. As the years following 2000 unrolled, the great lie remarked at the beginning of this book—the lie that "Fatima is finished"—would begin to be undone with dramatic effect.

The Vision of the Third Secret Revealed

It was in 2000—on June 26, to be precise—that Vatican Secretary of State Cardinal Angelo Sodano, bowing to mounting pressure from the faithful, including Father Gruner's Fatima Center,[286] superintended publication of the obscure vision of the "Bishop dressed in White" at a press conference attended by the world's media. Sodano and his successor as Secretary of State, Cardinal Tarcisio Bertone, have since maintained that what follows is the Third Secret of Fatima in its entirety. Herewith is the text of the vision in the third part of the Secret of Fatima, presented as if it were everything recorded by Sister Lucia:

> J.M.J.
>
> The third part of the secret revealed at the Cova da Iria-Fatima, on 13 July 1917.
>
> I write in obedience to you, my God, who command me to do so through his Excellency the Bishop of Leiria and through your Most Holy Mother and mine.
>
> After the two parts which I have already explained, at the left of Our Lady and a little above, we saw an Angel with a flaming sword in his left hand; flashing, it gave out flames that looked as though they would set the world on fire; but they died out in contact with the splendour that Our Lady radiated towards him from her right hand: pointing to the earth with his right hand, the Angel cried out in a loud voice: 'Penance, Penance, Penance!' And we saw in an immense light that is God: 'something similar to how people appear in a mirror when they pass in front of it' a Bishop dressed in White 'we had the impression that it was the Holy Father'. Other Bishops, Priests, men

[286] It was only in 2007 that Cardinal Bertone acknowledged it was due to Father Nicholas Gruner and *The Fatima Crusader* (among others) that the Vatican apparatus finally decided to reveal the Third Secret (at least in part). See Cardinal Bertone's book *L'ultima veggente di Fatima*, p. 57, "Il Giubileo di fine millennio era già così saturo di eventi religiosi. Perché aggiungere anche la pubblicazione del 'Terzo Segreto'? … Le pressioni dei 'fatimisti' erano fortissime, …" ["The Jubilee at the end of the millennium was already saturated with religious events. Why add [to all this] also the publication of the 'Third Secret'? … The pressures from the 'Fatimists' were very strong, …"] And who does Cardinal Bertone identify as 'Fatimists'? "Hard-core Fatimists, like the followers of Father Nicholas Gruner and the readers of his magazine, *The Fatima Crusader*" (*The Last Secret of Fatima*, p. 64).

> and women Religious going up a steep mountain, at the top of which there was a big Cross of rough-hewn trunks as of a cork-tree with the bark; before reaching there the Holy Father passed through a big city half in ruins and half trembling with halting step, afflicted with pain and sorrow, he prayed for the souls of the corpses he met on his way; having reached the top of the mountain, on his knees at the foot of the big Cross he was killed by a group of soldiers who fired bullets and arrows at him, and in the same way there died one after another the other Bishops, Priests, men and women Religious, and various lay people of different ranks and positions. Beneath the two arms of the Cross there were two Angels, each with a crystal aspersorium in his hand, in which they gathered up the blood of the Martyrs and with it sprinkled the souls that were making their way to God.
>
> Tuy-3-1-1944.[287]

What does it all mean? The definitive explanation could come only from Her Who had delivered the message. The Vatican's presentation lacked what the Vatican itself had revealed via its press release in 1960, when the Secret was suppressed by order of John XXIII: "the *words* which Our Lady confided as a secret to the three little shepherds..." The Virgin had explained to the three seers something as obvious as the vision of hell, which they had just seen in the first part of the Great Secret: "You have seen hell, where the souls of poor sinners go." Surely She would likewise have explained the utterly enigmatic vision (the Vatican had just published) of the "Bishop dressed in White". Yet the rather obscure text contained not a single word of explanation from the Virgin, much less the plainly needed explanation of its precise significance, including the how, where, why, when and who of the events depicted.

Clearly, something was missing. Suspicions in that regard could only have been heightened once it became apparent that the June 26 press conference would be a forum for Sodano's usurpation of the task of "interpreting" a vision that should have needed no interpretation, given the "words of the Virgin" that were obviously not being revealed. Sodano would treat the Secret as he had the rest of the Message of Fatima: not as a heavenly prophecy and warning for the good of the Church and all of humanity, but rather as a public relations problem to be handled by a "spin" to divert the public's attention from the truth. The Italian author and intellectual Antonio Socci would call this a "preventative interpretation."

The spinning of the Third Secret had already begun with Sodano's announcement of the vision's imminent publication during Pope John Paul II's pilgrimage to Fatima a few weeks earlier in May. On its face, the text of the vision depicts a white-clad bishop, evidently a future Pope, being executed by a band of soldiers on a hill outside a half-ruined city filled with the dead—a clearly post-apocalyptic scenario whose historical context is not provided by the text of the vision standing alone. As Pope John Paul II, suffering with Parkinson's Disease, sat silently by, however, Cardinal Sodano launched an "interpretation" that twisted the text into a mere depiction of events in the 20th century, culminating with the attempt on the life of John Paul II in 1981. On May 13, 2000, Cardinal Sodano said:

287 Congregation for the Doctrine of the Faith, *The Message of Fatima* (hereafter referred to as *TMF*), (Vatican City: Libreria Editrice Vaticana, June 26, 2000) p. 21, http://www.vatican.va/roman_curia/congregations/cfaith/documents/rc_con_cfaith_doc_20000626_message-fatima_en.html

> The vision of Fatima concerns above all the war waged by atheist systems against the Church and Christians, and it describes the immense suffering endured by the witnesses to the faith *in the last century of the second millennium*. It is an interminable Way of the Cross led by the Popes of the twentieth century.
>
> According to the interpretation of the "little shepherds," which was also recently confirmed by Sister Lucia, the "Bishop dressed in White" who prays for all the faithful is the Pope. As he makes his way with great effort towards the Cross amid the corpses of those who were martyred (bishops, priests, men and women religious and many lay persons), he too falls to the ground, *apparently* dead, under a burst of gunfire.
>
> After the assassination attempt of May 13, 1981, it appeared evident to His Holiness that it was "a motherly hand which guided the bullet's path," enabling the "dying Pope" to halt "at the threshold of death."...
>
> The successive events of 1989 led, both in the Soviet Union and in a number of countries of Eastern Europe, to the fall of the Communist regime which promoted atheism. For this too His Holiness offers heartfelt thanks to the Most Holy Virgin ...
>
> Even if the events to which the third part of the Secret of Fatima refers now seem part of the past, Our Lady's call to conversion and penance, issued at the beginning of the twentieth century, remains timely and urgent today. ...[288]

So, as Sodano would have it, a vision depicting a Pope and innumerable others being executed outside a half-ruined city filled with the dead signified John Paul II alone *not* being executed by a solitary assassin in the perfectly intact city of Rome. This was a patent attempt to neutralize the clearly apocalyptic implications of the vision—which, again, only the Virgin Herself could clarify. It would be precisely the conspicuous absence of the Virgin's own explanation that would lead to the collapse of the "official" version of the Secret.

An Ecclesiastical Fixer

The thoughtful reader will ask himself the question Father Gruner posed publicly from the moment Cardinal Sodano took "command" of the vision's publication and interpretation: As the Vatican Secretary of State is a mere Vatican functionary with no pastoral authority over the Church, by what right was Sodano "interpreting" the vision in the first place? The answer to that question lies in the ascendancy of the Vatican Secretary of State to the level of a veritable "prime minister" of the Church in keeping with the radical restructuring of the Roman Curia carried out by Cardinal Villot after Vatican II.[289]

The Secretary of State's "Party Line" on Fatima—that "Fatima is finished"—would now extend to the Third Secret. Just as the Secretary of State had put out the order to propagate the fiction that the Consecration of Russia was accomplished in 1984 (a development noted in Chapter 10), orchestrating the concomitant persecution of Father Gruner, so had he arrogated to himself the "interpretation" of the vision published in

[288] Vatican Information Service (VIS), May 13, 2000. (Emphasis added.)

[289] For a detailed discussion of this development see *The Devil's Final Battle*, Chapter 8 (also at http://www.devilsfinalbattle.com/book/BookChaptPDF/dfb_chapter8.pdf).

2000. Here we see how the post-Vatican II Secretary of State has acted as a kind of ecclesiastical politician, subordinating spiritual matters to the requirements of the "new orientation" of the Church and the "opening to the world" after the Council, including the policy of *Ostpolitik*.

No one was better suited to the blunt pragmatism required for the job than Cardinal Sodano, an ecclesiastical "fixer" skilled in the art of the cover-up. It was Sodano, in fact, who was instrumental in covering up the crimes of the infamous Marcial Maciel Degollado, head of the Legionaries of Christ, who molested boys, fathered children out of wedlock, abused drugs, and engaged in financial improprieties throughout his long career as an immensely successful ecclesiastical entrepreneur. As *America* magazine has observed: "The key Vatican figure in protecting Maciel in the 1980s and 1990s was Cardinal Angelo Sodano, the all-powerful secretary of state [sic] under John Paul II and now Dean of the College of Cardinals."[290] All-powerful indeed—so powerful that he took control of the Message of Fatima, although, as we shall see, Providence has confounded his attempt to neutralize it. The respected Catholic pro-life website Lifesitenews.com summarized the evidence of Sodano's complicity in the Maciel scandal, as documented in an exposé in *National Catholic Reporter*:

> Maciel developed a close relationship with Angelo Sodano, who served as Pope John Paul's Secretary of State, effectively the Vatican's Prime Minister, from 1991 to 2006 ... The Legion hired Sodano's nephew as consultant when they built their flagship institution, Regina Apostolorum University in Rome. ... [M]uch later, efforts to reveal Maciel's machinations and sexual improprieties were actively blocked by "pressure from Maciel's chief supporter, Cardinal Angelo Sodano." Berry reports that after nine former members of the Legion who claimed to have been sexually abused by Maciel filed a canonical case against the founder with the Congregation for the Doctrine of the Faith in 1998, Sodano "pressured" Cardinal Ratzinger to halt the proceedings.[291]

By late 2004, however, the future Pope Benedict XVI would put an end to the scandal. After a Vatican ceremony in November 2004 during which John Paul II honored Maciel, "Ratzinger broke with Sodano and ordered a canon lawyer on his staff, Msgr. Charles Scicluna, to investigate. Two years later, as Pope Benedict, he approved the order that Maciel abandon ministry for a 'life of penitence and prayer.'"[292] Maciel died shortly thereafter. Despite his deep involvement in the Maciel scandal, Sodano left office without consequences in 2006 to be succeeded by Cardinal Bertone, becoming Dean of the College of Cardinals. The journal *First Things* rightly observed that "Cardinal Sodano has to go. The Dean of the College of Cardinals [is] ... an ongoing embarrassment to the Church he serves."[293]

Yet in the year 2000, Sodano was still firmly in command of what could be called Operation Neutralize Fatima. Hence it was his patently untenable "interpretation" of the vision that controlled the press conference of June 26 at which the vision was published to the world sans any explanation by Our Lady. Then Cardinal Ratzinger, serving as

---

290 Austen Ivereigh, "Will Sodano Resign Over Maciel?", *America*, April 13, 2010, http://www.americamagazine.org/blog/entry.cfm?entry_id=2749.

291 Hilary White, "Sodano's 'Head Should Roll': Report Reveals Close Ties Between Vatican Cardinal and Disgraced Legion," Lifesitenews.com, April 14, 2010, http://www.lifesitenews.com/news/archive/ldn/2010/apr/1004140.

292 Jason Berry, "Money paved way for Maciel's influence in the Vatican," *National Catholic Reporter*, April 26, 2010, http://ncronline.org/news/accountability/money-paved-way-maciels-influence-vatican?page=2.

293 Joseph Bottum, "The Cost of Maciel," *First Things*, May 12, 2010, www.firstthings.com/onthesquare/2010/05/the-cost-of-father-maciel.

head of the Congregation for the Doctrine of the Faith (CDF), provided a theological commentary on the vision in *The Message of Fatima* (*TMF*), the booklet published along with the vision. In *TMF* Ratzinger adhered slavishly to Sodano's twisted interpretation, even as he called it a mere "attempt" to make sense of the vision without the Virgin's crucial assistance:

> Before attempting an interpretation, the main lines of which can be found in the statement read by *Cardinal Sodano* on 13 May of this year ...[294]
>
> For this reason the figurative language of the vision is symbolic. In this regard *Cardinal Sodano* stated ...[295]
>
> As is clear from the documentation presented here, the interpretation offered by *Cardinal Sodano,* in his statement on 13 May ...[296]
>
> First of all we must affirm *with Cardinal Sodano* ...[297]

Cardinal Ratzinger likewise followed Sodano in pronouncing the Third Secret a thing of the past:

> A careful reading of the text of the so-called third 'secret' of Fatima, published here in its entirety long after the fact and by decision of the Holy Father, will probably prove disappointing or surprising after all the speculation it has stirred. No great mystery is revealed; nor is the future unveiled. We see the Church of the martyrs of the century which has just passed represented in a scene described in a language which is symbolic and not easy to decipher.
>
> We must affirm with Cardinal Sodano that the events to which the third part of the 'secret' of Fatima refers now seem part of the past. Insofar as individual events are described, *they belong to the past.*[298]

Father Gruner with John Marto, the brother of Jacinta and Fancisco, in the house the seven Marto children all grew up in.

For Father Gruner, and for Catholics the world over, these affirmations were impossible to accept. For if the vision reveals "no great mystery" and concerns only 20th century events, there would have been no reason to keep it under lock and key at the Vatican since 1957, or to declare in 1960 that it would be kept "forever under absolute seal." Nor would there have been any reason for Cardinal Ratzinger to have stated in 1984 that the Secret speaks of "dangers threatening the faith and the life of the Christian and therefore of the world."

294 *TMF*, p. 32. (Emphasis added.)

295 Ibid., p. 38. (Emphasis added.)

296 Ibid., p. 39. (Emphasis added.)

297 Ibid., p. 42. (Emphasis added.)

298 Ibid., pp. 32, 42. (Emphasis added.)

Chapter 24
Something Is Missing

Whereas before 2000 a primary focus of Father Gruner's apostolate had been achieving the Consecration of Russia, after the press conference of June 26 the apostolate's related initiative respecting disclosure of the Third Secret acquired a new urgency. For the Vatican apparatus had clearly not only withheld a crucial part of the Secret—the Blessed Virgin's very explanation of the significance of the vision—but was also claiming its disclosure had been whole and entire, and that the matter of the Secret had been laid to rest. Given the very nature of the Secret as a dire warning for the Church and the world, the risk entailed in this deception could not be ignored. Hence, in the aftermath of the press conference, the apostolate pursued the question of the Third Secret with a new and tighter focus. The focus now would be on the missing companion text that must contain the "*words*" of the Virgin to which the Vatican itself had alluded in the 1960 press release announcing that the *words* of Our Lady in the Third Secret would not be revealed, as the world was expecting, but rather most likely kept "forever under absolute seal."

Here it is crucially important to bear in mind that Sodano's "interpretation" of the vision was said to be necessary only because, as Cardinal Ratzinger had stated in his commentary, the vision is "not easy to decipher." It could hardly be the case that in 1917 the Blessed Virgin had appeared on earth to deliver a cipher that would have to be deciphered in 2000 by—of all people, Cardinal Sodano—the Vatican Secretary of State. This was, after all, the same Vatican functionary who was at that very moment engaged in covering up the crimes of Father Maciel. The idea that Sodano was the appointed oracle of Fatima for the Church and the world was preposterous on its face.

Hence Father Gruner's conflict with the Secretariat of State expanded to a new front: unearthing the suppressed text of the Secret that accompanies the vision and provides its definitive interpretation. By the date of the press conference in 2000 members of the faithful throughout the world, thanks largely to the efforts of the Fatima Center, were already aware of a vast body of evidence, much of it provided by direct witnesses to the content of the Secret, pointing to the existence of a text that must have been withheld by the Vatican.

A full review of the evidence, presented fully in other sources,[299] is beyond the scope of this essentially biographical work. Suffice it to note here some keynotes concerning the elements of the Third Secret clearly not present in the vision alone:

- something so terrible that Sister Lucia could not commit it to paper without a direct order from her bishop in October 1943 and then a direct intervention of the Virgin Mary on January 2, 1944;
- *two parts*, one of which contains the words of the Virgin that are the "logical continuation" of Her statement "In Portugal, the dogma of the Faith will always be preserved etc." (source: Father Joseph Schweigl in 1952);

[299] For a detailed exposition and sourcing of the evidence on this score, cf. Christopher A. Ferrara, *The Secret Still Hidden* (New York: Good Counsel Publications, 2009), Chapters 2-3.

- a single page of some 25 lines of text (sources: Bishop Venancio [1959] and Cardinal Ottaviani [1967]);
- a text in the form of a letter to the Bishop of Leiria-Fatima in a sealed envelope (sources: Sister Lucia, Bishop da Silva, Father Jongen [1946] and the 1960 Vatican press release);
- a text that was lodged in the papal apartment during the pontificates of Pius XII, John XXIII and Paul VI (sources: Sister Pasqualina; Robert Serrou [1958]; Father Caillon; Archbishop Capovilla [2006], a still-living eyewitness);
- a text that contains difficult expressions Pope John could not read without a written translation prepared by a Portuguese native in 1959, unlike the text he read in 1960, which he understood without need of translation (source: Archbishop Capovilla);
- a text whose prophecy would become clear in 1960, by which time Vatican II (which would have a disastrous aftermath) had been announced (source: Sister Lucia);
- a "divine warning" about "suicidal" alterations in the liturgy, theology and soul of the Church (source: the future Pius XII in 1931);
- a prediction that after 1960 "the devil will succeed in leaving the souls of the faithful abandoned by their leaders," by causing "religious and priests [to] fall away from their beautiful vocation... drag[ging] numerous souls to hell," and that "nations will disappear from the face of the earth" (source: Sister Lucia to Father Fuentes in 1957);
- contents "so delicate" that they cannot be allowed "for whatever reason, even fortuitous, to fall into alien hands" (source: Cardinal Ottaviani in 1967);
- a text "diplomatically" withheld because of the "seriousness of its contents" and which predicts, *after 1980*, "great trials" and "tribulation" for the Church which "it is no longer possible to avert" and the destruction of "whole areas of the earth" so that "from one moment to the next millions of people will perish" (source: John Paul II at Fulda, 1980);
- details that could be "badly interpreted" (source: John Paul II in 1982);
- a "religious prophecy" of "dangers threatening the faith and the life of the Christian and therefore of the world" (source: Cardinal Ratzinger in 1984);
- matters which would make for the "sensationalistic utilization of its contents" (source: Cardinal Ratzinger in 1985);
- a prediction of apostasy in the Church that "begins at the top" (source: Cardinal Ciappi in 1995);
- "details" that would cause "disequilibrium" in the Church (source: Cardinal Ratzinger in 1996);
- a warning of a material chastisement of the world which accompanies the great apostasy in the Church, like that predicted in the approved apparition of Our Lady of Akita in 1973, whose message is "essentially the

same" as the message of Our Lady of Fatima (source: Cardinal Ratzinger to Howard Dee, as reported in 1998);

- a warning to avoid the "tail of the dragon" (the devil) referred to in the Book of the Apocalypse (12:3-4), which sweeps one-third of "the stars" (priests, bishops, cardinals and other consecrated souls) from Heaven and casts them to the earth (source: John Paul II on May 13, 2000).[300]

The published vision, standing alone, did not involve a single one of these elements. There could be no other reasonable conclusion: something was missing.

Besides the details provided by various witnesses and numerous other evidentiary facts indicating the existence of a companion text,[301] the vision's ambiguity and the conspicuous lack of any explanation by the Virgin led Catholics around the world to conclude that there must be a companion text still hidden in the Vatican. Doubting questions immediately abounded, and Father Gruner led the way in posing them:

- Where are the *words* of the Virgin which are the "logical continuation" of Her statement "In Portugal, the dogma of the Faith will always be preserved etc.," as Father Schweigl revealed?
- What is so terrible about this ambiguous vision that Sister Lucia could not commit it to paper without a direct intervention of the Virgin Mary?
- Where is the letter to the Bishop of Fatima, comprising some 25 lines of text?
- Given that *TMF* stated that the text of the vision had been kept in the Holy Office archives,[302] where is the text that a living witness said was kept in the papal apartment under the Pope's personal custody during the reigns of Pius XII, John XXIII and Paul VI?
- Why is the vision devoid of any reference to a crisis of faith in the Church and dramatic consequences for the world, alluded to by a train of witnesses who had either read the Secret or had indirect knowledge of it?
- Why is the text of the vision 62 lines when Cardinal Ottaviani spoke of a text of only 25 lines?
- What of the testimony of various witnesses concerning the location, paper size, and date of delivery of the text to the Vatican, which did not at all correspond to the "official" account, thus indicating the existence of another text that accompanies and explains the vision?[303]

The Secret's Connection to 1960

Moreover, as Father Gruner was quick to note, on its face the vision has absolutely nothing to do with 1960, the year the Secret was supposed to be revealed because it would be "more clear" then. Evidently in recognition of this problem, then Archbishop Bertone had claimed in *TMF* that during an unrecorded "conversation" with Sister Lucia at Coimbra on April 27, 2000, weeks before the press conference, she allegedly told him that the Virgin *had never said anything* about 1960:

---

300 Ibid.

301 See also, enumeration of facts set forth in Table 10, *The Devil's Final Battle*, Ch. 13 (also at http://www.devilsfinalbattle.com/book/BookChaptPDF/dfb_chapter13.pdf).

302 *The Message of Fatima* [*TMF*], p. 5.

303 Cf. *The Devil's Final Battle*, Chapter 13, for the pertinent facts.

> Before giving the sealed envelope containing the third part of the "secret" to the then Bishop of Leiria-Fatima, Sister Lucia wrote on the outside envelope that it could be opened only after 1960, either by the Patriarch of Lisbon or the Bishop of Leiria. Archbishop Bertone therefore asked: "Why only after 1960? Was it Our Lady who fixed that date?" Sister Lucia replied: "*It was not Our Lady*. I fixed the date because I had the intuition that before 1960 it would not be understood, but that only later would it be understood..."[304]

Tellingly, *TMF* failed to mention that on the envelope Sister Lucia had written: "*By express order of Our Lady,* this envelope can be opened only in 1960..." Nor did any of the presentations at the June 26, 2000 press conference or the text of *TMF* include a copy of the envelope as supporting documentation. We will see that in 2007 Cardinal Bertone, Cardinal Sodano's successor in office, would finally reveal the envelope—or rather, *two* such envelopes bearing the same express order of the Virgin respecting 1960. But during the June 2000 press conference, then Archbishop Bertone (serving at that time as Secretary of the Congregation for the Doctrine of the Faith) had the temerity to claim that Lucia declared to him in private weeks earlier: "*It was not Our Lady*. I fixed the date!" We say temerity, because the future Secretary of State knew then that his representation was flatly contradicted by what Lucia had written on the two envelopes he had chosen not to reveal at that time.

Father Gruner did not miss the significance of what Bertone was claiming here: Either Sister Lucia had lied about this crucial matter throughout her life, which was inconceivable, given that she is God's chosen recipient of the Fatima revelations, or the words attributed to her by Bertone were not hers, and thus it was Bertone who was the liar! Here, in and of itself, was reason to doubt the entire "official" account of the Third Secret.

The Telltale "etc"

Father Gruner's publications after the June 2000 press conference focused intensely on the famous "etc" in Sister Lucia's Fourth Memoir. According to Father Schweigl's testimony, noted above, the Third Secret includes the "logical continuation" of the Virgin's discourse following the phrase that ends with Sister Lucia's "etc"—"In Portugal, the dogma of the Faith will always be preserved etc." In fact, the attention of Fatima scholars had always been focused on the "etc" as the very key to the Secret, as it was obvious that the Virgin's words to the seers had not trailed off in the middle of a thought.

Yet, in a maneuver that undermined all confidence in the official account, *TMF* had evaded any discussion of the "etc" by taking the text of the Message of Fatima from Sister Lucia's *Third* Memoir, wherein Our Lady's prophecy concerning Portugal is not recorded, rather than the more complete Fourth Memoir, where the prophecy is recorded in part followed by the "etc". The conspicuous avoidance of the Fourth Memoir could only further engender suspicion. Why rely on the Third Memoir when the more complete Fourth Memoir was available? In his Introduction to *TMF* Bertone attempted to explain this curious behavior: "For the account of the first two parts of the 'secret', which have already been published and are therefore known, we have chosen the text written by Sister Lucia in the Third Memoir of 31 August 1941; some *annotations* were added in the Fourth Memoir of 8 December 1941."[305] Tellingly, Bertone's Introduction

304 *TMF*, p. 29.

305 *TMF*, p. 3.

did not specify what is contained in these "annotations," which is none other than the very phrase of the Virgin he had to know was at the heart of the entire controversy.

According to Bertone, then, the only difference between the Third and Fourth memoirs was "some annotations" by Lucia, the suggestion being that no one should think it amiss that the Vatican had ignored mere "annotations." The suggestion was less than honest, for the reference to the preservation of dogma in Portugal was *a direct quotation of the Blessed Virgin* ("In Portugal the dogma of the Faith will always be preserved etc."), immediately after which She Herself had said: "Tell *this* to no one. Yes, you may tell Francisco." *Yet Bertone and his collaborators, acting according to the imperatives of Operation Neutralize Fatima, had dared to mischaracterize the very words of the Mother of God as Lucia's personal "annotations"* and then bury those precious words in a footnote that *TMF* never mentions again.[306]

A Telling Discrepancy

Bertone's Introduction to *TMF* contained another point that, as Father Gruner would show, had decisive importance in the Third Secret controversy. According to Bertone, John Paul II did not read the Third Secret until July 18, 1981, a full three years into his papacy, when the text of the Secret was taken from the Holy Office archives and brought to him at Gemelli Hospital, where the Pope was recovering from the assassination attempt.[307] But according to papal spokesman Joaquin Navarro-Valls, as reported by *The Washington Post*, John Paul II read the Third Secret *in 1978, within days of his election*.[308] There is no record, however, of any text of the Secret being brought to John Paul from the Holy Office archives in that year.

Thus, whatever text John Paul read in 1978 must have been located elsewhere—evidently in the papal apartment, as attested by the witnesses and photographs already cited. It is highly significant that *neither Navarro-Valls nor the Pope ever denied the report that the Pope had read the Secret in 1978*, even though (with explosive implications) that report flatly contradicted Bertone's representations to the press.[309] It could hardly have been the case that John Paul II, the very "Pope of Fatima", would have waited for three years after his election to read the Secret. This major discrepancy between the accounts of Bertone and Navarro-Valls in itself indicated the existence of two distinct but related texts comprising the entire Secret.[310]

Dispensing with the Consecration of Russia

Leaving no aspect of the Fatima Message unburied, Bertone's Introduction to *TMF* purported to enlist Sister Lucia for the proposition that Pope John Paul II's consecration of the world in 1984 had sufficed for a Consecration of Russia: "Sister Lucia personally confirmed that this solemn and universal act of consecration corresponded to what Our Lady wished.... Hence any further discussion or request [for the Consecration of

306 *TMF*, p. 15. The footnote reads: "In the 'Fourth Memoir' Sister Lucia adds: 'In Portugal, the dogma of the faith will always be preserved, etc....'"

307 *TMF*, p. 5.

308 Bill Broadway and Sarah Delancy, "3rd Secret Spurs More Questions; Fatima Interpretation Departs From Vision," *The Washington Post*, July 1, 2000: "On May 13, Vatican Spokesman Joaquin Navarro-Valls said the Pope first read the secret within days of assuming the papacy in 1978. On Monday, an aide to Cardinal Joseph Ratzinger [Bertone], Prefect of the Vatican's Congregation for the Doctrine of the Faith, said that the Pope first saw it in the hospital after his attack."

309 The Associated Press, "Vatican: Fatima Is No Doomsday Prophecy," *The New York Times*, June 26, 2000: "'John Paul II read for the first time the text of the Third Secret of Fatima after the attack,' a top aide to Ratzinger, Monsignor Tarcisio Bertone, told journalists during a news conference to present the document."

310 Cf. *The Devil's Final Battle*, Chapter 13, "The Third Secret Consists of Two Distinct Texts," for further explanation.

Russia] is without basis."[311] But how could Sister Lucia "confirm" that the same sort of ceremony that did not suffice during the reigns of Pius XII and Paul VI—a consecration of the world with no mention of Russia and no participation by the world episcopate—had suddenly become sufficient?[312]

Curiously, Bertone cited only one solitary piece of evidence in support of his claim: a purported letter from Sister Lucia, identified only as "Letter of 8 November 1989," in which she is alleged to have written: "'Yes it has been done just as Our Lady asked, on 25 March 1984" ("*Sim, està feita, tal como Nossa Senhora a pediu, desde o dia 25 de Março de 1984*").[313] Even more curious: the addressee of the letter is not identified and no copy of it was provided as supporting documentation, even though other documents are reproduced in *TMF*'s appendices.

The purported letter, generated by a computer at the dawn of the personal computer age, contained a blatant error: a statement by "Lucia" that Paul VI had consecrated the world to the Immaculate Heart during his visit to Fatima in 1967, when in fact he had consecrated nothing at all. Lucia, who was present throughout the Pope's visit, would hardly have made such a mistake. Nor was it credible that an elderly cloistered nun, who had written thousands of letters by hand over her lifetime, would suddenly switch to a word processor at age 80 to peck out a one-page note to a Mr. Noelker, especially when even many business offices in Portugal were without personal computers at that time.[314]

Still more curious: the dubious "letter of 8 November 1989" was the only evidence Bertone cited even though, as *TMF* states, Bertone had "conversed" with Sister Lucia on April 27, 2000, only two months earlier, and could have obtained her direct testimony on this question at that time—or indeed at any other time. The failure to cite any direct testimony by Lucia, when such testimony was readily obtainable, spoke volumes. And note well: During the April 2000 "conversation" Bertone *did not ask Sister Lucia to authenticate the "Letter of 8 November 1989"* even though Bertone had to have known of the worldwide circulation of articles by Father Gruner's apostolate decisively debunking the letter.[315] The only reasonable inference was that Lucia had not been asked to authenticate the letter because it was indeed a fake that could not be authenticated.

To knowledgeable Catholics, it was not surprising that Bertone had been forced to rely *entirely* on a non-authenticated and previously publicly debunked 11-year-old "letter" to an unidentified addressee. That purported letter was the only thing Bertone could pit against a lifetime of contrary testimony by Sister Lucia, which had been surveyed exhaustively in the Fatima Center's publications.[316] Here it should be noted that when

311 *TMF*, p. 8.

312 Concerning the consecration of the world by Pius XII and several bishops on October 31, 1942, Sister Lucia wrote: "The Good Lord has already shown me His contentment with the act performed by the Holy Father and several bishops, *although it was incomplete according to His desire*. In return He promises to end the war soon. The conversion of Russia is not for now." Letter to the Bishop of Gurza, February 28, 1943; quoted in *The Whole Truth About Fatima*, Vol. III, pp. 60-61.

313 *TMF*, p. 8.

314 Flatly contradicting himself, Bertone would admit seven years later that Sister Lucia "never worked with the computer." *See The Last Visionary of Fatima*, p. 101. ("Sister Lucia never worked with the computer, nor visited any website.") This is one of the many self-contradictions in which the Cardinal has embroiled himself, as Socci has noted.

315 This letter, which was addressed to a Walter Noelker, was published and critiqued on pp. 10-11 of the May 1990 (No. 229) issue of *The Catholic Counter-Reformation* (*CRC*, English edition, published by Maison Saint-Joseph, F-10260 Saint-Parres-lès-Vaudes). This critique was explicitly referenced in *The Fatima Crusader*, No. 35 (Winter 1990-91), with a circulation of some 500,000 copies, in a story debunking the Noelker letter (on pp. 12ff, or at www.fatimacrusader.com/cr35/cr35pg12.asp).

316 For a detailed presentation of Lucia's testimony from 1946-1987—and even after 1987 her testimony by her silence, when she met John Paul II in 1991, speaks volumes—see *The Devil's Final Battle*, Chapter 8 (also at http://www.devilsfinalbattle.com/book/BookChaptPDF/dfb_chapter8.pdf). It is also worth noting that if Sr. Lucia had really changed her mind, the perfect time to announce her agreement that Russia had been consecrated in 1984 would have been immediately after her private meeting with John Paul II in 1991 at Fatima. But, after this audience, neither Sr. Lucia nor the Pope had a word to

John Paul II journeyed to Fatima in 1991, Lucia was ordered to attend an audience with him (although she was disinclined to do so). At no time during or after the encounter between the Pope and the visionary did either of them suggest that Russia had been consecrated seven years earlier.

Also noteworthy was the conspicuous absence of Lucia at the June 26, 2000 press conference. Was it feared that she would make some devastating revelation or refuse, if queried by the press, to confirm the "official account"? Such fears concerning the survivability of the Secretary of State's version of the Third Secret would be confirmed as the "official account" almost immediately began to unravel.

Huge 26 foot by 13 foot poster in the busiest mall in Rome—positioned at the elevator bank so more than 2 million people saw it in April and May 2011. The poster says: "Only the Pope can save Rome! By means of a special prayer of only 5 minutes."

say about the adequacy of the 1984 ceremony, although Sr. Lucia had previously declared publicly that it was *not* adequate.

Chapter 25

The Cover-Up Exposed

By the year 2001 the "worried signals" from the Vatican Secretary of State that had inaugurated the long persecution of Father Gruner by elements of the Vatican apparatus seemed to have lost much of their power to interfere with Father Gruner's legitimate canonical status and the Fatima Center's activities. The Vatican's response to Archbishop Arulappa's resounding affirmation in 1999 of his incardination of Father Gruner in the Archdiocese of Hyderabad in 1995 was met with an equally resounding silence.

To be sure, the Secretary of State made further efforts to continue the persecution. Chief among these was its intervention against a Fatima conference held in Rome by the Fatima Center from October 7-13, 2001, a month after the infamous terrorist attack in New York City on September 11. Although invitations to the conference extended to bishops had been signed by two bishops, a monsignor and four priests—not Father Gruner—the Secretary of State attempted to scuttle the event by publishing in *L'Osservatore Romano* on September 12, 2001—the day after the terrorist attack—an unprecedented unsigned "announcement" concerning Father Gruner and the conference:

> The Holy See has received several news reports concerning the so-called Conference for Peace in the World, which is being planned for Rome for October 7 to 13 and which has been organized by Fr. Nicholas Gruner of Canada. The Congregation for the Clergy, upon the mandate from a higher authority, wishes to state that Rev. Nicholas Gruner is under an "a divinis" suspension, which has been confirmed by a definitive sentence of the Supreme Tribunal of the Apostolic Signatura. The activities of Fr. Gruner, therefore, including the above-mentioned conference, do not have the approval of legitimate ecclesiastical authorities.

The canonically meaningless "announcement" was easily disposed of, however. For one thing, it failed to state any grounds for the alleged "a divinis" suspension—because there were none. It is crucial to note that *no one in the Vatican had purported to suspend Father Gruner*, and that the "suspension" was not attributed to anyone else. Who, then, had supposedly imposed it? While the Bishop of Avellino, under pressure from the Secretary of State, had indeed threatened Father Gruner with suspension "failing to be incardinated" elsewhere—after the Secretary of State himself had attempted to block incardination—*no decree of suspension had ever been promulgated*. At any rate, the issue had become moot in view of the incardination in Hyderabad.

Further, the "announcement" referred to a "higher authority" as its anonymous source, which is Vatican-speak for the Secretary of State. But the Secretary of State had no authority to suspend a priest, and his attempt to block the incardination in Hyderabad had failed. The alleged "suspension a divinis" rested, therefore, on thin air. It was a canonical sham designed to discredit Father Gruner and his work.

Finally, contrary to what the "announcement" falsely implied, neither the Fatima conference in Rome, nor any of the other activities of the Fatima Center's apostolate, required "the approval of legitimate ecclesiastical authorities" which the "announcement" falsely implied were necessary. Here, too, the "announcement" was a canonical sham. As the Code of Canon Law provides, members of the faithful, including priests, do not need approval by "ecclesiastical authority" to hold conferences or form private associations for the purpose of communicating with each other and with the sacred pastors on matters of concern in the Church.[317]

A changing landscape

The Catholic author Mark Fellows has aptly likened the Message of Fatima in general, and the Third Secret in particular, to a cork that keeps bobbing to the surface of the ocean despite every effort to sink it. No press conference at the Vatican could make Fatima go away. Quite simply, the faithful were not persuaded that Fatima was finished. Less than a year after the June 26, 2000 press conference, the worldwide incredulity of the faithful was given voice by Mother Angelica, foundress of the Eternal Word Television Network, who declared to a television audience of millions:

> As for the Secret, well *I happen to be one of those individuals who thinks we didn't get the whole thing*. I told ya! I mean, you have the right to your own opinion, don't you, Father? There, you know, that's my opinion. *Because I think it's scary ...*[318]

On October 26, 2001, a few weeks after 9/11 and the apostolate's 2001 Fatima Conference in Rome, the story on the Third Secret "broke wide open", as reporters say, when *Inside the Vatican* news service (along with various Italian newspapers) ran an article entitled: "The Secret of Fatima: More to Come?" The article reported: "News has just emerged that Sister Lucia dos Santos, the last surviving Fatima visionary, several weeks ago sent Pope John Paul II a letter reportedly warning him that his life is in danger. *According to Vatican sources*, the letter, claiming that events spoken of in the 'Third Secret' of Fatima had not yet occurred, was delivered sometime after September 11 to John Paul by the bishop emeritus [retired] of Fatima, Alberto Cosme do Amaral."

This was a controversy that would not go away, despite the best efforts of the Secretary of State to consign the Third Secret to oblivion. And Father Gruner's work would be instrumental in keeping the controversy alive. Over the next twelve years his apostolate's astonishing output of books, magazines, news articles, videos, TV shows, website content and regularly staged Fatima conferences (including Portugal in 2006, Brazil in 2007, India in 2008 and Rome in 2010, 2011 and 2012) would disseminate throughout the world a wealth of material on the true nature and content of the Fatima Message, the failure to consecrate Russia in the manner the Virgin had requested, and the probable contents of that part of the Third Secret yet to be revealed: the Virgin's own words explaining the meaning of a vision "not easy to decipher," as Cardinal Ratzinger had admitted in *TMF*.

On February 13, 2005, Sister Lucia passed on to her eternal reward at the age of 97, to be followed by Pope John Paul II on April 2. By the closing months of 2006 Archbishop Bertone had become Cardinal Bertone, successor to Cardinal Sodano as Vatican Secretary of State under Pope Benedict XVI. In a manner befitting the ecclesiastical politician he always was, Sodano "hunkered down in the apartment and offices he occupied as former Secretary of State and [defied] the Pope to remove him," threatening "that any attempt to remove him will be met by Sodano's revelation of 'where the bodies are hidden' from

---

317 Cfr. The Code of Canon Law [*Codex iuris canonici*], C.I.C 1983, Canons 212 §§ 2, 3; 215, 216, 299, 300.

318 "Mother Angelica Live," May 16, 2001.

the last ten years of John Paul II's pontificate—meaning the many things that went terribly wrong on account of the Pope's declining capacity during that period."[319]

As Bertone assumed his new office—forced to reside temporarily in Saint John's Tower on account of Sodano's refusal to relocate—the controversy over the Third Secret had not only failed to abate, it had reached a level of intensity it was now impossible for the Vatican to ignore. In November 2006 the appearance of a new book from a surprising source would shift to the Vatican a heavy new burden of proof concerning its "official" position that the Third Secret had been revealed in full.

A Remarkable Change of Mind

When he set out to write a book on the Third Secret affair, the Italian "public intellectual," Antonio Socci, was at first determined to demolish the claim of the so-called "Fatimists" that the Vatican was holding something back. As he stated in the introduction to his ironically and provocatively entitled *The Fourth Secret of Fatima,*[320] Socci had viewed the claim as a mere "dietrology," an Italian idiom for conspiracy theories that look behind (*dietro*) events for hidden plots. He was convinced that the vision of the bishop in white was all there was to the Third Secret, and that the "official account" presented in *TMF* had laid all questions to rest.

As Socci first believed, "Fatimist" literature on the Third Secret—much of which was produced and disseminated by Father Gruner's apostolate—was merely the result of "the burning disappointment of a Third Secret that controverted all of their apocalyptic predictions." The "Fatimists" had to be refuted, he thought, because the "polemical arms" in their arsenal were "at the disposal of whoever wanted to launch a heavy attack against the Vatican."[321] But then Socci encountered unexpected strength in the "Fatimist" case presented by Father Gruner, which he had never studied closely. At the same time, his own suspicions were aroused when Cardinal Bertone declined to grant him an interview, despite their friendly relations and Socci's intention to defend Bertone's position. That refusal opened Socci's eyes to the possibility "that there are embarrassing questions and that there is above all something (of gravity) to hide."[322]

As Socci explained: "In the end, I had to surrender. ... Here I recount my voyage into the greatest mystery of the 20th century and set forth the result I honestly reached. A result that sincerely contradicts my initial convictions ..."[323] In agreement with vast numbers of skeptical Catholics, Socci concluded that something must be missing: "[T]hat there is a part of the Secret not revealed and considered unspeakable *is certain*. And today—having decided to deny its existence—the Vatican runs the risk of exposing itself to very heavy pressure and blackmail."[324]

What completely changed Socci's mind and made him "surrender" was simply this: overwhelming evidence, the greater part of which had been marshaled and presented by Father Gruner and the investigators and writers associated with the Fatima Center. *The Fourth Secret of Fatima* (hereafter, *Fourth Secret*) made numerous references to the definitive Fatima scholarship of Frère Michel de la Sainte Trinité and Father Joaquin

319 Christopher A. Ferrara, "World Waits for Indult to Come and Sodano to Go," *The Remnant*, March 5, 2007, http://www.remnantnewspaper.com/Archives/archive-2007-0215-news_from_rome.htm.

320 Antonio Socci, *The Fourth Secret of Fatima* (Fitzwilliam, New Hampshire: Loreto Publications, 2009), English-language edition.

321 *The Fourth Secret of Fatima*, pp. 12, 13.

322 Ibid., p. 14.

323 Ibid., p. 14.

324 Antonio Socci, *Il Quarto Segreto di Fatima* (Milano: Rai and Eri Rizzoli, 2007), p. 173.

Alonso, the one-time official Fatima archivist, as well as *The Devil's Final Battle* by Father Paul Kramer, an edited compilation of Fatima material, and also to the 2000 edition in Italian of this very book, *Fatima Priest*. These publications were mainstays of the Fatima Center catalogue that had been disseminated throughout the world in multiple languages, including Italian. It is fair to say that Socci's book is permeated with information and insights gleaned from the Fatima Center's publications.[325]

Indeed, since the fateful Vatican press conference of 2000, the Center had been operating full blast despite the increasingly ineffectual efforts of the Secretary of State to interfere with its work. The Center's activities included international Fatima conferences attended by bishops and even cardinals as well as the laity. Each of these massive undertakings met with increasingly ineffective interference by the Secretary of State, as the following conference statistics would suggest:

- **2006 – "Last Chance for World Peace"** (October 6 – 13, 2006)
  Locations: Tuy, Pontevedra and Rianjo, Spain; and Fatima, Portugal
  Clerical attendees: 30 bishops, 74 priests and Cardinal Agre.
- **2007 – "Fatima: Only Way to World Peace"** (August 20 – 24, 2007)
  Location: Botucatu, Brazil
  Clerical attendees: 4 bishops, 160 priests.
- **2008 – "The Only Way to World Peace"** (January 30 – February 5, 2008)
  Location: Chennai, India
  Clerical attendees: 4 bishops, 318 priests.
- **2010 – "The Fatima Challenge"** (May 3 – 7, 2010)
  Location: Rome, Italy
  Clerical attendees: 9 bishops, 41 priests.
- **2011 – "Consecration Now!"** (May 9 – 13, 2011)
  Location: Rome, Italy
  Clerical attendees: 10 bishops, 41 priests and Cardinal Martino.
- **2012 – "Fatima: Your Last Chance"** (May 14 – 18, 2012)
  Location: Rome, Italy
  Clerical attendees: 3 Archbishops, 14 bishops, 61 priests, Cardinal Martino and Archbishop Capucci from Palestine.

In addition to these major initiatives were two full-fledged documentary films, *Heaven's Key to Peace* (2004) and *The Secret Still Silenced* (2008), and a continuous public relations campaign under the title "Target Rome" (October 2008, 2010, 2011, 2012). And, for the written record, the apostolate published worldwide a series of landmark books on the Fatima controversy, including this one: *The Devil's Final Battle* (2002 and 2010, 2nd edition), *Fatima in Twilight* (2003), *Sister Lucia: Apostle of Mary's Immaculate Heart* (2007), *The Secret Still Hidden* (2008), and *False Friends of Fatima* (2012).

Under Benedict XVI, who as Cardinal Ratzinger had described Father Gruner as "a serious man" (*un uomo serio*) during the 2000 press conference,[326] there appeared to have been a kind of tacit surrender within the Vatican bureaucracy to the reality that the Fatima Center had the right to exist and to propagate its message. It had become clear

---

325 See, e.g. *Fourth Secret*, pp. 19, 21, 23, 30, 46, 51, 65, 66, 68, 72, 75, 86, 89, 94, 101, 106, 111, 112, 113, 114, 116, 135, 138, 139, 140, 141, 143, 145, 146, 147, 149, 152, 154, 156, 159, 176, 178, 180, 181, 184, 185, 189, 190, 191, 193, 196, 198, 203, 205 (reference to *Fatima Priest*), 210.

326 Archival tape-recording and videotaping of remarks during Q&A session of the press conference of June 26, 2000.

that Father Gruner's work could not simply be snuffed out by meaningless bureaucratic dictates concerning completely unnecessary "canonical approval," or by false and irrelevant depictions of Father Gruner's canonical status.

The evidence the Center had made available to the world convinced Socci that the "dietrologies" of the "Fatimists"—i.e., loyal Catholics who have reasonable doubts about the official account—were actually correct: there must be a separate but related text of the Secret, not yet revealed, containing "the words of the Madonna [which] preannounce an apocalyptic crisis of the faith in the Church starting from the top." This second text is probably "also an explanation of the vision (revealed on June 26, 2000) where there appear the Pope, the bishops and martyred faithful, after having traversed a city in ruins."[327] That explanation, wrote Socci, would involve "the preannounced assassination of a Pope [the white-clad bishop in the vision] in the context of an immense martyrdom of Christians and of a devastation of the world."[328] Only such an explanation would make sense of the "difficult to decipher" vision.

A Devastating Eyewitness

In addition to the body of evidence the Fatima Center had marshaled, Socci gave wide publicity to the newly adduced testimony of Archbishop Loris F. Capovilla, the still-living personal secretary of John XXIII. As Socci recounted, in July of 2006 Capovilla was interviewed by an Italian Fatima researcher, Solideo Paolini, concerning the existence of the posited second text of the Third Secret. During that interview Paolini asked the Archbishop whether there was an unpublished text of the Secret, and the Archbishop replied evasively: "I know nothing. [*Nulla so*!]" Note well: he did not answer simply "No!" That answer puzzled Paolini, who expected that the Archbishop, "among the few who know the Secret, would have been able to respond to me that this is a completely impracticable idea and that everything had already been revealed in 2000. Instead he answered: 'I know nothing.' An expression that I surmised he wished ironically to evoke a certain *omertá* [code of silence]."[329]

Paolini's impression was confirmed by subsequent events. After his meeting with Capovilla, Paolini received from Capovilla by mail a package of papers from his files, along with a perplexing cover letter advising him to obtain a copy of *TMF*, which Capovilla must have known that Paolini, a student of Fatima, would already possess. Was this not, thought Paolini, "an invitation to read something in particular in that publication in relation to the documents sent by the same Archbishop?" That intuition was correct. Among the documents Capovilla had sent was a stamped "confidential note" by him, dated May 17, 1967, in which he had recorded the circumstances of a reading of the Third Secret by Pope Paul VI on June 27, 1963, only six days after his election to the papacy and before he had even been seated officially at the coronation Mass (which took place on June 29). But according to the Vatican's widely disbelieved "official account" in *TMF* and elsewhere, Paul VI did not read the Secret until nearly two years later: "Paul VI read the contents with the Substitute, Archbishop Angelo Dell'Acqua, on March 27, 1965, and returned the envelope to the Archives of the Holy Office, deciding not to publish the text."[330]

327 *Fourth Secret*, p. 82.

328 Ibid, pp. 63-64.

329 Ibid., p. 140.

330 *Il Quarto Segreto di Fatima*, p. 141; and citing *TMF*, p. 15 (English print edition).

The glaring discrepancy between the date recorded by Capovilla and that set forth in *TMF* prompted Paolini to telephone Capovilla, at precisely 7:45 p.m. on the same day he received the documents, to ask the Archbishop to explain the discrepancy. Capovilla protested: "Ah, but I spoke the truth. Look I am still lucid!" When Paolini politely insisted that, still, there was an unexplained discrepancy, Capovilla offered explanations that suggested "eventual lapse of memory, interpretations of what he had intended to say," whereupon Paolini reminded him that he had recorded the date of the reading by Paul VI in a stamped, official document. Capovilla then gave this reply: "But I am right, because perhaps *the Bertone envelope is not the same as the Capovilla envelope*."

Stunned, Paolini then asked the decisive question: "Therefore, both dates are true, because there are two texts of the Third Secret?"[331] After a brief pause, the Archbishop gave the explosive answer that confirmed the existence of a missing envelope and text of the Third Secret of Fatima: "Exactly so! [*Per l'appunto*!]"[332]

The "confidential note" completely corroborated Capovilla's testimony.[333] According to the note, on the date Pope Paul read the Secret (June 27, 1963), Monsignor Angelo Dell'Acqua—the same "Substitute" referred to in *TMF*—telephoned Capovilla to ask: "I am looking for the Fatima envelope. Do you know where it is kept?"[334] The note records that Capovilla replied: "It is in the right hand drawer of the writing desk called Barbarigo, *in the bedroom*." That is, the envelope was in the former bedroom of John XXIII, which was now the bedroom of Paul VI; it was *not* in the Holy Office archives, where the text of the vision was lodged.

The existence of two different texts comprising the entirety of the Third Secret of Fatima—the text of the vision and the text in the papal writing desk—now stood confirmed beyond any conceivable doubt. And Socci had announced that fact to the entire Catholic world in a book that could not simply be dismissed as the feverish ranting of "Fatimists."

The Secretary of State Defaults to the "Fatimists"

The publication of Socci's stunning conclusions—a development directly attributable to the persistent work of Father Gruner's apostolate—forced the Secretary of State to engage in rather frantic efforts at damage control. Those efforts began in May 2007, when Rizzoli—the same publisher that had published Socci's *Fourth Secret*—rushed into print a book by Cardinal Bertone entitled *L'Ultima Veggente di Fatima* ["The Last Visionary of Fatima"] (*Last Visionary*).[335]

Last Visionary, appearing in bookstores less than six months after *Fourth Secret*, was essentially a 100-page interview of the Cardinal concerning various Fatima-related subjects, followed by another 50 pages of appendices. This mass of verbiage surrounded a mere nine pages of comment comprising a purported response to the claims of Socci, who was never mentioned by name, and the "Fatimists," including Father Gruner, whose name was specifically mentioned in the text. The interviewer was a layman,

331 It would appear that Paolini became acquainted with the thesis of two companion texts comprising the entire Third Secret in the work *The Devil's Final Battle*, a publication of the Fatima Center.

332 *Il Quarto Segreto di Fatima*, p. 142.

333 The Italian original and English translation of the stamped "confidential note," dated May 17, 1967, are reproduced in Appendix I of *The Secret Still Hidden*.

334 Notice Dell'Acqua evidently presumed that the envelope was somewhere in the papal apartment, not in the Holy Office archives, of which Capovilla was not the custodian. Otherwise, Dell'Acqua would have asked the custodian of the archives, Cardinal Ottaviani, where the "Fatima envelope" was, rather than Capovilla, Pope John's former personal secretary.

335 Bertone, Cardinal Tarcisio, *The Last Visionary of Fatima* (Milano: Rai and Eri Rizzoli, 2007). All English translations from this point on are Christopher A. Ferrara's.

Giuseppe De Carli, a Vaticanist (reporter on the Vatican beat) and ardent admirer of the Cardinal, whose fawning questions not only posed no real challenge to Bertone's now-discredited "official version" of the Third Secret, but actually attempted to assist him in promoting what Socci had derisively described as "the official reconstruction." But *Last Visionary*, which never mentioned Socci or his book by name, utterly failed to address the substance of Socci's case. The eyewitness testimony of Archbishop Capovilla was simply ignored—a telling omission in a book that was supposed to have been an answer to Socci's explosive revelations.

On May 12, 2007, Socci published in his widely read Internet column this astonishing challenge to Bertone: "Dear Cardinal Bertone: Who—between you and me—is deliberately lying?"[336] Socci was responding to the Cardinal's veiled suggestion in *Last Visionary* (without mention of Socci's name) that Socci had misled the Catholic faithful in *Fourth Secret*. The significance of this public challenge to the credibility of the Vatican Secretary of State by one of Italy's most prominent laymen could not be overestimated; nor could Bertone afford to ignore it.

A Mountain of Evidence

By the time Socci's book was published, Cardinal Bertone, the new custodian of the Party Line, was facing a public relations crisis provoked by the same growing mountain of evidence that had changed Socci's mind and caused him to publish his breakthrough book affirming the existence of a hidden text of the Secret. We note here some of the key points developed by the sources Socci had studied, which had been cited by the Fatima Center and in Socci's independent work on the subject:

- Sister Lucia revealed that a text of the Secret is in the form of a letter to the Bishop of Fatima, but the text describing the vision is not a letter.
- Our Lady clearly had more to say following the momentous "etc," which clearly begins another, and thus the third, part of the Great Secret, but the text of the vision published by the Vatican as the entire text of the Third Secret contains not a word from Her.
- Our Lady explains everything in the vision contained in the first part of the Great Secret, but we are asked to believe that there is absolutely no explanation from Her concerning the vision in the third part—i.e., the Third Secret.
- Father Schweigl revealed that the Third Secret has two parts: one concerning the Pope, and the other "a logical continuation, of the words 'In Portugal the dogma of the faith will always be preserved etc'," but the text of the vision does not contain that logical continuation of the Virgin's words.
- The Vatican-initiated press release from 1960, announcing suppression of the Secret, describes the suppressed text as "*the letter*" that "will never be opened," containing "*the words* which Our Lady confided as a secret to the three little shepherds…", but the text of the vision is not a letter and contains no words spoken by Our Lady, confided by Her as a secret.
- Cardinal Ottaviani, who read and had custody of the Secret, revealed that it involved a "sheet of paper" bearing 25 lines of text recording "what Our

336 Article of May 12, 2007 in archive at http://www.antoniosocci.com; see English translation at http://www.fatima.org/news/newsviews/052907socci.asp.

Lady *told her* [Lucia] to tell the Holy Father…", but the vision spans 62 lines, and in it the Virgin does not tell Sister Lucia anything at all.

- A text of the Secret was kept in the papal apartment during the pontificates of Pius XII, John XXIII and Paul VI, and at least at the beginning of the pontificate of John Paul II, even though Bertone's "official account" speaks only of a text in the Holy Office archives.
- John XXIII read a text of the Secret that was so difficult it required a native Portuguese speaker to provide an accurate translation into Italian, yet he also read another text pertaining to the Secret, in the following year, that he could comprehend perfectly without the aid of a translator.
- The text of the vision *contains no particularly difficult Portuguese expressions*.
- There are two different Italian translations of the Secret: the one prepared for John XXIII, and the one prepared in 1967, neither of which we have been allowed to see.
- Three different Popes (John XXIII, Paul VI, John Paul II) read texts of the Secret on two different dates—years apart—during their respective pontificates, but all three of these second readings are mysteriously omitted from the "official account."
- Those who have read the Secret have revealed that it speaks of a coming state of apostasy in the Church as well as a planetary crisis, but the vision standing alone says nothing of apostasy in the Church or of a planetary crisis.
- Cardinal Ratzinger revealed that the Third Secret refers to "dangers threatening the faith and the life of the Christian, and therefore of the world," and further revealed a correspondence between the Message of Fatima and the Message of Akita, in which Our Lady*, in Her own words*, warns of a coming crisis in the Church accompanied by a fiery chastisement of the world. The text of the vision standing alone, however, contains no such warning from Our Lady.
- When pressed to explain in 2000 what text of the Secret John Paul II reportedly read in 1978, given that Bertone claimed John Paul did not read the Secret until 1981, Bertone was evasive and finally said merely that "in my opinion" John Paul did not read a text in 1978, when it would have been a simple matter to ascertain this from innumerable sources at his disposal, including the Pope himself—an omission clearly suggesting that Bertone knew the report was true.
- Archbishop Capovilla, personal secretary to John XXIII, confirmed to Solideo Paolini the existence of two texts and two envelopes relating to the Third Secret, one envelope and text of which, bearing his (Capovilla's) handwriting on the outer envelope and kept in the papal apartment, had never been produced. The exterior of this "Capovilla envelope" contains his name and the names of others who had read its contents at the instruction of Pope John XXIII, as well as the Pope's dictation: "I give no judgment."

- Capovilla had never retracted his testimony to Paolini, even though he had had every opportunity to do so.
- Bertone, in the process of producing *Last Visionary*, had evidently not even asked Capovilla to retract what he had revealed to Paolini, or had sought a retraction but was refused.
- Bertone had failed and refused to produce the reopened and resealed Capovilla envelope.
- The Vatican had issued no official denial of the allegations in Socci's book, even though Socci had literally accused Bertone of covering up the very words of the Mother of God.
- On the contrary, Pope Benedict XVI had sent Socci a note "concerning my book, thanking me for 'the sentiments which have suggested it,'" without the slightest indication that the book is in error.[337]

A Televised Disaster

With his "official version" still in ruins even after publication of *Last Visionary*, which had effectively conceded Socci's entire case for a cover-up by ignoring it, Bertone was reduced to the unprecedented step of appearing on the Italian talk show *Porta a Porta* ["Door to Door"] on May 31, 2007. The show was entitled "The Fourth Secret of Fatima Does Not Exist"—a clear reference to the title of Socci's book. Socci, most tellingly, was not invited to defend himself. Yet, although the field had been left open for Bertone to kick a goal into an undefended net, he fumbled the setup completely, not only failing to refute Socci but providing further devastating admissions and revelations, as Father Gruner's apostolate noted in its publications.[338]

This was the risk Bertone had no choice but to take, however, for had he remained silent in the face of Socci's book, he would have conceded the existence of a cover-up and his own complicity in it. On the other hand, if he made this unprecedented appearance on television, there was the potential for further slip-ups and inadvertent revelations. And that is exactly what ensued. The details of this televised disaster for Bertone's account are set forth elsewhere.[339] Here, a summary of key points will have to suffice:

- During the telecast Bertone, under mounting public pressure, finally revealed on camera that there are actually *two* identical sealed envelopes of Lucia's, bearing the "express order of Our Lady" that the contents were not to be revealed until 1960. Yet Bertone had been representing for the past seven years that there was only one envelope, and moreover had propagated the blatant falsehood that Lucia "confessed" she had never received any order from the Virgin linking the Secret to 1960 and forbidding its disclosure until then.
- Thus Bertone had been caught in two demonstrable falsehoods: that there was only one sealed envelope of Lucia's pertaining to the Third Secret, and that the Blessed Virgin had never connected the Secret to the

337 An exhaustive discussion of these and other points of evidence is to be found in Christopher Ferrara's *The Secret Still Hidden* (Pound Ridge, New York: Good Counsel Publications, 2008). Cf. Chapters 3-10 (also at http://www.secretstillhidden.com/book.html).

338 See, e.g. *The Secret Still Hidden*, Chapter 8, for a detailed analysis of Cardinal Bertone's disastrous appearance (also at http://www.secretstillhidden.com/pdf/ensshch8.pdf).

339 Ibid.

year 1960. Even more devastating, both falsehoods had been exposed *by the very evidence Bertone himself displayed on camera*, although he acted as if he did not appreciate the significance of his own revelation.

- Bertone further revealed a *third* envelope of Lucia's, unsealed and addressed to Bishop da Silva, which, together with the bishop's outer envelope, would make a total of *four* envelopes the faithful were supposed to believe had all been created for only one text of the Secret. Clearly, however, the proper configuration of the four envelopes was an inner sealed envelope and an outer unsealed envelope for each of two texts: the text of the vision published in 2000 and the text of the Virgin's explanation of the vision's meaning, which has yet to be revealed.
- The "official account" was further undermined by a historical fact that took on great significance after the revelations on *Porta a Porta*: When he held up Bishop da Silva's outer envelope to a bright light, auxiliary Bishop Venâncio saw only *one* envelope inside, and took exact measurements of both the envelope and the single sheet of paper within it, which contained 20-25 lines of text, just as Cardinal Ottaviani testified.
- The measurements of the envelope and the sheet of paper taken by Bishop Venâncio are entirely different from the measurements of the envelope and the sheet of paper revealed by Bertone on *Porta a Porta*.
- Only weeks before his appearance on *Porta a Porta*, Bertone himself had revealed in *Last Visionary* that in April 2000 Sister Lucia "authenticated" *sheets* of paper pertaining to the Secret. But during the *Porta a Porta* telecast Bertone revealed only *one* sheet, folded to make four sides, which contained the text of the vision.
- In *Last Visionary* Bertone had also revealed that there was an outer envelope, not Lucia's, bearing the note "Third Part of the Secret," but this envelope was not produced during the appearance on *Porta a Porta* nor has it been seen since then.
- During the telecast Bertone admitted that Cardinal Ottaviani had indeed testified "categorically" ("*categoricamente*") to the existence of a text of the Secret spanning only one page and 25 lines, whereas the text of the vision displayed on camera spanned four pages—four sides of a folded-over sheet of paper—and 62 lines. After a commercial break, Bertone offered the lame explanation that Ottaviani had somehow miscounted the 62 lines of the vision to arrive at 25 lines.
- Confronted with mounting evidence of a cover-up, Bertone adopted on *Porta a Porta* the new line of referring repeatedly to an "authentic" text of the Secret, an "authentic" envelope, and the "only folio that exists in the Holy Office archives," when he knew full well that there was a text and envelope in the papal apartment, thus suggesting, as Socci would note,[340] that he deems a second text of the Secret "inauthentic" and that, under a mental reservation, he feels free to conceal the existence of this "inauthentic" text.

---

340 *See* "Bertone nel 'vespaio' delle polemiche" ["Bertone in the 'Wasp's Nest' of the Polemics"], June 2, 2007, http://www.antoniosocci.com/2007/06/bertone-nel-%E2%80%9Cvespaio%E2%80%9D-delle-polemiche/. See also *The Fatima Crusader*, No. 86 (Summer 2007), pp. 43-48, at http://www.fatimacrusader.com/cr86/cr86pg43.asp

- Regarding this new notion of an "authentic" text, Bertone referred during the telecast to a document that "actually existed in the archives," insisting that "there was only this *foglio* (sheet of paper) in the archives of the Holy Office in 1957, when by order of Our Lady and the Bishop of Leiria, Sister Lucia accepted that the Secret be brought to Rome from the archives of the Patriarch of Lisbon…." Yet the document in question *was never in the archives of the Patriarch of Lisbon.* It is an undeniable historical fact that in 1957 copies of all Lucia's writings and the envelope containing the Secret were personally delivered by auxiliary Bishop Venâncio directly from the chancery in Leiria to the Papal Nuncio in Lisbon, Msgr. Cento, who took the documents directly to Rome.[341]

Socci posted on his website a reply to the telecast from which he had so suspiciously been excluded—a reply widely publicized by the Fatima Center. He observed that despite the absence of any real challenge to Bertone's version of the facts by the host or guests who participated in the telecast, the Cardinal had only succeeded in demonstrating that the doubt Pope John professed to have concerning the supernatural origin of the Third Secret at the time he decided to bury it

> could not refer to the text of the vision revealed in 2000, that does not contain anything "delicate." But only to that "fourth secret" that—as Cardinals Ottaviani and Ciappi revealed—spoke of apostasy and the betrayal by the upper ecclesiastical hierarchy. That "fourth secret" of which John Paul II, in 1982, said that it "had not been published because it could be badly interpreted." That "fourth secret" of which Cardinal Ratzinger, in 1996, said that at the moment certain "details" could be harmful to the faith…[342]

That "fourth secret," moreover, which concerns "dangers to the faith and the life of the Christian, and therefore the world," as Cardinal Ratzinger had revealed in 1984 was not mentioned in the June 26, 2000 revelation. Bertone's every effort to answer Socci had only dug a deeper pit for him and the other defenders of the Party Line. As Socci had said in defense of himself, Bertone had "offered the proof that I am right," that there is indeed a missing text of the Secret. This disaster prompted yet another unprecedented initiative by the Secretary of State.

The Cardinal Bertone Show

On September 21, 2007, with the "official account" irretrievably wrecked, Cardinal Bertone staged his own personal television show in an auditorium at the Pontifical Urbaniana University in Rome near the Vatican. The pretext was the "introduction" of *Last Visionary*, which had already been published and introduced at a press conference months before. Like the appearance on *Porta a Porta*, this spectacle only confirmed the existence of the very thing Bertone was attempting to conceal. Here, too, a summary of the key elements of this debacle will have to suffice:[343]

- During the telecast Bertone continued his mysterious failure to address a single question that would penetrate to the heart of any of the matters he knew to be in controversy. In particular, he avoided like the plague any

341 Cf. *The Whole Truth About Fatima*, Vol. III, pp. 480-481.

342 Antonio Socci, "Bertone nel 'vespaio' delle polemiche" ["Bertone in the 'Wasp's Nest' of the Polemics"], loc. cit.

343 For a more complete explanation, see Ferrara, *The Secret Still Hidden*, Ch. 10, pp. 167-197 (also at http://www.secretstillhidden.com/pdf/ensshch10.pdf).

questions about the "etc," the text in the papal apartment, the testimony of Solideo Paolini concerning the admissions by Archbishop Capovilla, the never-produced Capovilla envelope, and the mysterious sudden appearance of multiple envelopes never mentioned before.

- Called as a witness by Bertone, Bishop Seraphim of Fatima, who purportedly witnessed Lucia's authentication of the text of the vision in April 2000, made the heavily nuanced declaration on camera that "the Secret of Fatima has been revealed in an *authentic* and integral way," declining to affirm simply that the Third Secret had been revealed entirely and that nothing had been withheld.
- Unable to avoid any longer the subject of Archbishop Capovilla's explosive testimony, Bertone broadcast a heavily edited video interview of Capovilla conducted, not by an official Vatican representative, but by Giuseppe De Carli, the malleable journalist who had collaborated with Bertone on *Last Visionary*. The interview *never once addressed Capovilla's admissions to Solideo Paolini*, and De Carli never asked Capovilla to retract them.
- Quite the contrary, during the interview *Capovilla fully confirmed the existence of the Capovilla envelope* and the reading of its contents by John XXIII and Paul VI on dates different from those provided in the "official account" for the reading of the text of the vision published in 2000.
- Despite this devastating revelation, De Carli—but, most tellingly, *not Capovilla himself*—declared on camera that the "Capovilla envelope" (which the Vatican has never produced) and the "Bertone envelope" containing the text of the vision, are one and the same envelope. But this was a manifest absurdity from which De Carli would retreat during his later appearance at the 2010 Fatima conference sponsored by Father Gruner's Fatima apostolate in Rome (to be discussed below).

While this new disaster was unfolding in the auditorium, Socci and Paolini, who had waited outside in the hope of confronting Cardinal Bertone with a key question about the Third Secret, relating to the famous "etc", were forcibly ejected from the premises by security guards. Before they were ejected, however, they were able to play for the other journalists present an audiotape of a subsequent meeting between Paolini and Archbishop Capovilla during which the Archbishop states:

> "Besides the four pages [of the vision of the bishop in white] there was also something else, an attachment, yes."

As the reporter from the prominent Italian newspaper *Il Giornale* concluded, Capovilla's statement "would confirm the thesis of the existence of a second sheet with the interpretation of the Secret. The mystery, and above all the polemics, will continue." Tellingly, Bertone has never denied the existence of this "attachment," even though *Il Giornale* had declared that it "would confirm the thesis of the existence of a second sheet with the interpretation of the Secret."[344]

The final speaker on "The Cardinal Bertone Show" was Bertone himself. This was the Cardinal's moment to answer the many concerns raised by Socci and Catholics the world over concerning his version of events. But, as he had done for the past seven

---

344 "The Fourth Secret of Fatima does not exist," *Il Giornale*, September 22, 2007.

years, Bertone continued to duck every issue. Even in the act of doing so, however, he made another serious misstep: "On the famous Third Secret, on the truth of the Third Secret, I will not return. Certainly, if there had been some further element, of commentary, of integration, it would have appeared in her [Lucia's] letters, in her thousands of letters—something that isn't there."

It seems that every time he opened his mouth to speak on the subject, the Cardinal could not help but raise further doubts about the veracity of his account. Why would he say that *if* there were a missing part of the Third Secret it would have appeared in Sister Lucia's correspondence with various people around the world, rather than in a text she wrote specifically at the direction of the Virgin? Why would Lucia reveal an element of the Third Secret in her letters to third parties when, as we know, the Secret was transmitted in two envelopes which state they "can only be opened in 1960 by the Cardinal Patriarch of Lisbon or the Bishop of Leiria"? Did the Cardinal mean to direct our attention away from the two envelopes, or the never-produced "Capovilla envelope" bearing the dictation of John XXIII? And on what basis did he assert that there was nothing pertaining to the Secret in Lucia's thousands of letters? Had he read and studied them all?

Wikipedia Notes Bertone's Cover-up

Cardinal Bertone's every effort to salvage the credibility of his account since becoming Secretary of State had had the opposite effect. And the role of Father Gruner's apostolate in bringing about that state of affairs was implicitly acknowledged even by Wikipedia as a commonplace of current events in the Church. The Wikipedia biography of Bertone contains a reference to one of the Fatima Center's major publications on the Third Secret affair: *The Secret Still Hidden* by Christopher Ferrara, published in multiple languages, which carries forward and further develops Socci's exposé:

> After Bertone's book [*Last Visionary*] was published, Italian journalist Antonio Socci published an article entitled, "Dear Cardinal Bertone: Who—between you and me—is Deliberately Lying?" Catholic attorney Christopher Ferrara wrote an entire book called *The Secret Still Hidden* (content available online) aimed at exposing and debunking the claims of Cardinal Bertone with respect to Fatima. The book contains an appendix entitled, *101 Grounds for Doubting Cardinal Bertone's Account*.[345]

345 "Tarcisio Bertone," http://en.wikipedia.org/wiki/Tarcisio_Bertone. The Fatima Center circulated 70,000 copies of this work in English, 35,000 in Italian, 20,000 in Spanish, 4,000 in Portuguese and 5,000 in French—not to mention the thousands more people who read it on-line (English: http://www.secretstillhidden.com; Italian: http://www.ilsegretoancoranascosto.it; Spanish: http://www.elsecretotodaviaocultado.es; Portuguese: http://www.secretstillhidden.com/pt).

Chapter 26

A Fateful Roman Encounter

Even after the Secretary of State's "official account" had crumbled during the period 2007-2010, the Fatima Center continued its massive worldwide campaign of conferences and publications promoting the authentic Consecration of Russia and full disclosure of the Third Secret. The efforts of the Secretary of State to interfere with the Center's international conferences met with little success compared with earlier heavy-handed interventions in 1994 and 2001. Following the conferences of 2006, 2007 and 2008 already noted, in 2010 the Fatima Center staged a conference in Rome itself that would be a landmark event in the saga of the Third Secret.

From May 3-7, 2010 the famous Ergife Hotel was the venue for "The Fatima Challenge," whose theme was a direct challenge to the Secretary of State's "official reconstruction" of the Third Secret. The conference would become what Americans call a "game-changer," although the matter involved was hardly a game.

A major reason for this outcome was the appearance of none other than Cardinal Bertone's lay collaborator, Giuseppe De Carli, as a speaker on the conference's second day. What De Carli said in the course of his remarks underscored dramatically the reasons for worldwide skepticism concerning Bertone's representations. Indeed, immediately after the conference the mainstream Italian media, following the lead of the Pope himself in another May development, would declare that the case of the Third Secret had been "reopened."

A Remarkable Appearance at a Remarkable Conference

To his everlasting credit, by appearing at the conference De Carli did something no one in the Vatican party had ever done before during all the years of the Third Secret controversy: engage face-to-face with the "Fatimists" and respond to some of their objections to the "official" version. De Carli had agreed to appear for the stated purpose of introducing a second edition of *Last Visionary* bearing the new title *The Last Secret of Fatima* [*L'Ultimo Segreto di Fatima*], a copy of which he held in his hand (the book had just come off the press that morning). By the time his appearance was over, however, it was something far more significant than the "introduction" of essentially the same book he and Bertone had already introduced twice.

After De Carli's prepared remarks and the showing of an inconsequential film on Sister Lucia and her life in the convent at Coimbra, something quite unexpected happened. De Carli remained at the podium to take questions from the audience, despite his earlier indications outside the conference hall that he would have no time for Q & A. For more than an hour, De Carli would field questions (in Italian) from Father Gruner, Christopher Ferrara, and the Catholic attorney and apologist John Salza, all of whom were also speakers at the conference. The encounter was most revealing, as the Italian media would immediately recognize.

De Carli's three questioners knew a face-to-face encounter with Bertone's close collaborator in promoting the "official" account was an opportunity that probably would never present itself again. Given the small window of opportunity, the questioning focused primarily on facts that were undeniable and which De Carli would have no choice but to admit. For one, there was the existence of the yet-to-be-seen Capovilla envelope and the text it contained, lodged in the papal apartment rather than the Holy Office archives, where the text of the vision was kept. Bertone's failure to produce that envelope and its contents were unanswerable evidence of a cover-up.

The Capovilla Envelope

Accordingly, Ferrara repeatedly pressed De Carli to explain why the Capovilla envelope had never been produced. In response, De Carli repeatedly suggested, contrary to all the evidence, that the Capovilla envelope and the "Bertone envelope" displayed on *Porta a Porta*—namely the Bishop of Fatima's outer envelope—were one and the same. The first question and answer were as follows:

> **Ferrara**: Hello, Mr. De Carli, I am constrained by the limits of my Italian, but it seems that there are some obvious problems with your presentation. One problem is this: It is established as a fact that there is a so-called "Capovilla envelope" on which was written the name of Archbishop Capovilla, the heads of the Vatican departments, the judgment of John XXIII—to not *give* a judgment. And this critical envelope was in the papal apartment. So, a simple question: Where is this envelope?
>
> **De Carli**: The Bertone envelope *is* the Capovilla envelope; there is *no difference*. The Capovilla one is the one that ended up in the papal apartment. If you read the [Capovilla] interview in detail [i.e., the transcript presented during the "Cardinal Bertone Show" in 2007]... it explains how the envelope ended up in the hands of Paul VI, who was very interested—but a few days after his election, not months later—he wanted to read the text immediately. *Then the envelope remains there*. This is recounted by Msgr. Capovilla, who is a credible witness, the only living one. If you wish, you can give credit to what has been published by others, who are no longer with us. I give credit instead to a living person who, before me, recorded his testimony.

De Carli's answer flatly contradicted the very evidence he himself had presented during the "Cardinal Bertone Show" of September 21, 2007 discussed earlier: the envelope in the papal apartment was simply not the envelope produced on *Porta a Porta*, as the Capovilla envelope bears the Archbishop's handwritten list of the names of those who had read the contents and the dictation of John XXIII concerning his decision not to render any judgment on the text. And while De Carli further asserted that Capovilla's handwriting might be found on the back of one of the envelopes Bertone had displayed during his appearance on May 31, 2007, Bertone had shown the front and back of each of those envelopes to the cameras and no writing was present on the back of any of them.

Furthermore, the text of the vision Bertone displayed came from the archives of the Holy Office, now called the Congregation for the Doctrine of the Faith—not the papal apartment, where the Capovilla envelope and its contents were located. Pressed again on this point, De Carli made a stunning observation:

> **Ferrara:** I understand, but *living people* said that there is an envelope [the Capovilla envelope] there [in the papal apartment]—
>
> **De Carli [interrupting]:** It doesn't appear that way to me—
>
> **Ferrara:**—But *we never saw the envelope.*

De Carli: *I saw the envelope, and I said that what's reproduced in here* [indicating the book, *Last Secret*, formerly *Last Visionary*] is *exactly what I had photographed by my own photographer*, and not by the one for the Holy See, because ***I did not trust them completely***. I asked Bertone: "Seeing that we are here, would you let me go look at the Capovilla envelope?"... It is the same envelope. The Bertone envelope corresponds with the Capovilla envelope.

De Carli's distrust of the Vatican's photographer was understandable,[346] but his personally commissioned photograph of what he claimed was the Capovilla envelope does not appear in *Last Secret*. Under repeated questioning on how he could maintain that the never-produced Capovilla envelope was the same as the Bertone envelope, De Carli finally conceded defeat:

Ferrara: The document of Archbishop Capovilla[347] said clearly that there is an envelope on the outside of which is found my [Capovilla's] writing. On *Porta a Porta, Cardinal Bertone did not show this envelope. It is a fact. Therefore, there are two envelopes. With all due respect, you haven't answered my question.*

De Carli: *Yes, these are useful precisions*. However, do not fasten yourselves on these things, which are important but not critical. I personally went to see the writing on the envelope there. When Cardinal Bertone showed it on *Porta a Porta* it is not like he didn't want us to see it. *He took the envelope in his hands, which was simply turned to the other side.* And if you go back to listen to the recording, *Cardinal Bertone at one point read the sentences that Pope John XXIII dictated to Msgr. Capovilla to write on the envelope, but he did not turn it around to the camera so that we could see it*. But these are small things. The envelope is the same, it is the same. Then again, ***they could have tricked me***, showing me something different. But my clear *impression* was that the envelope is the same: the Capovilla envelope is equal to the Bertone envelope.

Having retreated to the position that it was his "clear *impression*" that the two envelopes were the same, while admitting "they could have tricked me," De Carli here made a devastating slip, attributable (one must assume in charity) to the pressure of the moment as opposed to any preconceived intent to deceive. For, as noted in the preceding chapter, on the *Porta a Porta* video it is clearly seen that Bertone *did* turn the envelope he displayed "around to the camera" to reveal *no writing on the other side*. Evidently, De Carli had retreated in confusion in his attempt to deny what was undeniable: that the Capovilla envelope is not the Bertone envelope, and thus the contents of the Capovilla envelope must remain well hidden in the Vatican.

---

346 In May 2011, while in Rome, Father Gruner attended a Wednesday papal audience. He, along with the pilgrim statue of Our Lady of Fatima, was permitted to enter the private viewing area behind Pope Benedict to receive his personal blessing after the audience. The Pope approached the private viewing area in the popemobile and blessed those people. According to official Vatican photos taken at the time, the photographer took six pictures in rapid succession (only seconds apart) which captured the Pope blessing Father Gruner and the statue. However, the photos published on the photographer's web site reveal that five of the photos had been edited to remove Father Gruner from the picture! **One photo shows Father Gruner standing behind a cleric dressed in brown, but the very next photo—taken only a few seconds later—does not show Father Gruner at all.** In this photo, a part of Fr. Gruner's black cassock, not fully erased, can still be seen against the brown cassock of the cleric standing in front of him.

347 His "confidential note" of 1967. *See, The Secret Still Hidden*, Chapters 6 and 10, and reproduction of the original typewritten text (English and Italian) at Appendix I, pp. 217-221.

The Virgin's "express order" concerning 1960

De Carli was also asked to address another element of incontrovertible proof of cover-up: that Bertone had misled the Church and the world concerning the Virgin's "express order" regarding revelation of the Third Secret in the year 1960 as indicated on *both* of the sealed envelopes Bertone had finally revealed on *Porta a Porta*. Here John Salza took the lead with a question that produced another staggering misstep:

> **Salza:** According to Cardinal Bertone, Sister Lucia never received any indication from the Virgin Mary that the Secret should have been revealed in 1960. Yet Cardinal Bertone said that Sister Lucia had confessed to him that she (Sister Lucia) chose that date, without direction by the Virgin. However, on *Porta a Porta*, Cardinal Bertone showed the two envelopes of Sister Lucia to the cameras, evidencing that it was a fact that it was by explicit order of the Virgin that the Secret should not be disclosed before 1960. And so how can we reconcile this testimony? Is it possible that the account of Cardinal Bertone is not true?
>
> **De Carli:** No. This 1960 question is one that *I have also posed to myself many times*, because Sister Lucia wrote on the envelope that "you must open it in 1960." But I think the answer by Cardinal Bertone is a convincing answer[!] Please note that we are dealing with a Sister *who could neither read nor write. She began to read and write when she was about 30, 35 years old—so 15 years, if not 20, after the apparitions.* She began to understand the value of words, but she never had a good understanding of time.

So, De Carli's attempt at an explanation was that Sister Lucia did not know how to write when she *wrote* on both of her sealed envelopes: "By express order of Our Lady, this envelope can only be opened in 1960 by the Cardinal Patriarch of Lisbon or the Bishop of Leiria." De Carli added the demonstrably false assertion that Lucia did not learn to read or write until she was thirty or thirty-five years old. In fact, the seer had achieved literacy while still a teenager. And this achievement was also by "express order" of the Virgin during the second Fatima apparition on June 13, 1917—*precisely so that Lucia could make the Message of Fatima known to the world in writing.* Thus we see Lucia writing to her bishop as early as 1922, when she was only fifteen years old.[348]

This notion of an ignorant, illiterate peasant girl who had no idea what she was doing when she wrote the Virgin's express order on the two envelopes is part of what Father Gruner described to De Carli as "fables told by those who do not believe in Fatima. The Fatima documentation is very well done, and it negates the theory according to which Sister Lucia did not know what she wrote. This is a fabrication." When Father Gruner pressed De Carli further on the matter, De Carli had to admit that he had no real explanation for why Bertone had claimed the Virgin never said anything to Lucia about the Secret being linked to 1960:

---

348 Lucia wrote a letter on June 21, 1921 to her mother only several days after she had left Fatima on June 16, 1921. Contrary to what De Carli affirmed, she had learned to read and write when she was only 14 years old or less. Lucia wrote additional letters to her mother on July 4, July 17, October 2, October 23 and December 18 of 1921, followed by letters to her mother and others on January 2, February 2, April 16 and June 4 of 1922. She was only 15 years old at this time and wrote quite well. Frère Michel de la Sainte Trinité quotes excerpts of some of these letters in *The Whole Truth About Fatima*, Vol. II, pp. 217-221. Lucia wrote her first account of the apparitions in a letter to her confessor on January 5, 1922 (before she was 15). See Father António Maria Martins, S.J., *Cartas da Irmã Lúcia*, (printed by Fraternidade Missionária de Cristo-Jovem, Samerio-Braga, 1978) pp. 80-84. This 4 1/2-page handwritten letter is photographically reproduced on pp. 468-476 of *Documentos de Fatima* (Porto, 1976).

> **De Carli:** *I do not know what to say.* That mystery of 1960 remains. There's an explanation that, in my opinion, is plausible and I think could be accepted, which is that, in my opinion, Lucia saw that date of 1960 as very far from her, so it was like saying: "Open this in the next century." She imagined that in 1960—remember that she wrote it in 1944, so 1960 is sixteen years after that date—she would probably no longer be.
>
> **Father Gruner:** Yes, but she said "according to *the explicit order of Our Lady*." In this writing she denies that it was her idea and says that it was the order of the Madonna. *Why did Bertone say that Lucia confessed to him that it was just her idea?*
>
> **De Carli:** I collected only what Cardinal Bertone told me. I cannot invent things. I write what I hear, what I see, what I think, and what I record. You can think whatever you wish....

The faithful would indeed think whatever they wished. They would think that Bertone has misled the faithful for years about the intrinsic connection of the Secret to 1960, the year in which the world awaited not only the revelation of the Third Secret but also the commencement of the ill-starred Second Vatican Council in 1962.

The Discrepancy of the Envelopes

On the question of the revelation by Bertone on *Porta a Porta* of not one, but *two* envelopes bearing Our Lady's "express order" concerning 1960, Father Gruner asked De Carli to explain why, in *Last Visionary* (now *Last Secret*), Bertone recounted having had Lucia authenticate only *one* such envelope. Perhaps not realizing that he was treading in a minefield planted by Bertone himself, De Carli provided an explosive answer:

> **De Carli:** I don't recall this detail, sorry, I just don't have recollection of that, that part of the book has not been changed. I myself saw that document. I took my photographer with me, who photographed it for me. *And there is an envelope which has written on it: "For delivery to the Bishop of Fatima," and a second envelope on which had been written: "to be opened after 1960."*

Note well: At the time his photographer took a photograph of the document published in 2000 (the vision), *De Carli was shown only one envelope bearing the Virgin's order concerning 1960*. Yet, on *Porta a Porta*, *two* such envelopes suddenly "jumped out of the top hat," to employ a phrase of Socci's. Thus it seems that De Carli *was* deceived in this matter, just as he had, apparently, been sold a bill of goods about Sister Lucia's ignorance and illiteracy. The truth of his own words—"They could have tricked me"—and his repeated expressions of distrust in Vatican photographers here stand confirmed. Given his evident lack of knowledge of the documentation on the historical details of the Third Secret controversy and the life of the seer, De Carli would have been particularly susceptible to being misled by those who wished to use him for their purposes.

The Secret "belongs to the past" canard

Still another patently indefensible element of the "official" position is that the Third Secret "belongs to the past," according to Cardinal Bertone, following Cardinal Sodano. De Carli's answer to the pertinent question was clearly at variance with Bertone's version of the facts, as De Carli himself seemed eager to note:

> **Father Gruner:** ... I do not understand why Cardinal Bertone told us that the age of lust for power and evil is over now—that is, on June 26, 2000, with the decision to reveal the Third Secret. We're seeing that this time of evil and lust for power for mankind *is not over yet*!
>
> **De Carli:** *This is certain.* By reading the Third Secret, we understand that the Third Secret is also valid today. *It is not just relegated to the past. I tried to show this in the book with a reflection by Cardinal Bertone, who then arrives at my thesis.* Read it carefully. The Third Secret *is not something that concerns only an event of the past, but is something that concerns us today, as well.* It has, therefore, a power that goes far beyond a mere historical memory.

While De Carli, at least, was willing to admit that the Third Secret does not belong to the past, contrary to what De Carli had suggested in his answer, Bertone's *Last Secret* does not reveal any such change of position by Bertone himself, but only his nebulous "reflection" (in a newly added chapter) that "it is good, therefore, that they [the events of Fatima] are consigned to the collective memory, leaving behind traces not deprived of meaning."[349] Otherwise, Bertone obstinately reaffirmed his "interpretation" that the Secret "is realized in the past..."[350]

Archbishop Capovilla's "Confidential Note"

Yet another piece of incontrovertible evidence brought to De Carli's attention was the "confidential note" by Archbishop Capovilla, wherein he recorded that on June 27, 1963 Paul VI had read a text of the Third Secret retrieved from the Barbarigo writing desk in the papal bedchamber of John XXIII—a fact radically at odds with the "official" account, which asserts that Paul VI read the Secret for the first and only time on March 27, 1965, and that the text he read came from the Holy Office. Recall that during the "Cardinal Bertone Show" on September 21, 2007, De Carli had attempted to explain away this devastating discrepancy by leading Capovilla to suggest during his interview of the Archbishop that Pope Paul read the same text twice—in 1963 and 1965—even though Capovilla himself demolished that contention *in the same interview* by stating that after the reading in 1963 "the envelope was resealed [*richiude* in Italian; "resealed" or "reclosed"] and *it was not spoken of further.*"[351]

But this "testimony" refutes itself. For if, as Capovilla himself affirmed, the contents of the envelope resealed in 1963 were "not spoken of further" after that year, *then how could he have known whether the envelope had been reopened yet again in 1965 and read for a second time*? Clearly, he could not have known this, and the attempt to suggest that he did, by putting words in his mouth via De Carli's leading question, was simply a deception. Here we see what invariably happens when one attempts to reconstruct a lie that has fallen apart by making additions to the lie's original structure: new and even more embarrassing defects appear in the edifice of falsehood, and it collapses even more dramatically upon close examination.

Thus Capovilla's own testimony, far from supporting Bertone's contrivance, ruled out a second reading in 1965, which would have required reopening the resealed (or "reclosed") envelope. What did De Carli have to say about this, now that he could be questioned directly? Curiously, his earlier reliance on Capovilla as the only reliable

349 *The Last Secret of Fatima*, p. 40.

350 Ibid., p. 89.

351 Cf. *The Secret Still Hidden*, pp. 189-190.

living witness was suddenly replaced by skepticism about the Archbishop's testimony:

> **Father Gruner:** Just one other point: Socci, referring to the interview by Solideo Paolini on this subject, said, "How come there are two dates: that of June '63 and the other one of March '65?"
>
> **De Carli:** This, too, is in my book. Because I wondered why there were two dates, but only one recorded officially. The fact is that we are not sure about the second date, the only one who gave us two dates is Mons. Capovilla. Now, he is a precise man and has marked that date in his diary, but it doesn't appear in the official archives. I don't have the certainty arising from the record of audiences of what was done by Paul VI, which in this case does not correspond to the archives of the Secretary of State and the Congregation for the Doctrine of the Faith. And if this is coming only from one man, even if it's his [John XXIII's] secretary, then I do not think it can be considered official. It has to be included in the interview [shown on the "Cardinal Bertone Show"], but we still consider the official date June 26 or 27, 1963 [sic]. I'm a little confused myself, too, with the dates.

Notice, first of all, De Carli's admitted confusion about the dates: he gave June 26 or 27, 1963 as the "official" date for the reading of the Secret by Paul VI, rather than March 27, 1965 (according to *TMF*, the "official" Vatican booklet published in June 2000). Clearly, he lacked a command of the most basic facts concerning the controversy, even though Bertone had employed him to produce a book about it. As for the claim that Capovilla's note does not "correspond to the archives of the Secretary of State and the Congregation for the Doctrine of the Faith," it should have been obvious to De Carli that there is more to the story than what is contained in those archives, for Capovilla categorically places a text of the Secret in the papal apartment.

Here De Carli effectively conceded that he had no answer to this evidence other than *to cast doubt on the testimony of the very witness he had pronounced most reliable only moments before.* Worse, while defending Capovilla's memory as reliable when it appears to (but does not really) serve the "official account," De Carli had cast doubt on the reliability of *a contemporaneous written record* of what the Archbishop had witnessed and concerning a reading of a text of the Third Secret by Paul VI in 1963, two years before the date given in the "official" account.

In dramatic departure from *Last Visionary*, *Last Secret* "adjusts" the "official" account to claim that Paul VI must have read the same text in 1963 that he read in 1965: "[he] read it two times, according to what has been reported by Monsignor Capovilla. Certainly on March 27, 1965, and he opted for its non-publication."[352] But Monsignor Capovilla had reported no such thing. Rather, during the edited interview televised in September 2007, De Carli put this "report" into Capovilla's mouth by asking a blatantly leading question designed to extract the answer De Carli (and Bertone) needed in order to address this gaping hole in the official version: "Paul VI read the same Message two times. Is that so?"[353] With good reason are such questions deemed improper in legal proceedings, for the leading questioner is essentially telling the witness what to say, thus rendering the answer worthless as proof of anything.

At any rate, why would Paul VI open again the very envelope he had *resealed* in

[352] *Last Secret*, p. 70.

[353] *The Secret Still Hidden*, pp. 189-190.

1963? Clearly, the envelope he read in 1965 was other than the one he had read two years earlier. From which it followed, as all the other evidence showed, that there are two companion texts pertaining to the Third Secret of Fatima.

Capovilla's testimony to Paolini

We have seen that at no time was Archbishop Capovilla asked by Bertone, De Carli or anyone else to deny specifically his admission to Solideo Paolini—"Exactly so!"—in response to the question whether there were two different envelopes and two different texts pertaining to the Third Secret. Confronted on this telling point, De Carli not only declared that Paolini was a liar who invented his conversation with Archbishop Capovilla, but also claimed to have in his possession yet another secret document the Vatican is not allowing anyone to see:

> **Father Gruner**: ... Why did he [Capovilla] not deny what Paolini said?
>
> **De Carli:** No, easy now, no. Let us speak of how that interview was obtained. It was a meeting, this Solideo Paolini, who went to Mons. Capovilla. It was a simple chat, and then he pulled from it an interview that truly and properly did not exist, *and much of that interview was invented wholesale.*
>
> **Ferrara:** Why did no one ask Archbishop Capovilla "yes or no" regarding the fact that he answered Paolini "Precisely so!" as an answer to his question if "There are two texts of the Third Secret of Fatima?" Why has no one asked him this?
>
> **De Carli:** Look, I have in hand [*i.e.*, available to him] a letter by Mons. Capovilla sent to the Secretary of State and to the Holy Father in which he denies he ever responded in such way to Solideo Paolini. He denies it. So either this Solideo Paolini is a liar, and has profited from it, or Mons. Capovilla is a liar. *I believe Solideo Paolini is a liar.*
>
> **Ferrara:** May I have a copy [of the letter]?...
>
> **Salza:** Why have you not published this letter from Capovilla, if it could answer all the questions?
>
> **De Carli:** Because it's private correspondence, I can't; I'm sorry.

In sum, De Carli publicly accused Paolini of being a liar and then refused to publish his evidence for the charge, claiming it was a "private" missive to the Pope and the Secretary of State! Yet he was in possession of a copy of that same "private" letter, and was now dangling its alleged existence before the entire world while refusing to produce it. Nor had the Vatican seen fit to publish Capovilla's denial, if such it was. It is telling indeed that *Last Secret* makes no mention of this secret but not-so-secret letter, even though De Carli, the co-author of *Last Secret*, had freely revealed its existence in connection with his promotion of that very book at "The Fatima Challenge" conference.

What about the "etc"?

The "official" account had always been fatally compromised by its glaring failure to ask Sister Lucia a single question about the very heart of the Third Secret controversy: that momentous "etc" Sister Lucia had placed at the end of the recorded Great Secret in her Fourth Memoir to indicate the beginning of its third and final part, consisting of the spoken words of the Virgin. We have seen that the only reasonable deduction is that the Virgin clearly foretells a crisis within the Church involving "the dogma of the Faith," which "will always be preserved" in Portugal but evidently not elsewhere. Pressed on the cover-up of the telltale "etc", De Carli pleaded a lack of memory:

> **De Carli:** *I do not remember this.* When I'm not sure I do not answer. With regards to that "etc"—following the phrase "Portugal will not lose the Catholic faith and Catholic nations etc" [sic], what's in that "etc"?—I said to Bertone: "Look, many have imagined that behind that 'etc' is another text which doesn't exist." And he answered—*I don't recall any longer what he answered to me. I am sorry, on this point I do not have a precise recollection.*

Pressed again to comment on the "etc" controversy, De Carli conceded—thus rejecting the "official" account—that the words embraced within the tellate "etc" did indeed represent the beginning of the Third Secret of Fatima:

> **De Carli:** The "etc" was by Sister Lucia. She had suspended that et cetera *because she had yet to write the last part of the Secret.* That et cetera said: "leave it for me." But that et cetera gathered a lot of attention by the bishops, by her confessors—not to mention journalists, "doomsayers" and apocalypse-sayers. And when Sister Lucia was finally pressed, put on the ropes, *she filled in the et cetera with the Third Secret.*

Now, if the "etc" represents something that Lucia later "filled in… with the Third Secret"—which indeed it was—then it is obvious that what Lucia "filled in" could only have been the *words* of the Virgin Mary following Her reference to the preservation of dogma in Portugal, *because the "etc" interrupts a sentence in which She was speaking*, not a vision that She was conveying, such as the vision published in 2000. Yet De Carli claimed a lack of memory about what Bertone told him concerning this utterly crucial point.

What could one say? Ten years after the controversy over the completeness of the Vatican's disclosure of the Third Secret began, there was still no answer from the Vatican party to the one question that would reveal the truth of the matter: *What are the words of Our Lady which conclude the Great Secret of Fatima by completing its third and final part*? It seems that the plan was to keep those words from the faithful forever, were it possible. Thus it had always been essential to the plan that the "etc" of the Fourth Memoir be avoided like the plague, which required the Vatican to employ the less complete Third Memoir in its commentary on the Message of Fatima in 2000. There was no other reasonable explanation for this behavior.

The testimony of Cardinal Ottaviani

Confronted by Father Gruner with the testimony of the late Cardinal Ottaviani that the text of the Third Secret he had in view was 25 lines in length, not the 62 lines of the vision, De Carli joined Bertone in affirming that *this was indeed Ottaviani's testimony*, but offered the "thesis" (as had Bertone) that Ottaviani had somehow mistaken a 62-line text for one with 25 lines:

> **Father Gruner:** On television, on the *Porta a Porta* [telecast] of May 31, 2007, there was a Vaticanist who asked: "But Cardinal Ottaviani said that the text consists of 25 lines, why then has this text 62 lines?" And Cardinal Bertone affirmed that Cardinal Ottaviani had said this, trying to explain how he had erred. I do not know—in your book is there an answer to this question?
>
> **De Carli:** Yes, this is also in my book. The thesis—since I cannot

> interview him because he is in the embrace of God—the thesis is that Ottaviani was wrong to say 25 lines, he was wrong.

Pressed further on the point, De Carli admitted that he had no real answer to the glaring discrepancy between what was published in 2000 and what Cardinal Ottaviani had clearly described:

> **Father Gruner:** But this explanation by Cardinal Bertone, who said that perhaps Ottaviani had not looked at the other side, and the fact that even adding these two sides the sum is... 31-32... not 25 lines—how could he be so wrong? And how is it that the Bishop of Fatima [who] looked up to the light—one can only say that there are [according to him] two envelopes [not four]—and said that there were 25 lines, how come this text has 62 lines instead? Bishop Venâncio put everything in writing. It's in the archives of Fatima.
>
> **De Carli**: *I cannot answer this*, and when I cannot answer I do not answer. I have the notes of the meeting between the Cardinal and Sister Lucia. Bertone showed to Lucia the 64 lines of text, which she then turned, turned again, examined; and the precise question is: "Sister Lucia, is this the text that you wrote in 1944, which was then placed in the envelope?" "Yes, it is my text." "And this is your envelope?" "Yes, this is my envelope."

De Carli's reference to Lucia's authentication of a *single* envelope, when Bertone had displayed *three* envelopes of Lucia's on *Porta a Porta*, prompted the next series of questions, with answers that highlighted dramatically the untrustworthiness of the "official" account.

A convenient "correction"

When Sister Lucia authenticated the text of the Third Secret in April of 2000, she told Bertone: "Yes, these are my *sheets* of paper (*fogli*) and the envelope is mine; they are the *sheets* (*fogli*) that I used and this is my writing. This is my *envelope*, this is my writing, this is my text."[354] Recall that on *Porta a Porta*, on May 31, 2007, Bertone had displayed a *sheet* of paper and three *envelopes* prepared by Lucia: her unsealed outer envelope and the two sealed envelopes bearing the Virgin's express order concerning 1960. Yet, according to Bertone's/De Carli's *Last Visionary*, published several weeks earlier (on May 10, 2007), Lucia had authenticated *sheets* of paper (*fogli*) and only *one* envelope—*exactly the opposite* of the document ensemble Bertone displayed weeks later on camera.

This enormous and never-explained discrepancy prompted questions that revealed another "adjustment" of the words Bertone had attributed to Sister Lucia, as allegedly recorded in his remarkably adaptable "notes":

> **Salza:** But in your book with Cardinal Bertone, he said that Sister Lucia said: "Yes, these are my *sheets* [*fogli*]"—using the plural form. But what was shown on *Porta a Porta* was only one sheet. Where are the other sheets?
>
> **De Carli:** This *is better explained* here [in *Last Secret*] because *we went back to check at the Archives*, which is one of the reasons why we did a second edition. There are two sides. The book reports it exactly because I repeat it several times: 4 pages on 2 sheets—two on one side

354 *The Last Visionary of Fatima*, p. 37; see also, *The Secret Still Hidden*, Chapter 8, pp. 128, 136.

and the other two on the other side. Because in the Cardinal's notes—keep in mind that when I wrote that book [*Last Visionary*] we were in 2006, Cardinal Bertone was moving to Rome, he had shelves full of books and had these diaries, at least 50 pages of his diary notes, we read them a bit faster.[355] So back then we relied on the 64 lines count, but now it is clear that there are two sheets (*fogli*) [!] of four pages.

Father Gruner: My Italian is not perfect, but in English we speak about a "sheet" like this [holding up one sheet of paper]. You can fold this sheet, but it is only one sheet. When Sister Lucia said that these are my sheets, she said that there was another piece of paper besides this.

De Carli: *You are right to point out this thing*. I should find the text. I cannot find it now [in the copy of *Last Secret* he is holding]. But the book specifies, in almost a maniacal manner, this thing about the sheets that Sister Lucia had in her hand. *It is no longer multiple sheets, but a single sheet*, divided into 4 sides, a single sheet exactly like he [Father Gruner] showed here—in half, 2 sides and 2 sides. It is repeated twice.

Salza: So you were wrong when you said that there are two sheets, and now you're saying that there is only one? We must be exact, here, because you have already said [here] that there are two sheets, and so the question is: Is there just one sheet or two?

De Carli: I'm looking at the text [of my book], because I can't remember all these details. Here is what is in the book: We talked about a large envelope, stamped with the seal of the Congregation for the Doctrine of the Faith. On the envelope [written in 1944] is the writing about 1960, and which contained another envelope, with a single sheet with lines, folded in two, and four sides handwritten by Sister Lucia.

Ferrara: The first book talks about sheets!

Salza: This is a change!

De Carli: We did a second edition of the book just to clarify better, also from an Italian point of view with regards to different language translations. And what we *wanted* to say is that it is a *single* lined sheet, folded in two, and four sides.

Salza: Therefore you made a mistake when you said that it was "sheets," in plural, right?

De Carli: I was wrong. Can't I make mistakes? Aren't we human?

Salza: But [today] you said this, two or three times, specifically.

De Carli: One can make a mistake. In fact, I wanted to check again the text [of the book] because it was important to clarify this point: a lined sheet, folded in two, written on four sides. But Fatima—it is not

355 The excuse that Bertone was moving to Rome and that he and De Carli were only able to read Bertone's notes in haste, and thus somehow mistook multiple pages for one page, lacks all credibility. Bertone was fully installed as Secretary of State by September 15, 2006. Socci's book was published on November 22, 2006, and De Carli did not begin to write his book in collaboration with Bertone until after Socci's book had appeared. There was more than ample time to read the notes carefully. Even if the notes had been read in haste, however, that still would not explain how they could have been so misread as to refer to multiple sheets of paper if they had stated that there was only one sheet. De Carli's excuse appears to have been an improvisation under the pressure of the moment.

> just a sheet written on four sides. Fatima is the marvelous secret of Mary who appears to the three shepherds! This is what really counts.

De Carli's statements were fraught with disaster for the "official" account. For one thing, even in the midst of attempting to explain that the Secret involved only one sheet of paper, he referred to *two* sheets,[356] evidencing his confusion on the matter. Further, the "mistake" about the number of sheets involved—one, rather than two or more—could not have been *his* mistake because, according to Bertone in *Last Visionary*, it was *Sister Lucia* who had referred to *sheets* of paper (*fogli*) and Bertone had provided, as noted above, a purported *verbatim quotation of the seer* to that effect. But, as has happened so often in the annals of the "official account," the words of "Sister Lucia" were altered to meet current exigencies. So, whereas in *Last Visionary* she is quoted as having said "these are my *sheets* of paper (*fogli*) ... they are the *sheets* (*fogli*) that I used," in *Last Secret* "Sister Lucia" now says "Yes, yes, this is my *paper* [*carta*]." As De Carli had put it: "it is *no longer* multiple sheets, but a single sheet..."

In other words, when it is necessary to change the "official account" to meet serious objections, what "Sister Lucia" said before is expediently revised, now that she is conveniently dead. Simple! But not so simple. For in his noncommittal letter of introduction to *Last Visionary*, reproduced without change in *Last Secret*, none other than Pope Benedict XVI relates that in preparing the "theological commentary" on the Secret when he was Cardinal Ratzinger (see Chapter 4 of *The Secret Still Hidden*) he had "prayed and meditated deeply on the authentic words of the third part of the Secret of Fatima, contained in the *sheets* [*fogli*!] written by Sister Lucia." Or, in the original Italian: "le parole autentiche della terza parte del segreto di Fatima contenute nei *fogli* scritti da Suor Lucia."[357]

So, *the Pope himself* reveals that the Third Secret involves *multiple* sheets of paper, whereas Sister Lucia, who once said this as well, "no longer" said it—at least according to Bertone and De Carli, now that the visionary was no longer alive to contradict them. But not even Bertone would dare to claim that *the Pope* was mistaken when he wrote *fogli* instead of *foglio*! Nor was Bertone in any position to "correct" the papal letter of introduction. He was stuck with it, and thus with the glaring discrepancy it revealed—the umpteenth—in his ever-changing story.

Why did he appear?

After having submitted to questioning that only demonstrated, yet again, why the "official account" had been deprived of all credibility, De Carli excused himself and left the conference. The net impression of his appearance was that of a decent man who, years earlier, had entered into a battle for which he was poorly prepared (as he himself admitted), had raised his flag for the wrong side, and now, perhaps, had begun to entertain serious doubts about the version of the facts he had been expected to defend. "They could have tricked me" is a phrase that could not be more revealing of a man having second thoughts.

In tribute to De Carli we must agree with the commentator who wrote: "As his case collapsed in one exchange after another, Mr. De Carli never displayed any sign of irritation or animosity, as usually occurs when a person's claims are radically challenged. He patiently

---

356 See question by Salza and answer by De Carli starting above.

357 *The Last Secret of Fatima*, p. 10.

listened and tried to reply to all questions, and gave the impression of an honest man, now rather confused, who had perhaps been drawn into an orchestrated deception of which he was unaware at the time." The same commentator noted that as De Carli was departing the conference, Father Gruner extended his hand, but instead of merely shaking hands with "the Fatima priest" De Carli "embraced Father Gruner and *thanked him for the work he was doing*."[358]

All in all, De Carli's appearance at the conference had contributed to making the event as a whole a tipping point for handling of the Third Secret affair within the Vatican. The Pope himself would soon make this dramatically apparent during his trip to Fatima from May 11-14, 2010.

The attendees of the "Consecration Now!" conference at the Vatican in procession in St. Peter's Square on May 11, 2011.

On October 11, 1990, Carolina, the blood sister of Sister Lucia, shortly before she died, told Father Gruner that she had visited Sister Lucia in the Carmel of Coimbra for more than 40 years and never had she been able to speak alone with her sister in the same room. They were always separated by a grille and many other sisters of the convent were in attendance at all visits. Unlike the hand-holding session in the same room by someone [Carlos Evaristo] holding the hand of a "nun" claiming to be Sister Lucia in October 1992 (see pages 94-96).

358 Edwin Faust, "The Latest Chapter in the Story of Fatima," http://www.secretstillhidden.com/pdf/epilogue_summary.pdf

Chapter 27
Breakthroughs for Fatima

"The Fatima Challenge" conference was yet another example of Father Gruner's almost superhuman persistence; and, once again, that persistence would be rewarded. On May 11, 2010, four days after the conference had ended, Pope Benedict journeyed to Portugal for a pilgrimage to the Fatima Shrine at the Cova da Iria on May 13, the anniversary of Our Lady's first apparition at the Cova. The Fatima Center's technical team had detected monitoring of the conference proceedings from an IP (Internet Provider) address within the Vatican. Surely, Cardinal Bertone had watched some or all of the proceedings, including De Carli's appearance on his behalf. And it is probable that the Pope himself had seen or been informed of the proceedings—a conclusion well supported by what the Pope said on the papal plane en route to Portugal.

The Pope Reopens the Third Secret "Dossier"

Speaking calmly and deliberately to reporters on the plane, the Pope reopened the entire Third Secret controversy by expressly rejecting—at last!—the by now universally doubted Sodano/Bertone "interpretation" of the Third Secret as merely a visional depiction of past events. Rather, said the Pope, the Secret prophesies what is happening in the Church today, is not at all limited to "the past," and predicts *future* events in the Church *that are still developing day-by-day.* The Pope addressed the question on camera as Bertone literally loomed over him from behind:

> **Lombardi:** Holiness, what significance do the apparitions of Fatima have for us today? And when you presented the text of the Third Secret, in the Vatican Press Office, in June 2000, it was asked of you whether the Message could be extended, beyond the attack on John Paul II, also to the other sufferings of the Pope. Is it possible, according to you, to frame also in that vision the sufferings of the Church of today for the sins of the sexual abuse of minors?
>
> **Pope Benedict:** Beyond this great vision of the suffering of the Pope, which we can in substance refer to John Paul II, *are indicated* ***future realities of the Church which are little by little developing and revealing themselves***. Thus, it is true that beyond the moment indicated in the vision, it is *spoken*, it is seen, the necessity of ***a Passion of the Church that naturally is reflected in the person of the Pope; but the Pope is in the Church, and therefore the sufferings of the Church are what is announced****....*
>
> As for the novelty that we can discover today in this message, it is that ***attacks on the Pope and the Church do not come only from outside, but the sufferings of the Church come precisely from within the Church***, from sins that exist in the Church. This has always been known, but today we see it ***in a really terrifying way***: that the greatest

persecution of the Church ***does not come from enemies outside, but arises from sin in the Church.***[359]

The content of the Pope's remarks amounted to a bomb that destroyed the "official" account. First of all, it is critical to note that the Pope's remarks were not off-the-cuff, but rather were in answer to a question *selected beforehand* by the Pope himself. As the *National Catholic Reporter* observed, the Pope "was hardly caught off-guard. The Vatican asks reporters traveling with the Pope to submit questions for the plane several days in advance, so Benedict has plenty of time to ponder what he wants to say. If he takes a question on the plane, *it's because he wants to talk about it, and he's chosen his words carefully*."[360]

The significance of the Pope's carefully chosen words cannot be overstated. The Pope went out of his way to bring up the Third Secret of Fatima, ten years after the subject was supposedly laid to rest by Sodano and Bertone; and he did so because he wished to speak of the Secret and its relation to the *current* and *future* state of the Church: "*future realities* of the Church which are *little by little developing and revealing themselves*."

Note well: *Future* realities, developing *little by little* and revealing themselves *today*, not merely "in the past." Here the Pope spoke of something *not seen in the vision* of the bishop in white: "attacks on the Pope and the Church ... *from within the Church*" which show in "***a really terrifying way***" that "the greatest persecution... arises from sin *in the Church.*" This went well beyond even the pedophilia scandal to a generalized assessment of the state of the Church in light of the Secret; it was a frontal attack on Bertone's and Sodano's position, which in fact had never been anything but their already widely rejected opinion in the matter.

Now, the vision says nothing at all about a crisis involving attacks upon the Church and persecution of the Church *from within her* on account of the sins of her own members. On the contrary, the vision depicts an external persecution of the Church in the midst of a post-apocalyptic scenario wherein a future Pope is executed outside a half-ruined city by soldiers who are not internal enemies. There is only one way to reconcile the Pope's remarks with the tableau in the vision; it is the same way both the "Fatimists" and Socci have proposed and this book itself proposes: There is a missing text related to the vision in which the Virgin explains in Her own words how an internal crisis of faith and discipline in the Church is accompanied by a chastisement of the whole world, including the bishops, priests and laity who are executed, "one after another," by the same soldiers who have already executed the Pope on the hill outside the destroyed city.

The Pope himself appeared to confirm the existence of precisely such a text when he said that "*beyond the moment* indicated in the vision, ***it is spoken***, it is seen [*si parla, si vede*] the necessity of a Passion of the Church, which naturally is reflected in the person of the Pope, but the Pope is in the Church and therefore what is announced are

359 "Oltre questa grande visione della sofferenza del Papa, che possiamo in sostanza riferire a Giovanni Paolo II sono indicate realtà del futuro della chiesa che man mano si sviluppano e si mostrano. Cioè è vero che oltre il momento indicato nella visione, ***si parla***, si vede la necessità di una passione della chiesa, che naturalmente si riflette nella persona del Papa, ma il Papa sta nella chiesa e quindi sono sofferenze della chiesa che si annunciano. Il Signore ci ha detto che la chiesa sarà per sempre sofferente, in modi diversi fino alla fine de mondo. L'importante è che il messaggio, la risposta di Fatima, sostanzialmente non va a situazioni particolari, ma la risposta fondamentale cioè conversione permanente, penitenza, preghiera, e le virtù cardinali, fede, speranza carità. Così vediamo qui la vera e fondamentale risposta che la chiesa deve dare, che noi ogni singolo dobbiamo dare in questa situazione. Quanto alle novità che possiamo oggi scoprire in questo messaggio è anche che non solo da fuori vengono attacchi al Papa e alla chiesa, ma le sofferenze della chiesa vengono proprio dall'interno della chiesa, dal peccato che esiste nella chiesa. Anche questo lo vediamo sempre ma oggi lo vediamo in modo realmente terrificante che la più grande persecuzione alla chiesa non viene dai nemici di fuori, ma nasce dal peccato nella chiesa." Transcript by Paolo Rodari, www.corriere.it/esteri/10_maggio_11/vecchi-parole-papa_fa994a90-5ce9-11df-97c2-00144f02aabe.shtml, confirmed by this author, who watched the video of the Pope's remarks.

360 "On the crisis, Benedict XVI changes the tone," *National Catholic Reporter*, May 11, 2010.

the sufferings of the Church."

> **Note well: The Pope refers to a prophecy *beyond the moment indicated in the vision,* involving both *words and images* relating to sufferings in the Church caused, not by the soldiers seen in the vision, but rather by the Church's *internal persecution* on account of the sins *of her own members*.**

The Vaticanist Paolo Rodari was quick to recognize the significance of the Pope's words, asking the question: "Was Socci right?" Wrote Rodari:

> It is true that the Pope did not speak of a fourth secret explicitly. But to read the response he gave today to the journalists, one cannot but think of Socci, who has always linked the contents of a hypothetical fourth secret to the corruption of the Church and to the sin which is born within the Church and is presently operative. Reading what the Pope said today, it seems that for him Fatima *is not reducible only to the past and thus only to the text of 2000.*[361]

If there were any doubt of this, the Pope all but extinguished it two days later on May 13 when, during his homily at the Mass to commemorate the anniversary of the first Fatima apparition, His Holiness declared:

> "One would be deceiving himself who thinks that the prophetic mission of Fatima is concluded." ["*Si illuderebbe chi pensasse che la missione profetica di Fatima sia conclusa*."]

This was another direct attack on the "official" version, and indeed on Bertone and Sodano personally for having promoted it as the Party Line: "*he* would be deceiving himself" meant particular individuals, and it was clear that both prelates had promoted assiduously and precisely the fiction that the prophetic mission of Fatima had been concluded or "fulfilled" with the failed assassination attempt, and that publication of the Third Secret—as Bertone had so absurdly contended in *TMF*—"brings to an end a period of history marked by tragic human lust for power and evil."

That the Pope had made this declaration on the most solemn possible occasion—his homily during the Mass at the Fatima Shrine—gave it the force of a teaching of the Church's universal pastor. Some 500,000 souls in the Cova alone—not counting the millions who followed him on live television—heard the Roman Pontiff say that whoever thinks (and thus asserts, as Bertone did) that the prophetic mission of Fatima is concluded has deceived himself.

It was only typical of Vatican bureaucratic maneuvering, however, that the English translation of the Italian homily neutered the Pope's words to read: "We would be mistaken to think that the prophetic mission of Fatima is concluded." No! It is not "we" who would be "mistaken." The Pope said that *he* who thinks Fatima is finished would be engaged in *self-deception*, not merely "mistaken." There was no doubt who the Pope meant by "he." Nor was there any doubt about who had been deceived and was leading others into deception.

In short, with a few well-chosen words the Pope had utterly negated the Sodano-Bertone "interpretation" of the Secret. It now joined other pseudo-official pronouncements

---

361 Paolo Rodari, "Fatima. Aveva Ragione Socci? ["Fatima. Was Socci Right?"], http://www.ilfoglio.it/palazzoapostolico/2675. As Rodari wrote in the original Italian: "E' vero il Papa non ha parlato del quarto segreto esplicitamente. Ma a leggere la risposta che ha dato oggi ai giornalisti non si può non pensare ad Antonio Socci il quale ha sempre legato il contenuto di un ipotetico quarto segreto alla corruzione della chiesa e al peccato che nasce all'interno della chiesa ed agisce nel presente. Leggendo oggi il Papa sembra che anche per lui Fatima non sia riconducibile al solo passato e dunque soltanto al testo del 2000."

in the discard bin of the post-Vatican II era in the Church. Even more dramatically, the Pope had not only repudiated Bertone's and De Carli's suggestion that *Last Visionary* (and later *Last Secret*) represented the "official position" of the Church, but also *his own former adherence to the "party line" dictated by the Secretary of State* when the Pope was still Cardinal Ratzinger. The same man who, as Cardinal Ratzinger, had written that "we must affirm with Cardinal Sodano: ... the events to which the third part of the 'secret' of Fatima refers now seem part of the past"[362] had completely reversed himself as Pope Benedict and adopted the "Fatimist" position. Thus did Father Gruner's persistence earn its reward.

Socci on Pope Benedict's "Operation Truth"

The Pope's momentous declarations during his pilgrimage to Fatima prompted a rapid-fire series of articles from Antonio Socci on the theme of the patent vindication of the "Fatimist" cause, which, as we have seen, became his cause once he had considered the evidence.

Writing in *Il Libero* on May 12, 2010, in an article entitled "So there was a Fourth Secret after all…", Socci exclaimed that the Pope's statements "bring back again into the mainstream news the whole dossier on the Third Secret. His words upset the 'official version' given in 2000, *which was never considered official*—neither by Ratzinger nor by Pope John Paul II." Referring to *Fourth Secret* and the "cheap shots" he had had to endure for writing it, Socci noted that Pope Benedict "reopens the discussion in the direction that I tried to investigate and that the documents themselves suggest." By declaring that the Third Secret concerns "realities of the *future* of the Church, which unfold and reveal themselves day by day" and which we "now see in a really terrifying way," the Pope, Socci continued, "reinforces the belief" that what he said about filth and corruption in the Church during his Way of the Cross meditations as Cardinal Ratzinger on March 25, 2005 was "perhaps, indeed, the revelation (even if not declared as such) of *the part of the Third Secret that was not revealed in 2000*. The part which contains *the words of Our Lady Herself*, as a comment on the vision."

On May 13, also in *Il Libero*, Socci published a searing commentary on the Pope's demolition of Bertone's/Sodano's entire position. It was now a matter of black and white, Socci wrote, that "*The 'fourth secret' (that is, a part of the Third Secret which has not been published yet) exists*, and the words of the Pope on the pedophilia scandal are the proof." The Pope, he continued, is "performing a great truth-telling work, even if this means *contradicting the interpretation given by the Vatican Secretaries of State*." Sodano's contention that the events depicted in the vision "seem to" belong to the past—from which Bertone had removed the words "seem to," converting Sodano's opinion into a pseudo-dogma—had been rejected by Pope Benedict, "who explains to us *the complete opposite*, which is that the Third Secret regards events which came *after* the assassination attempt of 1981… and even events which are still in our future." In fact, he added, "the assassination attempt of 1981 *is nowhere to be found in Benedict's words*, therefore it is not pointed out as 'the' fulfillment of the Third Secret."

Socci concluded that the Pope has "reopened the Fatima file in such a precise and obvious way that everyone who, in these past years, rushed to give his praise to the Curial version is now caught in a panic when confronted with the Pope's words…" Even Vittorio Messori, generally a reliable partisan of the Vatican line, expressed embarrassment that

---

362 *The Message of Fatima*, p. 43.

"Now, in the vast party of the 'Fatimites' [vast!] there will be excitement, to demonstrate that Pope Benedict XVI has betrayed himself..." But, wrote Socci, aiming directly at Bertone and his collaborators, the Pope:

> wants us to understand... that we must never be afraid of the truth, even when it is embarrassing or painful. *Because we do not serve God with lies*. When we lie with pretense that we are doing it for God, we are actually doing it for ourselves. God *does not need our lies to defend and build His Church.* It is better to do a *mea culpa*, because God is stronger and bigger than any of our sins. Obviously, *this behavior is not understood in the Curia*, not even by the 'Ratzinger fans.'

In a postscript to his article, Socci noted the remarkable about-face by Messori as well, "who, three years ago, had rushed to praise Bertone's version," but on an episode of *Porta a Porta* broadcast on May 12, 2010 had "without even batting an eyelash... said the complete opposite of what he has said so far." Messori had freely admitted that, quite contrary to Bertone, Pope Benedict "does not see the fulfillment of the Third Secret in the assassination attempt of 1981" and "does not consider it part of the past, but sees it projected into the future, because he is now considering a new fact—the pedophilia scandal—as part of the Secret (and it is obvious that the Pope cannot make all this up: *he must have taken this from the complete text of the Secret...*)." Yet Messori "did not show even the least sign of recognizing that he had been mistaken all these years, nor did he treat the consequences of what he himself had said. Same for the confident Bertone."

As Socci concluded: "Either Bertone is right (and the prophecy was fulfilled in 1981 and was concluded in the past) or Benedict XVI is right (and therefore the text of the Secret is wider, the prophecy still open and the martyrdom of a Pope and of the Church are still in our future). You cannot pretend that both versions can co-exist; it would not be logical. It would be desirable that love for truth would prevail, as well as a loyal recognition of our own mistakes... The call of the Pope for repentance, self-critical examination, and penance should be taken much more seriously."

So, almost overnight, Bertone now found himself an *opponent* of the papal view of the Secret, and rightly subject to public rebuke from the very man (Socci) he had tried to portray as a knave for disputing his patently incredible version of the facts. So much for the "official version" Bertone had labored for so long to impose upon the Church.

In yet a third article on these developments, published on his blog on May 15, Socci wrote of the *mea culpa* that Bertone now owed the Church. The article, entitled "Advice to Bertone: *mea culpa* and penance," focuses on the Pope's homily at Fatima and his resounding declaration to the whole Church that "He would be deceiving himself who thinks that the prophetic mission of Fatima is concluded." In light of the papal homily, even *Il Corriere della Sera* had announced in a headline: "The Fatima prophecy is not accomplished; there will be wars and terrors."

The Pope's words at Fatima, said Socci, "contain a warning to whoever does not wish to hear and does not wish to understand. Words of Benedict XVI that... are *the exact antithesis of the lies that, sadly, Cardinal Bertone has been spreading about for years* (caught above all by me). Here in fact is what he [Bertone] has said: 'The prophecy is not open to the future; it is realized in the past.' Thus he wrote on page 79 of his book [*Last Visionary*], repeating it a thousand times in those pages and also in interviews with journalists and on TV, where he has not hesitated to insult the one who simply spoke the truth and called for love of the truth and of the Holy Virgin, Mother of God."

"Now," Socci added, "finally the Pope has spoken and everyone can understand. That Bertone, in the face of the evidence (and the bad impression he gives of himself), has precipitously reached out to the Vaticanists to attempt a tragicomic reverse march (without a *mea culpa*), only adds to the sadness. Writes Tornielli in *Il Giornale*: 'now Bertone has *adapted his words*, stating that the prophecy can also be extended to the 21st century.' In a little while he will say that he has always said this... Any comment is useless."

And then this withering assessment of Bertone's tenure: "Except to note the many problems the current Secretary of State has caused the Pope, who deserves to have alongside him collaborators worthy of the task at this historical moment. Collaborators (I speak also of bishops) who will aid him in his mission. Collaborators humble and competent like him, not arrogant and inadequate. Collaborators he evidently has not found. This speaks to the drama of the situation of the Church and the solitude of the Pope."

Bertone, he concluded, could profit from reaching the age of retirement by "dedicating himself to prayer and meditation on the warnings and maternal solicitudes of the Queen of Heaven. In fact, the things of this world soon pass, and forever (including power and, above all, lies). Only the truth remains, which is Jesus Christ. That is, the Truth made flesh. And Who has said: 'There is nothing hidden that will not be revealed. Nothing secret that will not be brought into the light.'"

From the Vatican, there was only silence on the part of Cardinal Bertone. There was nothing he could say against Socci's well-deserved rebukes. For Socci was right to declare that the Pope has "reopened the file" on the Third Secret and that His Holiness is "trying to prepare the Church for this immense trial... entrusting everyone to the hands of the Madonna of Fatima. These are extraordinary hours." Indeed they are.

The Media Awaken

If it is reasonable to think that "The Fatima Challenge" conference and De Carli's appearance there had contributed to the Pope's inauguration of what Socci calls "Operation Truth" concerning the Third Secret, there is no question that what happened at the conference had prompted the Italian media to begin an Operation Truth of their own. On June 23, 2010 several major figures in the Italian press, including no less than Andrea Tornielli, appeared on the "Top Secret" television show on Rete 4, a channel operated by Mediaset, the largest commercial broadcasting company in Italy. The show discussed recent developments in the Third Secret controversy under the title "Fatima: An Unfinished Business"—*the very title of one of the talks delivered at "The Fatima Challenge" conference.*

As the show opened, the narrator declared: "The mystery about the Third Secret does not end with the publication of the Secret. Forty years of silence and reticence have led many people to believe that the Message contains something shocking. There are many questions which still remain open. If the prophecy refers to the failed attempt in 1981, why keep it hidden for 20 years? Those who cast doubts about the interpretation given... think that the Message of Our Lady is actually pointing to the future and would describe apocalyptic scenarios related to the crisis of the faith and the end of the Church."

During the broadcast there was an extraordinary exchange between Tornielli and

Claudio Brachino, a Mediaset journalist, which reflected the very themes Father Gruner's apostolate had been enunciating in its literature and conferences:

> **Brachino:** There are interesting elements in what John Paul II said during various interviews and declarations. In Fatima he spoke about the apostasy—we should tell the public what apostasy is.
>
> **Tornielli:** Yes, it's the "expulsion from the faith," the loss of faith, the ultimate and most terrible thing, because it means that we no longer believe. It should be noted that in his document *Ecclesia in Europa* John Paul II spoke about the apostasy in Europe, a term that indicates *the precise and heavy secularization of the Church, and the fall of any relationship with the absolute.*
>
> **Brachino:** We will discuss this and the apocalyptic vision, but I must insist on this important element: Even among the Catholics, all over the world, *there is suspicion about the official revelation; we're not talking about the secular world or protesters who want to challenge or dispute the Church's policy. We're talking about the so-called Fatimites and other parts of the world's clergy, who do not believe the official version.*

Here we see the widening scepticism regarding the "official" account that had arisen—in large part due to Father Gruner's educative efforts. The conviction that the whole and entire Third Secret relates to apostasy in the Church could no longer be considered unacceptable for Catholics.

This was followed by no fewer than three film clips of Father Gruner himself enumerating reasons to doubt the "official version." The narrator made the obligatory skeptical reference to "Fatimites," but then observed as follows: "However, one can not help but notice some inconsistencies in the text, with regards to the 1981 event of Saint Peter's Square. In the vision of the Third Secret, the 'Bishop dressed in White' falls, killed by a group of soldiers, and after him other men die. Pope Wojtyla, instead, was shot by a single killer, and survived. Is it possible, then, that the official interpretation of the Fatima text is wrong?"

After some typically dismissive comments by Vaticanist Giovanni Ercole about "extremists," the narrator returned to the prevailing theme of reasonable doubt of the "official" version: "But there is another testimony that makes Fatima an unfinished business: Father [Don] Luigi Bianchi, the priest of Gera Lario, in the province of Como, who was a friend of Sister Lucia and met her many times, when she was still alive." In a video clip Bianchi reveals that "The most important thing that I asked Sister Lucia was what she thought we had to expect from this new world, considering that humanity today seems to be so hostile. She said: 'The world is in serious danger.'" When asked by the narrator what precisely Lucia had told him about the Secret, Father Bianchi replied, "Sister Lucia told me that the Secret of Fatima is something *that is still in God's plan*." And that, as we have just seen, is precisely what the Pope said on the plane and during his homily at the Cova da Iria.

The narrator restated yet again the theme of a newly acceptable reasonable doubt: "So is it not yet possible to write the final word on the Fatima Secrets? The debate about the Third Secret of Fatima, which affected almost the entire 20th century, *seems not to be closed*, not even with the death of two of its greatest protagonists,

John Paul II and Sister Lucia." And with that introduction, Brachino and Tornielli conducted a discussion which simply *presumed the existence of two distinct but related texts* of the Third Secret, one of which, kept in the papal apartment, has never been revealed and has been deemed "inauthentic" by Bertone and company. This was precisely what Father Gruner and the "Fatimists" had maintained from the moment the vision was published without the plainly required explanatory words of the Virgin:

> **Brachino:** [A]re there two texts of the Third Secret of Fatima? Or are there multiple interpretations of the revealed text? So, are there two—implying that the Church has only revealed one text or just one part of it?
>
> **Tornielli:** *Well, certainly there are inconsistencies, there is evidence that shows the existence of two manuscripts. One that was kept in the apartment of the Pope and another one at the Holy See archives.* I don't think that we can call them two different texts of the Secret, because the Secret is what has been revealed, that is the vision; *it is possible, however, given what Sister Lucia has sent to the Vatican during the years, that there might be an attachment, or an explanation to it…* [I]t is clear that John XXIII and his successors *didn't consider it as being fully part of the Third Secret, but just as an interpretation given by Sister Lucia* rather than being part of Our Lady's apparition. In this sense it was declassified to a mere, personal interpretation.

Brachino, stating that "I have to push on this point," noted—adopting another "Fatimist" contention—that the famous "etc" indicated something was missing. To this Tornielli frankly replied: "Well, it *certainly gives you the idea of something that continues.* Indeed, in the same booklet published officially by the Vatican *there is no explanation to that sentence,* it remains suspended, and it seems to be referring to something else that *the published version of the Third Secret actually doesn't contain.*" Tornielli's deduction could have been lifted almost verbatim from any number of Father Gruner's publications on the issue.

At this point in the proceedings Brachino introduced the testimony of Archbishop Capovilla as recounted "by Socci's book on Fatima." Capovilla, Brachino noted, had "*admitted to Solideo Paolini in 2006 the existence of two different but complementary texts of the Third Secret.* One was kept at the Holy Office archives, the other one in the apartment of the Pope…" We have already noted Cardinal Bertone's conspicuous emphasis, during his appearance on *Porta a Porta,* on the text located in the archives, and his equally conspicuous avoidance of any reference to the text that everyone now knows was located in the papal apartments.

After showing the same video interview of Capovilla by De Carli that Bertone had aired in September 2007, Tornielli simply dismissed it as unpersuasive and, in a massive setback for Bertone and his "official" version, declared that the existence of a second text of some sort pertaining to the Third Secret is now *well established*:

> **Tornielli:** Yes, we have just seen the interview of Capovilla, in which he said that there is no fourth secret. *But we must remember one fact: Capovilla has repeatedly said that a text of the Secret, an "attachment," has always been kept inside the desk of the Pope, and has stated that it was he who revealed to Pope Paul VI, just a few days after his election, the place where the Secret was located: he told him that the text was kept*

> *inside John XXIII's desk called "Barbarigo".* When John XXIII read the Secret in 1959, he decided not to publish it, and Capovilla wrote a note on the envelope (this is confirmed not only by Capovilla, but also by Paul VI, who found that note on Capovilla's envelope). *Now, when it was shown on television in 2007 [on* Porta a Porta*], [Cardinal Bertone] showed the envelopes to the cameras, and there was no handwriting by Capovilla on it....* Not all the time when there is an evidence does it have to confirm a certain theory... ***But the existence of two texts in two different places seems to me now a well-established fact.***

Now the discussion was joined by Alessandro Banfi, a prominent Vaticanist, who praised "the reasoning that inspired Socci, with courage and great skill," to question the official version, and then asked and answered his own question, with devastating impact to the credibility of Bertone's position: "This is the matter which I think we should talk about: Is the successor of Peter in possession of a more complete version of the vision, with deeper and confidential information? *In my opinion it is quite credible*. But it was also more than possible a few weeks ago that this controversy could have never been solved. And now the Pope, as always, *has reopened the discussion about it*!" To which Brachino replied: "And he did indeed, as I said at the beginning of the transmission, in a very sensational way. Probably it was a decision that is part of Ratzinger's overall project, his new 'Operation Truth' for a different attitude within the Church, even with regards to herself."

These publicly administered hammer-blows to the Secretary of State's version of events were followed by discussion of "the dramatic problem of the apostasy" (Banfi), "the abandoning of the faith, but by the members of the Church themselves" (Brachino), "the abandoning of the faith inside the Church. Exactly." (Banfi). Then, following a video segment on Ali Agca and the 1981 assassination attempt, Brachino, Tornielli and Banfi took aim at the Sodano/Bertone "interpretation" that would require the events foretold in the Third Secret to "be interpreted as if they were referring to the past, and precisely to the assassination attempt against John Paul II on May 13, 1981, in St. Peter's Square." What Socci called the "preventative interpretation" was essentially deemed no longer operative, particularly in view of the Pope's statement during his flight to Portugal:

> **Brachino:** I want to ask Andrea Tornielli the following question: Between what is shown in the vision and what happened in St. Peter's Square, I don't think the two events coincide: in the vision the Pope died, but in 1981 he survived!
>
> **Tornielli:** The big difference is that Pope John Paul II didn't die, he fell "as if dead", to use the same expression used by Cardinal Sodano in 2000. But we must also say, as Ratzinger himself said in the presentation of the official Secret, that these prophecies are not a "film about the future"... *but that inconsistency is there.*
>
> **Brachino:** About this interpretation, Mr. Banfi, there are many things *that are actually leading us away from the true interpretation of the Third Secret that is being* given now [by Pope Benedict]. If not everything has to happen afterwards, *certainly not everything has happened already*!
>
> **Banfi:** True, the plot that leads to the attack against John Paul II has

> not been clarified yet: Okay, Ali Agca was caught and imprisoned, but it is hard to understand any connection, any link between that event and Providence, its secret designs, as Sodano tried to imply in his interpretation of the Secret. *So there's more than one contradiction that leaves us perplexed*. Moreover, the vision speaks of arrows and shots, so not just a single gunshot, but a collective attack. ***The vision suggests a Vatican which seems to have been bombed and is now just a heap of rubble; the remaining faithful would climb the hill towards the cross, and those soldiers would attack them, and the Pope, with arrows and bullets, killing them all.***

Brachino, just before playing a video of Pope Benedict's stunning remarks on the papal plane, returned to the theme sounded by Socci, declaring: "On May 13, 2010, another Pope, Benedict XVI, made some remarkable statements *which reopened the case*. On May 13, *a date that will remain forever in the history of Catholicism*." Brachino punctuated the video with a comment that indicated that the Italian media, joining Catholics all over the world, now recognized that a new chapter had been opened in the Third Secret controversy in a book that would not be closed until the whole story is read, a chapter in which the Secret as a prophecy of apostasy in the Church is revealed: "Here Benedict XVI brings to mind the speeches of Paul VI about the '*smoke of Satan within the Church*,' and it seems also to echo the great writings of Charles Hodge, who spoke about Christianity after Christ and without Christ. What comes to our minds is the dramatic question, in the form of poetry, posed by T. S. Eliot: 'Is it the Church that has abandoned humanity, or is it humanity that has abandoned the Church?'"

The Mediaset broadcast demonstrated that, years after the Vatican Secretary of State had ventured to put an end to the Third Secret of Fatima and the Message of Fatima as a whole, there was an ever-growing awareness among the faithful that the prophecies and warnings of the Virgin Mother of God to Lucia, Jacinta and Francisco were more alive, and more urgent, than ever. The "official" version had been completely overturned in the court of public opinion.

An Untimely Passing

Less than three weeks after the critical dissection of the official account on Mediaset, Giuseppe De Carli, age 58, passed away unexpectedly at Gemelli Polyclinic in Rome, reportedly while undergoing radiotherapy for a suddenly discovered inoperable throat cancer. Gemelli was the same hospital in which John Paul II had called for the text of the vision in 1981 while recovering from the nearly fatal wounds Ali Agca had inflicted on him.

Did De Carli know about his terminal illness when he appeared at "The Fatima Challenge" conference, stepping from behind the Vatican's stone wall of silence and evasion to encounter his fellow Catholics on the revealing ground of a free and open discussion in search of the truth? Or did he discover his illness after his appearance at the Ergife Hotel? We do not know. But we do know that, along with the conference as a whole, De Carli's decision to appear and attempt a defense of Bertone's indefensible position must have contributed to the impetus for Pope Benedict's "Operation Truth," an operation that, one must hope and pray, will lead at last to a full disclosure of the Virgin of Fatima's message-warning to the Church and all humanity, while there is still time to avert the worst of what it foretells.

Giuseppe De Carli died on July 13, 2010, the very anniversary of the day on which the Mother of God revealed the Third Secret in its entirety to the seers of Fatima. There are no mere coincidences in the designs of Providence.

Pope Benedict XVI, at the end of his Papal Audience on May 11, 2011, went 50 yards from the podium to bless various statues including the Fatima Center's Pilgrim Virgin Statue of Our Lady of Fatima. On the opposite angle of the camera, Father Gruner stands beside the statue with John Salza, who gratefully receive the Pope's blessing. The Fatima Center's Pilgrim Virgin Statue had also been blessed by Pope Paul VI at Fatima with the express purpose to travel and promote Our Lady's Message.

Chapter 28

A Path to Victory

By April of 2011 it was apparent that the Pope was well aware of the Fatima Center's continuing initiatives and that, at least indirectly, he was responding to them. On April 22, 2011, Good Friday, the Pope made an unprecedented appearance on a TV call-in show to take selected questions from the viewers. The very last question he chose to answer included this query: "... And, on the subject of entrusting, do you intend to renew a consecration to the Virgin at the beginning of this new millennium?"

As with the pre-selected questions during the flight to Portugal a year earlier, this was clearly a matter the Pope wished to address. He replied in a manner that suggested at least some doubt whether the 1984 ceremony performed by John Paul II was the consecration Our Lady of Fatima had requested:

> I *think* that the great, public act has been made. *Perhaps one day it will be necessary to repeat it again*, but *at the moment* it seems more important to me to live it, to make it real, to enter into this entrusting so that it might truly be our own.... Thus, *at the moment*, I do not intend to make a new act of public entrustment, but I would rather invite you to enter into this entrustment that has already been made...[363]

The Pope "thinks" that the public act has been done, but he stops short of declaring this definitively. He stops short because he is not certain. Why else would His Holiness even entertain the possibility of repeating the "entrustment" of 1984 if, as the Secretary of State's Party Line insisted, the 1984 ceremony certainly complied with Our Lady's request? And why would His Holiness say "at the moment" he did not intend to perform another ceremony in obedience to the Virgin's request if he were not aware of the possibility that at a later moment—perhaps very soon—the reality of the situation in the Church and the world might compel him to try again, as it was apparent that the promised conversion of Russia and a period of peace in the world had never arrived?

Indeed, Pope Benedict had repeatedly made pronouncements that depart from the inexplicable "optimism" of the post-Vatican II era and return to the line of his pre-conciliar predecessors and their grave warnings for the Church and humanity. There is no longer any pretense of a "renewal" of the Church after the Council:

> The darkness that poses *a real threat to mankind*, after all, is the fact that he can see and investigate tangible material things, but cannot see where the world is going or whence it comes, where our own life is going, what is good and what is evil. The darkness enshrouding God and obscuring values is *the real threat to our existence and to the world in general*.[364]
>
> In our days, when *in vast areas of the world the faith is in danger of dying out like a flame which no longer has fuel*, the overriding priority is to make God present in this world and to show men and women the way to God. Not just any god, but the God who spoke on Sinai; to that God whose face we recognize in a love which presses "to the

---

363 vatican.va/holy_father/benedict_xvi/speeches/2011/april/documents/hf_ben-xvi_spe_20110422_intervista_en.html

364 Pope Benedict XVI's homily for the Easter Vigil, April 7, 2012.

> end" (cf. Jn 13:1)—in Jesus Christ, crucified and risen. The real problem at this moment of our history is that *God is disappearing from the human horizon*, and, with the dimming of the light which comes from God, *humanity is losing its bearings, with increasingly evident destructive effects*.[365]
>
> How many winds of doctrine we have known in recent decades, how many ideological currents, how many ways of thinking... The small boat of thought of many Christians has often been tossed about by these waves—thrown from one extreme to the other: from Marxism to liberalism, even to libertinism; from collectivism to radical individualism; from atheism to a vague religious mysticism; from agnosticism to syncretism, and so forth.... *We are moving towards a dictatorship of relativism* which does not recognize anything as certain and which has as its highest goal one's own ego and one's own desires.[366]
>
> In the Old and New Testaments, the Lord proclaims *judgment on the unfaithful* vineyard. The judgment that Isaiah foresaw is brought about in the *great wars and exiles* for which the Assyrians and Babylonians were responsible. The judgment announced by the Lord Jesus refers above all to the destruction of Jerusalem in the year 70. *Yet the threat of judgment also concerns us, the Church in Europe, Europe and the West in general.* With this Gospel, the Lord is also crying out to our ears the words that in the Book of Revelation He addresses to the Church of Ephesus: "*If you do not repent I will come to you and remove your lampstand from its place*" (2:5).[367]

Thus the Pope himself has repeatedly heralded a coming apocalypse—like that apparently seen in the vision of the "Bishop dressed in White." He could not have put the matter more starkly: "a real threat to mankind" and "the real threat to our existence and to the world in general." And yet the Consecration of Russia could avert the scene of devastation that the vision presents to us, albeit without the precise warning the Virgin must have attached to the vision in the words we have yet to see.

Pope Benedict is evidently gravely concerned about a link between the crisis in the Church and the growing civilizational crisis of a once Christian West. As Christopher Ferrara has observed in his work *False Friends of Fatima*, the Pope seems to harbor the intention "to reverse the Church's course over the past forty years, to reverse its ruinous 'new orientation,' of which the 'new' Message of Fatima is a part." For that reason, notes Ferrara, Pope Benedict has taken several steps to restore order in the Church: "[He] has 'liberated' the traditional Latin Mass, declaring that every priest in the Church is free to offer it. He has refused any longer to distribute Communion in the hand at papal Masses. He has called for a 'hermeneutic of continuity' between Vatican II and the Church's constant teaching before the Council—in itself a devastating admission that something is wrong with the Council. He has lifted the 'excommunication' of the bishops of the Society of Saint Pius X, initiating theological discussions with the Society's representatives precisely on the question of Vatican II's conformity with Catholic Tradition."

---

365 Letter of His Holiness Pope Benedict XVI to the bishops of the Catholic Church, March 10, 2009.

366 Cardinal Ratzinger's homily for the Pro Eligendo Summo Pontifice Mass, 18 April 2005.

367 Pope Benedict XVI, homily for the opening of the 11th Ordinary General Assembly of the Synod of Bishops, Rome, October 2, 2005.

In addition to these measures of true reform and restoration, will this Pope finally accomplish the definitive Consecration of Russia in the manner Our Lady requested? Throughout 2011 Father Gruner continued to work and pray for that outcome. And yet again his persistence would find a reward, if not in fact the fulfillment of Our Lady's request.

A New Frontier

On April 15, 2011, the Fatima Center entered an entirely new frontier in its campaign for the Consecration and full disclosure of the Third Secret. On that date the apostolate's latest initiative, Fatima TV, conducted its first digital TV broadcast on Channel 213 in Rome. That the channel number coincided with the date of Sister Lucia's death (February 13) was another of those "coincidences" that could not fail to suggest a providential intervention on the apostolate's behalf.

With the audacious initiative of acquiring a TV channel in Rome, the apostolate had introduced into the very heart of the Church a voice in the most powerful medium of social communication ever devised; and that voice would be a standing rebuke to the plans and policies of a Vatican apparatus that had for far too long impeded the accomplishment of the great mission the Mother of God had assigned to Her Church at Fatima.

About two weeks before the launch of Fatima TV, Father Gruner gave an interview in the studio of the new channel to representatives of Rai Uno, Italy's largest state-sponsored television network. Over the next two hours he provided the interviewer with a thorough overview of the entire Fatima affair, with special emphasis on Cardinal Bertone's role in the Vatican cover-up of the missing text of the Secret. That Rai Uno had deemed Father Gruner an authoritative source on Fatima in general and the Third Secret in particular, a source worthy of a primary interview on the subject, was itself a breakthrough for the legitimation of the "Fatimist" position. What was once dismissed as "Fatimist" extremism was rapidly assuming the character of respectable Catholic opinion even in the eyes of the formerly skeptical—even in Rome itself.

While only a few sound bites from the interview were included in Rai Uno's later program on Fatima, it was obvious that the network had confronted Cardinal Bertone with the substance of Father Gruner's contentions. On April 30, Cardinal Bertone appeared on the major Italian radio station, GR 1, for an interview with its director, Antonio Preziosi. In the course of the interview, which related primarily to the pending beatification of John Paul II, Bertone made an astonishing admission respecting both the Consecration of Russia and the Third Secret: "The third mystery of Fatima is accomplished *in part* in the description given by Sister Lucia, but as (then) Cardinal Ratzinger said, the Immaculate Heart of Mary *will* triumph. It is necessary to cultivate hope and not be catastrophists."[368]

This was a statement ripe with implications decidedly at odds with the Party Line Bertone had hitherto been promoting. For "the description given by Sister Lucia" was none other than the vision published in 2000, so that if what the vision depicts is but a partial fulfillment of the Secret, then there must be more than the vision. Where is it? And if the Triumph of the Immaculate Heart remains an event that will happen in the future, and is thus not unfolding before us now, then what becomes of the Party

[368] "Il terzo mistero di Fatima è compiuto in parte nella descrizione che è stata fatta da suor Lucia, ma come ha detto (l'allora) cardinale Ratzinger il cuore immacolato di Maria trionferà. Bisogna coltivare la speranza e non essere catastrofici". Andrea Tornielli, "Il Terzo Segreto non é compiuto," http://2.andreatornielli.it/?p=1562.

Line that Russia was consecrated to the Immaculate Heart in 1984? The Blessed Virgin promised that Her Immaculate Heart would triumph precisely upon the moment of Russia's consecration; in fact, the Consecration is *part of that triumph*: "In the end My Immaculate Heart will triumph. The Holy Father will consecrate Russia to Me, which will be converted, and a period of peace will be granted to the world." Yet, twenty-seven years after the 1984 ceremony, Bertone now admitted that the Triumph of the Immaculate Heart had not occurred, referring instead to the indefinite future. But he could hardly do otherwise, given the manifest failure of Russia to convert and a general state of world affairs that bespoke anything but a triumph for the Mother of God.

Moreover, the suggestion that one ought to cultivate hope instead of being a "catastrophist" was quite telling. Hope in what? Evidently, hope that the Triumph of the Immaculate Heart would *avert catastrophe*. But how could catastrophe be averted if Mary's triumph was still only an event in the indeterminate future? Had there been a valid consecration in 1984, as Bertone would have the public believe, there would be no need for hope in 2011 that catastrophes would be averted, for the Triumph of the Immaculate Heart would already be manifest and there would be no reason to fear any catastrophe. And just what did Bertone have in mind when he introduced the concept of catastrophe into the discussion? Does he know something the faithful do not know?

Andrea Tornielli did not miss the significance of Bertone's remark, linking it to the Pope's own explosive statements on the flight to Portugal during his pilgrimage of 2010. Noting that "there does not exist an official interpretation of that text [the vision published in 2000]"—another victory for the "Fatimist" position—Tornielli observed that Bertone's admission that the Secret had been accomplished only "in part" was "in full harmony with what was affirmed by Benedict XVI on the flight that carried him to Portugal… as well as in a passage of the homily for the Mass celebrated at Fatima."[369]

Father Gruner's relentless pursuit of the truth had earned him the serious attention of Rai Uno and thus Bertone. That development had no doubt helped to provoke yet another chink in the crumbling edifice of Bertone's pseudo-official account of the Third Secret, which had already been jettisoned by the Pope himself at Fatima.

Pope Benedict Consecrates Italy to the Immaculate Heart

On the same date as the launching of Fatima TV (April 15), the Fatima Center commenced a massive publicity campaign for the Consecration of Russia. Among other initiatives, the Center's Rome headquarters arranged for the placement of a giant poster calling for the Consecration in Porta di Roma, the city's busiest shopping mall. An arresting image of Our Lady was accompanied by the words: "Only the Pope can save Rome! By a special prayer of only five minutes." That is, the campaign tied the fate of Rome in particular to the fate of the world in general, failing Russia's consecration.

All told, more than a million people saw the poster at Porta di Roma, and millions more saw posters at other locations in Rome or heard advertorials and radio advertisements for the Fatima Center's upcoming "Consecration Now!" conference (to be held May 9-13). Pilgrims attended the Pope's Wednesday audience on May 11, 2011 with a large "Consecration Now!" banner directly in the Pope's line of sight. Among those pilgrims were Father Gruner and John Salza, who received personal blessings from the Pope in the private viewing area behind the Pope's *sedia*. (In a censorship operation

---

369 Tornielli, loc. cit. ("Va qui ricordato che, come venne spiegato al momento della pubblicazione del Terzo segreto, nel giugno 2000, non esiste una interpretazione ufficiale di quel testo… Parole in piena sintonia con quanto affermato da Benedetto XVI sul volo che lo portava in Portogallo, un anno fa, come pure in un passaggio dell'omelia della messa celebrata a Fatima.")

typical of the Secretary of State's tight control over information flowing both in and out of the Vatican, as noted above, and in footnote 346, Father Gruner's likeness was digitally edited out of five of the six photographs of the blessings taken by the papal photographer.)

By linking the Message of Fatima to the welfare of Rome, the campaign brought Fatima home to Romans with astonishing effect. The Fatima Center's office at Piazza Risorgimento was flooded with phone calls. The callers were informed about Our Lady of Fatima's request concerning Russia and of the chastisements She warned would follow if Her request were ignored, including the "annihilation" of "various nations." But the tenor of these conversations was not gloom and doom. Rather, as the Center's newsletter noted, "we told them about the wonderful mercy of Our Lady, Who has given the Church and the world Her promise of protection in exchange for a simple act of consecration."

Pictured above, in English translation, is one of the 70 outdoor signs (13' X 9.75') displayed around Rome two weeks prior to the Conference.

The publicity campaign had undoubtedly had its effect on the Pope, for only 11 days after saying he would do no Consecration, and only six days before the commencement of the "Consecration Now!" conference, His Holiness announced that he would "entrust" Italy to the Immaculate Heart—yet another substitute for what Our Lady requested! On May 26, 2011, Pope Benedict, together with the Italian bishops, would conduct a public "Act of Entrustment" of the people of Italy to the Immaculate Heart in the great Roman basilica of Saint Mary Major.[370]

"Is the Pope preparing the world for THE BIG CONSECRATION?" the Center's newsletter later queried. Father Gruner offered this assessment: "I believe he is. I pray that he is. I will do all I can to encourage the Holy Father, as I know you will by your support for Our Lady's Apostolate, which is so crucial at this time." As Father Gruner astutely observed: "Pope Benedict has set a precedent. He has put it in the mind of the bishops that together they can consecrate a nation—by name—to Our Lady. If Italy, why not Russia?" Why not, indeed?

Another Breakthrough Conference

While the Pope was preparing to consecrate Italy to the Immaculate Heart, the Fatima Center's "Consecration Now!" conference, held at the Ergife Hotel in Rome from May 9-13, 2011, produced further unprecedented advances for the work of the apostolate. In attendance for the proceedings was no less than Cardinal Renato Martino, former Prefect of two Vatican Congregations and the Vatican's permanent observer

[370] Cf. "Pope Entrusts Italy to the Virgin's Protection," May 27, 2011, Vatican Information Service, http://visnews-en.blogspot.com/2011/05/pope-entrusts-italy-to-virgins.html.

at the United Nations. He had thus served directly under the very Secretary of State whose complicity in blocking the Consecration of Russia and concealing the yet-to-be disclosed text of the Third Secret were principal subjects of the addresses given. Yet this Vatican Cardinal listened attentively and appreciatively to those very speakers.

A veteran Vatican journalist also in attendance remarked to Father Gruner that "Something has changed in the Vatican." In a moment that indicated just such an historic shift, Father Gruner approached Cardinal Martino to thank him for his attendance, and the Cardinal, taking Father Gruner's hand, uttered one word in Italian that could not have been more significant: *Coraggio*! Courage. The implication being that Father Gruner was engaged in a cause that required precisely what he had exhibited for so many years: the courage of perseverance in the face of opposition that, humanly speaking, seemed impossible to overcome. But Father Gruner would be the first to point out that all things are possible with God, Who mediates His graces through Her Who had come to give both dire warnings and precious promises to the Church and the world at Fatima.

If further proof of the growing mainstream acceptability of the "Fatimist" position were wanting, it was provided by the attendance at the conference of two prominent Vaticanists: the world-renowned Andrea Tornielli and the rising star Paolo Rodari. These first-rank Italian journalists and commentators not only attended the conference but also addressed its participants, who once would have been dismissed as a "Fatimist" fringe group but were now being taken quite seriously as a legitimate constituency of the faithful.

Tornielli's address clearly linked the post-Vatican II crisis in the Church to the contents of the Third Secret of Fatima—a stunning assessment, coming from a Vatican-accredited journalist whose career revolves around access to the corridors of power and influence in the Vatican controlled by the Secretary of State. Referring to his biography of Paul VI, Tornielli dropped a bombshell: that Pope Paul had specifically linked the mass defection of priests after Vatican II to the Third Secret, and that this is what had prompted his papal pilgrimage to Fatima on May 13, 1967. It cannot have been a mere happenstance that Paul VI chose the occasion of his sermon at Fatima on this date to lament that the "renewal" of the Church after Vatican II was going wrong: "What an evil it would be if an arbitrary interpretation, not authorized by the Magisterium, transformed this renewal into a disquieting disintegration of her traditional structure and constitution, substituting for the theology of the true and great teachers, new and particular ideologies intended to detach modern thought from the norm of faith..."[371] The same Pope would famously lament five years later that

> By some fissure the smoke of satan has entered into the temple of God: there is doubt, uncertainty, problems, unrest. Doubt has entered our consciences, *and it has entered through the windows which were meant to have been opened to the light*. This state of uncertainty reigns even in the Church. It was hoped that after the Council there would be a day of sunlight in the history of the Church. *Instead, there came a day of clouds, of darkness, of groping, of uncertainty*. How did this happen? We will confide Our thoughts to you: there has been interference from

371 "Quale danno sarebbe se un'interpretazione arbitraria e non autorizzata dal magistero della Chiesa facesse di questo risveglio un'inquietudine dissolvitrice della sua tradizionale e costituzionale compagine, sostituisse alla teologia dei veri e grandi maestri ideologie nuove e particolari, intese a togliere dalla norma della fede quanto il pensiero modern..." Homily at the Sanctuary of Our Lady of Fatima, May 13, 1967, http://www.vatican.va/holy_father/paul_vi/homilies/1967/documents/hf_p-vi_hom_19670513_it.html.

an adverse power: *his name is the devil...*[372]

It was one year after this stunning admission that Pope Paul would further admit publicly that perhaps he himself had contributed to the debacle of what was being vaunted as the Church's long-overdue "opening to the world" following the Council: "the opening to the world became a veritable invasion of the Church by worldly thinking. We have perhaps been too weak and imprudent."[373]

These historic papal admissions of the vast ecclesial disturbances following the Second Vatican Council were clearly consistent with Tornielli's revelation that Paul VI knew that the Third Secret related to the post-conciliar internal crisis in the Church. Yet the vision published in 2000, standing alone, clearly gives no indication of any such internal crisis. The only reasonable inference was that the text of the Secret that Pope Paul read in 1963—a reading not mentioned in the "official account," which refers only to a reading in 1965—must be the missing companion to the vision. That companion text must explain the vision's full significance, relating the catastrophe it depicts to a collapse of faith and discipline within the Church accompanying the attack by external enemies seen in the vision.

For his part, Rodari boldly outlined the serious contradictions in Cardinal Bertone's account of the Third Secret and noted that in recent days it appeared that, in the face of mounting evidence of a cover-up, there was now "a will to say something" in the Vatican, as indicated by Bertone's comment that the Third Secret—contrary to everything he had said before—has been fulfilled only "in part." Both Tornielli and Rodari admitted the possibility that Bertone was concealing a text containing the part of the Secret not disclosed by the vision alone, a suspicion that by now had ripened into a presumptive truth in the mainstream Italian media.

That a Vatican Cardinal and two Vaticanists of the first rank had appeared at this conference in a manner sympathetic to its themes marked a new stage in the progress of the cause for which the Fatima Priest had been laboring for decades. By the end of 2011, Father Gruner could discern the opening up of a broad new path toward victory for the cause. For now even respectable voices in the mainstream of public opinion, and even from within the Vatican apparatus, were acknowledging the absolute seriousness of the Fatima event and the failure of the upper hierarchy to fulfill the mandate the Virgin had given Her Church at that place nearly a century before.

372 Paul VI, *Insegnamenti*, Ed. Vaticana, Vol. X, 1972, p. 707.

373 Speech of November 23, 1973.

Chapter 29

A Last Chance

From May 13-18, 2012, the Fatima Center staged in Rome yet another Fatima conference in the Vatican's shadow. The theme, "Fatima: Your Last Chance," reflected the growing urgency of the Fatima Message at a time when even Pope Benedict was warning that "moral consensus is collapsing, consensus without which juridical and political structures cannot function. Consequently, the forces mobilized for the defense of such structures seem doomed to failure... *The very future of the world is at stake*."[374] Here the Pope indicated a return to the line of sober realism concerning the so-called modern world that had characterized the teaching of all of his predecessors before the delusional "optimism" attributed to the Second Vatican Council.

An Extraordinary Intervention

It seemed that every conference staged by the Center since "The Fatima Challenge" in 2010 was destined to produce yet another breakthrough for the movement to bring about, at long last, a fulfillment of the Fatima mandate by a true and proper Consecration of Russia and complete disclosure of the Third Secret. The breakthrough this time was into the sphere of political activity. The Honorable Mario Borghezio, an Italian representative to the Parliament of the European Union, delivered an extraordinary address on a theme to which he had been drawn by the apostolate's work: the duty even of political authorities, for the sake of the common good of all men, to seek Russia's consecration to the Immaculate Heart. Borghezio made this stunning announcement:

> I will ask the Catholic Members of the European Parliament (but nothing stops others from joining us in this initiative) to support and sign a motion in order to bring the Message of Fatima, through the European Parliament, to the attention of the over 400 million people of the European Union, represented by the 27 member States. Afterwards, I will also try to involve the Catholic members of the Europe-Russia Commission, of which I'm an effective member, to hear and obey the Message of Heaven to consecrate Russia to the Immaculate Heart of Mary.

Borghezio noted that he was already deeply involved in opposition to the globalist and anti-Christian agenda of the EU Parliament itself, "which unfortunately is causing much suffering and disappointments with its decisions—decisions which I, together with other Members of Parliament, tried to oppose and resist." But now he was calling for a spiritual resistance movement led by the very Mother of God, thus breaking the pernicious and quite imaginary "wall of separation" between religion and politics demanded by the powers that be.

A Catholic Declaration of Independence

Given the dire moral, political and economic state of European and world affairs, Borghezio declared, Russia's consecration to Mary "is a duty of every single Catholic politician because I believe that the Message of Fatima is addressed mostly and fundamentally to whoever has political responsibilities! In this period of history, there

[374] Benedict XVI, "Christmas Greeting to the Roman Curia", December 20, 2010.

are dangers threatening peace—like a possible nuclear war, the problems with Iran and terrorism, from which Italy has suffered a huge blow just a few days ago—but also dangers that, at a superficial view, might seem less important. I'm talking about the financial and economic crisis."

Borghezio's landmark address concluded with an act of political courage almost unheard of in a "modern world" that has turned its back on God. He dared to condemn the betrayal of Europe's Catholic heritage by its political and economic leaders, and to call upon the faithful to rise up against the traitors:

> This is another very important point: the Europe of the Cathedrals, the Europe of the churches, the Europe of the humble Faith, the Europe of the people who work, pray, sacrifice and suffer and are now regrettably under control by the world banking system and its usury! Now, that Europe, the Europe of our people, is not dead, because WE are that Europe!

But Borghezio was not calling for any sort of revolution in the rebellious modern sense, but rather a spiritual turning about in the hearts and minds of both rulers and subjects that would, as Antonio Socci had put it in his exposé of the Third Secret cover-up, "overthrow the mentality dominating modernity." The Message of Fatima, said Borghezio, "asks the world to open its eyes, mainly regarding freedom: terrorism, financial crisis, wars, even a nuclear one—God be merciful to us—three terrifying dangers that threaten humanity, and all three have to do with a fundamental point: freedom!"

What Borghezio had called for was nothing less than a Catholic declaration of independence from the powers that had for so long been dominating the modern world and arraying themselves in opposition to the Church's salvific mission to all nations. Soon Borghezio would make good on his commitment to bring the Message of Fatima into the very nerve center of Europe's aridly secularist, post-Christian regime: the EU Parliament. And Father Gruner would be a prominent part of that historic event.

A Key Endorsement from Beyond the Grave

Some three months after the "Last Chance" conference, evidence surfaced that another high-ranking member of the Secretariat of State had rejected the Secretary of State's Party Line on Fatima, thus further corroborating the veteran Vatican journalist's advice to Father Gruner that "something has changed in the Vatican." The evidence was in the form of an endorsement of Christopher Ferrara's *The Secret Still Hidden* by no less than Archbishop Pietro Sambi, who had served as Papal Nuncio to the United States and was thus a member of the Secretariat of State's top tier. This endorsement appeared in the August 2011 issue of the prestigious Catholic review *Inside the Vatican*, a month after Sambi's death. An article by editor-in-chief Robert Moynihan, entitled "Passing of a Friend," pays tribute to Sambi and discusses some of his fond memories of the man. One of these was a discussion of the question whether the Vatican was concealing part of the Third Secret:

> We were discussing the Third Secret of Fatima, the allegations that the Vatican has not published the entire text of the Third Secret as revealed to Sister Lucia, and the response of Cardinal Tarcisio Bertone, the Vatican Secretary of State, in a book where Bertone states that there is nothing more to be revealed.
>
> Archbishop Sambi said, "Excuse me." He got up, went out of the room,

> and came back with a book. "Here," he said. "Do you know this book? You should read it." It was Christopher Ferrara's *The Secret Still Hidden*.
>
> "Wait," I said. "You are the Pope's representative in the US, and *you are urging me to read a book that questions what the Secretary of State wrote*?"
>
> Archbishop Sambi replied, "All I am saying is that there are interesting things worth reading in this book. And in the end, we are all after the truth, aren't we? The truth is the important thing ..."[375]

This stunning endorsement—from beyond the grave—of a meticulous indictment of the Secretary of State's cover-up of the Third Secret, coming from one of the Secretary's highest-ranking attachés, was yet another tribute to the work of the Fatima Center, whose driving force was a lone, persistent priest from Canada. The truth is indeed the important thing. And as the Year of Our Lord 2012 moved toward its conclusion, the truth about the Third Secret and the Message of Fatima as a whole was rising to the surface with irresistible force.

Zenit Abandons the Party Line

By the fall of 2012 it seemed that barrier after barrier was falling before the advance of the cause to which Father Gruner had first dedicated himself thirty-five years earlier. In yet another testament to Father Gruner's perseverance, the prominent "mainstream" Catholic news agency Zenit, which boasts 520,000 subscribers and is semi-officially a press arm of the Vatican, ran a major story that implicitly endorsed the entire program of his Fatima apostolate.

The article by Edward Pentin must be considered a minor revolution in mainstream Catholic opinion, which for so long had belittled the "Fatimists" and their insistence that Russia had never been consecrated to the Immaculate Heart. Pentin remarked the coming 1700th anniversary of Emperor Constantine's victory at the Milvian Bridge on October 28, 312, which the Emperor attributed to the miraculous intervention of Christ, prompting the Emperor's conversion, which began the conversion of the entire Western world.[376] Pentin quoted Edmund Mazza, a professor of history and political science at Azusa Pacific University in Los Angeles, for the proposition that the so-called modern world "has forgotten its Christian origins ... People are concerned about saving the planet, global warming, and so forth, and there's certain legitimate concerns here, but what we've lost is an awareness of the salvation of the soul." As a result, "*we're either nearing the End Times or we're in the End Times*, because what we have is the disintegration of Christian civilization."

Mazza specifically linked this situation to the unheeded Message of Fatima: "It [the Message of Fatima] foretold the Bolsheviks would take over Russia, institute a secular socialism where government controls everything, tells everyone what to do, and where government contradicts the people's religion, Christianity in particular." "And what do we see today?" he asked. Answering his own question he noted,

> In America, the Church is being persecuted now quite openly; individual Christians, let alone Church institutions, are going to be

375 "Third Secret Breakthrough; *Inside the Vatican* Reveals: Papal Nuncio to US Endorsed Chris Ferrara's Book *The Secret Still Hidden*," *The Remnant*, August 6, 2011, www.remnantnewspaper.com/Archives/2011-0815-ferrar-nuncio-inside-vatican.htm; cf: "Papal Nuncio, Archbishop Pietro Sambi Endorses Christopher Ferrara's Book: *The Secret Still Hidden*", at http://www.fatimacrusader.com/cr100/cr100pg56.pdf.

376 Edward Pentin, "The New Evangelization of the Modern World," October 11, 2012, http://www.zenit.org/article-35701?l=english.

> forced to pay for contraception and abortifacients, to go against their moral principles. It's Diocletian's persecution all over again: if you refuse to follow the norms of state, you're going to suffer.

Pentin ran with the Fatima theme, observing:

> During the apparitions, Our Lady of Fatima talks about the 'errors of Russia,' meaning the errors of atheism and socialism which would lead to the deaths of 60 million people in the 20th century. 'Russia will spread her errors throughout the world,' She warned, 'raising up wars and persecutions against the Church, the good will be martyred, the Holy Father will have much to suffer, various nations will be annihilated.

In this connection Pentin quoted Edward Lucas, a correspondent for *The Economist* who spoke at the same conference as Mazza, to the effect that "instead of spending millions of dollars on weapons as it did during the Cold War, Russia is now a state of espionage and deception, with a former KGB agent as its president—a remarkable reality if one imagines the Nazis had won World War II and then, after it had collapsed, they remained in power." In other words, Russia had clearly not converted; her errors continue to spread about the world. Here Pentin quotes Mazza to the effect that Russia's errors are like "a vampire that refuses to die. 'If you want to kill a vampire, you can't shoot it, you've got to use a wooden stake.'"

And what was the wooden stake that would kill the vampire? Here Mazza introduced the revolutionary change of opinion: "Jesus and Mary gave us the solution: *the Consecration of Russia*." Mazza, Pentin noted uncritically, had observed that while John Paul II "consecrated the whole world in 1984… Russia *has still not been singled out for consecration*." And then the amazing clincher—not from any "Fatimist," but from Mazza, a college professor in Los Angeles writing for perhaps the most widely read Internet Catholic news service:

> The only thing that will kill the errors of socialism and the dictatorship of relativism that the Pope has talked about is this: *We need the Pope and the bishops to take five minutes of a public ceremony in which they consecrate Russia to Mary's Immaculate Heart.*

As John Vennari noted, Mazza's reference to "five minutes of a public ceremony" is one of the themes the publications of the Fatima Center had sounded often: a brief public ceremony that will change the world, if only the Pope and the bishops will make that minimal effort. In fact, the theme of "a five-minute prayer" was precisely that of the Center's Roman publicity campaign in 2011, which had clearly provoked the papal consecration of Italy in that year. And then another clincher, this time from Pentin by way of Zenit: "The Year of Faith may be the perfect time to do so."

Thus did a mainstream news service with close ties to the Vatican matter-of-factly present the view that only the Consecration of Russia to the Immaculate Heart could avert disaster for the West, that this Consecration has not yet been performed, and that the Year of Faith proclaimed by Pope Benedict would be the perfect time to perform it. There could hardly have been a more resounding public validation of the primary aim of Father Gruner's apostolic work of the past thirty-five years.

Breakthrough at Strasbourg

But there was still another, even more dramatic, breakthrough into the wider world for the cause of Fatima. On October 23, 2012, Father Gruner and Christopher Ferrara appeared at the headquarters of the Parliament of the European Union in Strasbourg, France to speak in support of an absolutely unprecedented motion in modern political society: *a declaration by the EU Parliament calling upon Pope Benedict XVI to carry out the Consecration of Russia to the Immaculate Heart of Mary.* Two members of the Parliament, the Honorable Mario Borghezio and the Honorable Lorenzo Fontana, sponsored the motion and invited Father Gruner and Mr. Ferrara to speak in its support at the time of its official introduction.

The text of the historic measure refers to the threat of "great danger at the present time to world peace and the serenity of all European peoples" and notes that "the Blessed Virgin Mary has promised a long period of prosperity and peace, if and only if, the Holy Father will consecrate Russia in a solemn and public manner, as precisely specified by Her in the Message of Fatima." Accordingly, the motion provided for a declaration by Parliament formally requesting that "His Holiness, Pope Benedict XVI... fulfill the will of the Queen of Heaven" by performing the Consecration in order to address European and world problems. Speaking before the international press corps in the parliamentary press hall, Father Gruner and Mr. Ferrara made presentations urging Parliament to pass the motion, including a discussion of the content, undeniable authenticity, and absolute urgency of the Fatima Message for the Church and humanity at large. The two speakers were introduced to the world press by MEP's Borghezio and Fontana, who appeared alongside them at the press conference. After the presentation, at least six more members of Parliament added their endorsements to the motion.

As of this writing, the EU Parliament has not acted on the motion, but even if it never comes before that body for a vote, its mere introduction was a dramatic and salutary provocation in one of the world's most important public forums. That the legislative nerve center of the New World Order in a post-Christian Europe was the site of this initiative, and that it came in the midst of an ever-deepening worldwide spiritual, moral, social and economic crisis, seemed to represent a final stage-setting for the conclusion of the drama that began almost a century before at the Cova da Iria.

Giuseppe De Carli, co-author of Cardinal Bertone's book *The Last Secret of Fatima*, was willing to come forward to try to defend his position at the "Fatima Challenge" Conference on May 4, 2010. De Carli learned many facts from the conference that had apparently been withheld from him. On his departure from the conference he warmly embraced Father Gruner and said: "Thank you, Father Gruner, for the great work you are doing." Days after, at Fatima on May 13, 2010, he heard Pope Benedict XVI tell him and the whole world, "He would be deceiving himself who thinks that the prophetic mission of Fatima is concluded." On July 13, 2010, Mr. De Carli passed away.

Chapter 30

The Final Act

If Father Gruner's Fatima Apostolate were a commercial corporation engaged in some profit-making enterprise, the graph of its gains over the years 2000-2012 would trend sharply upward and the board of directors would heartily approve a large raise and bonus for the CEO whose visionary leadership had led the company to ever-greater success. But the apostolate is no mere corporation, and its head has not reaped any financial rewards. Its mission statement aims at something far higher and nobler than a calculus of profit and loss.

Father Gruner would be the first to acknowledge that revelation of the Third Secret in its entirety, the Consecration of Russia, and the consequent Triumph of the Immaculate Heart are ends of infinite worth, so that anything less than their full accomplishment would be infinitely far from the mark. God does not bargain for less than what He has required through the prophets He sends to admonish and instruct men in each age of salvation history. Thus, where the Message of Fatima is concerned, better is not nearly good enough.

And yet, throughout a quarter-century of tireless labor, Father Gruner had demonstrated that determined leadership and the prudent use of the means of social communication could produce great gains for the spiritual cause to which he has devoted his priesthood since 1977. God has always deigned to employ human instruments to effectuate the designs of Heaven, and by God's grace Father Gruner had served with distinction as one such instrument. But he is only one small part of a grand design, conceived in Heaven before the beginning of the world, whose center and summit is the most exalted human instrument of all: Mary Immaculate, Mediatrix of All Graces—including the singular graces to be unleashed by the fulfillment of what She requested in His name at the Cova da Iria nearly a century ago.

As the year 2012 drew to a close, Father Gruner continued laboring, praying and offering the Holy Sacrifice of the Mass for the consummation of the divine design revealed to the Church and the world at Fatima. As this new edition of his biography appears, he continues to work seemingly endless days, managing the complex affairs of an international organization that has thrived despite all efforts to destroy or discredit it in places on high. He subsists on the plain food provided to him, and when sleep can no longer be deferred, he retires to the sparsely furnished bedroom of the modest old home his parents left him in the working class town of Fort Erie. He drives his unimpressive car or takes a plane to one meeting, conference or rally after another, and his stamina is repeatedly being taxed to the point of collapse. Those who come to hear him speak are likely to see him struggle to avoid weeping at the tragedy unfolding before the eyes of an unbelieving world, but weeping as well at the joy of the heavenly promise whose inevitable fulfillment lies at the end of it all.

Only God knows whether the Fatima Priest will live to see the accomplishment of the mission of the Virgin of Fatima to a fallen and ever more rebellious world. But he has already lived at least long enough to witness the hastening approach of that glorious fulfillment. And no matter how much time God has allotted to Father Nicholas Gruner, history will record his part in what must be the final act of the drama that is Fatima.

Select Bibliography

BOOKS

Floridi, Alexis Ulysses, S.J. *Moscow and the Vatican*, Ardis Publishers, 1986.

François de Marie des Anges; Frère. *Fatima: Intimate Joy, World Event*, Immaculate Heart Publications, Buffalo, New York.

Book 1, *Fatima: The Astonishing Truth*, 1993
Book 2, *Fatima: Mary's Immaculate Heart and Your Salvation*, 1993
Book 3, *Fatima: The Only Way to World Peace*, 1993
Book 4, *Fatima: Tragedy and Triumph*, 1994

Golitsyn, Anatoliy. *New Lies For Old*, Dodd, Mead and Company, New York, NY 1984.

Golitsyn, Anatoliy. *The Perestroika Deception* - The World's Slide Towards The 'Second October Revolution' (Weltoktober), Edward Harle Limited, London, England 1995.

Gruner, Nicholas; Father. *World Enslavement Or Peace ... It's Up to the Pope*, Fatima Crusader Publications, Fort Erie, Ontario, Canada, 1988.

Johnston, Francis. *Fatima The Great Sign*, Tan Books and Publishers, Rockford, Illinois, 1980.

Kelley, Francis Clement; Bishop. *Blood Drenched Altars*, Tan Books And Publishers, Inc., Rockford, Illinois, 1987.

Lucia, (Lucy) dos Santos; Sister. *Fatima in Lucia's Own Words*, edited by Father Louis Kondor, SVD, Postulation Centre, Fatima, Portugal, 1976.

Manifold, Deirdre. *Fatima And The Great Conspiracy*, seventh edition, Firinne Publications, Galway, Ireland, 1993.

Michel de la Sainte Trinité; Frère. *The Whole Truth About Fatima*, Immaculate Heart Publications, Buffalo, New York.

Vol. I, *Science and the Facts*, 1989;
Vol. II, *The Secret and the Church*, 1989;
Vol. III, *The Third Secret*, 1990.

Trinchard, Paul; Father. *The Awesome Fatima Consecrations*, Metairie, Louisiana, 1992.

Walsh, William Thomas. *Our Lady of Fatima*, The Macmillan Company, New York, NY 1948.

MAGAZINES AND NEWSPAPERS

The Fatima Crusader magazine, Issues 1-106, 452 Kraft Road, Fort Erie, ON, Canada, L2A 4M7.

The Catholic Counter Reformation in the XXth Century, Maison Sainte Therese, 255, Chemin de la Resereve, Shawinigan RR2, P. Que - G9N 6T6, Canada.

Catholic Family News, MPO Box 743, Niagara Falls, New York 14302, USA.

1942 - Dr. Gruner (Baba) and Nicholas.

1945 - Jessie Gruner holding Nicholas. Behind from left to right are his brothers Michael, Peter, Christopher and Anthony.

1955 - The Gruner family in their garden on Caledonia Road in Montreal. Front, left to right, are Nicholas, Pinocchio their dog, and Cecilia. Middle row: Anthony, Michael, Jessie, Jennifer, and Malcolm. Back row: Christopher and Peter.

L'OSSERVATORE ROMANO

GIORNALE QUOTIDIANO POLITICO RELIGIOSO

UNICUIQUE SUUM NON PRAEVALEBUNT

Copia L. 500 — Copia arretrata L. 800

Anno CXXIV - N. 72 (37.564) CITTA' DEL VATICANO Lunedì-Martedì 26-27 Marzo 1984

Tre eventi

NELLA GIORNATA GIUBILARE DELLE FAMIGLIE IL PAPA AFFIDA ALLA MADONNA GLI UOMINI E LE NAZIONI

Liberaci dalla fame, dalla guerra

Nel ricordo del «Fiat» pronunciato da Maria al momento dell'Annunciazione, il Papa ha affidato al «suo Cuore Immacolato» ieri, domenica 25 marzo — in spirituale unione con tutti i Vescovi del mondo — gli uomini ed i popoli, ripetendo l'atto di affidamento, compiuto a Fatima il 13 maggio del 1982. Con voce forte e solenne il Santo Padre ha invocato la liberazione dell'umanità dalla fame, dalla guerra, da ogni male, aggiungendo una speciale invocazione perché la Vergine illumini quei popoli per i quali Ella stessa ha chiesto, a Fatima, la consacrazione e l'affidamento.

Il solenne atto di affidamento è stato continuato nel pomeriggio, quando il Santo Padre Giovanni Paolo II nella Basilica Vaticana, al momento del congedo, ha di nuovo affidato alla Bianca Signora di Fatima «le sorti del mondo, degli uomini, dei popoli al Tuo Cuore Immacolato — ha detto testualmente — per arrivare al centro stesso del mistero che è più forte di tutti i peccati dell'uomo e del mondo, in cui si può vincere il peccato nelle sue diverse forme, in cui si può incominciare, inaugurare un mondo nuovo».

Questo il testo dell'atto di affidamento alla Madonna:

La Famiglia è il cuore della Chiesa. Si innalzi oggi da questo cuore un atto di particolare affidamento al Cuore della Genitrice di Dio.

Nell'Anno Giubilare della Redenzione vogliamo confessare che l'Amore è più grande del peccato e di ogni male, che minaccia l'uomo e il mondo.

Con umiltà invochiamo questo Amore:

1. *«Sotto la Tua protezione cerchiamo rifugio, santa Madre di Dio»!*

Pronunciando le parole di questa antifona, con la quale la Chiesa di Cristo prega da secoli, ci troviamo oggi dinanzi a Te, Madre, nell'Anno Giubilare della nostra Redenzione.

Ci troviamo uniti con tutti i Pastori della Chiesa, in un particolare vincolo, costituendo un corpo e un collegio, così come per volontà di Cristo gli Apostoli costituivano un corpo e un collegio con Pietro.

Nel vincolo di tale unità, pronunziamo le parole del presente Atto, in cui desideriamo racchiudere, ancora una volta, le speranze e le angosce della Chiesa per il mondo contemporaneo.

Quaranta anni fa, e poi ancora dieci anni dopo, il tuo servo, il Papa Pio XII, avendo davanti agli occhi le dolorose esperienze della famiglia umana, ha affidato e consacrato al tuo Cuore Immacolato tutto il mondo e specialmente i Popoli, che per la loro situazione sono particolare oggetto del tuo amore e della tua sollecitudine.

Questo mondo degli uomini e delle nazioni abbiamo davanti agli occhi anche oggi: il mondo del secondo millennio che sta per terminare, il mondo contemporaneo, il nostro mondo!

La Chiesa, memore delle parole del Signore: «Andate... e ammaestrate tutte le nazioni... Ecco, io sono con voi tutti i giorni fino alla fine del mondo» (Mt 28, 19-20), ha ravvivato, nel Concilio Vaticano II, la coscienza della sua missione in questo mondo.

E perciò, o Madre degli uomini e dei popoli, Tu che conosci tutte le loro sofferenze e le loro speranze, Tu che senti maternamente tutte le lotte tra il bene e il male, tra la luce e le tenebre, che scuotono il mondo contemporaneo, ac-

(continua in sesta pagina)

> ***Madre della Chiesa! Illumina il Popolo di Dio sulle vie della fede, della speranza e della carità! Illumina specialmente i popoli di cui tu aspetti la nostra consacrazione e il nostro affidamento. Aiutaci a vivere nella verita della consacrazione di Cristo per l'intera famiglia umana del mondo contemporaneo.***

CONTINUAZIONE DALLA PRIMA PAGINA

Liberaci dalla fame, dalla guerra

cogli il nostro grido che, mossi dallo Spirito Santo, rivolgiamo direttamente al Tuo Cuore: abbraccia, con amore di Madre e di Serva del Signore, questo nostro mondo umano, che Ti affidiamo e consacriamo, pieni di inquietudine per la sorte terrena ed eterna degli uomini e dei popoli.

In modo speciale Ti affidiamo e consacriamo quegli uomini e quelle nazioni, che di questo affidamento e di questa consacrazione hanno particolarmente bisogno.

«Sotto la tua protezione cerchiamo rifugio, santa Madre di Dio»! Non disprezzare le suppliche di noi che siamo nella prova!

2. *Ecco, trovandoci davanti a Te, Madre di Cristo, dinanzi al tuo Cuore Immacolato, desideriamo, insieme con tutta la Chiesa, unirci alla consacrazione che, per amore nostro, il Figlio tuo ha fatto di se stesso al Padre: «Per loro — egli ha detto — io consacro me stesso, perché siano anch'essi consacrati nella verità» (Io 17, 19). Vogliamo unirci al nostro Redentore in questa consacrazione per il mondo e per gli uomini, la quale, nel suo Cuore divino, ha la potenza di ottenere il perdono e di procurare la riparazione.*

La potenza di questa consacrazione dura per tutti i tempi ed abbraccia tutti gli uomini, i popoli e le nazioni, e supera ogni male, che lo spirito delle tenebre è capace di ridestare nel cuore dell'uomo e nella sua storia e che, di fatto, ha ridestato nei nostri tempi.

Oh, quanto profondamente sentiamo il bisogno di consacrazione per l'umanità e per il mondo: per il nostro mondo contemporaneo, in unione con Cristo stesso! L'opera redentrice di Cristo, infatti, deve essere partecipata dal mondo per mezzo della Chiesa.

Lo manifesta il presente Anno della Redenzione: il Giubileo straordinario di tutta la Chiesa.

Sii benedetta, in questo Anno Santo, sopra ogni creatura Tu, Serva del Signore, che nel modo più pieno obbedisti alla Divina chiamata!

Sii salutata Tu, che sei interamente unita alla consacrazione redentrice del Tuo Figlio!

Madre della Chiesa! Illumina il Popolo di Dio sulle vie della fede, della speranza e della carità! Illumina specialmente i popoli di cui tu aspetti la nostra consacrazione e il nostro affidamento. Aiutaci a vivere nella verità della consacrazione di Cristo per l'intera famiglia umana del mondo contemporaneo.

3. *AffidandoTi, o Madre, il mondo, tutti gli uomini e tutti i popoli, Ti affidiamo anche la stessa consacrazione del mondo, mettendola nel Tuo Cuore materno.*

Oh, Cuore Immacolato! Aiutaci a vincere la minaccia del male, che così facilmente si radica nei cuori degli uomini d'oggi e che nei suoi effetti incommensurabili già grava sulla vita presente e sembra chiudere le vie verso il futuro!

Dalla fame e dalla guerra, liberaci!

Dalla guerra nucleare, da un'autodistruzione incalcolabile, da ogni genere di guerra, liberaci!

Dai peccati contro la vita dell'uomo sin dai suoi albori, liberaci!

Dall'odio e dall'avvilimento della dignità dei figli di Dio, liberaci!

Da ogni genere di ingiustizia nella vita sociale, nazionale e internazionale, liberaci!

Dalla facilità di calpestare i comandamenti di Dio, liberaci!

Dal tentativo di offuscare nei cuori umani la verità stessa di Dio, liberaci!

Dallo smarrimento della coscienza del bene e del male, liberaci!

Dai peccati contro lo Spirito Santo, liberaci! liberaci!

Accogli, o Madre di Cristo, questo grido carico della sofferenza di tutti gli uomini! Carico della sofferenza di intere società!

Aiutaci con la potenza dello Spirito Santo a vincere ogni peccato: il peccato dell'uomo e il «peccato del mondo», il peccato in ogni sua manifestazione.

Si riveli, ancora una volta, nella storia del mondo l'infinita potenza salvifica della Redenzione: potenza dell'Amore misericordioso! Che esso arresti il male! Trasformi le coscienze! Nel Tuo Cuore Immacolato si sveli per tutti la luce della Speranza!

Reproduction of the March 26, 1984 issue of *L'Osservatore Romano.* (See enlargement above Pope John Paul II's words.) This has been reproduced and published three times in *The Fatima Crusader* over the years because the opponents of the consecration of Russia have conveniently, since 1984 to the present, continued to omit to report what the Pope actually said when he clearly indicated he had not done the consecration. Above, we reproduce the undisputed evidence that was published again in the February 1989 issue of *The Fatima Crusader.*

On December 8, 1983, Pope John Paul II wrote to all the bishops of the world, asking them to join in with him on March 25, 1984, in consecrating the world to the Immaculate Heart of Mary. He included with his letter his prepared text of consecration. On March 25, 1984, the Pope, making the consecration before Our Lady of Fatima, **departed from this prepared text to add the words highlighted here.** As you can see, they were reported in *L'Osservatore Romano.* The words he added at this point indicate clearly that the Pope knew then that the consecration of the world done that day did not fulfill the requests of Our Lady of Fatima. After performing the consecration of the world proper, a few paragraphs above, **the Pope added the highlighted words which translate: "Enlighten especially the peoples of which You Yourself are awaiting our consecration and confiding.**" This clearly shows he knows Our Lady is awaiting the Pope and bishops to consecrate certain people to Her.

1994 - Official opening of the Fatima Center near the Peace Bridge between Buffalo, New York and Canada. Father Gruner and Father Nault [RIP April 1997] (front) and Father Michael Jarecki [RIP October 2012] (behind the altar boys) lead the procession.

On August 22, 1994, Father Nault [RIP April 1997], Father Gruner and Father Victor Soroka [RIP January 2008] in front of the plaques listing the thousands of supporters who made possible this dream of purchasing this printing plant, thereby at that time more than doubling the size of The Fatima Center.

Father Maschio [RIP September 1996], Father Gruner and Father Nault. Father Maschio, a legend in his own time, spent more than 40 years in Bombay and other parts of India establishing great works of charity and piety. Father Maschio predicted that many bishops around the world would be helped by Father Gruner's efforts to explain and promote devotion to Our Blessed Mother.

Archbishop Limon, S.V.D. [RIP June 1996], in his cathedral at Dagupan, Philippines, after the Mass and public procession in 1989. On October 7, 1992, he joined Archbishop Toppo of India and Archbishop Jose Cordoso Sobrinho, O.Carm., of the Archdiocese of Olinda e Recife, Brazil, when the Bishop of Fatima gave his blessing to Father Gruner's Conference at Fatima, October 8-12, 1992.

Immaculate Heart of Mary Orphanage founded by Archbishop Arulappa and Father Gruner.

1. Father at the new orphanage building built by benefactors from his apostolate.

2. At the opening of the new orphanage building on January 25, 1999, Father Gruner accepts a gift from one of the children as Archbishop Arulappa [RIP Feb. 13, 2005] (left) looks on.

3. Father Gruner with some of the orphans helped by his apostolate.

Father Gruner (center) officially opens his apostolate's new orphanage building in the Archdiocese of Hyderabad, as Archbishop Arulappa blesses it. Anthony Sebastian, orphanage manager (left), looks on.

New World Order obelisk erected in Elberton, Georgia in 1980 stands 19'3" high and weighs 237,746 lbs. The stone inscription in 8 languages (photographically reproduced here) outlines a call to wipe out 9/10ths of humanity.